A PLACE FOR EVERYONE

A History Of State Education From
The End Of The 18th Century To The 1970s

BY *NIGEL MIDDLETON*

WHEN FAMILY FAILED
*The Treatment of Children in the
Care of the Community during
The First Half of the
Twentieth Century*

A PLACE FOR EVERYONE

*A History Of State Education From
The End Of The 18th Century To The 1970s*

by

NIGEL MIDDLETON
and
SOPHIA WEITZMAN

LONDON
VICTOR GOLLANCZ LTD
1976

© Nigel Middleton 1976

ISBN 0 575 02028 8

The material in this Book which is Crown
copyright is reprinted by
permission of the authority

MADE AND PRINTED IN GREAT BRITAIN BY
THE GARDEN CITY PRESS LIMITED
LETCHWORTH, HERTFORDSHIRE
SG6 1JS

DEDICATION

To the several generations of civic and community
leaders who at council, committee, board or other
meetings have spent countless unpaid hours in consultation and argument to further the provision of
school and college places for everyone; and especially to those in my native city of Sheffield whose
record is a proud one. They gave me my chance
when things were far from easy. So may they please
accept this dedication as thanks for "my place", for
my life has been the fuller for it.

CONTENTS

ILLUSTRATIONS

PREFACE AND ACKNOWLEDGEMENTS

IN ALL MY reading one story has captured my imagination and
that is of the radical writer De Condorcet in the turmoil of the
French Revolution, dodging the security police while he finished
his book. In failing health he saw his proofs safely away before
allowing himself to be caught and executed. I do not know
how true the story is, but no writer can help being touched by
it as it links with his own work, for every book is the life blood
of its author.

Something of this feeling came to me when, after considerable trouble, I obtained access to Dr Sophia Weitzman's papers.
I was looking for evidence of the growth of community support for children and I had read several of the official histories
of the second world war with profit. Dr Weitzman had been
engaged on the history of education but had died before she
could complete her work. When I looked through the hundred
laundry boxes housing several drafts of her manuscript plus the
collections of reports and summaries, I knew in a few minutes I
was in a treasure house. Across the years I felt myself reaching
agreement with a kindred spirit. I never met her but I found
much of my research already completed. As I went away it
seemed to me so wasteful to leave that collection of finished
and half finished material to collect dust awaiting the casual
plunder of later scholars, especially as we shared a common
interest in the opportunity afforded the child with little but the
State to provide an education. Luckily I enlisted the help of her
brother, David Weitzman, QC, MP, and it is due to his personal intervention with the Prime Minister, Harold Wilson, that
I was allowed to use one part of her writing, a 50,000 word
survey of the history of education. I have considerably edited the
material but her work is so vital to the early chapters that my
deceased collaborator must have her name included on the title
page of this book.

I held over the writing of the general survey of the treatment
of children to build up this account of the provision of state
education. In doing this I was guided and encouraged by the

late Professor. A. C. F. Beales, doyen of historians of education who overlooked the work until his death. His successor at King's College, London, Professor K. Charlton has also been most helpful. As Dr Sophia Weitzman had been working as the official war historian of the education service, I sought out my old tutor, Professor Richard Titmuss, who had organised the production of several of these volumes. Although in failing health, his support was enthusiastic in my efforts of salvage and he gave me many leads to follow up.

It is not possible to list all the large number of people who have helped me. They include many individuals of the Civil Service, both serving and retired; they were without exception courteous and did all in their power to assist me. In trying to reconstruct matters which took place some thirty or more years ago, it was soon obvious how quickly memories fade and evidence disappears. I therefore owe a unique debt to the many politicians, officials and their families who gave me generously of their time to answer my questions. Much of the material on the Education Act of 1944 was illuminated in this way to enable me to complete a jigsaw of events which I believe is not fully recorded anywhere.

In an interview Lord Butler generally agreed with my account of the events surrounding the passing of his great Act and commended my detective work. I hope my interpretation of events will not be seen as diminishing the efforts of those concerned with government in the 1939–45 War and after. It illustrates fully the pressures which are on those in charge of a nation's affairs, and how long-term trends are affected by the urgencies of the moment. In talking to people in office or recently away from responsibility, the heat of the moment often colours accounts of their activities. I have tried to make allowances for this and to be fair to all concerned.

In assembling a great deal of evidence, both oral and written, I have developed certain sociological interpretations in an attempt to evaluate events, and follow long-term trends. Thus a remarkable experience was a long conversation I had with Mr T. O. Wilson, CBE, formerly Chief Education Officer for Oxfordshire, who began his service by administering the setting-up of the 1902 Act. To talk to him was to brush aside the fog of seventy years and to be made aware of several factors which affected his daily work. His unique personal evidence points to the general need to try to salvage such experiences before they are lost to us.

I owe a debt of gratitude to Miss A. K. Davies, Principal of Wall Hall College, and to Hertfordshire Education Committee for their support in the early stages of this work. The Northern Ireland Polytechnic have also contributed to help me finish the manuscript. I must not forget my long-suffering wife who has borne with my writer's isolation and preoccupation for many years with generosity and sympathy.

A much neglected source of sociological evidence is to be found in the work of cartoonists who show a contemporary viewpoint with an aptness which may puzzle; but if their point is grasped, it is always valuable as a reflection of the moment. Several examples are used here, among them a selection from *Punch*, always a rich lode for social comment, and I have been allowed to use its cartoons captioned "Cobden's Logic", "The Raw Material", "Taking The Edge Off It", "Priority Plans", "The New Boy", and "The Three R's; Or Better Late Than Never".

The *Observer* gave permission for the cartoon of Margaret Thatcher and Trog's trenchant comment, "One Nation— Perishable".

Syndication International allowed the reproduction of Zec's cartoon, "Under The Counter".

Mark Boxer allowed the use of his cartoon of Edward Short. Brian Jackson's caption is published by permission of *The New Statesman*.

Associated Newspapers Group Ltd gave permission for the use of the Jon cartoon of the Eton and Harrow match.

The Times Newspapers Ltd gave permission to use the cartoon about putting an infant's name down for the Holland Park Comprehensive School.

Sir Peter Ramsbotham gave permission for the use of Heap's cartoon of his father, Herwald Ramsbotham, later Lord Soulbury.

I am grateful to the following publishers who have allowed the use of passages from their books to the enrichment of this text :

The Bodley Head for Thelma Cazalet-Keir's *From The Wings*.

Hamish Hamilton for the Earl of Birkenhead's *The Life of Lord Halifax* and also Lord Butler's *The Art of the Possible*.
William Heinemann Ltd for F. Blackburn's *George Tomlinson*.
Hodder and Stoughton Ltd for Richard Haldane's *An Autobiography*.
Longman Group Ltd for Lord Eccles' *Life and Politics*.

The following early protest against comprehensive education was writtten by Samuel Butler (in 1820) to Lord Brougham who was sponsoring a Bill to set up a system of parish schools financed from the rates. Butler was a Barchester-type cleric who during the 38 years he was headmaster of Shrewsbury School collected a series of rich livings, until finally appointed Bishop of Lichfield and Coventry by Lord Melbourne; he was one of Queen Victoria's favourite authors.

The intention of the founders of the Grammar Schools appears to have been to diffuse as widely as possible the attainment of learning, by affording in most cases gratuitous, or at least cheap means of instruction in those languages, a knowledge of which is indispensible for academic education and the liberal professions. While the probability was that what are generally called the middle classes of society would chiefly take advantage of these institutions, there was no exclusion either of the highest or lowest.

But commonsense evidently points out that the lowest classes would not *wish* in many cases to bring up their children to liberal professions; and if they had this laudable ambition, would not be able, in many instances, even when their children had completed their school education, to support them at the universities, or place them out in liberal professions in life.

It is equally obvious that the very highest classes would, from motives of pride, or even conscience, generally decline to take advantage of eleemosynary foundations. The probability therefore was, and has been confirmed by the experience of all ages since these institutions have been established, that the middle classes of society would *principally* be benefited by them. From thence we are supplied with our clergy, our lawyers, our physicians; and here by far the greatest part of the ordinary and some of the highest order of the gentry of the realm receive their own education, and as they advance in life send their children to receive the same benefits.

They will not care if the son of a person greatly their inferior receives the *same* benefits of a learned education with their own children—if they have common liberality, they will foster and encourage the boy, if he is modest and deserving, well knowing that from such education, in such institutions, have arisen many of the brightest ornaments of their country both in church and state. But they will feel and apprehend a great deal, and justly too, if the Grammar Schools are to be made schools for teaching English reading, writing and accounts—in other words, Parish schools.

They will know and feel, without the least ill-will or disrespect to the lowest orders of society, that their children can learn no improvements in manners or morals by associating with all the lowest boys of the parish, and they will feel it necessary and inevitable, to forgo ... the benefits of an institution which they cannot enjoy without exposing them to so great a risk.

... if these clauses pass, these parents must place them elsewhere, probably at greater expense and with less advantages of competent instruction—the injury which must result from the measure will appear, indeed, enormous.

A PLACE FOR EVERYONE

Look there! Do you not see a man hang by the neck? Oh, it is a sad sight. A rope is tied round his neck to what they call the gallows: and there he hangs till he is quite dead. See what a crowd there is round him, to see him hang! I dare say there is his mother, and his friends. How full of grief they must be, to see him come to such a sad end! But you will want to know who it is. It is Dick Brown. When he was a boy, he would pick

LOOK WHAT HAPPENED TO DICK!

Early school text books were usually moral tracts. This page from *Children's Tales*, written in 1829 by the Rev. William Carus-Wilson, warns of the long-term results of taking apples from a neighbour's orchard without permission. (*Re-drawn from the original*)

PART ONE

I

The Start Of It All—
Different Ways For Master And Man

"The Rich and the Poor. Two nations; between whom there is no intercourse and no sympathy; who are ignorant of each other's habits, thoughts and feelings as if they were dwellers of different planets; who are formed by a different breeding, are fed by a different food, are ordered by different manners, and are not governed by the same laws."

> Benjamin Disraeli's introduction to his novel *Sybil,* 1845
> Conservative Prime Minister in 1868 and 1874–80

THIS WORK EXPLORES the development of educational opportunity for the children of ordinary families, those without notable wealth or position, showing the progress made from earliest times to the present. Lest this should appear to be too ambitious a venture to be contained in one volume, it must be added that the early portion is only briefly surveyed and the story in detail begins in the early part of the nineteenth century. The latter part of the book is largely concerned with the last overhaul of the national education system brought about by the Education Act of 1944; it covers the preliminary discussions, the parliamentary processing of the Bill, and follows its application over the following quarter of a century, with some assessment of the present state of affairs. The aim is to make the past illuminate the present.

Much analysis of popular education is carried out in isolated fragments so the persistent central issues are often overlooked. The first of these is the connection between the economic, social and political factors of the time as they affect the general national scene and so, incidentally, education. The second is the extension, or otherwise, of opportunity for the child of average ability to make a way in life through personal effort and ability. In following these two issues it soon becomes apparent that education, especially in the early years of its development, is a minor matter which hardly troubles the biographers of the great political figures and seems at times confined to the footnotes of history. Moreover such is the frailty of politicians and their fortunes that the story is a repetition of great hopes followed by disappointment. It is only in the long run that aims, long seen as necessary, are finally fulfilled.

This first chapter gives an outline of educational development from earliest times to the start of the first national schemes in the nineteenth century. It is a lead-in to the build up of the full provision of school places for everyone.

State education is a beneficial social service which confers great advantages on the individual as the most important influence generally available for improving social and financial opportunity. Without educational skills the individual is usually confined to varying types of manual work, largely of a dead-end type. Pay generally increases in direct ratio to the skills mastered; so, for the majority, the key to a more rewarding life is to be found in the schools, in many of which promise outstrips provision. Although government has openly acknowledged liability for the provision of education for 150 years it has always baulked at the costs. As a result various systems of rationing have grown up. These administrative services ensure that even though, with the growth of the concept of comprehensive education, from nursery schools to higher education, a fully open system is in sight, it remains a long way from being realized. The reasons for this lie not only in the priorities in spending public money, but also in the persistence of social division. An identity with a certain section of the community is, for many parents, more important than the academic quality of the school.

From the start educational development threw up two separate and distinct systems of schools. The first, a classics-based system grew up to become the grammar schools, designed to produce controllers and managers of the community, together with the professions required to support them. The second was not initially seen as an education system, but primarily as a means of indoctrination for the children of the large section of labourers, so that they would accept their place in a developing industrial society. The two systems were poles apart and educational history from the eighteenth century to the present is largely concerned with attempts to bring them together.

The main thesis of this work is to trace the development of these two systems of education from feudal times to the present. The consideration of the growth of education at two levels, i.e. a binary model, enables a vast amount of historical material to be placed in proper perspective, thus providing a frame of reference for the interpretation of the mass of loosely related facts that educational historians have accumulated. It is easy to point out many exceptions to the main line of development, but they do not invalidate the argument presented here : which is, that for at least 500 years education has been carried on at two levels.

The division has its origins in the family situation where parents taught their children. Naturally this mainly centred on their own way of life, for it was almost axiomatic that the children would follow in their parents' footsteps. Therefore the leading families showed their children how to run and control the community, whilst those with more mundane rôles taught their own work, such as looking after the animals or tilling the soil. In both cases much of the teaching was incidental, usually through the children taking part in community activities. Girls' education remained centred on the home and domestic round, so it is the development of the education of boys that is significant.

The academic training for the small section of ruling families quite early crystallized into a study of the classics. As in the undeveloped countries of the world today, dialects were many and incomprehensible outside their areas, so the language of government and commerce, and indeed the only means of clear communication within the nation, was different from the speech of the people. For over 2,000 years to be able to conduct affairs at anything but a local level, a knowledge of Greek and Latin or later French, was essential. Moreover by acquiring a knowledge of them young men were guided to joining the ruling élite. In Britain the centres for such knowledge were the grammar schools which were built mainly in towns as the first national network of schools to be bastions of Protestantism. This mainly happened in the sixteenth century but included many schools of earlier foundation.

These provincial grammar schools varied greatly, but for the most part they consisted of the provision of a building and a resident tutor. The accepted qualification for the post was a clergyman who could teach the classics, plus, usually, some history and geography. For extra subjects outsiders were employed by the master, and additional fees were charged for certain instruction. The master also derived a further income from feeding and boarding students who required it. Pupils were mainly drawn from the sons of the local gentry, professional men and the better-off farmers. There was often some small provision for poor but bright local boys to be taught; but fee paying, both for basic tuition and extras, was part of the economics of the grammar schools. The pupils were almost exclusively male, aged between the ages of thirteen and sixteen, although in some cases younger children were taken. The school roll seems to have been usually no more than twenty. On admission, boys were expected to have basic skills in literacy and number. Standards of tuition and numbers varied, depending on the ability and standing of the incumbent. Most school histories tell of periods when through illness, ageing or simple inability of the appointed master, the numbers and income slumped to reveal almost complete ineffectiveness, often for several years; and it appears the school governors usually had to wait for the incumbent's retirement or death before making a new appointment. The new master would then be faced with the task of building the school up to reasonable educational standards and an economic enrolment. The régime was traditionally authoritarian with moral indoctrination reinforced by long sermons and thrashings. These schools probably catered for no more than about five per cent of the male children, and that proportion did not materially change until the middle of the nineteenth century when the value of education was realized and a measure of industrial affluence brought such schools within the reach of more families.

The religiously-inspired origins of most grammar schools provided some measure of foundation funds, usually based on land rents, but even if the income was adequate at the outset, changing values decreased their assured income, so that all but a handful seemed to pass from one financial crisis to the next. The few well-founded schools became identified with the aristocratic and landed families who used them for the education of their sons, but even these superior grammar schools, which later developed into the original public schools, were not without their economic difficulties.

Thus this nationwide network of schools, teaching more or less the same curriculum, provided a unifying culture, complete with lingua franca, for the section of the community they served.

Children from the lower walks of life fared very differently. Their education was strictly vocational, based on family training to fit a young man to take his work place in the community. Life for all was precarious and it was perhaps this factor that helped develop the widespread system of young men going to other families to be brought up and taught their business in life. This had started in feudal times and was widely used by all classes of people. In the more exalted families young men went to similar households to serve as pages or squires; this later developed into boarding in clergymen's houses, for tutoring, and is the origin of the house system in public schools. Merchants' sons, like Dick Whittington, were sent to business associates to gain wider experience. In another walk of life skilled tradesmen took boys on a form of contract to teach them a trade. These engagements were strictly supervised by the craft guilds who did not want to see their trades overcrowded, or their skills diluted by the adoption of shoddy practices. This control produced considerable documentary evidence which reveals much about the arrangements. They show that although the form of contract changed with the demands and conditions of the times, the situation is fixed in the history books by the Elizabethan Statute of Apprentices of 1563, although this is but a static picture of a series of developments.

There were, however, a great number of engagements that were not formalized by contract. These were generally known as labour apprenticeships and, as the researches of Peter Laslett,[1] have shown, they were well established in Tudor times. His reconstruction of the social structure of villages from parish records shows that households varied directly in size with the affluence of the family. The children of the labourers left their homes as soon as they could get about on their own to take a place with a local merchant or farmer.[2] They would be set to earn their keep by bird scaring, animal minding and other tasks well established in the work routine as suitable for children; the girls graduating to domestic servants and the boys to labourers. Both sexes often stayed the whole of their lives in the service of one family. These arrangements were widespread for Shake-speare,[3] in *The Taming of the Shrew*, makes the gentleman Vincentio say of his son's servant, Tranio, that his father "is a sail-maker in Bergamo" and "I have brought him up ever since he was three years old". The Poor Law used the same formula for finding places for pauper children; and the enabling legal authority was periodically renewed from Elizabethan times onwards. It was restated for the last time in 1933, and the practice finally lapsed with the Children Act of 1948. The resulting household pattern is reflected in Gregory King's tables of population drawn up in 1688.[4]

Although these practices were mainly induction into work, they implied a measure of pastoral care, and some indication of this was usually written into apprenticeship agreements. In the uncertain pre-industrial economy everyone worked all the hours the season of the year required, the children acting as auxiliaries to the stronger adults. Labouring children had no special privileged position; indeed, as the weakest and least efficient part of the work group, they were at the bottom of the pecking order, but still an integrated member of the workforce and the household. Although conditions were often harsh and hours long, expectations were low and authoritarian discipline accepted. The important thing was to have a niche in the established social order so that the master took responsibility for the servant and the servant owed a loyalty to his master. Contemporary law catered for this situation fully and a servant betraying his master could, in certain circumstances, be punished by death for it was looked on as a form of treason. It was a terrible thing for someone to lose their "place", for a "masterless man" was a type of outlaw, without civil rights. He had no place to stay and could be whipped simply for being found in a village without employment.

In the latter part of the eighteenth century these traditional ideas and values, unchanged from feudal times, showed signs of breaking down. A drive for farming efficiency had developed which produced a scramble for the enclosure of the common lands. This process had started in Tudor times but proceeded with gathering intensity into the nineteenth century. Before 1760 some 300,000 acres were added to the total of twenty million acres of arable land in England and Wales, but between

1790 and 1810 the needs of the French wars made the figure 10 million acres. Changes of this magnitude put the plough literally and figuratively across the face of Britain. The benefits went to the landowners and the larger farmers who could afford to buy land. In contrast the labourer and the small yeoman farmer slipped from being companions in work to mere paid employees. At the same time there was an erosion of those benefits of the system based on local paternalism. The pressures on the family-style work units swept away the old tempo of work and gave way to outright exploitation.

This badly affected the arrangements by which young people had been trained for centuries to fit into society; there was a complete change. Evidence of the more informal agreements is difficult to come by, but the deeds of apprenticeship, even before 1700, began to be increasingly less of a safeguard for the youngsters. The training period, which had been generally seven years, was shortened in some cases to as little as a single year. Interest in the quality of the instruction, taken by the controlling bodies, decreased and this is evidenced by the fact that whereas there had previously been a succession of cases for abuse of agreements brought before the courts, during the 1760s these ceased altogether in the London area. From then on the agreements were debased : the occupations were often of little worth, the training time trivial and, most important of all, a complete absence of the pastoral element, such as living in with the employing family, which meant being part of the family work group. This was an uneven process, probably more noticeable in the areas affected by industrialization.

From this stage the children began to work from their parents' homes and the change was considerable. Previously they had been part of a work group with some communal interest in the product, for, as much of the life was shared and payment made largely in kind, everyone benefited from good results and followed the work through all its stages with interest. The factory work group which replaced this, was an impersonal one, the employees only coming together for the work and apart from their pay they had little interest, for the processes were broken down and few saw the whole production through.

Overcrowded living conditions in the new urban areas ensured the final collapse of the old style of life and its values. There was an unprecedented rise in population giving rise to the hordes of children growing up in the slums of the rapidly expanding towns. Many lived virtually on the streets, owing only an uneasy allegiance to parents they saw all too briefly. The resulting rise in lawlessness and crime baffled the authorities. The eighteenth century was one of rigid but uneasy authority. The century saw the Stuart putschs of 1715 and 1745 and a growing fear of the masses which culminated in the Gordon riots of June 1780 when the mob controlled London for several days. There were bouts of feverish commercial speculation with several financial crashes. External pressures came from the long French wars, the loss of the American colonies and the traumatic reverberation of the French Revolution. All these factors produced a deep questioning of the state of society. Bentham and Burke sought solutions in the change of political principles, Adam Smith in economic revision, Wesley and Whitfield in return to a simpler form of Christianity, while the monarchy was widely seen as responsible for the national decay. On every side there were indications of a worn-out social order with consequential demands for major reconstruction. The success of the French Revolution thoroughly alarmed the owners of wealth and property as they saw their French counterparts dispossessed, exiled, imprisoned or executed. While anxiety over the unruly lower orders multiplied the question asked on every side was, "Could it happen here?"

It was against this background that the advocates of a constructive approach advanced their proposals for universal education to replace the pastoral influence and disciplined control which the parent or master had given in the old-style apprenticeship situation. It was in effect the expansion of some existing arrangements that provided precedents for the education of the labouring classes. John Locke in 1697, when in government employment, had written a memorandum suggesting a system of schools based on the workhouses, but available to all children. In the resulting schools, children from the ages of three to fourteen were trained in the elementary skills required by local industries: usually spinning, knitting or similar activities. Religious instruction was given, but the elements of reading and writing were not always taught. The aim was to ensure that the children would be kept "in much better order ... and from infancy inured to work, which is no small consequence to the making of them sober and industrious all their lives after".[5]

There were only a few schools which developed along these lines, but the Society for the Promotion of Christian Knowledge, a voluntary body firmly linked with the Church of England, also started charity schools of the same type. This movement reached its peak in 1760 when it catered for 30,000 children. Reading was taught from a "spelling book" made up of "sentences from the scriptures", and the teaching was fortified by constant religious services. There was much emphasis on knowing one's place in society and being content with it, so on leaving the school "to go out into the world as servants or apprentices, a Bible, a Common Prayer Book and 'The Whole Duty of Man' " were given to pupils so that they could "read to advantage and improvement as long as they lived".

Even these unambitious establishments, although designed to inculcate industry, discipline and suitable religion, were considered by some to have gone too far. Bernard Mandeville writing in 1772 satirized this viewpoint when he wrote "in a free society where slaves are not allowed, the surest wealth consists in a multitude of laborious poor". To be certain that they will remain happy with their lot "under the meanest circumstances, it is requisite that great numbers of them should be ignorant as well as poor. Knowledge both enlarges and multiplies our desires, and the fewer things a man wishes for, the more easily may his necessities be supplied." In the same vein he suggested that "going to school, in comparison to working is idleness, and the longer boys continue in this easy sort of life, the more unfit they will be when grown up for downright labour, both as to strength and to inclination".[6]

Even the pioneers of popular education expressed thoughts along these lines. One of these, Mrs Sarah Trimmer strongly advocated the education of "children in the lower classes of life", but at the same time added the rider that "it cannot be right to train them *all* in a way of life which will probably raise their ideas above the very lowest occupations of life, and disqualify them for those servile offices which must be filled by some members of the community, and in which they may be equally happy with the highest, if they will do their duty". However there was to be some social mobility allowed because she considered the best of her pupils, "the first degree of the lower orders" would be suitably qualified "for teachers in schools supported by charity, for apprentices to common trades and for domestic servants in respectable families".[7]

There was no general enthusiasm to take advantage of these facilities for the pressures on a labourer's family in the newly developing money economy required the help of all the family to make ends meet. The removal of a child from the family support group with consequent loss of earnings, could not be easily accepted by a poor family and this situation had considerable effect for a further 150 years; but more immediately it prevented the voluntary supported schools from becoming viable and ensured the eventual arrival of a state system. As a substitute to serve the needs of the working child, the Sunday School was developed. Starting in the 1780s they flourished while the charity schools declined and by 1787 they claimed no less than 250,000 pupils. The founder, Robert Raikes, saw them as offering "instruction to the poorer part of the parish, without interfering with any industry of the week days". The formula was similar to that used in charity schools : briefly, reading and instruction in "the plain duties of the Christian religion, with a particular view to their good and industrious behaviour in their future character of labourers and servants".[8]

The venture depended on the middle classes, both for the funds and the instructors, so claims were made about the "great reformation [which] had taken place among the multitudes" employed in the factories as a result of attending Sunday School. It was claimed, they changed "from being idle, ungovernable, profligate and filthy in the extreme", so that they "have become not only cleanly and decent in their appearance, but are greatly humanized in their manners—more tractable, and attentive to their business, and of course, more serviceable than they (the employers) expected to find them." These arguments made sense to businessmen and as more and more children went into the factories, Sunday Schools flourished. It was also in their favour that they offered some protection from the growing lobby for full-time education. By the 1830s some one and a half million children were attending Sunday Schools, which was about half the children between the ages of five and twelve. The possibility of universal education was clearly demonstrated.

The hours of instruction were usually long and the discipline could be severe. Their success was due to the fact that they were open to all without charge, when even a seat in church had to be rented. They were usually run by able and successful local businessmen who saw the value of offering small prizes for those who did well. Local religious rivalries could escalate these rewards in the hope of attracting new children. For many children, living in squalor, driven at work by curse and blow for long hours of drudgery throughout the week, they were the first contact with a different atmosphere. Equally important was the fact that besides the inevitable bias of religion, they offered an opportunity to become literate, a big advantage for those with ambition to escape from the treadmill of the factory. Many schools ran classes for illiterate adults.

By the start of the nineteenth century mounting public concern for the treatment of children caught in the tide of industrialization was shown by the formation of several societies. Their lobbying, however, only revealed the ineffectiveness of community authority and the lack of local-government machinery to administer schools. But, most important of all, it did show that public concern had not reached a level when *laissez faire* beliefs could be thrust aside. As a result, while successive governments uneasily hovered on the brink of taking action but could not see what machinery was needed nor where the funds were coming from, two voluntary societies, with strong religious motivations set about revitalizing the charity-school idea. They both sought to keep their costs down by using the monitorial system, by which a single master briefed older, able pupils to teach the rest, each selected boy then taking a group under his supervision. A group of Free Churchmen was first in the field, when it founded the British and Foreign School Society in 1808 with the declared object of establishing schools for the children of workers. The Church of England anxious that the Nonconformists should not outmanoeuvre them, founded the National Society for the Education of the Poor in the Principles of the Established Church some three years later.

The thought of the period considered education and religious teaching as identical. The entry of two societies sponsored by rival religious interests brought conflict into the educational field. Their struggles already had a long and bitter history arising from the Reformation. The Nonconformists of the period had mostly grown up in small self-contained communities, later combining into loose associations united in a wish to produce a religious expression which excluded the established Anglican Church with its links with the landowning oligarchy. From the start the local groups had found themselves in conflict with the Anglican Church doctrinally and in more fundamental ways, such as discrimination over employment and housing, or even obtaining land to build a place to worship. The many chapels up and down Britain represent great struggles and sacrifice on the part of their founders; their very lack of pretension often bears witness to the difficulties they had to overcome. It was the ardour of these early founders that created their institutions and this ardour had to some extent been fanned by opposition of the established Church. The Roman Catholics and the Jews, who came later on the educational scene, faced similar prejudice.

From the outset the Anglicans claimed education as a matter for the control of the establishment and this meant under their aegis, while the Nonconformists would accept only Bible teaching; other interests wanted religious matters excluded entirely from schools. Each of the Churches saw themselves fighting for the survival of their own faith and in the atmosphere that developed compromise solutions were difficult to arrive at and uneasy to maintain. The many links of the minority bodies with political radicalism gave further dimensions for disagreement thus ensuring the struggle found fresh issues; 150 years later the disputes still had considerable life.

The rival "British" and "National" schools spread all over the country, to create something approaching an overall national education service for the labouring classes. They were usually small one-room buildings with the children crowded in under the supervision of a single teacher of variable qualification. Most of the children spent no more than two years in them, with frequent absences. They usually left before they were eleven to start work. Parents were required to find weekly fees ranging from 2d. to 4d. for each child, but most schools had recurrent financial difficulties. The fees excluded the poorer children and the pupils tended to be from the homes with a regular income.

The master, the key to the success of the school, had first to be a disciplinarian, for the success of the factory methods of instruction depended on drill-like routines and learning simplified lessons by rote. It was dreary and dull so that only the strictest control could keep the noise of the chanted lessons within bounds. The situation was given a religious gloss, but the middleclass subscribers, on whom the school depended for its finance, looked to the master "to civilize" his charges, thus making them more amenable factory fodder; successful educational attainment was a secondary consideration.

In this way Britain, emerging as the premier industrial nation, inherited two different systems of education, the grammar schools for the sons of the better off, and the voluntary-society schools for the children of the labourers. The first had a curriculum biased towards the classics with a culture identification with the owning and managerial classes; the second had a curriculum covering basic number, reading and writing, with a heavy indoctrination towards regimentation and obedience.

STILL A 2-TIER SYSTEM

The better grammar schools were run by graduate clergymen who maintained links with the universities where they had been educated and from time to time sent pupils. At this crucial period in the development of national education, they emerged as a key group with several centuries of experience and authority through running the only nation-wide education system, the grammar schools, the unifying factor of which was their identification with classical culture. They were schools for an élite and this was the badge of their culture; gentlemen who could exchange a few classical allusions and an appropriate tag, identified one another as of the same class. The leaders of such a culture had nothing to hinder them deciding educational policy in high places or at lower levels taking over "the supervision of the parochial schools for the poorer classes". Dr Arnold of Rugby fame made the point in 1839[9] that the status of school masters was not high and what standing they had derived from "connexion with the profession of clergyman, for that is universally acknowledged in England to be the profession of a gentleman".[10] It was a superiority that was to be maintained for most of the century largely through the appointment of government inspectors from the ranks of the graduate clergy, and by the clergy acting in various supervisory capacities for their local schools. Considerable feeling developed between the various sections of the profession which reached a peak at the turn of the century when the teachers' associations attacked Morant. Both the grammar schools and those for the children of the working people had a rôle in buttressing the existing social order. Industrial expansion at the start of the nineteenth century created an increasing number of "the middling classes" who did not fit easily into either of the existing systems. They sought a variety of solutions for their educational needs, several showing a decided bias towards the sciences. By co-operative efforts they provided a number of schools and colleges designed to meet their own requirements which would have provided a basic training and identification with science and engineering. It looked for a time as though there could be an infusion of new ideas and content into British education. This movement occurred at a time when the classically-orientated schools were generally in poor condition and their hold on the school system and national stream of education was threatened. For centuries the domination of the classics had successfully kept the sciences excluded from the universities as unsuitable for academic study. Such knowledge had thus been restricted to the workshops, so that although its applications produced great wealth, it still had an aroma of trade and manual labour, which made it unacceptable to the old style school master.

Hopes of a renaissance in British education faded away when Dr Arnold took over Rugby School in 1828. He had already won the approval of the mercantile and middle classes by his broad theology in which he advocated a reconciliation between the Anglicans and Nonconformists, which offered successful industrialists of the period a way to the more socially acceptable Church of England. Yet he was a classicist of the old school who saw his main task as the production of Christian gentlemen through a suitable classroom curriculum allied with the healthy development of the body through games in an updated version of the ancient Greek tradition. He was certainly aware of the claims of the physical sciences to be included in an educational curriculum, but in his opinion, it was "too great a subject to be studied 'in parts' and it must either occupy the chief place in the school curriculum or be left out altogether". He concluded that "rather than have physical science the principal thing in my son's mind, I would gladly have him think that the sun went

. .

round the earth, and that the stars were so many spangles set in the bright blue firmament. Surely the one thing needful for a Christian and an Englishman to study is Christian and moral and political philosophy."[11] In this manner he rejected science for his ideal curriculum for he claimed "study of language seems to me as if it was given for the very purpose of forming the human mind in youth; and the Greek and Latin languages seem to be the very instruments by which this is to be effected".

It is interesting to see how durable was this restrictive attitude. In 1921 a committee was appointed by the Board of Education to inquire into the teaching of English in England. Its report stated, "The Classics then remain, and will always remain, among the best of our inherited possessions, and for all truly civilized people they will always be not only a possession but a vital and enduring influence. Nevertheless, it is now, and will probably be for as long as we can foresee, impossible to make use of the Classics as a fundamental part of the national system of education." The committee had to find a second best substitute. "We are driven, then, in our search for the experience to be found in great art, to inquire whether there is available any similar and sufficient channel of supply which is within the reach of all without distinction." They concluded that English literature is "a means of education not less valuable than the Classics" if used in the way "the best teachers of the Classics have often succeeded".[12]

Arnold's success at Rugby set the pattern for English secondary education and re-asserted the position of the classicists. He rallied a powerful interest and in a short time his disciples were everywhere in key educational positions. The emerging middle classes had not the assurance to deny the links with the gentility which Arnold and the public schools held out to them, so Britain went into a period of intense industrial development with her educational eyes on the past; the slave-based states of Greece and Rome were seen as the ideal societies or at least the source to look for authoritative statements to settle social questions. As a result her only pattern of secondary education for industrial managers and specialists had evolved for a pre-scientific agricultural economy. When the Education Act of 1902 gave secondary education a sound financial basis for the

2—APFE * *

first time, the question was already settled, so most of the schools used their new resources to expand on the old pattern. Public schools of the type devised by Arnold were by then well established as a means of absorbing the new wealthy middle classes into the existing system. This process, linking the new rich to the established families, together with the reform of the universities, clearly confirmed the authority of the classicists and facilitated their hold on the national system of primary education during its formative period after 1870, so that the relations between the two systems of education remained largely as they had been in their origins in the eighteenth century.

The universities as the founts and strongholds of the classical tradition had another part to play in securing the ascendency of their cult, for by insisting on classical languages as entrance qualifications they shaped the grammar-school curriculum. This influence was extended in the 1850s by the universities becoming responsible for external examinations taken by the grammar schools as the final achievement of their teaching.

All these arrangements underlined the difference of the two systems of education, clearly establishing the superiority of the grammar schools. At the same time the education of the teachers for the elementary schools developed outside the classical system and had usually no Greek or Latin in its content. The teachers were thus considered indifferently educated, a fact emphasized in the title of training colleges given to the institutions in which they obtained their professional qualifications. Such a division frustrated attempts to absorb the colleges into the university system. It was soon seen that the large numbers involved threatened the existing balance and organization of the institutions designed for the leisurely education of an élite, so any thought of an all-graduate profession including elementary-school teachers, was clearly out of the question. On the other hand grammar-school teachers had traditionally always been graduates, which implied a measure of classical scholarship. The gulf between the two types of teachers was immense, for while the grammar-school teachers spent three years at universities where even the constituent colleges had a world-wide status, those serving the national system qualified by study at an institution of little standing, usually for a year; many even became certificated by attendance at teachers' centres without residential instruction. It was not until the 1960s that equality between the two sections of the profession could be seen as more than a pious hope, although few grammar-school teachers were professionally trained.

It is interesting to note the quick acceptance of the state primary schools for by 1900–1 82.5 per cent of children were attending elementary schools and 30 years later it was 92.2 per cent. In recent years *The Times* has run several articles on its woman's page to explain the liberal aspects of the state system. In contrast the pressures to preserve the binary system of secondary education have been enduring and consistent. Multilateral education was a natural development of all-age schools created by the simple additions of forms for older children as more stayed on. Under the patronage of progressive local authorities, this was coming along, as in other countries, developing from the initiation of the system in 1870. These enlarged schools with assured finance pressed ahead, developing outside the classical systems of secondary schools, until in the 1890s, some were challenging the existing classical secondary pattern. On this development being checked, the Education Act of 1902 was necessary to provide secondary education based on the traditional type of schools, to meet the increased demand. It was designed to preserve the *status quo* between the two types of school by a system of creaming by scholarships, while still providing places for those who could pay. In this way there was a renewal of the secondary system by the provision of regular finance, while the residual schools were deprived of their brighter pupils and the stimulation which their education had brought to the system.

In 1926 the Hadow Report, the "Education of the Adolescent", spelled out the division anew as grammar and technical streams which provided full secondary education, while the senior (later modern) schools, which took some 80 per cent to 90 per cent of all pupils, did not. These latter schools were hardly more than the elementary schools, with some extras added and this was quickly recognized by both pupils and parents. The same report also spelled out the multilateral solution but this attracted little following until the early 1950s. The singular failure of the British system of education to cater for the substantial majority, that is the non-academic children, largely stems from the wish to run public services on the Poor-Law principles of immediate cheapness, coupled with a singular lack of concern for the progress and welfare of children.

The lack of success of the educational system is shown in the standard of those popular papers with total daily sales of ten million copies. One of these was aptly described by an intelligent ten-year-old as a "comic for grown ups". Disc jockey, John Peel, said of another the content was so trivial that he was always surprised all words of over six letters were not divided by hyphens as in initial reading books. Sub-editors on such papers are largely restricted to a specially prepared vocabulary so that the material caters for a reading age of about ten years old; and this is practically the sole reading matter in perhaps 50 per cent of homes. The inadequate performance of the schools in this respect strikes at the very root of democracy, for such people cannot understand easily what is proposed or planned either at national or local level. The ubiquitous hire-purchase agreement is merely reduced to a jumble of words leading up to the line marked for signature. Explanatory leaflets and regulations for social benefits and the like, are largely incomprehensible. Income tax is a mystery. This is living in blinkers and leads to much manipulation, both commercially and poltically, which may suit certain interests, but is neither just nor desirable.

There are other effects of prolonged élitism, notably the reverence for the habitual, glorified by the label of tradition, which is widely used as a means of deterring reform, for empty ritual can extend the use of outworn procedures. In the educational context, it has exalted the excellence of the grammar and public schools at the expense of the residual schools, to the detriment of the whole system, for the prestigious cannot easily be criticized or reformed. Consequently there has been little adaptation along lines suitable for modern conditions. The result has been the production of suitably conditioned factory hands, rather than potential mechanics with an adequate background of scientific knowledge for machine age work. Yet as early as 1776, Adam Smith in his widely read *Wealth of Nations* advocated such teaching when he pointed out that "there is scarce a common trade which does not afford some opportunities for applying to it the principles of geometry and mechanics". Attempts to do just this have been repeatedly frustrated and few schools of any type can boast a curriculum which caters for the needs of industrial life, while in many grammar and public schools the classical curriculum would still be recognizable to the schoolmaster of Tudor and Stuart times.

The binary approach to schools has discernible effects in every educational situation. Agitation for nursery schools for poor families has continued with little success for nearly 70 years, but the recent interest of middle-class women in nursery education has quickly brought the matter to a head. The same interests distorted the primary-school curriculum through the influence of eleven-plus selection. It is reflected in the lack of enthusiasm for comprehensive secondary education and the poverty of educational building, especially in poor areas where the parental lobby is not large or informed. The approach is being repeated in higher education, by which one student will go to an older university with great status and social cachet as well as access to a world-renowned teaching staff, while another with equal entry qualifications may be at home with only the services of the Open University for guidance. The tag which accompanies the same grade of qualification will remain for 40 years of working life. The list is long and virtually inexhaustible because the binary approach to education is both rooted in, and also feeds the social-class system. The Conservative party has consistently espoused the cause of the secondary modern schools, but a party of their MPs had reluctantly to admit to Lord Boyle that they would not send their own children to them. In such an approach, which affects the whole nation, are the seeds of wasteful industrial conflict, to say nothing of the incidental human waste all along the line through lack of opportunity. A rational unified education system is overdue.

Setting Up The Rickety System—
The Nineteenth Century To 1870

The Reverend St John Rivers explained to Jane Eyre about his parish. "Morton when I came to it two years ago, had no school : the children of the poor were excluded from every hope of progress. I established one for boys : I mean now to open a second school for girls. I have hired a building for the purpose, with a cottage of two rooms attached to it for the mistress's house. Her salary will be thirty pounds a year : her house is already furnished, very simply, but sufficiently, by the kindness of a lady, Miss Oliver, the only daughter of the sole rich man in my parish—Mr Oliver, the proprietor of a needle factory and the iron foundry in the valley. The same lady pays for the education and clothing of an orphan from the workhouse; on condition that she shall aid the mistress in such menial offices connected with her own house and the school, as her occupation of teaching will prevent her having time to discharge in person. Will you be this mistress?"

He put the question rather hurriedly; he seemed half to expect an indignant, or at least a disdainful rejection of the offer. In truth it was humble—but then it was sheltered, and I wanted a safe asylum; it was plodding—but then, compared with that of a governess in a rich house, it was independent. It was not ignoble—not unworthy—not mentally degrading. I made my decision.

"I thank you for your proposal, Mr Rivers; and I accept it with all my heart."

"But you comprehend me?" he said. "It is a village school : your scholars will be only poor girls—cottagers' children—at the best farmers' daughters. Knitting, sewing, reading, writing, ciphering, will be all you have to teach. What will you do with your accomplishments? What with the largest portion of your mind—sentiments—tastes?"

Charlotte Bronte, *Jane Eyre*, 1847.

AS ALREADY OUTLINED the nineteenth century began with two clearly defined systems of education, the grammar schools for the middle classes and the voluntary-society schools for the manual workers; both were patently unsatisfactory because neither had a viable financial basis on which the development of any social institution depends. England was slow off the mark to remedy this, largely because the national taste is for the pragmatic, rather than working out complete solutions. The reason for this lies in the class situation which persuaded, with anecdotal evidence, much of it Biblical, that society was arranged in tiers and happiness was in acceptance of the rank in which an individual found himself. This involved acceptance of playing the rôle appropriate to that social grading. There was great persuasion that little education was required for the greater part of the population. It proved a most successful doctrinal trick for most of the victims accepted its findings willingly enough. There is little evidence in Britain that the lower orders have ever had much enthusiasm for increase in the term of compulsory education.

Parliament controlled the country's finance and thus had the last word in what was to happen. Parliament itself was controlled by the property-owning classes, who naturally saw government as primarily concerned with maintaining order and protecting property. The quality of all types of education was giving cause for concern by the 1820s, but the intervention of the State in any matter so personal as education ran counter to current political and economic philosophy. While the grammar schools eventually effected their renaissance through the successful innovations of Dr Arnold at Rugby, which were widely imitated, the schools for the children of manual workers were a larger and more unwieldy task. Parliament as constituted at that time had no wish to concern itself with social welfare which would involve the raising of money. Moreover there existed no central or local machinery for the administration of services such as education.

The problem persisted, and it was finally decided to frame the question as one of relieving the destitute and "the labouring poor" as regards the education of their children. Material relief had been the concern of the government since Tudor times, although the inclusion of education was an extension of the duty. In 1833 a small annual sum was granted by parliament towards "the building of school houses for the poor", to be distributed, not through the local Poor Law Boards, but through the voluntary societies concerned with providing schools. On 10 April 1839 an Order in Council set up a committee of the Privy Council "to superintend the application of any sums voted by parliament for the purpose of promoting public education."

The importance of this embryo central authority cannot be overstressed in the development of national education. These sub-committees were a survival of the period before the Revolution Settlement of 1689, when most of the business of government had been carried on by various committees of the Privy Council. With the establishment of cabinet government, individual departments with a minister responsible had superseded them, but from time to time similar committees had still been appointed to carry out special tasks. Most of these committees were temporary, but in some cases they became a standing committee. In time this could even develop into an executive department with a Member of Parliament to answer for its affairs in the House; it could advance further to an independent Department of State with its own section of the civil service. Most departments concerned with social and economic matters, such as Health and Trade, originated in this way. During the period of their evolution they often continued to function through the Privy Council, thus escaping responsibility to the legislature. It was in this way that the committee of the Privy Council, set up in 1839 for supervising the expenditure of public monies on education, eventually developed.

As successive Factory Acts freed more and more children from work to attend school, parliamentary grants-in-aid grew from £30,000 in 1839, to £100,000 in 1849 and £260,000 in 1853. The volume of work grew till it threatened to swamp the Privy Council office and absorb staff appointed for general duties. In 1853 no fewer than 28 clerks belonging to the Privy Council were devoting their whole time to educational business, in addition to the six officials properly employed in this manner. Despite the weight of work, the education provided was limited to teaching the three Rs to some children of the poorer classes.

Other curricular subjects were the province of the committee of the Privy Council for Trade, generally called the Board of

Trade, whose interest arose from the regulation of apprenticeships. In 1836 the Treasury had allocated them £1,500 for "the setting up of a Council and a Normal School of Design". Provincial schools had followed and in 1849 a Department of Practical Art had replaced the council. The Royal Commission on the Exhibition of 1851 drew attention to the poor state of the teaching of the arts and sciences. This resulted in 1853 in the Board of Trade Department of Science and Art with an annual vote of £41,586, divided into two sections; arts and sciences. One of its duties was the encouragement of elementary instruction in art and science, for which purposes it was in touch with the Committee of Council on Education.

There were still other authorities in the field. The War Office had army schools, the Admiralty had navy schools while the Commissioners of the Poor had workhouse schools. The Charity Commissioners had a more general responsibility in their concern for the growing number of educational endowments which in 1837 yielded an annual income of £312,544. About half the schools provided for were elementary schools, but their endowment put them outside the jurisdiction of the Committee of Council on Education, and they were therefore not subject to inspection, although many were in a notoriously parlous state. The Grammar School Act of 1840 gave the Courts of Chancery, under whose jurisdiction they came, powers to widen their curricula, but the procedure was cumbersome. Suggestions made to the Privy Council in 1841 and 1849 to set up a public authority to supervise charitable trusts were fruitless as Bills designed for this purpose failed. Eventually, in 1853, the Charitable Trusts Act set up such a body, but modification of existing schemes required the sanction of an Act of Parliament. Although many of the trusts were concerned with schools of different kinds, no powers of an educational character were given to the commissioners, nor was any provision made for consultation with the Committee of Council on Education.

Such a tangle of untidy and confusing administration attracted considerable attention. As early as 1852 Sir James Kay Shuttleworth unsuccessfully proposed one central body, a "Committee of Public Education and Charities" with representation in parliament. In 1854 the Board of Trade's Department of Science and Art, in its first report, made the point that elementary knowledge in their field could not make "much progress until it formed part of national education and was taught by the masters themselves" in the schools, which "could only be developed under the Committee of Council on Education". There was even greater concern over the extent to which the Privy Council facilities were occupied with educational matters; but the keenest criticism centred on the growing educational expenditure, its exact amount unknown, over which the legislature had no direct control. The amounts were entered as "miscellaneous services" in the Supplementary Estimates, so they were neither specifically "appropriated" nor subject to the close scrutiny of the House. In 1853 a Select Committee of the House required that this financial situation be regularized.

The Privy Council in their report of 1 February 1856 proposed that the Educational Establishment of the Privy Council and the Board of Trade Science and Art Departments should be "united under one direction and be represented in both Houses of Parliament"; this united establishment was to be called the Education Department. A member of the Privy Council should be the Vice-President, acting under the direction of the Lord President of the Council; the original two establishments were, for the time being, to continue to function as previously. The new department was also to report "on such questions concerning education as the Charity Commissioners referred to them". It was also to inspect army and naval schools. An Order in Council to this effect was approved by Parliament on 6 March 1856. In this way the constitutional status of an executive department was achieved, with its own civil service personnel.

The work of the department henceforth proceeded as in other government departments, policy being considered and decided by political chiefs, the Lord President and the Vice-President, who brought major issues to the Committee of the Council. The detail of administration became the task of the staff, whose head, the Permanent Secretary, was largely responsible for drafting and even initiating legislation through the shaping of minutes, codes and regulations, as well as advising the political chiefs.

Nevertheless despite an augmented staff the new department found its work grew so great "the system threatened to break down at the centre".[1] Much of the pressure came from a newly instituted method of assessing grants to schools by capitation. It was part of a larger plan which did not survive the parliamentary process intact. Proposed local bodies to assist in levying a local rate and routine administration did not materialize, so an inordinate amount of work fell on the central office although much of this was routine queries concerning the interpretation of regulations.

Proposals for modifying the making of grants introduced the notorious Revised Code of Regulations, which introduced "payment by results". This was not conceived so much as a measure for economic use of the education vote, which in 1860 amounted to £840,000, but primarily as a means of delegating some of the detailed work swamping the central office to managers of schools.[2]

In spite of all the efforts of the reorganized Education Department, there were never enough school places. An examination of the statistics reveals the size of the problem, and does much to explain the intractable administrative situation they presented to a single central office. In 1861 the Newcastle Commission reported 2,165,926 children in schools of every description which represented 1 in 7.7 of the total population, with 1 in 10 in average attendance. This was held to compare favourably with the compulsory system in Prussia which had an attendance of 1 in 6.25.

Other interpretations of the situation were not as favourable. Mr H. A. Bruce, Vice-President of the Committee of Council, when introducing his unsuccessful Bill for the Education of the Poor in July 1867 noted that the Prussian attendance was nearly equal to the numbers on the registers, so the true comparison was ten per cent attendance in England against sixteen per cent of the population in Prussia. He also drew attention to the superiority of the Prussian schools over their English counterparts; for the Newcastle Commission had reported few to be satisfactory, many indifferent, and a large number "almost wholly bad". Mr Bruce estimated that England and Wales with a population of 21 million should have one sixth "at elementary schools for the labouring classes", that is some 3,500,000 pupils with an expected attendance of 2,600,000.[3] The actual numbers in 1866 attending schools assisted by the State was

1,200,000 with an average attendance of 903,561. Thus about two-thirds of the potential students were absent.

He also showed that school grants were equally unsatisfactory, for the report for 1863 told of only 4,000 parishes receiving State assistance, while another 11,000 had nothing. Although the poorer country parishes were slow to be given assistance, he felt the greatest deficiencies were in the populous towns where the bulk of the uneducated children were concentrated for these were "perhaps intellectually superior to the children of the poor in the agricultural districts". There were wide differences in the distribution of assistance; for example in Cumberland and Westmorland two-thirds of the schools were assisted, while in Somerset not one parish in five received aid.

Mr Bruce stressed the sorry situation in the large towns. The Bishop of London had collected returns which showed 47 per cent of children in his diocese were not attending schools of any kind. Manchester reported an average attendance of 46 per cent. Fragmentary but extensive evidence showed "about half the labouring population are unable to write even their own names".[4]

The Children's Employment Commission of 1863 confirmed this account of educational progress among factory children. In one workshop it was reported : "The ragged, half starved, untaught children, or taught, if at all, a bit now and then, often in successive schools, chiefly the ragged or 'free' ..." The investigating official examined 270 of them under eighteen years of age and reported on their educational attainments.

Of these, 40 were below ten years of age, 10 of them being eight, and 5 only six years of age. The average age of the remaining 230 was 12¾. It would be difficult in any record of the actual state of instruction among a similar number of children of the working classes, to find an average state of intelligence so low as that exhibited by the answers to the questions addressed to them. A very small proportion can be said to have been taught, or to have retained, any elementary knowledge capable of exercising any appreciable effect upon their characters, or of being of any solid use in their daily life. The ignorance of a great many indeed, considering their age and that they live in the midst of a society keenly alive to social and political duties, cannot be contemplated, as it is portrayed by themselves, without pain and sorrow. A long list of illustrations might with ease be extracted from the evidence, exemplifying this state of ignorance; betraying in very many cases an almost entire want of acquaintance with the elementary truths of religion, and in almost all, a complete absence of all common secular instruction, or so slight and imperfect a command of reading, writing, or ciphering, as not to make either of the least practical value.[5]

The inadequacy of the educational facilities was increased by the growing child population and also intensification of efforts to make existing legislation effective against continuous and widespread evasion. Reports of 1863 described wholesale disregard for the Mining Act of 1861 which prohibited the employment underground of boys between the ages of ten and twelve. Contemporary accounts revealed widespread defiance of the Factory Acts as they related to children. Many industries were still untroubled by regulation and the Children Employment Commission of 1862 had no difficulty in finding evils comparable with earlier reports. To meet this situation the Factory Acts were extended in 1867 to all workshops with 100 workpeople. Regulations were expanded to end employment under the age of eight, and allow only half-time work between the ages of eight and thirteen. In the rural areas a report in 1867 had told of thousands of children in agricultural work gangs openly flouting controlling legislation. Fresh regulations were framed to meet this situation and the age for gang labour was raised to ten.

Public support for a national education system was hamstrung by an identification of the State's responsibility in this respect only to the children of the poor. For over a century the education of the people remained in the minds of many as no more than a particular kind of poor relief. At this stage of development it was also considered the duty of the central authority not to initiate development but to assist the voluntary efforts of the well intentioned. The overcrowding and inadequacies of the schools attracted growing criticism; in the language of the day, "educational destitution" was seen as the cause of many social problems. Moreover although the accent was still on social control of the lower orders, the counsels of the intellectual leaders who had long been agitating in the cause of public education, began to catch the public ear. Developments in science and technology obviously demanded a new kind of learning; the complications of government and administration, both at home and overseas, as well as in commerce and industry, all seemed to require men stamped in a new mould. The revelations of official inquiries following the widely publicized bungling of the Crimean Campaign of 1853–6 followed by the Indian Mutiny in 1857 underlined the need for new ideas.

It was not only the schools for the children of labourers, but all types of schools which were seen to be inadequate and a variety of official inquiries were appointed. They divided the schools into three divisions which reflected the social composition of the nation. The Clarendon Commission of 1861–4 investigated the leading nine grammar schools, under the title of public schools, named as Eton, Winchester, Westminster, Charterhouse, St Pauls, Merchant Taylors, Harrow, Rugby and Shrewsbury. These and several others which managed to get themselves included in the same category emerged as superior grammar schools, remaining financially independent through their endowments and expensive fees. They were almost entirely boarding establishments and were closely associated with the most influential families.

The Taunton Commission of 1864–8 concerned itself with schools not in receipt of parliamentary grants, that is the large number of private, proprietary and endowed schools which catered for the middle classes. Among the data considered by this commission was a memorandum by the Registrar General breaking down the 1864–5 population for England and Wales of 21 million into classes. The Commission's main concern was the three million rated as middle class because they occupied houses assessed at an annual value of £20 or over; it was estimated that they had 974,000 children between the ages of five and twenty. The schools for this section of the population were divided into three sections: the endowed schools, wholly or partially maintained by charitable endowments; private schools, the property of the master or mistress conducting them; and lastly proprietary establishments belonging to individuals or companies. The first category included all those originally intended either wholly or partially "for education above the elementary"; consisting of 705 grammar schools and 2,200 non-classical schools. The commission's main concern was with the grammar schools, for the others were devoted by foundation and practice to the education of the labouring classes. Detailed enquiries were made of only forty of the nonclassical schools; those with means exceeding £500 a year. The pressures on such establishments to adopt a grammar school format, with its higher fees and status, were considerable so, over the years, many moved into middle-class education. The 10,000 private schools recorded by the Commission are an indication of the general interest in education.

The education of those who were not able, or not prepared to pay, was initially investigated by the Newcastle Commission of 1858–61, charged with looking at the provision of "sound and cheap elementary instruction to all classes of the people". This inquiry revealed a sketchy system of schools only indifferently attended, their pupils mainly drawn from the manual workers' three million children aged between five and twelve. In 1865 a select committee was set to inquire into prospects of improving this makeshift system by more grants and further inspection.

The scope of these inquiries makes it plain there was concern for every level of the school system. Each had the same general aim of improving education; all were in agreement on the low standards which prevailed, all saw the need for government support and called for improved central administration. Despite this unity of purpose there was no suggestion of a general comprehensive plan; so each inquiry ignored anything outside its own sector and the measures which followed were on the same pattern. Although all aspects of public education were widely debated between 1867 and 1870 in both Houses of Parliament, the debates and subsequent legislation were in separate watertight sections. Suggestions to open the better schools to the lower orders were ignored and backbench attempts to discuss the creation of a unified scheme were brushed aside.

Not for the first time, the interest of the middle classes in the control of the grammar schools was openly demonstrated. The arbiters of this social strata, the county families, had throughout the century felt themselves to be under increasing pressures. Although later marriage and the adoption of contraception meant fewer children, their higher standard of living ensured that proportionately more survived with expectations of superior life-styles and calls on the family wealth. A big challenge came from the many new families making the most of the advantages of the new industrialism to climb the social ladder. The older, established families had already seen the diminution of their special position, based on the possession of land and connection with influential personalities. The import of grain and meat from the Americas had adversely affected the first, while the curtailment of well-paid government sinecures had weakened the opportunities for the second. The spread of the examination system from the universities to the professions and even for entry to government departments, hit them hard. Reluctance to become engaged in manufacture and trade limited their options. Although they appreciated the growing opportunities overseas, previous family experience also supplied information of the unhealthiness of more than one white man's grave.[6]

The renaissance of classical education by Arnold of Rugby was their main hope. Now it was not only cultural identification, but also as the means of qualifying for entry to the professions and services, where the old extended family connections could still count for something. It was obviously important to restrict access and preserve what was possible of the old élitist position. As a consequence secondary or grammar-school education remained shaped to their requirements; that is loaded with middle-class values and virtually exclusively male.

There were other influential views which weighed against a universal system. Prominent among these was John Stuart Mill who observed. "While it is almost a self evident maxim that the State should require and compel the education up to a certain level of every human being who is born a citizen" this did not justify the provision of State schools for all; for, he held "a general State education is a new contrivance for moulding the people to be exactly like one another". However although he was against a universal system on the Prussian model, Mill considered "the State might compel, and the State might defray the cost of the education of the poor".[7] At that time the State did neither of these; neither compelling attendance at schools, nor to any adequate extent meeting the cost of those who did attend.

The evidence of the extent of State assistance was so inadequate that protagonists could produce widely differing arguments. In 1867 the government spokesman, the Duke of Marlborough, claimed that the unaided areas contained some 564,000 children, while the opposition spokesman, Earl Russell held the number to be approximately a million.[8] Nevertheless the Departmental Committee investigating the state of education were able to glean enough to accept a conclusion of widespread "educational destitution"; it also found that the Education Department, as it was constituted, was quite unable to cope with the educational problem. Robert Lowe in his evidence, pointed out that the initiative lay with individuals, the department could only then follow their lead; he stressed that there should be powers to initiate action to extend and improve the existing schools for the people.

The report concluded that "a material and fundamental alteration" was necessary in "the whole system of national education", by which was meant working-class education. It was recommended there should be a Minister of Public Instruction of cabinet rank to encourage study of science and the arts, as well as popular education. Local bodies should be set up with powers to levy an education rate, while parents should have a statutory right to withdraw their children from religious instruction as a means of meeting objections to State aid for denominational schools. While preserving the division of the curriculum, still limiting the scheme to the labouring poor and proposing local bodies on the lines of the Poor Law, this report also looked forward to local action and a proper financial backing for the schools instead of uncertain voluntary contributions.

Matthew Arnold writing in 1865 underlined another snag when describing the situation as approaching the time when the working classes will demand "public schools, and not schools which the clergyman or the squire, or the millowner, calls 'my school'. And what is the capital difficulty in the way of giving public schools? It is this : that the public school for the people must rest upon the municipal organisation of the country. But we in England have our municipal organisation still to get".[9]

The endowed schools were similarly recommended by the Taunton Commission for material reform, which also foundered on the lack of suitable local-government bodies to undertake supervision. Since 1853 the Charity Commissioners had had considerable powers over charitable funds, but the cumbersome procedure for change involved reference to Parliament. It was proposed that the powers of the Charity Commission should be strengthened and supervisory bodies on a county basis set up. The report lamented the lack of a local-government structure and the resulting difficulty in creating a suitable body to control local educational endowments, tentatively suggesting direct election as the "most trustworthy guarantee of permanent activity and efficiency. But it may be doubted whether an intelligent interest in the subject is at present sufficiently general, to enable the public at large to take the management of schools so entirely into their own hands."[10] Consequently *ad hoc* county boards were proposed based on members from Boards of Guardians, the bodies administering the local Poor Law, plus half their number nominated by the Crown. It was thought this type of body, although not really representative would become "amenable to public opinion". If the majority of the Guardians wished to have an elected board, this would be allowed, for although the resulting body was thought likely to make mistakes, there would be benefit in the long run as "much narrow minded opposition to liberal plans would disappear at once". It was proposed that large towns should set up their own bodies made up of town councillors and trustees of the larger endowded schools in the area, thus avoiding the odious Poor Law connection. In all cases the local District Commissioner of the Charity Commission would be an ex-officio member to supply specialist advice. These forward-looking proposals for representative bodies were later withdrawn, the supervision of funds being undertaken by officials called District Commissioners, engaged on civil service contracts.

In both working-class and middle-class education, the establishment of a stronger central authority was advocated, together with effective local authorities, yet these new organs were to be distinctly separate. The psychological barriers of the Victorian class system could hardly be more clearly demonstrated. It should also be noted that in the proposals put forward there was little prospect of progressive advance. The suggested local representatives for education were from the Boards of Guardians and the town councils, ensuring that they would be a further exten-

COBDEN'S LOGIC.

"I DON'T know, perhaps, any country in the world where the MASSES OF THE PEOPLE ARE SO ILLITERATE AS IN ENGLAND."—*From Mr. Cobden's Speech at Rochdale.*

"Sound Statesmanship requires such an extension of the franchise as shall admit the Masses of the People to political power."—*From the Same Speech.*

Punch – 5 December 1863)

sion of the authority of property owners and businessmen who made up the bulk of such bodies.

About this time the schools acquired a nomenclature which indicated the valuation of the systems. The education provided in the public schools was linked with the universities and termed "higher" or "primary" education; the endowed schools catering for the middle classes were called "secondary schools", while the schools for the manual workers' children were called "elementary schools".

The primary schools were dealt with under the Public Schools Act of 1868, which delegated to individual governing bodies the task of carrying out their own reformation. Seven commissioners were appointed for a fixed period to overlook the new arrangements, which had to be submitted to the Privy Council for approval, for these were "the schools of the highest political and social importance". In the debate on the Act, Sir Stafford Northcote, replying for the government, brushed aside a proposal that the endowments of certain schools should be more properly used for the benefit of the people of the metropolis, arguing that the Clarendon Commission, whose report had been the basis of the Bill, as well as the Bill itself, were only concerned to improve "the higher education of the country". It was in the same debate that these schools were first described as "primary schools", meaning those of the first rank, a term later extended to include the universities.[11]

In 1869 the Endowed Schools Act dealt with secondary schools; it did not proceed with the suggestions for local bodies, but it did something to strengthen the central authority and extend the secondary school system through a special temporary commission, set up to initiate schemes reorganizing endowments and to encourage new secondary schools for girls as well as boys.

Although in the two grades of grammar schools there was comparatively little change, in the field of elementary education, after prolonged controversy, the State moved decisively into a new area of responsibility. In June 1866 the Liberal administration was defeated and for two years a Conservative minority government maintained itself in office. In the middle of this precarious political situation, in 1867, Bruce, a Liberal, introduced a Bill for the Education of the Poor which had a second reading on the 10 July, but was withdrawn five days later.

On the 16 July the Reform Bill of 1867 passed the Commons. Its main clauses lowered the franchise qualification to all holders of houses worth £12 a year, which doubled the electorate and completely altered the political climate, for this gave the artisan in steady employment the vote. A significant acknowledgement of this fact was the re-emergence of Bruce's Bill in 1868 under the more elevated title of The Elementary Education Bill.[12] At the same time Conservatives introduced their own Bill in the Lords, and the debates on these measures revealed the differences between the two parties.

Several party spokesmen had already made their views clear in the debate on the reform of public schools. Quaker William Forster, the Liberals' expert, welcomed "the reform of the public schools; he expected the endowments to be so arranged that clever boys of a low sphere of life might be able to obtain a high-class education by rising from the national schools, with the assistance of exhibitions, to the secondary and primary schools". Mr Neate, MP for Oxford, had opposed the same measure as delusive and reactionary, for he suggested it was perhaps too late to bring the sons of the wealthy and great again under the same roof for the purpose of education with the sons of farmers and tradesmen; but it was not too late to take back from those funds, which were originally intended chiefly for the benefit of the sons of the farmers and tradesmen, some part of which was now, exclusively appropriated to the benefit of the rich. Sir Harry Verney protested at the exclusion of the poorer townsmen from their own local schools of Harrow and Rugby. The Tower Hamlets Member, Mr Ayrton, saw the measure as maintaining a "fashionable system of education for the fashionable classes" and "with those great endowments they were going to do for the education of the poor and the great body of the people of the country absolutely nothing".[13]

These minority protests against "the appropriation by the rich" of the endowments intended for the support of poor scholars, together with suggestions that children of the poorer classes should be given some opportunity to win their way to public schools had no effect, because class segregation was regarded on both sides of the House as axiomatic. It was not only a wish to limit opportunities for advancement which motivated such views but a feeling that education should not become a State charge. Lord Montagu, opposing Bruce's Elementary Education Bill contended that "Every expression which limited the Bill to the education of the poor had been studiously omitted. ... It was a measure providing simply for elementary education ... and it might be taken advantage of by the middle classes". Mr Bruce interrupted with a cry of "Hear, hear!" Lord Montagu noted "the declared object of the right honourable Gentleman, but must differ from him as to the wisdom of the course he was pursuing".[14]

Similarly neither political party contemplated making school attendance compulsory, for both were agreed that with the existing supply of schools and teachers this would have been "quixotic and impracticable". This point was made by Bruce in presenting both his Bills although he clearly indicated the need for eventual compulsion. In introducing the 1868 Bill he pointed out that a national system of education could only be a gradual growth and the success of the schools depended on the efficiency of the masters, but "you could not at once create a supply of the masters. If you had a railway to make, you could ensure a sufficient number of labourers; but the mere issue of an advertisement would not give you skilled teachers."

Neither party proposed to interfere with the existing voluntary system, although both agreed on its inadequacy. The Conservatives sought to minimize the weaknesses, but both based their plans on supplementing it; the differences arose from approach. Clearly more money must be available and there must be an authority to spend it; the choice lay between local and national fund raising with similar issues about the point of control. Briefly the choice was between centralization or dispersal of policy making.

The Liberal Elementary Education Bill of 1868 proposed decentralization of authority and the provision of funds from local taxation. This had been suggested in the select committee report, but the problem was the constitution and size of the administrative unit area. Concrete proposals for local control had originated in Lord Russell's unsuccessful Bill of 1853 when the borough had been the proposed unit, while other proposals had favoured association with the Poor Law Boards of Guardians, notoriously illiberal bodies. The Liberal Bill planned to set up representative local education authorities with the power to levy an education rate; these school committees were to be elected in corporate towns by the town council and in rural areas by the ratepayers. The committee could supplement local school accommodation where it was thought inadequate but their powers to interfere in the running of schools were considerably restricted. The original Bill introduced permissive rating, but Bruce's second Bill proposed powers for compulsion, which were only to be used after voluntary action had failed to remedy demonstrable "educational destitution". It was foreseen that "the religious difficulty" would arrive from financing education with public money, so there was to be no distinction between denominational and nondenominational schools, although parents were to have a statutory right to remove their children from religious instruction.

The Conservatives opposed the Bill strongly stigmatizing the financing of schools from the rates as inequitable. This was not an unexpected objection, as the party strength lay with the landed classes, on whom the rate would fall heavily. They minimized the defects of the existing system, particularly in the rural areas where the landowners held sway, but the situation in the towns could not be denied, so they attempted to attribute it to a lack of public spirit on the part of the Liberal manufacturers. It was also argued that the compulsory rate would destroy the voluntary system, as contributions would fall off and parents would refuse to pay pence for fees. The Conservatives roundly condemned such proposals as destructive and mischievous. The religious difficulty was invoked to suggest that the introduction of educational rates would lead to secular schools as in the USA, together with the loss of that vital ingredient in education, the inculcation of sound moral and religious principles. The operation of a conscience clause as a condition of the schools receiving grants was said to put a premium on lack of principle. Thought should also be given to the unfortunate children who because of their parents' denominational allegiance would be excused religious instruction in school and go out into the world without a basis for right moral action.[15]

Later the Conservative minority government expressed their proposals in their own Bill, which had the avowed object of conserving the existing system, "founded in great wisdom", so as to incorporate it in a "national system". In contrast to the Liberal Bill, priority was given to the reform of the central authority under the direction of a Secretary of State, who, it was proposed, should have "the whole range of educational matters under his consideration and control" which implied, besides elementary education, interests in the science and art department and the endowed schools, as well as education in Scotland and Ireland. The proposed Secretary for Education was to be charged to investigate educational problems in the whole country and to present suitable schemes for parliamentary approval.

The Liberal opposition criticized this Conservative Bill for wrong priorities, for they claimed not much could be gained from appointing a minister until he could be given control of a really national system which could not be built on the existing voluntary structure. Moreover it did nothing to create machinery to initiate action where it was urgently needed, namely in the big industrial towns.

In the conflict of proposal and counterproposal neither Bill made the statute book. The only reforms that resulted from this period were relaxations in the rules governing grants to schools. The rule requiring all schools to be "connected with some religious denomination" was abolished to meet the Nonconformist objections, and it was hoped that they would now feel able to accept State grants for the schools they managed, which up to that time many had refused. It was also thought this might encourage more new schools to accept grants, as even purely secular establishments would be eligible for help. A second relaxation, of doubtful advantage, indicates the difficulty of staffing. Grants had been available only to schools with a certificated teacher, but in rural districts, where the authorities were poor and the district small, this condition prevented many schools from receiving assistance; while not abandoning the rule, under certain conditions, a proportion of the grant could now be allowed.

Parliament was dissolved in the latter part of 1868, and a strong Liberal government resulted enabling them to proceed with their own educational programme presented by Forster. It was nevertheless a compromise measure, to meet the needs of practical politics. The radical demand for a completely new national system of schools with a different orientation of the curriculum would have aroused indignation in a dozen important interests, not least the various religious bodies. Moreover the economic and staffing resources were not available. For these reasons the ultimate 1870 Education Act was a compromise between the existing system of State assisted voluntary schools and the radical demand for free non-sectarian schools under popular control. It was the first piece of modern social legislation, full of innovations, from the adoption of a secret ballot in elections to the introduction of substantial delegated legislation. Yet its greatest advance was in the form in which it put the measure into effect.

Four ways had been proposed for the reform of the education system. First, further support for the voluntary societies; but the failure of this formula was the cause for a new measure. Forster in a confidential office memo dated 21 October 1869 wrote, "Notwithstanding the large sum of money voted for education, there are vast numbers of children utterly untaught, or very badly taught, because there are too few schools, because many schools are bad schools, and because many parents either cannot, or will not, send their children to school". The large sum voted was about half a million pounds, whereas the cost of the Crimean War had been £37 million.

Secondly, there had been the possibility of extending the Factory Acts, either by prohibiting the employment of children to persuade them to attend school or by linking work with education, thus making the employers responsible for instruction. This method had a sorry history of evasion and in the debate Mr Mundella, MP for Sheffield, called such Acts "a farce" and showed no regard was paid to them.[16]

A third proposal concerned the extension of the Industrial Schools Act of 1866 to recruit children into the schools. It had been specifically framed to deal with children who were minor delinquents or, in modern terms, in need of care and protection. It was clearly a punitive measure, and that it could be even proposed as the basis of a national education system illustrates a prevalent attitude to the children of the lower orders.

The fourth choice, the Poor Law, was the traditional organization for making help available to the poor. It was a harsh system, universally detested, by which the other classes provided a minimum assistance to the labouring poor. The accent was on cheapness and its routines were planned to humiliate and so prevent application for help from all but the really needy. As the time-honoured existing machinery for helping the lower orders, it was to many Victorians, the obvious method of providing education for those who could not find the fees for their children.

Although the Poor Law never had control of education, the tenets of the period, influenced by the doctrine of *laissez faire* and a mandate of complete parental responsibility for children, ensured that the elementary schools remained in many minds a type of poor relief. This was a stigma that remained, particularly as regards education over the age of eleven, to be largely dispersed only by the 1944 Act. The language of the older, repressive philosophy, the basis of the Poor Laws, kept intruding into the arrangements for a national education scheme. Educational writing of the period has constant reminders of the Poor Law for, although overtly concerned with popular education, many still carried in their minds an analogy with the system which they knew so well in its material relief of the poor.

In the parliamentary debates on education there was much concern for the neglected parishes and the phrase applied to the resulting situation was "educational destitution", an epithet redolent of Poor Law jargon. In putting forward the terms of the 1870 Bill, Forster deliberately used the language of the Poor Law and stressed the parts of his proposed system which were similar to the older, widely accepted philosophy. He invoked the time-worn Poor Law formula of official schemes co-operating with charity. He told the House his object was "to complete the present voluntary system, to fill up the gaps, sparing the public money where it can be done without, procuring as much as we can the assistance of the parents, and welcoming as much as we rightly can the co-operation and aid of those benevolent men who desire to assist their neighbours".[17]

Another Poor Law belief was that assistance to parents would cause them to neglect their children. Forster paid lip service to this when he announced that in considering the question of intellectual relief there would be "the most careful absence of encouragement to neglect their children" and this approach was put forward as an essential part of the measure. He cautiously stressed that for those parents who could not pay school fees, there would be free tickets and gave a pledge that "these free tickets shall have no stigma of pauperism attached to them", for that would have meant the non-co-operation of many self-respecting poor families.

Thus each of the four ways which suggested themselves to the contemporary mind faced with framing a national education system was tied to the past, in one way or another a part of a system based on class segregation and exploitation. As such they had nothing to contribute to the reconstruction of society which was felt to be urgently needed through the realization that a number of other countries with well developed education systems had achieved dramatic military and economic advances. There was a fear that Britain would be left behind. In explaining his 1870 Bill, Forster told parliament :

> Upon the speedy provision of elementary education depends our industrial prosperity. It is no use trying to give technical teaching to our artisans without elementary education; uneducated labourers—and many of our labourers are utterly uneducated—are, for the most part, unskilled labourers, and if we leave our workfolk any longer unskilled, notwithstanding their strong sinews and determined energy, they will be overmatched in the competition of the world.

The swing of the balance of the nation's economy from agriculture to industry which had taken place in the 1860s had brought about the need for a different kind of work force; a break with the past was inevitable. The Education Act of 1870 was the first major measure to do anything constructive for a people who had been ruthlessly exploited in the process of industrialization.

It is true that the Act did not go far enough for the Nonconformists and radicals who even before the new education scheme had become law, had formed the National Education League in Birmingham in 1869 to fight for "free, compulsory and secular" schools. It is true, as one of their number, John Morley,[18] wrote in 1873, that the 1870 Act "was the least possible with [its] rickety framework of permissive boards and permissive compulsion"; but that was by design. Forster had framed a deceptively mild measure so that he could introduce the tip of the wedge of universal education. To any student of politics it was clearly the first step in the tactics of progressive social legislation, the geometry of which was dubbed by a later Permanent Secretary at the Board of Education, Selby Bigge, "the time honoured method of gradual advance".

ENI)·

The chief significance of the Act was in its provision of a school place for every child, safeguarded by a framework which in ten years was to lead to universal compulsory attendance. It was thus the first step in creating a better life chance for every one. Forster realistically said in proposing his Bill that he aimed to cover the country with good schools and to get the parents to send their children to them. With the help of later supporting legislation, this is basically what the 1870 Act did.

The machinery for achieving this was ingeniously designed not to cause initial alarm. The whole country was divided into a number of districts in which the state of educational provision was investigated by the central authority. If the schools were found to be "sufficient, efficient and suitable" there would be no State intervention, although the right was reserved to re-examine the situation later. Where things were found to be unsatisfactory, the voluntary authorities were allowed a period of grace to put their house in order; if this was not effective then the State would step in. The intervention was through the use of a new local authority the School Boards. These, as originally conceived were to raise a local rate to set up and maintain their own schools; they were also to assist the local voluntary schools.

The Act empowered them to make bye-laws to compel the children to attend between the ages of five and twelve on pain of small fines. This was raised to thirteen in the final draft and there were also specified examples of "reasonable excuse" for non-attendance, such as illness, unavoidable causes or there being no school within two miles.

The central authority introduced overall controls, as grant aid required all schools, both voluntary and Board alike, to submit to certain conditions such as achieving satisfactory standards of tuition, accepting inspection and enforcing the conscience clause. The aided schools through receiving government grants had long been accustomed to accept the first two conditions, but now inspection which had been on a denominational basis with

THE THREE R's; OR, BETTER LATE THAN NEVER.

RIGHT HON. W. E. FORSTER (CHAIRMAN OF BOARD). "Well, my little people, we have been gravely and earnestly considering whether you may learn to read. I am happy to tell you that, subject to a variety of restrictions, conscience clauses, and the consent of your vestries—*you may!*"

(*Punch* – 26 March 1870)

inspectors approved by the senior clergy, was to be on a territorial basis. The conscience clause was the condition arrived at in parliamentary debate to narrow the disagreements between the parties on religious teaching. Forster explained that now that public money was being spent on secular education there was growing support for the view that there ought to be both liberty of religious teaching and also liberty of withdrawal by the parent; and it was on this principle that he framed the conscience clause.

On the religious issues the Bill was debated at length, and the clause allowing parents to withdraw children from religious instruction was made more effective by the further requirement that such instruction was to be given only during the first and last lessons of the day. The provision became known as the Time-Table Clause. Religion in Board schools raised many nice issues, but compromise came with the acceptance of the amendment moved by Cowper-Temple to include a clause which forbade the teaching in Board schools of any formula or catechism distinctive of any particular sect.

Forster in presenting his Bill had planned it otherwise, explaining that:

> If we are to prevent religious teaching altogether, we must say that the Bible shall not be used in schools at all. But would it not be a monstrous thing that the book, which, after all, is the foundation of the religion we profess, should be the only book that was not allowed to be used in our schools? But then it may be said that we ought to have no dogmatic teaching. But how are we to prevent it? Are we to step in and say the Bible may be read but may not be explained? Are we to pick out Bible lessons with the greatest care in order that nothing of a doctrinal character might be taught to the children? . . .
>
> I say that it is (a labour) of detailed supervision which does not belong to the central government, and in which the great probability is that the central government would fail.[19]

The school regulations which carried the Cowper-Temple clause into effect were clear and simply worded. The Bible should be read and explained together with instruction in the principles of morality and religion suitable for the capacity of the children. There should be no attempt to attach the children to any particular denomination; the matter was left to the discretion of the teachers and the managers, with rights of appeal to the local School Board in case of dispute. The right of withdrawal of children from religious instruction was clearly stated. It was obligatory to display a copy of the relevant parts of the 1870 Act in the school. Many schools placed this notice at head height directly facing the entrance door. In view of the length of the religious dispute and the depth of feeling engendered, this compromise was singularly successful and attracted little litigation. It was the cornerstone of further compromise, especially in the framing of agreed syllabuses of religious education after 1924.

In the final stages of the Bill the unrepresentative nature of existing local government with which the School Boards were to be associated was raised. Forster agreed, "It is almost a disgrace to this country that we have this difficulty at all ... we are behind almost every other civilized country, whether in America or on the continent of Europe, in respect of rural and municipal organization; and this drawback meets us not only in connection with education, but when many other social questions affecting the people come before us."[20]

The School Boards finally emerged as directly elected in secret ballot by the burgesses in the towns, and the ratepayers in the country areas. These *ad hoc* representative bodies, especially in the towns, became the interest of the radicals and the vehicle of much democratic educational progress.

The same section also defeated a proposal that voluntary schools should be aided from the rates. The Board schools were therefore the only ones maintained out of local funds, although they too, in general charged a small fee, which, together with the exchequer grant, made up the school fund. School Boards could also raise loans for buildings. Although the voluntary schools were to receive more generous exchequer grants, the Board schools operated on a more realistic financial basis and it was not long before the difference in facilities began to tell.

The provision of education through State intervention had at last been accomplished; "the education of the poor" tag of the original 1867 Bill had been lost, but the new measure reinforced with its very title the identification of the State with elementary education. The old attitudes of patronage remained and continued to dominate the evolution of the administrative machinery of the emerging system. The State still had nothing to do with the grammar schools and the two styles of schools went on separately as before, thus re-defining the class barriers which already divided society.

Those who looked beyond the immediate issues, like Lyon Playfair, MP for the Scottish Universities, attacked the formation of a narrow system which "confined a department to mere elementary education and cuts it off completely from all secondary and higher education". Forster and the Liberal government of the period, occupied with the practical politics of the measure, argued that it was not in the power of any central educational department to influence the quality of education unless the children could be induced to attend the schools first and this could only be accomplished by local, not central government.

The result was that the Act of 1870 set up a decentralized system, with "local administration and local rates, aided by money voted by Parliament and expended under local management" with, it is true, "central inspection and control". This basis determined the future relationship of the State, the local-education authority and the parent. It ensured that there was no bureaucratic education system imposed from above, and the flexibility of the English pattern of schools followed. However, certain disadvantages came from the loss of the Conservative proposal for a unified system under a responsible minister for this could have given more opportunity to produce a truly national system with integration of the two levels of schools. But, in its main aims the creation of a school system and ensuring that the children of the labouring classes attended, the Act served its purpose.[21]

It should be understood that there was no universal enthusiasm for compulsory schooling among poor families, for wages were low and they needed all the monetary support their offspring could contribute. This was widely accepted by the courts as a reason for non-attendance. The employers, frequently closely linked with the local authorities, were reluctant to lose a traditional part of their labour force, especially a section which they knew to be cheap and trouble free. The children themselves usually preferred the status of paid workers to that of non-earning scholars. The costs of schools were seen as falling heavily on the local tax payer, and many saw no need to increase that burden to educate labour to standards which they considered unnecessary. There was considerable survival of eighteenth-century attitudes especially in the rural areas. More subtle barriers arose when the unlettered father faced the change in his family budget with uncomprehending resentment. He was also soon made aware of other pressures concerned with regular attendance, together with the need for better feeding and care of his children. Even if the courts were reluctant to enforce the law, there was nevertheless a stigma attached to a failed court action. The father also felt his position as head of the family challenged by the new authority of the schools, while children who became literate were placed in a position of advantage over their illiterate parents. These varied threats to the father's position as the undisputed head of his family lay behind the reluctance of manual workers to accept the advantages offered by the schools.

III

Getting Them In And Trying To Do Better
1870–1902

"I don't know what all this fuss is about education. Look at the Pagets. None of them can read or write . . . and they got on all right."

Lord Palmerston to Queen Victoria.

(The Pagets had estates in Staffordshire, Anglesey and Dorset amounting to 20,000 acres. The family fortune had been founded through services to Henry VIII in the Reformation. The family titles included that of Marquess of Anglesey and Earl of Uxbridge.)

THE LATTER PART of the nineteenth-century saw the intensification of the struggle of the old order to control the new; on every side there is evidence of great bitterness as the managerial and owning classes tried to contain the rising aspirations of the manual workers. In the educational field the last 30 years of the century were taken up with two questions; achieving universal, compulsory but free education; and raising the indifferent standards of the schools, so that youngsters of poor background should have a chance of "education beyond the elementary" stage. In obstructing these modest aims the hydra of reaction made full use of the confusion brought about by rapid social and economic changes. The schools were only a peripheral part of the social struggle, but a comment on the causes of unrest in the general scene will help in understanding the many difficulties which emerged at every stage in the development of a truly national education system. These forces operated at different levels of intensity in the simmering social cauldron, and they can be loosely grouped under four heads.

Firstly there were the large movements of population which arose from recruitment to the growing industrial machine with resulting ethnic and religious rivalries. This had started in the

seventeenth century with an influx of Scots, Welsh and Irish
to the developing towns. The continued flow depended largely
on the conditions prevailing in the area of origin for people were
driven out rather than attracted by better living conditions in
the towns. Alongside these groups were the displaced English
rural workers. Before the arrival of radio with its intrusion of a
standard speech into every home, accent and vocabulary varied
widely, as Shaw pointed out in *Pygmalion*. In many cases
the dialect of one area was largely unintelligible to those living in
another.

Most of the people displaced in this way were, for industrial
purposes, unskilled labour; moved on by eviction or famine, they
were desperate to win a toe hold in a new area. In their extreme
need they would accept wages under the established rates, which
were already inadequate. Victims of the Irish famine[1] arriving
in the 1850s or of the Highland clearances[2] of the 1860s were
in no position to bargain or consider the solidarity of the working classes. The differences of language, which could be total
with many Welsh, Highland Scots and West coast Irish, were
aggravated by religious differences, for their local brands of
religions were not always identifiable with the English versions.
Catholicism, whether allied with Irish nationalism or not, caused
much suspicion, especially if there were Irish Protestants in the
area, as in Liverpool. The arrival of some 120,000 Jews in the
1890s, Yiddish speaking, visibly foreign and wretchedly poor,
added another variant to the conflict. There were other smaller
groups from Europe who arrived, often as political refugees,
and naturally allied themselves to radical political movements.
An envied group was the specially-skilled Germans who arrived
from the late 1880s onwards to work as clerks, mechanics, motor
drivers; they often built up thriving businesses as pork butchers
and continental-style grocers.

These various groups were generally viewed with suspicion
as a threat to a precarious way of life, for loss of job in the
nineteenth century was the first step to the workhouse. Factory
conditions were bad, the work life short, and competition at all
levels jungle-fierce.

Alongside this steady flow of new labour into the towns, was
the second factor motivating nineteenth-century society; the
struggle for the benefits of industralization. At the start of the

century there were whole armies of labouring men roaming
Britain to work in coolie-like conditions to build the infrastructure of an industrial country. They were mainly employed on
digging out the paths of canals, railways, the roads, the drains
and the construction of many new buildings. They were at the
outset brawling, drunken roisterers, their constant violence a
byword;[3] but later they began to inch their way up the social
scale, which they had done so much to enrich. Through their
churches and emerging trade unions they sought to escape from
exploitation by the community, to partnership in it. A central
feature of the Victorian labour scene is the long fight by unskilled labour for recognition as responsible citizens with a right
to a stake in the national community.

It is understandable that such activities should be opposed
by the property-owning interests who believed that the cheaper
the labour, the higher the profits. Britain with a glut of unskilled
manpower gave little thought to labour-saving, and management skills were therefore neglected. This was in contrast to
the USA where labour was in shorter supply and had to be
used carefully, with consequent higher productivity.

Another interest also sought the benefits of industrialization:
the skilled manual workers usually referred to as artisans, often
with the prefix "respectable", to contrast them with the unskilled
element. Their life style was entirely different and seen as
superior to that of the labourers' hand-to-mouth existence. It
was their children who benefited most from the new schools, for,
with less pressure on them to seek employment, they attended
regularly and stayed on longer. These skilled men owed their
importance to maintaining the industrial apparatus; at the
lower levels they set up the machines for the unskilled to operate,
but at higher levels they modified and even designed new
mechanisms to suit the needs of the occasion. Alongside the
industrial experts were those with the more traditional skills in
masonry, metals, wood and other materials. These specialists,
both within the industrial complex and as private businessmen,
were constantly called on to adapt their techniques to the
changing demands of new products. In general they functioned
as junior managerial staff and identified themselves with the
owners, for they were well paid with considerable personal
security. Their favourable position arose, not only from their

importance to the owners, but also because they were formed
into trade unions, usually grouped by craft. These organizations
although local and small seem to have provided considerable
protection through provident funds and by creating a method of
communicating national and local developments in their
business.

The attitude of the artisans was one of constant opposition to
the fight for better conditions, for as they saw it, the labourers'
rise would threaten their favourable position; preoccupation
with the differential is still a feature of trade union negotiations.
These men were an intelligent and informed élite, some of whom
built up tidy businesses. They were politically active and found
little difficulty, after the Franchise Act of 1867 gave them the
vote, in accommodating themselves within the two existing
political parties, making Gladstone and Disreali their political
idols. This was in contrast to the unskilled workers, whose political needs required a new philosophy, which finally produced the
Labour party.

The third factor influential on the social scene was the
religious one and the intensity of religious feeling alive in the
nineteenth century is hard to comprehend today. In a period of
little personal security, even for the wealthy, religion was the
one certain thing. The resulting fervour invaded the schools
because at all levels education was identified with moral training; indeed, in the case of the children of the labouring classes,
little else mattered in certain influential quarters. It should be
realized that the original organization of the State Church, the
Church of England, had evolved during the agricultural period
of the country's economy and the pattern has still not adapted
to the population changes of the industrial revolution.[4] As a
consequence their educational strength lay in the small village
schools, where the local squire usually held control of the living.
From the eighteenth century the Anglican Church had been
aware of a loss of influence. Its massively entrenched position as
the financed organ of the landowners gave it great assurance,
but robbed it of the power to adapt to the great social changes
which accompanied industrialization. Anglicans saw their main
threat as Nonconformism, an amalgamation of dispersed religious groups largely supported by skilled manual workers. The
resulting rivalry, which had its roots deep in the Reformation

and the Civil War, expressed itself in the Sunday Schools, with extension to the voluntary-school movement at the start of the nineteenth century. Later Catholic and Jewish claims in the same field aggravated the situation, as both communities proved successful.

One cause of the intensity of religious feeling was the insistence in seeing the evils produced by the concentration of people in the impersonal industrial towns as caused by lack of morals. It was widely propagated and believed that the sorry state of depressed families came from idleness and lack of effort on their part. Moreover it was claimed squalor, drunkenness, immorality and all the other ills of nineteenth century society, especially evident in the towns, could all somehow be avoided by unremitting hard work and blind religious faith. Each denomination saw its view as the sovereign and just remedy of the social diseases of the age. The first objective surveys of conditions, which began in the 1890s, demolished the basis for this comfortable middle-class belief, but it has considerable residual force even today.

Locally, the rivalry to claim children unattached to any religion was especially fierce between Anglicans and Nonconformists. Both made great play to attract them to their Sunday Schools with small prizes and treats, such as a Christmas concert with a meal, as well as outings at Easter and midsummer. On Sunday afternoons working men preferred their children out of the house so that they could have privacy for a marital embrace and a sleep. Children would work out ways of dividing their attendances to qualify for two sets of "treats", for the same carefully selected scriptural texts would often serve in both Anglican and Nonconformist classes as proof of Biblical knowledge.

The fourth ferment of the Victorian scene was the arrival of new knowledge, which was not easily accepted because it challenged long-held beliefs. The growth of rationalism and scientific ideas had a long and considerable influence starting with the French thinkers associated with the revolution. There was no lack of able minds to advance the causes of republicanism, rationalism, atheism, free thinking, as well as progressive political ideas, although taxes on publications restricted circulation of these writings. The leading educationalists were usually graduates of the older universities in holy orders who could not accept new ideas of this type. Worse was to come and it is difficult to overestimate the effects in these quarters of the publication in 1859 of Darwin's *Origin of the Species;* it tilted at the very foundation of their world, which lay in the first chapter of *Genesis.* It was this same group who barred the introduction of a broader curricuum, especially the introduction of science and realistic history. Against the ground-swell of new ideas, the classically-orientated educationalists, their position strengthened by their religious cloth, fought to maintain control of the schools of all types. It was their influence that shaped the system, and insisted that the schools for the children of manual workers were largely concerned with training and socialization rather than intellectual development, thus ensured that the restrictive philosophy of the founders of popular education took a long time to lose force. This limited development was maintained by keeping the training of elementary teachers outside the universities; thus clearly defining them as uncultured practioners in an inferior system.

All these various ingredients were compounded to produce regional variants of the national scene of turmoil and change. Local issues, even without taking into account the personalities concerned, were frequently further complicated by varied influences which could produce unique antagonisms or alignments of forces. It should be realized that the bulk of the people were so poorly educated and informed there was ample scope for evasion, misrepresentation and sowing confusion. The issues were often contained in small borough-sized societies, their boundaries defined by the limits of horse transport, yet linked by the railway to the greater arena of the national capital. As a result the Anglican property owners would oppose plans emanating from the chapel-attending artisans, but both would combine against an unruly Irish Catholic labouring community. All three would however feel obliged to unite in campaigns against proposals interpreted as promoting immorality or manifesting free thinking Darwinism. Questions related to schools were thrashed out in such complex local conditions.

It was against this social background that the Education Act of 1870 began to take effect. It had an initial success in the provision of school places; and in the first five years the number almost doubled. The potential school population in 1870 was

some 4 million, of which 1.5 million were on the registers of
government-aided schools; this represented 40 per cent of working-class children between six and ten and about a third of those
between ten and twelve. By 1875 the voluntary agencies had
provided over a million more places and the School Boards half
that number. School attendance proved more difficult and in
1876 there were only 1.8 million daily attendances for the 3.25
million places.[5] The powers of compulsion lay with the School
Boards, but only 13 million out of the total population of 22
million lived in areas subject to these authorities. Not all boards
made attendance byelaws and it was estimated that just over 11
million lived in areas where school attendance was enforced.
The Acts of 1872 and 1874 extended the powers of the school
boards, but in 1874, when the Liberals lost power, the process of
gradual enforcement lost momentum.

The Conservatives, conscious of the support of manufacturers, farmers and businessmen who were not eager to lose a
source of cheap labour, and ill disposed to the independence of
the School Boards, rejected proposed extension to cover the
whole country. Their educational proposals were therefore more
in the nature of provision for legal employment over the age of
ten, rather than an extension of the school period. They set
their policies against "direct compulsion", the Liberal aim, and
proposed instead that in areas where there was no School Board,
the Poor Law authority, the Board of Guardians, could set up a
school attendance committee with similar powers to make bye-
laws and impose fines on the parents of non-attending children.
In explaining this policy much was made of the drawbacks
of the School Boards; they were "very costly machinery",
"inflicting turmoil", with "the disturbance of triennial elections"; above all they "would sound the knell of the voluntary
schools" and lead in the long run to what "the country would
detest and abhor, namely one general system of secular education". Direct compulsion to attend was represented as requiring
"constant visits to houses and streets where people lived and
would call for a large body of visitors and attendance officers".
It was therefore "unsuitable for this country".[6]

The resulting Act of 1876 clearly defined every parent's duty
to provide efficient elementary instruction in reading, writing
and arithmetic for his children under pain of penalties, if the

local-attendance authority wished to impose them. Children over ten and under fourteen could be employed if they produced a certificate of educational proficiency in the "Three R's" and had a record 250 attendances, which in effect set a ceiling on educational achievement. There was an even more liberal interpretation of the clause which became known as "The dunce's certificate". It had also been widely realized that the courts gave a wide meaning to "reasonable excuse" as a means for keeping a child away from school; with a general acceptance that family need for the child's earnings justified non-attendance. This interpretation was in accordance with Poor-Law rulings which forbad family assistance where a child could be sent into some employment, even if it was of a dead-end nature and meant an end to further hopes of education or training.

The School Attendance Committees are significant in that for the first time educational administration was linked with local government, although the powers were limited to matters connected with school attendance. Thus the 1876 Act made it possible to bring all children into schools. However, when the local authorities set up the committees, there was no haste to enforce attendance, and the procedure proved unwieldy. The results tell their own story. By 1880 the areas subject to attendance byelaws contained nearly 18 million out of a total population of 26 million. Although 4.25 million school places were available, there were only some 3.75 million on the registers; the percentage average daily attendance had risen from 67 per cent in 1875 to 70 per cent, which meant that only 60 per cent of school places were used.[7]

In the spring of 1880 the Liberals returned to office. A. J. Mundella, the radical MP for Sheffield, a long standing advocate of children's rights and "direct compulsion" of school attendance, was appointed Vice-President of the Privy Council Committee on Education. The existence of more than 4 million places removed the main argument used in 1870 against compulsion and the Education Act of 1880 imposed an absolute duty on all local school authorities to enforce school attendance, also abolishing "the dunce's" work permit. This measure established the principle that the requirements of education and not work should govern the lives of the children of the labouring classes, although the courts still continued to accept pleas of "reasonable excuse", which was contrary to this.[8]

The new policies were supplemented by further legislation which quickly proved effective in increasing attendance and lengthening the period to be spent at school. The School Attendance Act of 1893 raised the age of compulsory schooling to eleven and this was amended in 1899 to twelve. Children employed in agriculture could claim exemption for half-time work at the age of eleven, but if they did so, they had to continue at school until thirteen. An Act in 1900 gave the authorities powers to raise the compulsory leaving age to fourteen, reinforcing their powers of compulsion by increasing the maximum penalty from 5/- to £1, about the weekly wage of a labourer.

These measures were effective as the figures prove. In the thirty years since 1870 the population had risen from 22 to 32 million; in the same period the number of children on the rolls of the public elementary schools had risen from just over 1 million to 5.7 million, while the average daily attendance had gone from 67 per cent to 82 per cent. The average duration of school life had extended from 2.55 years in 1870 to 5.19 in 1880 and 7.5 in 1897; by the turn of the century it was estimated to be 8.5 years. Most important there were signs that education was becoming more important to the parents, for the number of half-timers, had fallen to less than one in sixty. This was a real advance, for in 1876 with under 2 million on the registers there had been 200,000 children in half-time employment; in 1900 out of 5.7 million there were 89,000, reflecting not only a drop in numbers but a fall from 10 per cent to 1.5 per cent of the children on roll.

One reason for these advances was the Elementary Education Act of 1891 which, although it did not abolish fees for elementary education outright, made it virtually free for the vast majority by making a grant for fees of 10/- per head on the average attendance of every child between the ages of three and fifteen; by 1900 over 5 million enjoyed free schooling and another half million paid only reduced fees. To show the importance of the voluntary part of the system it is worth noting that of the 5.7 million enrolled, 3.0 million were at voluntary schools run by the denominations and 2.7 million were at Board schools.[9]

Regarded statistically the progress in education over the period from 1870 to the end of the century was impressive and seemed to justify the Liberal policy of decentralization and development under local control, even though there had been no proper local machinery of government. There was a price to be paid for this rapid growth, for, by even moderate criteria, the quality of the education was far from satisfactory.

The main cause of the low standards was the quality of the teachers who had difficulty in obtaining access to the secondary schools and, therefore, knowledge of the classical curriculum, which were the first steps to higher education and increased status. There were increasing opportunities in the professions and in commerce, so that recruiting drew largely on its own unsatisfactory sector of the system. In 1870, 8,281 inspected elementary schools with 2 million children had been manned by 12,467 certificated teachers; most schools were single-teacher establishments and the overall student-teacher ratio was 160 for each certificated teacher; there was a supporting strength of 1,262 assistants and 14,612 pupil teachers. When compulsion came in 1880, the 17,614 inspected schools had 4 million children with 31,422 certified teachers, giving a ratio of 130 per certificated teacher. An additional complement of 7,652 indifferently trained assistants did little to raise the quality of the teaching; they were mainly women and 2,352 were unqualified. Furthermore the employment of 32,123 pupil teachers, many of them children of thirteen and fourteen, as full-time teachers responsible for classes was, in effect, but another version of the old monitorial system.

It was not only staffing but buildings also which held back development from the standards of the early nineteenth century. They were often makeshift, unsuitable and even unhealthy. Inadequate and inconvenient class rooms hampered teaching, while overlarge classes of unwilling pupils dictated methods and compelled the schools to a repressive atmosphere, for discipline was always the first consideration in such conditions. School architecture was in its infancy with the teachers' needs the last consideration. In rural areas, the school, when not the church or a village hall, was usually long, narrow and barnlike. Sometimes moveable partitions divided the structure into two or more classrooms. Town schools, usually better financed, adopted more pretentious styles such as ecclesiastical Gothic, or mockeries of Tudor or Jacobean. Inside the layout usually consisted of one main room which could be divided; other classrooms were added as the site allowed. A gallery was a feature of many schools both in towns and in the country; this served for a variety of purposes : from a pulpit for the head teacher to a convenient parking place for the infants. Later some London schools copied the "Prussian" model with a central corridor flanked on either side by classrooms. Little thought was given to siting schools or the elementary requirements of ventilation, heating and lighting, while sanitary arrangements were persistently primitive. In the towns it was not unusual to find chapel basements, railway arches and the like converted to schools, although often dark and airless. Others were sited on busy streets where the noise of traffic made it difficult for teachers to be heard or children to concentrate. Heating was usually by open fires, while windows were placed high up to prevent looking out, and quite often there was no playground, or it was small and irregular in shape.

School furniture and equipment was of the sparest; the children sat on long wooden benches designed so that large numbers could be crowded in. Even though daily attendance was likely to be around 75 per cent the classrooms were usually crowded, with several activities going on at the same time; children in the rear rows writing, while those listening to an oral lesson sat at the front. There were too few teachers to divide the school into class groups suitable to be taught together. The range of age and ability was usually wide, for schools catered for all ages from three to the leaving age. In such conditions teaching methods remaining antiquated and mechanical.

The prevailing attitudes to the elementary schools were determined by the view that education should be appropriate to the social class of the pupils. This attitude was reinforced by the system of "payment by results", whereby parliamentary grants largely depended on the success of individual students in approved subjects. This system had been introduced in 1862 in the period of administrative confusion; but remained to prove that money for elementary education was spent on the type of instruction considered appropriate for children taught at the public expense. It remained in force until 1897, with various modifications, which, although outwardly broadening the curriculum, in practice required only memorization. The system firmly established the authority of the inspectorate. Not only was the inspector the arbiter of the children's response but a merit grant also depended on his verdict, relying as it did on the school organization, discipline, intelligent instruction and quality of the children's work. A three point scale carried appropriate decreasing payments for the grades excellent, good or fair.

The result of this system were in every way unhappy for a premium was placed on the rigid adherence to accepted methods, so teaching degenerated to mere cramming to memorize a jingle of questions and answers. The resulting authoritarian structure affected the whole of school life; the teacher was the overseer, the children his charges, Her Majesty's Inspectors the official taskmasters. The business of the administration was the assessment of grants; it expressed a philosophy by which the paper form meant more than the children. Its abolition was a sign that new ideas were gaining ground and the time for improving the limited service offered was at hand.

There were still two systems of education, with the gulf between them vast and their interests opposed to each other. Firmly established as the core of education for the middle classes was, as we have seen, the classical syllabus built around Greek and Latin. The claims made for it ranged from training in logic, clarity of written and spoken language, to the more dubious one of learning from accounts of slave-based, agricultural economies in a Mediterranean climate two thousand years ago, lessons which could unhesitatingly be applied to the problems of urban industrial Britain; for example the development of payments to citizens was seen as causing the collapse of the Athenian "golden age" and however dubious this was, it was frequently advanced as a cause for halting the development of social services, even as late as the 1930s.[10]

In contrast the public elementary school was seen as mainly concerned with socialization and the bare elements of literacy and number; it was thus in no position to challenge the intellectual supremacy of the classics. A science-based curriculum obviously had advantages in training children who would work with their hands, but it found little favour. This had been advanced by Adam Smith in 1776[11] when advocating parish

schools; he noted the need for elementary geometry and mechanics because they could be applied in every common trade.
He was not alone in this belief and although such studies found
no place in the voluntary schools, they developed in the mechanics institutes till in 1850 there were no fewer than 622 of
these establishments in England and Wales, with an enrolment
of 100,000 members, mostly manual workers. Support for scientific education came from the army, especially as Prussian victories over Austria in 1866 and France in 1870 were put down
to the victor's high standard of schools which made much of
scientific studies. There was a growing body of industrialists who
for business purposes travelled widely on the continent and in
north America; they compared what they saw with the haphazard facilities available in Britain and the almost complete
neglect of science in the elementary system.

The controllers of education at all levels were the classically
orientated, and had inherited a centuries old tradition that
refused to accept the sciences as worthy of inclusion in academic
institutions. Unfortunately Aristotle (384–347 BC), who appreciated the natural sciences, had declined to accept training in
crafts or the theory derived from them as part of formal education. In his *Politics* he condemned such knowledge because it
will "absorb and degrade the mind". Later classical luminaries
down the ages had embroidered this valuation. Thomas Aquinas
(1223–74) pronounced that "if physical theory is inconsistent
with received metaphysical teaching, it cannot be admitted,
because metaphysics is the supreme science, not physics".[12]
Repeated attempts to establish science in the British universities
failed, so that the developments which transformed the embryo
power revolution based on water and wind, in the great leap
forward following the utilization of steam power, took place
outside the universities; as a consequence the sciences were
associated with trade and utility, outside the understanding of
the classically-orientated theologians who not only held sway in
the universities, but had come to decide the educational policies
of the elementary schools.

The course for nineteenth-century educationalists was set in
1828 when Dr Arnold took over Rugby school. He had won the
approval of the rising mercantile and middle classes by his
broad theology which advocated a reconciliation between the

Anglicans and the Nonconformists, although he was a classicist of the old school. He saw his task as the production of Christian gentlemen through a suitable classroom curriculum allied with the Ancient Greek tradition of the healthy development of the body through games. Arnold's success set the pattern for secondary education and his disciples and imitators were everywhere, for he had re-established the traditional grammar school curriculum, largely unchanged since medieval times.

It was a deeply entrenched position and the development of the elementary school curriculum became part of a dispute over wider issues. There were other factors which hampered development, including the status of the classicists as educationalists and the costs of providing facilities. The greatest barrier was at the popular level where the case for utilitarian education in the schools was met by describing this as a type of professional training; it was therefore a private matter and the concern of parents who should be prepared to pay. Education beyond the bare essentials was largely captive in the middle-class grammar schools and there fossilized in the formal study of the languages, literature, history, and geography of a Mediterranean world of two thousand years ago.[13]

The question had been discussed at length before the 1870 Act and recommendations made to teach certain science subjects in both elementary and secondary schools, but little emerged from these proposals. Later the Science and Art Department of the Board of Trade began to encourage the formation of organized science schools for older pupils although they made slow headway; they offered a three-year course through either day or evening classes. In 1885 there were three, in 1896 there were 125 and in 1901, 212 such schools. At the same time a number of grammar schools began to offer scholarships to the more able pupils from the elementary schools; in some cases this was by a stipulation added to existing awards which reserved places for such candidates.

Some of the larger school boards in the industrial areas proposed to set up central schools where older pupils could continue their education through practical courses linked with local industries; the syllabuses included such subjects as chemistry, geometry, algebra, geology, machine construction and geology, as well as modern languages.[14] Official circles reacted in a variety of ways. There was a good deal of toleration because it was felt that only the exceptional working-class child could benefit from secondary or further education. It was also discovered that this school board initiative constituted "special training", which was outside the legal scope of public-education authorities and so could not be financed from public funds; moreover it was felt such policies encroached on the middle-class province of secondary education. These attitudes barred the way of the development of working class education beyond the elementary stage.

The whole matter came to a head in the 1880s when a number of official bodies investigated the whole question of education, including technical instruction. The first of these, the Royal Commission on Technical Instruction (1881–4), was brought about by the sorry showing of British exhibits at international exhibitions. The argument for this type of education was pressed home not only on utilitarian grounds but also because it aroused interest and stimulated intelligence. It was advocated that there should be a progressive system of schools as on the continent, where pupils could pass from elementary to the highest technical education without a break. Inspired by the holding of the International Conference on Science, meeting for the first time in London, there was insistence on the importance of the scientific empirical method; the Commission urged general extension of manual, technical and scientific education of all types, together with the study of modern languages in place of the classics. Trade and industrial organizations were seen as likely to assist local authorities in providing study facilities.

Such recommendations struck deep into what was regarded as the exclusive professional territory of the traditional educationalists, who had nothing to offer for the education of the children of labourers. Moreover when the prosperous life-style of the artisan was compared with the makeshift existence of the labourer, the argument had great value on many counts, especially as they provided realistic aims for popular education.

Worse was to come. The rising standards in the public sector threatened the superiority of the secondary schools. The best endowed, like the public schools, worked in close association with the universities, but many of the others were reported as "very little above the level of the ordinary elementary schools", a damning indictment considering the gulf between the classes. Although secondary education was considered a private matter outside the scope of State action there was widespread concern; but nothing could be done for, although under some supervision by the Charity Commissioners, neither that body nor the Education Department had authority to inspect grammar schools.

In 1884 a select committee was appointed to inquire into educational administration and it recommended the upgrading of the department to take charge of both elementary and secondary education, with a political chief of ministerial rank. This proposal would have given some public control of middle-class education, but was not acceptable. Public opinion would not accept the expenditure of taxpayers' money on education beyond the elementary stage, and so long as the department was confined to elementary schools only, although these were for the bulk of the population, the work did not merit a chief of ministerial rank. This was a repetition of inquiries held in 1865 and 1866. To the first of these, Mr Lingen, the Secretary of the Education Department, declared that no statesman of the age and rank of a Lord President or a cabinet minister would be willing to undertake the drudgery of the daily business of education, which was worse than in any other department. Moreover the function of the Committee of Council over which he was required to preside, was confined to aiding the schools for the poor. Several witnesses before the 1884 inquiry expressed similar views.

To make progress it was essential that some machinery should be devised so that the local authorities should be able to concern themselves with middle-class education and thus facilitate access to secondary education; the old stumbling block, the inadequacy of local government organizations, appeared again. It was not too bad in the towns where the Municipal Corporations Act of 1835 gave 184 boroughs an elected government, albeit only by ratepayers of substance; subsequent legislation had given an extended franchise and in these areas working-class organizations were becoming more vocal and active; they were especially alive to the growing number of workers with parliamentary and municipal votes.

The country areas still remained under the arbitrary rule of the squirearchy, acting as Justices of the Peace in Quarter Sessions and on many *ad hoc* bodies created over the years to cope with the growing demand for community services. There was growing resentment at the arbitrary exercise of power, sharpened by the contrast between the poverty of the labourers and the wealth of the landowners. The landowners and farmers were concerned at the archaic system of rating which weighed heavily on land and asked little of industry. The situation was often made more prone to conflict by the unreasoning attitudes of employers to farm workers' unions; as well as labour's allegiance to Chapel worship rather than the Anglican Church, where the incumbent was frequently the nominee of the local landowner. This religious difference spread to the schools, for the Noncomformist worker often had no choice but to send his children to the school controlled by squire and his clergyman.

There were a number of attempts to meet the discontent caused by the lack of representation, but the turning point came with the Reform Act of 1884 which gave the rural smallholder the franchise; it was then no longer possible for the Conservative squirearchy to resist reform, because, although denied a voice in local affairs, there was now a lever on the national political scene. Moreover, the rural voter through a series of political accidents became a key interest which led to the acceptance by the Conservative government of local-government reform, which hitherto had been a Liberal programme. The resulting measure, the Local Government Act of 1888, provided for representative county councils as well as sixty-one county borough councils, which took over all financial and administrative functions for their areas with the exception of police and the poor law. This allowed many functions of the central government to be transferred to local bodies which greatly facilitated the local administration. The Exchequer was able to make over large sums of assigned revenue, in place of the grants-in-aid to individual schools. The Conservative administration, to pacify their landowner supporters, also included in the Act a re-adjustment of rating, which did much to pacify the opposition in the House of Lords to expenditure on middle-class education, as well as the development of higher elementary schools. The whole measure was too much for a right-wing parliament, and in debate the sections creating subordinate district councils were thrown out, so that the reform of rural administration was only partially achieved. This failure to create subordinate authorities caused the School Boards to continue to function, a survival which could only delay the integration of elementary and secondary education.

The financial advantages reconciled the country gentlemen to the loss of their arbitrary power, and they proceeded to capture the new organizations, proving especially successful with the county councils; it has been said that the Act did not bring about the abdication of the old ruling class, but converted them to constitutional rulers of the countryside. Nevertheless, the consequences of the Act approached the revolutionary, for, as the constitutional representatives of a wide electorate but no longer called on to contribute lavishly to local expenditure, the gentry ceased to blindly resist social change and even in some cases became enthusiastic advocates of the new developments.[15]

Meanwhile there were signs that the educational climate was changing, as was shown by the Cross Commission (1886–8) set up to investigate the workings of the Education Act. It had been organized by the Conservative government of the day, under the chairmanship of the Bishop of London, to protect the voluntary church schools which were seen as threatened by the progress of the School Boards; it was too blatantly packed and an outcry was raised which not only succeeded in changing the chairman, but introduced a strong progressive contingent on to the Commission. The report was published before the reform of local government, consequently the majority report was not only innocuous but dated; the most interesting passages are to be found in the report of the forward-looking minority on the Commission. The main report on elementary education considered the existing system satisfactory and proposed only modest reforms, mainly concerned with increasing the financial support of the voluntary schools. The minority made out the case for radical reforms starting with the abolition of the voluntary schools and the reorganization of elementary schools "under local representative authorities, over sufficiently extensive areas, with full powers of management and responsibility for maintenance, with well graduated curricula, a liberal staff of well trained teachers and buildings sanitary, suitable and well-equipped with school requisites".

On higher education they were similarly divided. The majority deprecated the establishment of higher elementary schools as contravening the principle that secondary education, which they identified with middle-class education, should be financed from public funds, but surprisingly they stressed the need for technical instruction after the elementary level. The progressive minority advocated the establishment of higher-grade schools on the lines suggested by the Technical Commission, in which children over the age of fourteen could receive an education of a more practical bent than was available in the ordinary run of secondary schools. In the language of the day, they argued that such schools were needed to serve "an entirely different class of pupil from those who desired secondary education", that is a classically-orientated course as provided by the grammar schools. This report is therefore notable for giving the first official recognition of the need for post elementary education for the non-academic child from a working-class background; it threw a long shadow towards the Hadow Report 38 years later.

In 1889, a pressure group of eminent intellectuals, the National Association for the Promotion of Technical and Secondary Education, managed to pass the Technical Instruction Act, which gave the county and equivalent councils the power to provide, or assist, technical or manual instruction from public funds. The inclusion in the Act of sanitary bodies as authorities empowered to take advantage of this educational provision shows the incompleteness of the reform of local government.

In Wales there was also a further measure, the Welsh Intermediate Education Act of 1889 which set up in the principality special local authorities with the power to raise a half penny local rate for intermediate and technical education. Specific provision was made for "intermediate education" in Latin, Greek, Welsh, English language and literature, as well as modern languages, together with mathematics, natural and applied science with a full range of technical education. It was in effect a mandate for local authorities to organize secondary education, for who could say where intermediate ended and secondary began. It gave the Welsh children a start over their English counterparts.

In 1890 the Conservative government budget partially miscarried, through the inclusion of an additional duty on beer and spirits to be credited to the county councils for, among other things, the purchase of publicans' licences of redundant public houses; the powerful temperance movement managed to mobilize public feeling on the question. This part of the budget had to be abandoned, although the money had already been voted; the constitutional point was pressed that revenue allocated could not be left unappropriated and Arthur Acland, a Liberal, intervened to make the claim for technical education. He fought for three days to have the fund of "whisky money" allocated for this purpose; in the end the government agreed that the Welsh counties could spend it under the terms of the 1889 Act. England had no such measure or equivalent educational bodies, but the revenue was allocated to the county councils to spend as they thought fit, but with a rider which directed it to educational use; the question had become a *cause célèbre,* and where there were local activists to press the point the authorities could hardly refuse. Moreover the results reacted with some effect throughout the haphazard administrative framework.

It was possible within the financial limits of the "whisky money" to apply it very generally, because the Act used the definition of technical education adopted by the Royal Commission on Technical Instruction which, by using the term in a theoretical rather than a limited practical reference, interpreted it to comprise " instruction in the principles of science and art applicable to industries". Once this definition was accepted, the new councils were constituted virtual local education authorities, not only for technical instruction in the narrow sense of the term, but also for "education beyond the elementary" stage, which in effect was the promotion of secondary education.

This development brought into being two distinct central authorities, each with its own separate local organs for the administration of State-provided education. First, there was the Education Department of the Privy Council, with its framework of School Boards and School Attendance Committees, concerned with elementary education; secondly, the Science and Art Department of the Privy Council, a separate branch of the Committee of Council for Education with the technical committees of the county and county borough councils, which had entered the field to administer technical education which was "beyond the elementary". This latter body had undergone constant

reorganization after its transfer in 1856 from the Board of Trade
to the Education Department of the Privy Council. In 1884 it
had reverted to the organization provided by the Order in
Council of 1856, with a separate secretary and a permanent
head; it was thus a separate branch of the Education Department of the Privy Council, not amalgamated with it and still
preserving a degree of autonomy.

In the pressure groups that had long worked for the promotion of scientific education were recognizable links with the
non-academic interests, which looked for development of facilities to compare with the best institutions found abroad. They
were prepared to continue their campaign.

The wide interpretation of technical education, together with
the fortuitous availability of whisky money, turned the Conservative flank which had reluctantly to accept local-government
reform. Middle-class refusal to relax their control of the grammar schools and the continual underrating of the working
class child, had barred open access to secondary education.

It was here that the local enthusiasts took up the cudgels so
that 41 of the English counties and 61 of the county boroughs
allocated the whole sum for educational purposes, while the
remaining 15 authorities allocated part; the English educational
authorities collected £473,560 in 1892–3 which rose to
£654,463 by 1895–6. The greatest single allocation was made
in London, where Sidney Webb, already a leader of the newly-
formed London County Council, took the opportunity to found
a Technical Education Board to plan its use. It was composed
of twenty council members, plus fifteen nominated by bodies
active in education, such as the School Boards, the various
teachers' bodies and the London Trades Council. Much of the
fund went towards the creation of an elaborate system of
scholarships, covering the whole of a student's life from the age
of eleven to university graduation.

Sidney Webb made his attitude clear when he told the Bryce
Commission in 1894; "We accepted from the beginning that a
large proportion of the work of technical education was in the
promotion of the teaching of those subjects which fall within
the definition in secondary schools. Consequently from the beginning we regarded the secondary schools of London as a very
important factor in the technical education of London." He

planned how to achieve this end saying: "We have undoubtedly to build the greatest capacity catching machine the world has ever seen. Time has yet to show to what extent we shall be successful in discovering treasures of genius of ability and practical wisdom among the children of the people of the poorer sections of the community, as among the more favoured in pecuniary fortune."[16]

There was no doubt about his success. The scholarships brought a stream of clever boys and girls to the languishing endowed secondary schools, to the expanding technical institutions and to the unfilled classes of the universities. Payment was made under a system of annual grants in such a way that inspection was justified. The stimulus of a regular income together with a watching official eye brought a new life to moribund old foundations and stimulated the development of the institutions. The benefits were obvious to the students, the colleges and the community; there could be no turning back and indeed reinforcement of this success was to dominate the educational budget for the next half century.[17]

At the same time the School Boards and voluntary managers made their contribution to the growth of higher education, making the most of the fact that the 1870 Act had not defined the limits of elementary education, nor did it specify any age limit for the attendance of pupils at elementary schools. Considerable use was made of these loopholes to develop classes beyond the top standard of the elementary code. There was plenty of scope for this because up to 1882 six standards had been recognized and no child could be counted for an attendance grant after passing the top standard; compulsion, followed by the Mundella Code of 1882, added a seventh standard. Up to 1880 the age limit of eighteen had been included in the codes, but after a short attempt to reduce this to fourteen no age limit was mentioned. Later codes, especially the Revised Instruction of 1885, stressed there was no reason why scholars should not stay on after passing the top standard, even though they brought in no income other than their fees. The practice of staying on began to spread, although these higher classes were filled by the children of the better-off families prepared to pay a higher fee to make up for the lack of Exchequer grant. In time, these "higher grade schools" won support from the Science and Art

Department. In some areas, the pupils from the top standards and above were gathered into a separate establishment which became a special type of central school; this was a practice first developed in the industrial areas of the North and the Midlands, where there was a need in industry for young people who could take advantage of technical training.

The School Boards were bound by law to use the educational rate only for schools, "the principal part of which was elementary", and they had no authority to go beyond this. Their support for higher-grade and central schools was in effect dependent on the sanction of the auditors of the Local Government Board, the central authority for local government; there were frequent quibbles over expenditure. To overcome this difficulty, at the suggestion of the Education Department, higher-grade schools were transformed into Organized Science Schools, which were eligible for greater support from the Science and Art Department. This suggestion was first made in 1880 and was widely acted upon. The Report of the Royal Commission on Technical Instruction when issued in 1884 further encouraged the School Boards in their higher-grade work. The legislation of 1889 and 1890, together with the recommendations of the Cross Commission of 1888, gave the movement fresh impetus; Organized Science Schools or classes, providing three year post-elementary courses, grew from two in 1882, to between 93 and 125 by the end of the century, depending on how they were defined.[18]

All this was progress although administratively untidy. From this empirical development two problems emerged which would have to be eventually faced. First, the multiplication of agencies dealing with higher education was uneconomic and confusing. Secondly, the cardinal rôle of the Science and Art Department, through the terms of the Technical Instruction Act of 1889, gave the development of secondary education a technological bias; although this was generally welcomed in the industrial areas, it was elsewhere attacked as distorting the accepted pattern of secondary education and hampering true development. At local level bitter rivalries, heightened by class identity, flared up between the old grammar schools and the new higher-grade schools. The School Boards were accused of misusing public money in an effort to drive the old secondary schools out of business; they were denounced as "unseemly" for introducing elementary-school attitudes and standards into secondary education. It appeared that secondary education should be only acquired on middle-class terms.

The 1880s, a decade of inquiries, reports and recommendations was followed by a decade of action. New men at the Education Department soon showed their colours by a stream of liberal directives. In 1890 Sir George Kekewich became Secretary to the Education Department with the declared aim of promoting "the greater happiness in their work for both teachers and children". He discouraged corporal punishment, keeping in after school hours, cramming and punitive home work, at the same time advocating enlightened teaching methods. Sir Arthur Acland who came in with the Liberal government in 1892 reinforced the work of this progressive civil servant.

The Code of Education for 1890 largely abolished the system of payment by results. From 1891 elementary education became virtually free and in 1893 the school-leaving age went up to eleven. The new spirit was even evident in the language of official circulars, which reverted to a style in use before the Revised Code of 1862. The directives of this period were modern in content, stressing the need to encourage the child's spontaneous activity in the teaching of juniors and infants. It also suggested giving full scope to practical occupations suitable to the children's abilities and interests, the need to develop the senses, the habit of questioning, training the powers of observation and the ability to reason.

The curriculum was expanded to include not only practical subjects but also outdoor activities. The Codes for 1890 to 1896 extended the range of subjects to be taught in the elementary schools to include geography, history, science, drawing and singing as part of the general school pattern. At the same time cookery made rapid progress, but laundry work and manual instruction (usually simple woodwork), developed more slowly. In 1893 housewifery and dairy work were authorized, and in 1895 domestic economy. In 1895–6 school visits to art galleries and buildings of historical and national interest were allowed. Savings banks and libraries were started in many schools. Some School Boards in the Midlands even introduced physical training in contrast to the more usual military-style drill.[19]

An attempt was made to regulate the size of classes by assigning a staff value to each teaching grade and limiting the number of pupils accordingly. In 1890, the head teacher was assigned a value of 60, qualified assistants 50, pupil teachers and women supplementary teachers 30, with probationers 20. The 1894 Code for the first time regulated the size of classes by limiting the numbers which could be enrolled under the control of a teacher to no more than 15 per cent above his assigned staff-value, so head teachers could accept only 69, assistants 58 and probationers 23. This should be compared with the 1870 notion of 80 as a reasonable class.[20]

A departmental enquiry was ordered in 1893 by Acland to investigate the condition of school buildings, for it was at last being realized that schools needed to be carefully designed and purpose built; to facilitate this, schedules were drawn up to ensure that adequate standards of sanitary conditions were observed in future buildings.

A start was also made in legal provision for handicapped children. The whole atmosphere emanating from the centre was one leading to a gentler approach, banishing the régime of strict control and oppression which had originated in the crowded and inadequate conditions at the beginning of national education. The new spirit was given expression in the Education Department's report of 1897–8, which declared, "A school is a living thing and should be judged as a living thing".[21] Reconstruction needed facts, so in 1896 a special bureau was set up to provide statistics and other educational data for guidance in future plans. Most far reaching of all was the establishment from 1890 onwards of departments of education in a number of universities. The emerging new discipline linked with the development of the social sciences to produce teachers fired by the vision of a child-centred education system. It looked forward to a new type of school, not prisons for children but places for their self-fulfilment.

The developments of the 1890s have been rightly hailed as "a revolution in education", but many of the new ideas were slow to make headway, particularly in the more backward areas. The conservatism of teachers made them cling to the methods that they had found effective, and many schools remained indifferent because there was never sufficient money to clear the backlog of adverse conditions. Nevertheless, having achieved quantity of attendance, from this time on there was a declaration of intent to strive for a better quality of service for children attending the elementary schools.

All this did nothing to solve the two major problems facing the developing system : first, simplifying the dual system of control by the School Boards and voluntary bodies; secondly, the situation beyond the elementary stage of education, which remained wholly undefined. The moves towards a more humane and just approach threw into relief the need to resolve situations that were clearly obstacles to future progress.

There were already signs of stress, particularly in the voluntary sector. In 25 years numbers in the schools had gone up from 1 million to well over 4 million; nearly 60 per cent of these were in voluntary schools and this increase placed a heavy burden on the Churches, despite the increased Exchequer grants, for there was no assistance from the rates. The annual income from the contributors had hardly increased whereas the commitment had more than doubled; these in 1882 totalled £0.72 million compared with the Board schools' £0.8 from local rates; by 1895 the voluntary contribution had become £0.834 million while the School Board income had become £1.942 million. As the amount of Exchequer grant depended on the school's income from other sources, the voluntary schools were doubly hit. The result can be seen by comparing income per pupil; in 1895 the Board schools averaged an income of £2.5 against £1.95 for the voluntary schools. As a result the voluntary schools could not compete with the amenities of the Board schools and found it increasingly difficult to meet the improved standards required by successive educational codes.

The voluntary bodies became shrill in their demands for further financial assistance, pointing out that if they ceased to operate the ratepayer would be faced with a greatly increased bill for education. Their capital costs of providing for the 60 per cent of children in voluntary schools was estimated at £25 million, with a further £2.5 million to be found annually. The really weighty arguments were not financial but religious; the identification of education with religion was very strong and thus non-doctrinal religion as offered in the Board schools was unacceptable to many parents; if they were forced to send their

children to Board schools they would demand a revision of
the religious compromise on which the 1870 Act was based.
On the other side the radicals bitterly opposed further provision
of public finance for voluntary schools, without a corresponding
extension of public control. The Conservative party with its
strong Anglican links came out in support of the voluntary
schools; the controversy developed along party lines into an
increasingly highly charged social issue, the chances of compromise receding the longer it was allowed to continue.

Mr Gladstone's Liberal government of 1892 attempted to
grasp the nettle by introducing a Bill on the lines of the Welsh
Intermediate Education Act of 1889, which had been a great
success. It was proposed that the county councils were to be
given powers, either by themselves or in conjunction with the
School Boards or other bodies, to raise a halfpenny rate to
augment whisky money for the provision of secondary education. A wide definition of secondary education was adopted,
namely;

> a course of education which does not consist chiefly of elemen-
> tary instruction in reading, writing and arithmetic, but which
> includes instruction in Latin, Greek, the English and other
> modern languages and literature, mathematics, physical, natural
> and applied sciences, history, geography, one or more branches
> of technical and manual instruction as defined in the Technical
> Instruction Act of 1889, or some such studies, and generally in
> the higher branches of knowledge.[22]

The Bill pleased no one; the grammar schools, the public schools
as well as the School Boards all held that it was premature. The
classicists rallied their ranks; the Vice Chancellor of Oxford
University convened a conference on secondary education, open
to all interested parties; not unexpectedly this conference condemned the Bill and recommended that an inquiry should be
held into the whole system before legislation.[23]

It could hardly be denied that the question was urgent, for
the authorities were being faced with demands from the better
type of parents for secondary places for their children; these
were heeded because recent reforms had given many artisans
and people of moderate prosperity both a local and national
vote. There was also pressure from industrialists who, finding a

shortage of suitable men to train as technicians, began to import
Germans for key jobs. The local councils continued to do the
most they could under the terms of the Technical Instruction
Acts and there was a resulting surge in spending on advanced
education in colleges, endowed and other secondary schools, as
well as a number of elementary schools; in England alone the
£12,762 spent on this count in 1892–3 became £43,700 in
1895–6. The Department of Science and Art also extended
its support and in 1894–5 the departmental report listed 2,673
science schools and 9,545 science classes, catering for over
190,000 students and accounting for an expenditure of
£141,745. Although in theory this was confined to technical
education, liberal interpretation made it indistinguishable from
traditional secondary education, save that it lacked a classical
bias.

In 1894, the task of investigating secondary education was
entrusted by the Liberal government to a Royal Commission
under the chairmanship of George Bryce, a known advocate of
integration. They reported the following year with a balanced
survey of the situation and some constructive proposals. Starting from the Schools Inquiry Commission of 1868, of which the
chairman had been a member, it recalled that report had urged
the establishment of a national system for secondary education.
A survey was made of the scene as the members found it a
quarter of a century later. They recorded an obvious need for
more secondary facilities and indicated that the School Boards
had "slipped into the void"; the higher-grade schools, which had
resulted, were seen as "really secondary in character". The
developments towards a secondary system had come about piece-
meal without reference to any overall plan and as a result there
was administrative confusion and overlapping of functions; this
led to uneconomic expansion aggravated by petty jealousies. The
results of pragmatism were described by the commission, who
saw "the field of secondary education . . . as already almost all
covered with buildings so substantial that the loss to be incurred
in clearing it for the erection of a new and symmetrical pile"
could not be contemplated, but these existing buildings "were
so ill-arranged and ill-connected and therefore so inconvenient,
that some scheme of reconstruction seemed unavoidable".

It was necessary to bring the administration of secondary

education under a single central authority, and the commission recommended the establishment of a Minister of Education who would also take over the Science and Art Department with the educational work of the Charity Commissioners. His task was not to impose uniformity on the schools, but to preserve and promote local initiative in secondary education. His rôle was to be supervisory only and he was "not to override or supersede local action but to endeavour to bring about among the various agencies ... a harmony and co-operation which are now wanting".

An advisory body was to be set up to assist the minister, thus meeting the objections of those opposed to the intervention of government in the secondary field; twelve members were proposed, to be divided equally between crown nominees, the universities and experienced members of the teaching profession. No such watch dog had been thought necessary for the elementary schools and the difference in status is at once apparent. The development of secondary education was to be by education committees working through the counties and county boroughs. The majority on the committees were to be council members, with a third of the number appointed by the minister in consultation with the universities, the rest were to be co-opted by the local council; in boroughs the members were equally divided between the council, the school boards and the Minister. The committees were to have financial resposibilities for expenditure of rates and Exchequer grants, under supervision of the central authority.

The commission was at pains to make the point that a wider discretion must be left to these committees than to the School Boards for the interference of the State was to be "virtually restricted to aiding and advising local authorities", for regulation of secondary schools on the authoritarian pattern of elementary supervision would be "positively harmful".

The position of private schools was mentioned and the commission noted, "We are far from desiring to see secondary education pass wholly under public control and into the hands of those who are practically public servants, as elementary education has done". A rider was added that there should be no "needless competition" with such schools and the minister was charged with preventing this. Machinery was to be created by which independent schools could obtain official recognition of their efficiency.

A theme running clearly through the whole report is the distinction between secondary and elementary education. Although secondary education was no longer to be limited to the middle classes, it was not envisaged as a normal stage in the education of the nation; it was still to depend largely in the accidents of parental status or special aptitude. At the same time, there was a realization that the needs of an increasingly complex modern society demanded wider educational opportunities, which the State must accept the duty of promoting, including instruction in technical and vocational subjects. The point was made that the difference between technical and secondary education was not one of kind but of emphasis, for they declared "secondary education was the education of the boy or girl not simply as a human being who needs instruction in the mere rudiments of knowledge, but is a process of intellectual training and personal discipline conducted with special regard to the profession or trade to be followed".

By the time the Bryce Commission made its report there had been a change of political masters and the Conservative-Unionist ministry of Lord Salisbury was in power. Predictably they were impressed with evidence of waste of public money and anxious to assist the voluntary schools, but showed little interest in the rest of the report. In 1896 a Bill was framed to deal with the problems of both the voluntary schools and education beyond the elementary stage. Briefly it was proposed to redress the financial balance between the School Boards and the voluntary bodies along lines that had been drawn up by a conference called by the Archbishops of Canterbury and York. An upper limit was imposed on the education rate which the School Boards might levy and conditions were eased to facilitate increased grants to the voluntary schools. Proposals were included for the provision of denominational religion in the Board Schools at the wish of a "reasonable" number of parents.

In the sphere of education beyond the elementary stage the Bryce Commission's suggestion for a new central authority was ignored, and both secondary and elementary education was to come under the control of county and county borough councils. The School Attendance Committees and the School Boards were to be abolished. It was a Bill designed to disturb every hornet's nest in the educational field. In 1894 the Liberals had succeeded in completing the work of local-government reform, so the newly created municipal borough revolted at the prospect of subordination to the county authorities. The delicate religious compromise was threatened and the loss of the School Boards roused their many supporters. The Liberals opposed the Bill fiercely, and even the government was itself divided. The Bill was withdrawn.

In the following year, 1897, the government succeeded in passing its proposals for the relief of the voluntary schools, but the secondary education problems remained. The 1896 Bill had at least clarified the issues and established the political groupings. It was generally recognized the government had been wrong to try to co-ordinate local-level administration without similarly linking the central authority; indeed it had been an attempt to intervene in a field in which the government had no acknowledged duty. There must be open recognition by the State of its duty to provide secondary education with a reorganization of the central authority to do this. Attempts to impose co-ordinating local authorities on a multiplicity of competing educational bodies might conceal the confusion, but it would not cure it. Before a logical administrative structure could be constructed the ground must be cleared, but this could only lead to political controversy, especially after the attempted cavalier changes of the 1896 Bill. With the reform of local government completed the *ad hoc* School Boards had become anomalies and indeed constituted the largest obstacle to co-ordination of educational administration. The small ones were the subject of much adverse gossip, but those in the large towns had become local symbols of educational achievement; their schools covered the area, certificates with their imprint were treasures in many homes. They were especially well thought of in the industrial towns where they had successfully met an urgent need for schools and the Liberals who had created them took a partisan interest in their survival. This sentiment had come to the fore in the debate on the unsuccessful Conservative measure of 1896; it was clear that any plan to eliminate the School Boards would meet bitter opposition.[24]

It is about this time that a new influence began to appear in

the Education Department. The government was so packed with
the relatives and friends of one aristocratic family, it was known
as the Hotel Cecil; the results departmentally were predictably
deplorable. The head of the Education Department was the
Duke of Devonshire who had little interest in the intricacies of
state education; the decisions lay with the "eccentric and irre-
sponsible" Sir John Gorst, who was blamed for the debâcle of
the portmanteau Bill of 1896. He was not on speaking terms
with the Permanent Secretary, Sir George Kekewich, who had
been appointed in 1890 and initiated a new spirit in elementary
education. He had encouraged the work of the School Boards,
and, especially in London, had stimulated the development of
higher-grade work; the results had both exceeded the hopes of
the progressives and alarmed the traditionalists. Conservative
policies for School Boards and secondary education aimed at
destroying what he had built up.

This situation was exploited by the able and ambitious Robert
Morant, who had arrived after being expelled from Siam where
he had been tutor to the Royal Household. Educated at Winchester, he had read Greats at New College, Oxford, and was
theologically qualified. With a new career to make he entered
the Education Department in a junior capacity in the newly
created research department. He indicated how, by the exercise
of delegated authority under the Education Acts, it would be
possible to prevent the School Boards from developing their own
type of secondary education and thus destroy a trend which
alarmed classical educationalists; it was not necessary to pass
new legislation, but merely to clarify what was meant in the
administrative instruction, i.e. The Code, by elementary education. As the discoverer of the means to break the political im-
passe over the School Boards, the educational strongholds of the
radical towns, Morant's future was assured; he became Gorst's
secretary. From this point on, alongside the bungling of the
politicians, can be seen the moves of a calculating and able
administrator carefully advancing his own plans for reform.

The opposition of Liberals from both sides of the House would
have blocked measures to interfere with the powers of the School
Boards, so it was decided by administrative means to clearly
divide the two types of education, elementary and secondary,
and place the latter in the hands of the county councils; legislation

on the lines of the Bryce Commission could follow later. The county councils were invited in 1897 to assume certain responsibilities to the Science and Art Department in the field of secondary education. The next move was to limit the activities of the School Boards, as far as possible, to elementary education. To prepare the ground, the department called a conference of headmasters concerned with secondary education, including those from higher-grade schools and schools of science. The new policy, which was later issued as a Parliamentary Papers,[25] on the relationship between elementary and secondary schools was spelt out. Secondary education "gave importance to general mental training" and had certain social significance; this distinguished it from education beyond the elementary standard, such as was provided in the higher-grade schools, which was devoted to subjects of "immediate utility"; the curriculum limitation of this type of education was made plain. It was tactfully indicated there would be no more departmental backing for education beyond the elementary except along these limiting lines. The headmasters whose schools were affected by the decision accepted this doctrine as the price of official recognition of their right to continue to provide some higher education.

The School Boards were less amenable in accepting the restriction which the government sought to enforce. In 1898, the London School Board claimed to be the proper provider of higher education in its area, and stoutly resisted the claim of the London County Council to be the authority for secondary and technical education. The Education Department had not expected outright refusal and moved to demonstrate the illegality of such a claim by forcing a showdown. As there had been no statutory definition of elementary education, there had been a long string of difficulties over charges for higher education, which, in the strict interpretation of the law, the School Boards had no authority to spend money on. The local government Board auditors had queried items of expense and in a long history of these disputes they had usually been upheld. Despite this, powerful authorities like the London School Board, with the backing of the Education Department under Kekewich, had been able to provide a considerable amount of higher education. To curb the defiance of the London School Board the financial controls were invoked and well primed with what was required;

in June 1899 the District Auditor, Mr Cockerton, disallowed expenditure on older children and surcharged the members of the Board. His decision was subsequently upheld in the High Court and in the Court of Appeal.[26] The plot was well arranged and followed up with a press attack on the London School Boards for misusing money from the rates, which was reinforced by subsidiary court actions by a group of ratepayers and an individual case brought by a solicitor. Once started, nothing was left to chance to break the power of the School Boards.

The Court of Appeal did not give judgment in the Cockerton case until April 1901, but in the meantime the government made its policy on higher education clear in an instruction called the Higher Elementary School Minute of 4 April 1900.[27] This enforced the distinctions drawn in the Headmasters' Conference of 1897. The conditions were so restrictive that few schools could meet them. They must not be commercially or scientifically biased yet the main attraction for brighter youngsters had been the passport to a good salaried post; they could only keep pupils to fifteen and must select from those not bright enough to compete with the recognized secondary schools. The higher elementary school movement, which had promised so much, was reduced to a shadow of its former self. It was sacrificed to prevent it competing with the traditional grammar schools, although it taught the very subjects which were most popular at evening school: those needed by industry. It is ironical that the skills such schools provided were the very ones in short supply and being met by importing Germans to act as clerks and technicians. The ruling also removed from the School Boards the ability to educate their own pupil teachers.[28]

It should be noted that it was government policy and not the legal judgment in the Cockerton case that prevented the School Boards from developing a new category of education for the mass of the nation's children. In their judgment in the High Court on 2 December 1900, the judges held that elementary education was "the education of children", but considered that childhood could extend to sixteen or seventeen. They ruled that any education suitable for pupils up to that age could be given by a School Board, so long as it was provided under the Code of the Education Department, for the Education Acts showed that it was the clear intention of parliament to place elementary schools under the sole administration of Whitehall. They held that School Boards could provide instruction that was "more than elementary" so long as they provided it under a Whitehall Code; if they went beyond what was allowed by the Code they could not call on the rates for the excess. The Court of Appeal in April 1901, thought the age of sixteen or seventeen "rather high" for childhood, but did not suggest a lower date. It was the alteration of the condition laid down by the government that restricted the work of the School Boards; the legal judgment merely pointed this out.[29]

In the meantime the government passed legislation to reorganize the central authority for education. It was recognized that the 1896 Bill had been a "mistake in principle", for the reorganization of the central authority was "an indispensable preliminary" to the creation of satisfactory local authorities for secondary education.[30] It was also thought that in time a single central authority would prove more economical than the existing variety of authorities. After careful consideration, the Board of Education Bill was introduced and passed in 1899. The new board was modelled on the recently constituted Board of Agriculture, but differed little from the old Committee of Council on Education. The President was in effect a Minister of Education; the first draft of the Bill had proposed a Secretary of Education, but the legal experts pointed out a single secretary would be a disadvantage in that "there is no one to act for him in case of illness."[31] The authority was no longer merely an "executive activity" of the Privy Council, but now a full department of state, responsible to parliament for its activities and finance. There was some widespread disappointment that the chief of the department was not given ministerial rank with a seat in the cabinet, but that promotion had to wait until the next major departmental reorganization in 1944. The old Education Department and the Science and Art Department finally merged and provision was made to take over the educational powers of the Charity Commissioners and the Board of Agriculture, while the new board was charged with "the superintendence of matters relating to education in England and Wales".

University and secondary school interests prevailed on the government to adopt the education council suggested by the Bryce Commission. The government had considered the pro-

posed committee "a rather peculiar institution" and valued it
as "not essential", but a conference on secondary education in
1898 gave a decided lead on the matter and significantly urged
it should also advise on matters related to technical as well as
secondary education. Such pressure from its own supporters
caused a standing consultative committee to be set up, drawn
from the universities and other bodies with an interest in secondary education. Provision was also made for inspection of secondary schools.

The Liberals condemned the Act as "a meagre measure" as
it left the confusion of local authorities untouched, which was
seen as the only way to effective reform; the government indicated this was to follow. The Act had also managed to alarm
both the classical and technical interests about the development
of secondary education; the issue centred on the internal organization of the new board. The university of Oxford and the bigger
public schools were anxious that technical and secondary education should be distinguished by the creation of separate sections
for each within the office of the board; this would prevent
the old Science and Art Department emerging under a new
guise to impress a technological pattern on the whole field of
secondary education, to the obvious detriment of the classical
curriculum. The Technical Education Committees of the local
councils, with strong links with local industries, claimed they
were already responsible for much truly secondary education
and that their activities would be constricted if a single branch
of the central office did not co-ordinate the supervision of both
technical and secondary education. A temporary solution established a single branch for both, but this was only until the
appropriate local authorities could be brought into existence.
There was another ground for concern, namely inspection;
secondary schools could apply for inspection and thus win recognition of efficiency, but they had to bear the cost of inspection.
Poor schools could obtain help from the county technical fund,
but such help was only likely at the price of accepting a technical bias in the school's curriculum.

There was considerable apprehension at the prospect of
government control whether exercised from the board as a
central office or through local authorities;[32] in their concern the
secondary schools looked to the universities and the public

schools for protection, for it was seen no government dare bully them.

Although as yet the State only had responsibility for elementary education, it can be seen that there was strong distrust at its intervention in secondary education. Any suspicion of the rigid control that was considered appropriate for the schools for the children of the manual workers, was seen as intolerable in the schools for the middle classes. At the same time many small and antiquated grammar schools were in a permanently precarious financial state as their income from endowments and fees was insufficient to allow them to expand. This was an area of Conservative party interest because many of their followers had received their education at these schools. Alongside this, the restriction on the school boards' activities affected some 150,000 children eager for secondary education; these came from the emerging lower middle classes and artisan families, only recently enfranchised with their political allegiance wooed by both parties.

Not surprisingly the first task of the new Board of Education was the solution of the problem of secondary education. The recent history meant that public opinion of all types was alerted and the Board was obliged to proceed with caution. Having eliminated the School Boards from the administration of secondary education, the next step was to establish distinct local authorities for this sector, for all the many indications were that any association of secondary and elementary education under one official control would invite great reaction. To this effect a Secondary Education Bill was launched in June 1900[33] to extend the powers the education committees of the county and county boroughs had over technical education from the Technical Instruction Acts, and to cover secondary education generally. The Bill only reached its second reading on 23 June 1900 at the end of the session; parliament did not discuss secondary education again until May of the following year. By that time the national climate of opinion had been changed by a Fabian Society publication written by Sidney Webb called "The Education Muddle and the Way Out".

Webb's avowed object in educational reform was briefly, "to enable all, even the poorest, children to obtain not merely some, but the best education they are capable of".[34] He saw this as being achieved by having "a Minister for Education, with control over the whole educational system, from the elementary school to the university, and over all educational endowments". His formula to solve the secondary "education muddle" was administrative unity by providing "in each district of convenient size, one public educational authority, and one only, responsible for providing and controlling all the education maintained in the district out of public funds, whether it be literary, scientific, commercial, artistic or technological in type—whether it be for any of these types, primary, secondary or university in grade". He held that only in this way could there be a hope of curing the waste and want, which in English education went hand in hand, and allow the provision of a balanced and coherent system.[35]

At the same time he made it clear that the School Boards had outlived their usefulness and could not be converted to universal education authorities, for over a third of the country had no boards; it would not be possible to establish them, in view of the distaste they aroused, in areas where the voluntary-society-school interests were strong. In any case the existing bodies for administration for the most part controlled areas which were far too small to comprise a convenient unit for the purpose of secondary education. Moreover it was undesirable to allow the denominational strife, which had often centred round the boards, to spread into the field of secondary education hitherto largely free from sectarian squabbles.

On the other hand, Sidney Webb did not favour a clean sweep of all existing educational authorities in order to begin again with a fresh division of the country into suitable districts; the upheaval would be too great to be contemplated. The elections for education authorities had proved to be contests on theological grounds; to continue these would be to perpetuate the bitter religious animosities. It was true that since the establishment of the School Boards in 1870 many people had come to feel there was "something inherently reasonable and natural in having a separately elected body to look after schools", but he considered the appointment of *ad hoc* bodies was not outmoded as a method of local government. It should be the aim of policy to establish in each locality a single elected body responsible for every function of local government, and to this end, he proposed the existing county councils should be made responsible for education of all types and grades. The School Boards should be abolished and their schools transferred to the county councils, which should meet educational costs from the county rate.

The large towns required another treatment, for in London and many county boroughs, including the larger industrial cities, like Manchester, Birmingham and Liverpool, the School Boards worked well and had built up a reputation for progressive efficiency, so here the problem of unification was more complex. The town councils should be established as authorities for all education, other than that within the sphere of the School Boards, with financial powers similar to those they had for providing water and drains; but for the time being the School Boards should remain.

Both town and county councils should work through education sub-committees, which should be responsible for providing and maintaining schools of such kind and grade as the circumstances required. Although they appointed head teachers and their officials inspected the schools, detailed administration should be left to local committees, in some cases the parish council. In the case of growing towns that had not yet achieved county borough status, local initiative should be encouraged by the delegation of the whole management of the local schools to the existing borough councils.

Sidney Webb acknowledged that it was not practical politics to abolish the voluntary schools which provided variety in the education system, with opportunity for experiment. He proposed that they should be brought under the control of the local authorities, which would be empowered to make a grant-in-aid to voluntary schools, accepting official inspection and representation on their boards of management.

In an examination of the central authority, it was pointed out that no less than ten cabinet ministers had powers in the field of education and this was far from being a unity of administration. He proposed the Board of Education should be given power to inspect and audit the accounts of every scholastic institution in receipt of public money, as well as those maintained out of endowments or trust funds of any kind. This would have included many establishments, from the universities to the reform schools, and would have brought the whole educational scene under the supervision of a single central authority.

Through all this can be seen Sidney Webb's comprehensive theory of public education. He insisted that it was not enough for the State to provide a ladder for a few students of high academic ability to climb from the elementary schools to the university; he held the needs of a democratic society required that every child, the dull no less than the brilliant, should be enabled to develop individual faculties to the full.

The pamphlet by such a notable progressive as Sidney Webb created great interest, not least of all in government circles. In May 1901 when Sir John Gorst introduced a fresh Education Bill it became clear it had created a change in official policy, there was acceptance of administrative unity, and the adoption of some of the pamphlet's arguments on local administration, though less radically expressed. In an echo of Webb, the School Boards were condemned as survivals of an outmoded system of local government, although it was not proposed they would be deprived of their existing powers. All over England and Wales the county and county borough councils would be constituted the local authority for education; the School Boards would be the subsidiary authority mainly concerned with elementary education. Where there were no School Boards, the county council would supervise schools of all grades, elementary as well as secondary and technical. In this way a uniform system of local authorities would be established which, in time, could absorb the powers of the School Boards. Whisky money and the technical rate, increased to 2d., would be available for secondary education in general. The county councils were to work through education committees, the exact composition of which was to be worked out, but would require Board of Education approval.

Non-county boroughs and urban districts, which under the Technical Instruction Act of 1889, had power to levy a penny rate for technical education, were to keep their power as an exception to the new pattern of administrative unity. This was designed to meet the needs of the industrial areas. Once again echoing the Fabian pamphlet Gorst indicated the need for "a great deal of delegation of management", proposing that the smaller authorities should continue their work in the field of

THE RAW MATERIAL.

THE RIGHT HON. SIR JOHN E. GORST, Q.C., M.P. "YOU 'VE A GREAT CAREER BEFORE YOU, MY LITTLE MAN! UNDER MY NEW SCHEME THERE IS NOTHING TO PREVENT YOU FROM BEING SENIOR WRANGLER, OR PRESIDENT OF THE ROYAL SOCIETY, OR EVEN—AHEM!—VICE-PRESIDENT OF COMMITTEE OF EDUCATION!" UNEDUCATED URCHIN. "GARN! WHO ARE YOU GETTIN' AT?"

(*Punch* – 15 May 1901)

technical education also becoming the sole agents for this purpose, answerable to the county education committees. They would have the county contribution to add to their penny rate, and the hope was expressed that as these specialist facilities built up they would come to serve districts far wider than their own.

The measure was met by fierce Liberal opposition mainly motivated by the Nonconformist objection to the treatment of the voluntary schools. The government was showing signs of strain and, as the session was busy, the Bill was abandoned, but a part of it was salvaged to become law in July 1901. This measure was necessary to fill the void created by the cramping effect of the Cockerton ruling on the School Boards. It conferred on the local authorities the right to sanction expenditure by the School Boards on higher education. The new Act in this way established the county councils as the appropriate local authority for secondary education; it was a further stage in the eclipse of the School Boards.

The intensity of radical Nonconformist feeling against rate support for the Anglican schools needs some explanation for it is a conflict with roots going back to the Reformation and the Civil War. In the eighteenth century there was a revival of Nonconformism as a reaction to the widespread corruption of the age; their religious stand was an expression of the resentment at centuries of arbitrary rule by landowners who, through owning the main means of livelihood, controlled employment and housing. Having a virtual monopoly, the squire could dictate his own terms, which would be enforced by him or his friends as magistrates. Initiatives by the landowners in taking the common land hit the cottagers hard and there was much frustrated resentment. Alongside the inevitable violence, there was a movement to withdraw from the Church which condoned such measures. In the latter part of the eighteenth century there were few villages or towns without a group of men who gathered together to worship in their own way, their religious service a simple expression of their high ideals. Many of these were manual workers, but their adoption of a personal code of industry, temperance and honesty gave them a measure of success; their wish to be independent of the landowners took them into skilled crafts and trades.

They were drawn into constant collision with the wealthy Anglican Church, controlled by the landowners through their ownership of the livings. To these were appointed only those who would use their cloth and moral authority in reinforcing a respect for the *status quo* or, as it was explained, "the state of nature in which God left it", thus rendering even the wish for change sinful. The boast of the Nonconformists was that they were "specially committed for the establishment of full civil and religious liberty" and they "never coveted the peace which is the insipid fruit of indifference".[36] Before the formation of working-class political organizations and full adult franchise, Nonconformism was the institution that gave a voice to that majority which had no share in parliament. They had developed legitimate and effective techniques, like demonstrations and petitions, by which they could make their numbers and the justice of their cause effectively felt. They had a long list of successes for they had carried the Reform Bills, abolished slavery, forced Free Trade to be adopted, and their greatest triumph; the abolition of the payment of tithes to the Anglican Church. The payment of rate support to Anglican schools was but a new twist to an old grievance which they had finally redressed in 1868, immediately after the 1867 Reform Act had given the vote to many of them.

One of the chief grievances the Nonconformists had related to the rural areas where there was no choice but to send their children to the single school, usually an Anglican Church school, where the parson's catechism was drummed into them with all manner of social and other pressures used to ensure that the Wesleyan or Baptist child attended the religious lessons. Such monopoly was widespread in the rural areas, but in the towns the Anglicans had made little headway, for urban agitation against tithes had prevented Anglican establishments being made. In the towns the Nonconformists had built up their strength, becoming active in local politics, usually being constructively radical as they followed their tradition of orderly progress towards better conditions; it was an easy step from Christian ideals to social justice. Having learned to value and work for a community purpose, they were already a force in the expansion of the trade unions and the emerging Labour party.

These activities brought about a change in attitude to secular authority. In 1870 they had accepted with some misgivings the Cowper-Temple Clause which forbade the teaching in the Board Schools of any formula or catechism distinctive of any particular sect. Thirty years experience of this working arrangement and they were prepared to hand over their schools to the School Boards on which they had a democratic voice. In 1870 they had supplied about 20 per cent of the voluntary effort, with 1,549 out of 8,281 schools and some 242,000 of the total of 1,152,000 children; in 1900 only 458 out of the 14,000 voluntary schools were Nonconformist, the bulk of the rest were Anglican. They had handed over their schools to the Boards, not simply to escape expense, but because they accepted what they saw as the future administrative pattern. It was a solution which they found acceptable and they saw no reason why other religious bodies should not do the same. They had watched the deteriorating position of the Anglican schools believing they would inevitably become Board schools.

Many saw in the Conservative government, with its evident links with titled landowners and the Anglican Church, the old enemy; the prospect of being obliged to give rate support to the schools of "the richest Church in the world" was seen as another version of the hated tithe payments; it was alleged that already the State was paying 18/6 in the £1 of the costs of Anglican schools and "yet little or nothing in the nature of control was demanded for this enormous subsidy".[37] Recent development had affected the Nonconformists considerably. The School Boards had taken over their schools to become their educational authorities. Moreover as a steadier and better-off section of the community, it was their children who had benefited from the extension of the work of the elementary schools; consequently the Cockerton judgment struck at their beliefs of individual effort and democratic management of community affairs.

The Conservatives claimed a sizeable Nonconformist vote in the towns, but, would put this vote at risk, for the party's links with the Anglican interest were more fundamental and made it imperative that a further attempt must be made to save the church schools. To them the intrusion of the State into an area as personal as education was a restriction of personal choice, and excited the same response that threats of nationalization arouse today. The party represented property, position and privilege with an openness that is unthinkable in contemporary politics; so it felt itself threatened on every side by the emerging working-class movements, as it was certain all the parts it stood for would be swept away by them. The fear of any organization of labourers was long standing; and in preserving the church schools they fought to retain the moral content of education, which was one way of halting the spread of pernicious influences.

After the relief of Mafeking,[38] it became apparent the Boer War was approaching a satisfactory conclusion and in the resulting euphoria the government staged an election which rejuvenated its powers by giving an overall majority of 134. With the Lords overwhelmingly Conservative, there was no obstacle to new educational measures, although the opposition in the country was much greater than at first apparent; the Conservative 51 per cent of the vote gave them a massive 402 seats, yet the Liberals polled 45 per cent for only 184 seats. The size of this opposition outside the House was shown by a vehement campaign whipped up by the Nonconformists against the Government.

Meanwhile the internal situation in the Board of Education was somewhat involved, for a peculiar situation had developed. Morant had used his post as secretary to Gorst, now Vice-President, to become acquainted with everyone who mattered in the Conservative ranks, concentrating on the cabinet and those MPs with an interest in education policy, as well as building up influential Anglican contacts. In six months he had become the principal person in the department and he gave a strange glimpse of the board's workings, which explains his ascendancy :

> The Duke of Devonshire, the nominal Education Minister, failing through inertia and stupidity to grasp any complicated detail half an hour after he had listened to the clearest exposition of it, preoccupied with Newmarket and in bed till 12 o'clock; Kekewich trying to outstay this Government and quite superannuated in authority; Gorst cynical and careless, having given up even the semblance of interest in the office; the cabinet absorbed in other affairs, and impatient and bored with the whole question of education.

The Prime Minister, Lord Salisbury, was already on the decline which ended in his death, so Morant appealed over the heads of his seniors in the department, and his political chiefs, to the scholarly Arthur Balfour, the Prime Minister's nephew and apparent successor, warning him, "Unless you are going to take the helm in Education . . . nothing will be done". He was invited to the Balfour home to discuss the situation and as a result was exclusively engaged by the cabinet committee to draft the next Education Bill; both Gorst and Kekewich were ignored, neither seeing the Bill until it was printed. Morant wrote to Gorst, saying he assumed he might "put his name at the back" as the President of the Board of Education, and the responsible departmental minister. Gorst replied, "I have sold my name to the government; put it where they instruct you to put it!"[39]

The situation had deteriorated for one half of the elementary system was in danger of collapse and the handling of previous policies had thoroughly alarmed every interest in the educational field. In 1900 there were 5,675 Board Schools with 2.6 million children which were mainly in the towns. There were 14,444 voluntary schools with 3 million children, mostly smaller schools serving rural areas, many quite isolated. The urgency came from the fact that some 60 church schools were closing each year; many were in debt and a variety of schemes to halt this decline were not effective.[40] Even the urban church schools were affected and the Bishop of Rochester wrote to the Prime Minister: "If the schools are not in some way relieved many will go within the year—enough to greatly weaken the cause, and, by creating the impression that 'the game is up', to bring down others in increasing numbers and at an accelerating rate. I am speaking of what I know."[41]

The Vicar of Leeds wrote to Morant about how things were in the north: "I am told that Sheffield declared that they cannot hold on for more than a year without help. At Bradford a resolution was actually drafted proposing to close all their church schools on a given day unless help was forthcoming . . . in Leeds we shall find it very hard to maintain the unequal struggle much longer."[42]

The 1902 Bill had advantages over its predecessors in being ably prepared by Morant and presented by the Prime Minister designate, Balfour, who used his material with unflappable precision. It was an impassioned debate lasting 57 days, the longest to that date, and even then guillotine procedures had to be used; but with the government's unassailable majority the result was never in doubt. The debate outside parliament split the country, for the Nonconformist campaign against "Rome on the rates" was well organized and maintained even after the measure was made law. It made a big impression on Winston Churchill, for 40 years later the virulence of an educational dispute charged with religious issues affected his approach to the 1944 Education Act.

The terms of the final Act were a compromise between the Fabian scheme of unity of control and the requirements of the Anglican and middle-class interests. The School Boards were abolished by a free vote of 271 to 102, giving virtually a single pattern of educational authorities, based on the county and county borough councils. It had been necessary to create minor authorities, boroughs with a population of 10,000 and urban districts with 20,000, giving them powers over elementary education only.

The new authorities for elementary education were placed under an obligation to efficiently maintain all public elementary schools in their area, including voluntary schools. Elementary schools were divided into two categories, provided and non-provided, both to be assisted out of the rates. Provided schools were the old rate-aided elementary schools taken over from the School Boards or established with public money; the non-provided were the former voluntary schools which had been established by voluntary subscription. The local education authority would be responsible for the provision and maintenance of all provided schools. In the case of non-provided schools the managers remained responsible, not only for provision of the school buildings but for keeping them in good repair, besides making alterations and improvements reasonably required by the local authority; the authority was liable for making good all fair wear and tear.

The Local authorities were to be given increased aid from the Exchequer and their functions were to be carried out through the agency of education committees, the constitution of which had to be approved by the Board of Education. There was provision for the inclusion of members with specialist educational experience and for a variety of interests; it was expressly laid down that women were eligible for membership. All public elementary schools were to have governing bodies appointed by the local authorities and the local authority was responsible for the secular instruction. In non-provided schools the authority appointed only a minority of managers and their consent was needed for the appointment and dismissal of teachers, but they could not oppose dismissal if it was in connection with the religious teaching in the school. The authority had powers of inspection and if any school fell short of the required standards they could close it.

Religious instruction, as always, provoked the most vehement debate. All rate-aided schools, both elementary and secondary, had to apply a "Conscience Clause" on Cowper-Temple lines, and arrange the timetable for easy withdrawal of children from religious instruction. Parents could request other denominational religious instruction at any of the council's schools. In non-provided schools the managers were to dictate the nature of the religious instruction in accordance with the terms of the original trust deed of the school.

In the field of secondary education the county councils were required "to consider the educational needs of their area and to take such steps as seem to them desirable, after consultation with the Board of Education, to supply, or aid the supply of education other than elementary and to provide the general co-ordination of all forms of education". They were given power to raise a rate not in excess of two pence in the £1, and obliged to use whisky money for higher educational purposes. This section covered secondary and technical education as well as the provision of training colleges for teachers.

Considering the stable from which the Act came it was a surprisingly progressive measure, for not one person concerned in framing it can be considered sympathetic yet alone optimistic, in approach to the education of the lower orders. Much of the benefit came from the establishment of unity of control, the acceptance of which had been assisted by the Fabian tract which had prepared the large towns for the loss of their School Boards, showing them that through their local authorities they would still have a democratic voice in education policy, albeit within a different framework. The rural areas still lagged behind but no more than they had done; the county area was too large in the days before the motor car and the simple geographic facts were a barrier to working-class participation in county politics. Nevertheless, even in rural counties it was made easier to apply a national yardstick and insist on the lowest basic standards, so that they progressed even if at a slower rate than the municipal authorities. Unity of administration, finance and control made for a uniformity of progress not possible before; the extremes of religious teaching or indifference in secular instruction could be placed under scrutiny and challenged. Uniform conditions for teachers made it easier to enforce contracts of service and raise professional standards.

It is perhaps not realized that education was still not effective with even half the children, especially those from the families of the lower grades of labourers. Their feeding, housing, clothing and domestic circumstances were measures of their severe material deprivation; they existed, as surveys by Booth and Rowntree showed, at the best slightly above subsistence level.[43] Their physical and psychological condition limited their educational ability to a struggle to master the rudiments of number and literacy. Not until 1918, when this submerged majority gained the vote, could they even begin to achieve the material conditions that allowed education to be effective for their children. This is especially important when considering proposals for secondary education, for the depressed condition of the bulk of the children was taken for granted and with it their lack of response to education. Improvement was not even considered and they were seen as never being able to master anything but the basic skills.

As regards secondary education the Act gave an utterly blank authority to proceed under Board of Education approval, which, in the circumstances, meant Morant.

To understand the attitude in 1902 to secondary education it is useful to run over Richard Haldane's speech in a debate. He was a leading Liberal spokesman on education and later became the Lord Chancellor in the first Labour government. In a lucid exposition of the Liberal party's educational philosophy, he opened by calling attention to the growing realization of the importance of education, especially of secondary and industrial education. He made a clear distinction between elementary and secondary education. The former, parliament had determined, should be universal and free, while the latter could be largely self-supporting. In this latter case it was not so much that money was required in many places as organization. It was not the business or interest of the country to give everybody secondary education, not even everybody who asked for it. The only interest of the country was to see that everybody who was fit to receive secondary education did so; this was a legitimate State interest, for it would get out of it, by the improvement of the child's faculties, a return for the money expended. Only in such cases was it the duty of the State to give any secondary education at all. This duty was best discharged by picking out from the elementary schools the most promising pupils and inducing their parents to forego the wages, which were often so important to the family, by giving suitable scholarships. This would cream the very best of the children in the elementary schools into the secondary schools, where they would receive such instruction as would make them much better citizens.

The class connotation in this speech reveals how little the mass of labouring people was valued in 1902; in the light of such a climate of opinion it is the most progressive measure which could have reached the statute book at that time.

IV

It Would Be All Right For Some!
1902–1918

"The wages paid for unskilled labour in York are insufficient to provide food, shelter and clothing adequate to maintain in a state of bare physical efficiency, even if the diet is less generous than that allowed in the Workhouse.

"And let us clearly understand what 'merely physical efficiency' means. A family living upon the scale allowed for in this estimate must never spend a penny on railway or omnibus; never go into the country unless they walk : never purchase a halfpenny newspaper or buy a ticket for a popular concert; never write letters to absent children, for they cannot afford the postage. They cannot save, join sick club or Trade Union; they cannot pay the subscriptions. The children have no pocket money for dolls, marbles, or sweets. The father must not smoke or drink. The mother must never buy any pretty clothes for herself or for her children. 'Nothing must be bought but that which is absolutely necessary for the maintenance of physical health, and what is bought must be of the plainest and most economical description.' Finally, the wage-earner must never be absent from his work for a single day."

B. Seebohm Rowntree, *Poverty: A Study in Town Life*, 1902.

THE PERIOD BEFORE 1914 was marked by the peak of a peculiar political influence which was clearly reflected in the social policies adopted. The 1867 Reform Act had doubled the electorate; the 1884 Act and economic changes made even more people eligible for the franchise. Usually to be the male occupier of property worth around £10 a year sufficed, which gave the vote to many in steady, better-paid, manual employment. The sudden increase in numbers voting gave great political power to a special section of the community : the male heads of lower-middle-class households; these were small businessmen, clerks and skilled artisans. They felt reasonably secure and comfortable, so they were not interested in reforming the

Poor Law, the problems of unemployment or the provision of nursery schools. The first two problems appertained to their social inferiors, the unskilled workers; whilst the latter was linked in their minds with a wife having to go out to work, which they did not favour. These little masculine despots responded to jingoism, certainly in religion, and the ringing call to put it all right at a stroke. Political buccaneers like Lloyd George and Churchill, no less than the more dramatic clergymen, knew how to appeal to them by a telling phrase with a Biblical ring.

Although depressingly ignorant and bigoted, it was the peculiar political weighting of these prototype Alf Garnetts, with Billycock hats and heavy watch chains, who set the pattern of educational development for the next 50 years. As a skilled élite, élitism was their way of life; when Samuel Smiles advocated self-help these were his most ardent followers. Educationally they were interested in their children getting on. This meant some improvements in elementary schools, their own *alma maters,* but most of all they wanted access for their children to secondary education. As both Conservatives and Liberals wanted their support, they had their wishes.

After 1918 when the electorate was virtually trebled by the granting of nearly complete adult suffrage, the previously dominant influence was swamped by the mass of votes cast by the newly enfranchised men and women from the unskilled sections of the community. Their unique political weighting lost much of its value for, during the next 30 years, the domestic political issues reflected the basic needs of the long-submerged majority. Political demands centred on the problems of unemployment and its associated distress. This unskilled section of the population placed education some way down their political shopping list and it was not until the 1950s, when their needs for more basic services had been satisfied, that their demands in this direction were given forceful voice. Until then the policies laid down in the political reign of skilled manual workers remained in force largely unchallenged.

Following the prolonged and stormy passage of the Education Act of 1902 through Parliament, there remained many areas of dispute. The complete victory, ensured by the massive Conservative parliamentary majority, embittered the Liberals and their Nonconformist supporters. Pledges to repeal the Act only added to the resentment and encouraged agitation against it. Yet the voluntary schools remained a majority of the elementary schools; of 20,833 schools in 1912 12,637 were voluntary, 10,877 being Church of England schools and 1,082 Catholic schools. Moreover in nearly 8,000 areas the only school available was a church school. The very large measure of independence which the Act had left to the managers proved a serious impediment to the work of the local education authorities. The managers retained powers over the appointment and dismissal of staff and so they still informally imposed denominational or service conditions on applicants. These arrangements were disliked by the teachers and prevented the organization of a proper system of promotion or even movement of staff. Frequent disputes arose over the improvement or closure of unsatisfactory schools, as religious rather than educational criteria were invoked.

Religious instruction in schools continued to cause much resentment. Under the 1870 Act all schools in receipt of public aid, whether voluntary or local-authority schools, had to enforce a timetable conscience clause which confined religious instruction to the first or last periods of the school day to facilitate withdrawal.[1] Interpretation of this clause had long been the centre of dispute. The Education Department had consistently taken the line that withdrawal from religious instruction should mean secular instruction in another part of the school but many of the schools were small making withdrawal in this way virtually impossible. Children were told to sit in a corner and not listen to the religious lesson being given to the rest of the class. After 1902 this question flared up again with renewed vigour. Many small country schools took their children to church on certain days and the question now arose as to whether this could count as an attendance for the grant-claim within the school-attendance byelaws. To clarify this issue the board issued in 1903 a model byelaw, "the Anson byelaw", which authorities could adopt. This permitted parents, who gave notice of their intention in writing, to remove their children from school during religious instruction. Although this was adopted in time by many authorities, the atmosphere in many denominational schools was such that parents were not disposed to write a letter; in many cases the existence of the clause was not known. In both instances resentment continued. It should be noted that resistance to payment of rates to support church schools lasted three years under the slogan, "No control, no cash". Significantly the refusal was longest in Wales where the Anglican Church was still established and tithe supported.

An election in January 1906 brought the Liberals into power with a large majority. In their manifesto they were pledged not only to repeal the Education Act of 1902 but also to "secure a national system of education, based on popular control and free from religious and sectarian influences, which could open the road to the university for every boy and girl, however humble their origins". This message addressed straight at the Nonconformist skilled worker was matched by a similar Labour party policy which helped them win 29 seats, their initial emergence as a parliamentary force. The President of the Board of Education, Augustine Birrell, framed the appropriate measure to repeal the support for voluntary schools, and amend the law on religious instruction. This passed the Commons but in the Lords was met by Conservative tactics, "simple, childlike and brutal" as the Bill was amended beyond recognition. Birrell fumed, "What is the good of winning great electoral victories, when you find on going a few yards down the lobbies of the House, all the foes you routed in the open field, installed, established and apparently immovable, mutilating all your work."[2] Even King Edward considered the Lords had gone too far; and this proved to be the opening exchanges in a battle for power between Lords and Commons.[3]

In December 1906 the Labour leader, Keir Hardie, reminded the Commons that the Trades Union Congress "with two million affiliated members, had four times in succession declared for a national system of education under popular control, free and secular, from primary school to university". Although many trade unionists had no vote, the Liberal party was conscious of losing the support of the manual workers, so further Bills followed: one in 1907 and two the following year, all unsuccessful. A private member's Bill also failed.[4]

There were further setbacks in the same quarter. The Liberals had made an electoral pact with the Labour party and part of this was for the statutory provision of school meals. There was no intention of fulfilling this promise promptly, although official reports over several years showed many children to be in a state of semi-starvation.[5] In London alone some 13 per cent of those attending elementary schools were habitually in want of food; about half of these had access to a voluntary-society meal, usually watery soup and bread. A lucky draw in the private members' ballot gave a newly elected trade-union MP, William Wilson, a chance to introduce a Bill for school meals. The Board of Education and the Local Government Board were completely unprepared for this unprecedented intrusion into the activities which had up to then been reserved for the Poor Law. Morant produced a departmental Bill in two days which the Government promised time for; the Labour group withdrew their Bill for the certain passage of a more modest measure. The final endorsement was delayed nine months for it was an expense the Liberals did not want and yet were shamed into accepting. It allowed local authorities to spend up to a half-penny rate on providing meals for school children, either through their own organization or a voluntary society. This modest Bill was used by only 131 out of 322 education authorities and it mainly operated in times of strikes or great depression; the school-meals service as a national system did not operate until the second world war. This is a significant measure because it was the first effective intervention of Labour in parliament and it shows the difference in objectives of another section of the community; the skilled workers wanted secondary education for their children, while the unskilled wanted food. It was also the first relief service that was outside the control of the Poor Law and, because of its lack of punitive conditions, caused some confusion in that department as they saw the deterrent framework of their service threatened.[6]

In 1907 the Labour group were again ready with a private Bill which called for compulsory playgrounds and medical inspection in schools.[7] For the second time, amid jeers, a government Bill was quickly produced which required education authorities to provide medical inspection of school children and gave permission for the arrangement of treatment. The reports of the school medical officers which appeared in the following year revealed such a mass of untreated defects and disease that no civilized government could long resist authorizing a proper school medical service, but this did not arrive until 1918.

The impotence of the Liberal administration was demonstrated still further by their inability to assist the adolescent. Three widely publicized reports all pointed to the inadequacy of facilities and agreed on measures to correct them[8] : namely, the raising of the school leaving age, the abolition of the half-time system and the provision of day-continuation schools. Public opinion was not generally ready to accept any extension of compulsory education and the various official reports thought it prudent to leave the actual decision—to proceed with altering the existing age of twelve—to the discretion of local authorities, although continuation classes to the age of seventeen, were generally envisaged.

Agitation for radical reforms continued both in and out of parliament. The Liberals pinned their faith on the support of that section of the community which had brought them to power in 1906, but the Conservatives were resilient and the Labour party only slowly gathered strength. From early in 1910 the Liberals were, in effect, a minority government dependent on the support of the eighty Irish MPs who, being Roman Catholics, opposed the secularization of schools. It is significant that from the time the Liberals were seen as incapable of dispensing social justice both they and the Nonconformists began to lose power while Labour gained support.

There were other forces moving against the development of a free and open education system. The strongest centred in the staff of the Board of Education where, through his success with the Education Act of 1902, Robert Morant had ensured that he became the Permanent Secretary. He had seen, in 1900, that only the careful use of the South African situation had enabled the Conservatives to gain an electoral victory but it soon became increasingly obvious to him that in their current condition they were a spent political force. He had reason to be apprehensive of the return of the Liberals because of the part he had played in the 1902 Act. But he worked fast and by the time the Liberals arrived to take up the reins of power

in 1906 he had not only set up a system of secondary education but had also repeated Dr Arnold's feat of the 1830s in
once again re-asserting the supremacy of the classically-
orientated educationalists.

The Education Act of 1902 gave one of those rare occasions in government for a clean start for what is laid down
usually proves remarkably difficult to change. Much depends
on the initial division of the departmental budget for once this
is fixed many vested interests are created and major realign-
ments are increasingly difficult to make. This proved to be the
case on that occasion and the priorities then decided continued
in force for over 40 years. To evaluate what happened it is
necessary to make further assessment of Robert Morant who
dominated the board during this key period of educational
development, for his ministers seem to have been overshadowed
by him.

Enough has been said of the staff of the Hotel Cecil to
wonder whether anything could be more disjointed than the
Devonshire/Gorst partnership; but they were followed by Lord
Londonderry, who Morant treated like a backward pupil: "He
instructed him, controlled him, dominated him; and, inwardly,
despised him".[9] This was the Conservative minister in charge
while the foundations of the system were being completely
revised. Morant was a man of great energy who fought with
able determination to achieve selected objectives. With something of the ardour of the missionary clergy, he dedicated himself to furthering the cause of humanity, but his theological
training gave him a narrowness and an uncritical acceptance
of his beliefs which led him to be ruthless, for he saw ends
justifying means. His compassion was moved by the widespread
material distress among working people; he saw this as a barrier
to further progress. But it was in this shabby world that the
elementary schools operated. He could not conceive that anything of educational quality could come out of the packed classrooms of stunted children taught by teachers obviously lacking
the culture he associated with scholarship. Prominent among
the school managers who pressed the interests of their local
schools were tradesmen openly alert for any profit their local-
authority connections could bring. The Webbs had been critical
of their greed for contracts. Morant was probably similarly

affected and could hardly see them as compatible with educational progress.[10]

In a search for what could be done, he turned to the tried system of a classical education as a counter to the squalid materialism which dominated the children and the elementary schools. An injection of this type of learning would sort out the mistaken pattern which he saw untidily developing on every side. In a prophetic passage which shows the extent of his influence he wrote in 1898, urging the creation of :

> ...a true and complete organization of [England's] schools, not merely of her primary education, but also of that most valuable asset of the national welfare—higher and middle schools; so that each and every grade of education, and each and every type of school may have a clear presentment before it, both of the functions which it is intended to fulfil, of the results which it is framed to produce, and of the area which it is created to supply. Thus and thus only, can each and every school, and each and every grade of education, have its due share of national development.[11]

The higher schools which he envisaged as the apex of the national system were the secondary grammar schools, while he relegated the development from the elementary into a subsidiary rôle, which finally became the secondary modern school.

The value of the grammar school, apart from its traditional unity arising from its links with the old-style universities, came from an unshakeably high valuation put on the study of the classics. This arose from a belief widely endorsed by some educationalists during the nineteenth century and to the 1920s known as faculty psychology : the mind could be separated into special faculties, and suitable training of one of these would benefit the whole by a process of transfer of ability to assimilate knowledge.[12] This proposition was evident in Arnold's justification of his Rugby curriculum. It is also seen in documents which came out of the Headmasters' Conference of 1897 in which the difference between secondary education and education beyond the elementary was that the first could transfer learning and the second could not. This was a theory too valuable to the educational classicists to be abandoned lightly, for not only could certain subjects be seen as "given for the very purpose of forming the human mind in youth" but undesirable subjects could be declared unsuitable.

The provision of secondary education was agreeable to both main parties, but the problem of financing it was formidable. The Boer War had cost £270 million and a request for £25 million to rebuild the schools and prevent the clash over the voluntary schools, which had climaxed in the passage of the 1902 Act, had been flatly refused. It was therefore essential to launch the State secondary-education scheme cheaply and to ensure that as much as possible was borne by the local authorities. An analysis of the situation shows how little option there was in the form to be adopted. There were roughly three divisions of the community.

The first of these, the labourers, although the greatest in numbers did not count politically because they had no vote. The second were the skilled industrial workers mainly in the towns and linked with Nonconformism. They presented no difficulty in the acceptance of secondary education; they were imbued with local patriotism and were a constant and weighty lobby for educational improvements. They had a wide appreciation of the work of the schools and although they may have preferred the formula of higher education to have developed out of their elementary schools, if their higher grade schools were given the accolade of being declared secondary schools, it would sweeten the pill of higher rates to pay for their elevated services. The rural areas were the third force and, as the stronghold of the landed interests and the Anglican church, they still had more than a touch of the eighteenth century; they were at the best lethargic to education. Although something like 85 per cent of all children between the ages of five and fourteen were attending the elementary schools, the rural schools were very poorly served; they housed mainly the children of agricultural labourers and were indifferently staffed. It would be impossible to build a secondary-school system on such a foundation. Moreover these were also the centres of religious controversy and the rural areas had strong links with the House of Lords whose power was only curbed in 1911.

Whatever had to be done would have to be readily acceptable to the areas outside the large towns. There could be no question of wholesale building for the money was not there; but there

was the precedent of the 1870 Act by which the State obtained
the use of sites and buildings by the offer of a grant. There was
already a network of schools, most of them indifferent, but the
experience of the elementary system showed that a regular
income backed by inspection could raise standards. Thus when
the areas outside the large towns were considered with their
requirement of many small schools, only one solution was possible; an approach on the lines of the 1870 Act to the local
schools. Moreover the settlement offered had to respect both
social structure and local sentiment for setting up a system in
opposition to local schools, many of long standing, would be
asking for trouble no matter how unsatisfactory they were. The
moves had to be made tactfully so as not to rouse the already
apprehensive secondary-grammar-school lobby supported by the
universities and public schools.

Accordingly, expenditure on the development of secondary
education was given priority. Throughout the latter part of the
nineteenth century there had been continuous development of
a single stream of education from the age of three to seventeen.
The younger end was well developed and generally accepted
while the arrangements for older children varied a great deal;
but in places like Leeds and West Ham higher-grade schools
approached a pattern pointing to the comprehensive education
of the 1970s. Both of these developments were halted to channel
resources into the board's planned secondary-school development. It is one of the tragedies of British education that this
decision was taken because it would have provided an established means of avoiding selection, with its long-standing history of distortion of primary education and the social division
now inherent in grammar school education.

The hardest blow of all was the decision to withdraw the
grant from children under the age of five, which was a calculated choking-off of schooling which took some 43 per cent of
all children between the age of three and five. Much was
made of the indifferent teaching and the hazard to health but
in reality it was an area in which a cut could be made. The
decision was all the more deplorable because at the time the
McMillan sisters were developing their methods of nursery
education for this age group with singular benefit to hard-hit
families. This policy of refusing to accept the under fives as part

of the normal system arrested the spread of nursery-school education. Only in the 1960s has the lobby for this service again begun to be heard. It can be seen this reshaping of the system involved savings taken from the parts mainly used by the children of the working classes, in order to build up a service which became largely a middle-class stronghold. These policy changes were never debated in open forum and the secondary reorganization was contrary to "the statesmanlike and far sighted recommendations of the Royal Commission on Secondary Education of 1895".[13]

Further development from the elementary schools was halted when the higher-education schools were covered by separate regulations published in 1905. However there remains a carefully nurtured "rump" which, between 1905 and 1917, never exceeded forty-five schools and had under 10,000 pupils. While they existed it could not be said that higher education developed from the elementary school had been killed off; moreover they still had a use, for they were taken as the model for the reorganized senior schools created by the Hadow Report of 1926[14] or, to use a more recent terminology, the secondary-modern schools of the Education Act of 1944. It was the final degradation of a development from which so much had been hoped.

The effect on the elementary schools could well have been a standstill because there was nothing directly done for them of an educational nature until 1918; but, nevertheless, there was some considerable progress largely through the improvement in the condition of families. There were scores of measures which had some bearing on the welfare and happiness of children ranging from the registration of midwives and checks on baby farming to the regulation of betting, hours of drinking and children's employment. The Royal Commission on the Poor Laws published in 1909, although openly ignored by the Liberal government, was widely discussed in the country and by its effects on the civil service started a new approach to the social welfare of the family.

Moreover, the simplified administration of the schools and the diminuition of the authority of the clergy over the schools had many small effects. The reduction of some 3,300 sundry authorities to 300 local authorities meant the appointment of

Great Gaddesden School Board.

Hemel Hempsted,

June, 189 .

Sir,

    I am requested by the School Board to inform you, that in case you should require any Boys for Hay-making during the present season—upon filling up and signing the Form enclosed herewith, and sending it to either of the Teachers of the Gaddesden Row Board School—the Great Gaddesden National School—or the Potten End School ; leave will be given to such Boys as you may require, for a period of 4 weeks.

Your obedient Servant,

W. GROVER,

Clerk.

School boys for haymaking in the 1890s

supervisory staff who could enforce a universal standard. They could intervene where, owing to the feudal nature of some of the village communities, local landowners or an influential farmer controlled even the simplest decisions. In some cases school children were still looked on as labour which could be called on for haymaking or whenever required. The intervention of an authority outside their sphere of influence checked the more obvious abuses.[15]

    Meanwhile the planned development of State secondary education took place in two stages. The first occurred in 1904 with the implementation of the 1902 Act. The board's secondary syllabus was a careful compromise which left much room for individual development. The basic stipulations were three.

Over a 4-year course there was to be a weekly amount of $4\frac{1}{2}$ hours spent on the Arts subjects—English, history and geography; science and mathematics claimed $7\frac{1}{2}$ hours a week; there was to be $3\frac{1}{2}$ hours on a language other than English, and if the school developed two or more languages one of them had to be Latin. This balanced allocation allowed about the third of an average week for other studies. Acceptance of this formula was the basic condition for a school to be entitled to a State grant which would pay about half the salaries of the teaching staff.

The Endowed Schools Acts had assumed that endowments plus fees would supply a financial basis for a satisfactory secondary-school system, but at no time had this been satisfactory. However many of the better type of secondary schools, usually those in centres of population, had advanced along the lines suggested, some with well-developed mathematics and science wings, but they were exceptional. The Bryce Commission of 1895 while dwelling on the excellence of Manchester Grammar School contrasted this with the indifferent standards of schools in the surrounding towns. This was a pattern found all over the country and it has been estimated that only 30,000 pupils were receiving in the grammar schools of 1895 an acceptable secondary education, out of 75,000 attending endowed schools and 35,000 in proprietary schools.[16] These figures illustrate the cause for middle-class alarm when the despised free State schools began to improve their standard above that of fee-paying schools.

It also goes some way to explain the syllabus for as the Spens Report of 1938 points out, "The board took the existing public schools and grammar schools as the general cadre or archetype for secondary schools of all kinds". It was made clear that the mirror for development was not to be the higher-grade schools of West Ham and Leeds, but a shadow of Eton and Harrow. An industrial country was training its potential managers in a tradition which was a modification of the middle ages with values to match. To ensure that these benefits were appreciated, Mr James Headlam of Eton and Cambridge, with a first in classics and later a Professor of Greek and Ancient History, was sent to inspect the former higher-grade schools. He pronounced their neglect of Greek and Latin "would have a most harmful effect on the intellect and character of the nation."[17]

Except in the large towns, England at the turn of the century, was still in borough-size communities with the outlying villages clustered round a market town. Most of these towns had fee-paying schools which gave some form of secondary education to boys of the middle classes, but there was little for girls. The standard of the schools varied a great deal but, because of financial difficulties, the terms of the 1902 Act were universally welcomed. In effect the best schools were evident to everyone in the district and they were the ones selected for grant. Girls' schools had to be established, in many cases from scratch, and this accounts for the large number of girls' high schools as distinct from the older title of grammar schools. There was some resistance to proposals to mix the sexes in areas where numbers did not warrant separate schools. It is interesting that the middle classes would not find money to give secondary education for their daughters until stimulated to do so by government grant aid; a similar pattern was repeated with university education. The period was one in which the use of the motor car developed which, together with the growing use of motor buses usually run by small operators on the lines of the old carrier's cart, allowed the schools to draw on larger areas. At the same time, local authorities were under pressure to improve country roads to allow farmers to get produce to market quickly, and this made money for educational development particularly tight.[18] Nevertheless the local authorities were led to stand the greater part of these increased charges; local-authority expenditure went up during 1900-1 to 1910-11 from £7 million to £14 million, while government grant increased only from £9 million to £13.5 million.[19]

The regulations showed that the board were prepared to accept some indifferent establishments. Not only was the minimum number taking the course fixed at twenty but the following passage is revealing:

A defect which is notorious in many schools is that in certain subjects (often from causes for which the school authorities are not responsible) instruction of scholars is cut down to "marking time" or the repetition of lessons already learned. Instruction which is not progressive, while it may be of some use as drill and discipline, is of little real educational value. It gives only a superficial and transitory acquirement, while at the same time it fails to interest or to stimulate the scholar.[20]

The next phase of development extended opportunities for secondary grammar education. There had been a small provision of scholarships in the 1904 Regulations, but these were widened in 1907 under special Free Place Regulations which further opened the door to secondary education. Preferential grants were offered to secondary schools which provided 25 per cent of their places free for children from elementary schools; this gave a guaranteed regular income to the schools and for most of such schools their expansion dates from this measure. It should be noted that this income from the local authority enabled fees to be lowered for paying students. The scheme was widely accepted, and a few working-class children began to find their way to secondary schools. This provision also led to more better-off children attending elementary schools where they would be eligible for scholarships; if they did not get one they could still take advantage of the reduction in fees that the local-authority support made possible.[21] Nevertheless this brought a type of unity to the two systems and, at the outbreak of war, some 89 per cent of children between the ages of five and fourteen were attending grant-aided schools. The chances of a child from the elementary system winning a place at a secondary school had shortened from 200 to 1 in 1895 to 40 to 1 in 1914; to a betting man that was still an outside chance. By 1910–11 the 160,000 free places in secondary schools were impressive until its inadequacy was revealed by the 600,000 students attending night school, most of whom were seeking qualifications which were closely allied to secondary education.

Once again an outmoded and bankrupt system of schools had been given a new lease of life by the injection of public money; little was asked in the way of control of these schools. Moreover, these were schools which, although serving a large part of the community, had never been used by the labouring people. Such was the difference in life-style, that the few who won places in them were not made particularly welcome; their speech, dress, status and way of life set them apart from the rest of the children. It was soon established that the free places went for the most part to children nearest in background and manners to the children already attending. In this way the children of the labourers, over three quarters of the population, had very little benefit from the measure. Much could have been done to make the schools more tolerant but they were already established institutions with their régime settled to attract fee-paying children from the better-off families. Thus although the main assured income came from the State the orientation towards a small section of the community remained. In this way the two-tier system was extended because more children received a secondary grammar-type of education, but it was done in such a way that the dividing line remained; it was merely redrawn a little way down the social pyramid, still leaving some 90 per cent in the elementary school. Thus it was established that the best the elementary school could do was to help a child to leave it. Those who remained, if not actually failures, were at least inferior to those who won their way out of the system.

By 1910 the parliamentary struggle to curb the power of the Lords, brought great bitterness to Liberal and Conservative rivalry. When the King accepted government advice to create peers, the Lords had to accept defeat, leaving the Conservatives angry at the loss of their upper chamber vote; they retaliated as they could. In 1911 an injudicious instruction signed by Morant was seized on as a means of embarrassing the government. The teachers' organizations took the opportunity to attack Morant's attitude to their profession and the central bureaucracy he had built up. Press backing carried the campaign for nine months, causing the resignation of the President and the transfer of Morant to the newly-formed national insurance department. These changes caused the withdrawal of a Bill to raise the school-leaving age to fourteen, with powers to extend to fifteen and provide continuation classes until sixteen.[22]

The Liberals continued to be alarmed at their loss of support in the country and policies were redefined to restore the position. In December 1912, a cabinet committee initiated planning for a fully national system of education. It involved a comprehensive reorganization of the schools and it was ready for presentation in 1914, when the war intervened. Parts of it were salvaged in other legislation but its main value today is as a bench mark in the acceptance of the State obligation to provide a complete education for every child. The leading Liberal expert, Richard Haldane, was the Prime Minister's closest friend and too senior to hold the post of education minister. He had been educated in Germany, his Nonconformist parents mistrusting the Anglican atmosphere of the English universities. Repeatedly he urged the need to match Germany's well-developed and logical system of schools. Haldane[23] spoke several times at length on the new Bill; in March 1913, when addressing the National Union of Teachers, he outlined government policy acknowledging that the State had a deep and direct interest in seeing that the people were educated just as it had in seeing they were healthy. The Liberal party aimed to put English workers "on a level with those of other countries" and it was also their objective to "break the line of demarcation between manual and mental labour". To this end elementary and secondary education would be treated as successive stages of the same national system. The new reorganized system would provide that all children, "without any discrimination of rank" would pass through the elementary schools "to the secondary schools appropriate to their natural gifts and capacities".

To a people who had not yet been disappointed by Hadow's reforms of 1926 and the resulting secondary-modern schools, such proposals held considerable promise. It called for a wider interpretation of secondary education, with "the establishment of different types of secondary schools", which were to be technical and vocational as well as "literary". To make the new plans possible the first necessity was to raise the school leaving age to fourteen, with permissive authority to raise to fifteen. Children who were "beneficially employed" could leave after discussions with the local authorities, when each case would be judged on its merits.[24]

The present pattern of education can be seen emerging as it was necessary to re-plan the school curriculum to appeal to the older children by making schemes of study which related school to the world outside, and to include practical periods as well as some vocational training. This was already in accordance with the best elementary-school practice; the larger towns had already begun to develop special classes and even centres for such tuition.

A phrase which had been applied to secondary schools from around 1911 was intermediate education, while university education was called higher education, expressing a unified system from the elementary schools on the lines of continental practice. It should also be noted that the Code of 1904 divided the elementary school into three divisions, "infant" up to six, "lower" dealing with "younger scholars" aged seven to eleven, and the "upper" division with the "older scholars". The last were then authorized to be given practical and special subjects "suitable to their age, circumstances and capacities", with grants available for "adequate equipment and efficient teachers".[25]

The 1914 Bill sought to achieve its ends by the stimulation of the local authorities who had developed their education services somewhat unevenly depending on the value they put on the service and also on the state of local finances. Grants were to be shaped to encourage development and authorities which failed to respond could lose their educational powers. A network of provincial advisory associations were to be set up with staff and offices to make suggestions and if the local authorities wished they could delegate to them some of their educational powers. It was also realized that there must be a general revision of local-government financing, not only for educational purposes, and it was proposed to adopt a system of block grants covering several years; these would replace assigned revenue such as whisky money.[26]

There was also an attempt to deal with the religious questions which troubled the service. It was proposed that during religious instruction children could be completely withdrawn from the school unless there was separate secular instruction. Parents would also be given the right to send their children to religious instruction elsewhere. Local authority powers over the appointment of teachers were extended to include some to instruct in nondenominational religious instruction for provided schools; similar appointments could also be made for non-provided schools by arrangement with the managers. In localities where there were no provided schools and there were 30 children whose parents objected to them attending the available voluntary schools, the parents could call on the local authority to provide a new non-denominational school or to make transport arrangements to the nearest provided school.[27] In single-school areas the local authority was to be given power to appoint and dismiss all teachers; in future the teachers in such schools were to limit religious instruction to topics of a non-denominational character.

This Bill was not presented to parliament but it can be seen that it included many contentious passages. It appears to underestimate the strength of the religious bodies as well as not allowing for the growing power of the local authorities. With the Liberals and Conservatives each with 272 MPs, the balance of power lay with the 84 Irish Nationalists and 42 Labour members; the government was in no position to put through a major reform on a controversial subject like education.

The political atmosphere was completely changed by the war which quickly built up into an all-out struggle so that all sections of the community had to be enlisted in the war effort. Social problems neglected for decades took on a new urgency. The national campaign for munitions brought a great demand for labour with a corresponding rise in wages. This brought a reversion in attitudes, for children were once again largely considered as workers. In 1916 it was discovered that less than 20 per cent of children over the age of fourteen were receiving any formal education, although there was a small but steady rise in children attending secondary schools up to that age. There was also a decline in evening work where much technical education took place, while at the same time the expansion of factories emphasized the importance of such instruction.[28]

To meet this situation the consultative committee to the Board of Education was asked to resume its consideration of educational scholarships in their "scientific, industrial and commercial bearings", which had been suspended at the outbreak of war.[29] At the same time a departmental committee under Herbert Lewis, Parliamentary Secretary for Education, was appointed to investigate "Juvenile Education in Relation to Employment after the War".[30] Both reports called for an expansion of opportunity within the field they investigated. The consultative committee called for a wider range of scholarships to be provided from public funds to enable boys to make their way from secondary schools to technical colleges and universities. The Lewis Committee, concerned with the general body of children, followed the lines of the draft Bill of 1914.[31] It was felt that the public would not accept a higher school-leaving age than fourteen, with its inevitable loss to parents of their children's wages, whilst the provision of maintenance grants would not be favourably received by taxpayers. It was therefore proposed that beyond fourteen all children not in full-time instruction to the age of sixteen should attend continuation school for eight hours a week until they were eighteen.

Meanwhile the war had become deadlocked in costly trench warfare causing Asquith in December 1916 to give way to Lloyd George as Prime Minister. The new leader, the son of a school master, had a long-standing interest in education; moreover he realized the value of social reform as a means of raising national morale. He invited H. A. L. Fisher, a distinguished academic, to become the President of the Board of Education at the same time making more money available for a service badly hit by wartime inflation. Teachers' salaries had been similarly affected and measures were taken to induce local authorities to improve them. By August 1917 the new President was ready with a measure which incorporated much of the material in the 1914 Bill, although, to avoid sectarian strife which could endanger the wartime political truce, it was considered advisable to omit most of the parts relating to religious matters. The Lewis Committee's suggestions on continuation schools were included.

The Bill immediately attracted bitter opposition in several quarters.[32] The local authorities disliked the administrative reforms, calling the submission of plans to the board for approval and the proposed elimination of the smaller authorities (the Part III Authorities) an attack on their independence. The Bill was designed to put them into "strait waistcoats designed and manufactured by the officials of the Board". The projected Provincial Advisory Associations were seen as "alien to the principles of English local government". Roman Catholics attacked the whole Bill with some heat.[33] The more moderate section pointed out it would throw a heavy financial burden on the Catholic community if they were to preserve their own schools. It was also feared that the advanced instruction for older students would include sex education which, with instruction in birth control, was being given to workers in many factories as well as to the men and women in the armed services. The extremists, who included the hierarchy of the clergy, attacked the whole principle of universal higher education. The Catholic Archbishop of Liverpool declared that the majority of the working classes would not be persuaded that "their children needed any more schooling to prepare them to be labourers like themselves", and urged positive resistance to the Bill.[34] A union vote among cotton operatives in a 50 per cent poll showed 81,500 were in favour of the continuation of the half-time system with under 33,000 for abolition.[35] Wartime full employment and high wages had brought security and a measure of prosperity for the first time to many homes and workers wanted to hang on to it.

The most important opposition came from employers who feared the loss of a supply of cheap labour. The Federation of British Industries declared itself satisfied that "a large percentage of children were incapable of benefiting by education beyond the elementary stage". Sir Henry Hibbert, spokesman for the cotton manufacturers, proposed a maximum of half-time education up to sixteen, which would be more educationally fruitful and would also fit in conveniently with the working of the mills. However, one Lancashire firm, Tootal Broadhurst, Lee and Co., accepted the suggestion by setting up their own continuation school.[36]

In face of such varied opposition the Bill was withdrawn for revision and re-presented in January 1918 with a number of concessions that made the measure acceptable to the local authorities and the moderate Catholics. As this made the reforms more imminent the employers redoubled their opposition. The cotton industry was joined by the shipbuilders, the mine owners, the builders and the farmers, who all swelled the chorus against not only the proposed day continuation schools, but also restrictions on the employment of children out of school hours. Newsagents alleged they would have to close down, dairymen said they would have to start work earlier and even the theatrical interest saw their productions threatened, so that Shakespeare might be driven from the stage. It seemed as though the whole economy of the country depended on the fourteen to eighteen age group, and that one day a week to continue their education would dislocate the whole of industry. There was a marked similarity to nineteenth-century protests on the withdrawal of young children from factories.[37]

On the other hand it was felt that day-continuation schools would perpetuate the class divisions in education through the two different types of treatment : continuation courses for the poor and secondary schools for the better off. The proposed alternative was free, publicly-controlled secondary schools with maintenance grants for the poorer pupils.[38] In other quarters there were protests about the provision of vocational training from public funds. The real objection to the Bill was the cost, which was alleged to be at least £10 million annually, of which £8.7 million would be for the day-continuation schools. The Lords were shocked at this "limitless expenditure" and sponsored a proposal to put the education department under "strict treasury control".[39] Despite verbal concessions the employers' lobby remained active, while vocational training was described by another interest as "Prussian". Substantial alterations followed to meet the employers' objections : the implementation of day-continuation over the age of sixteen was to be delayed for seven years and there was a reduction in the hours of attendance. Fisher felt he had managed to keep his Bill intact in principle, but some Liberals saw his concessions as "surrender to the Ulster of Education—Lancashire".[40]

The Roman Catholic opposition remained and they, sensing their strength, requested financial equality with the local authorities. To assist their cause the President was bombarded by hundreds of printed cards sent from the front by Catholic soldiers. Criticism was made of the abolition of elementary-school fees as unfair to non-provided schools, coupled with a demand for voluntary continuation schools. This latter demand was disturbing the religious settlement and taking the religious controversy into the secondary field; the President only offered an amendment which underlined the duty of councils to take into account, when preparing their schemes, proposals to establish "efficient and suitable non-provided schools and colleges". Moderate Catholic opinion, which included most Catholic teachers, supported the Bill and their opposition was withdrawn.[41]

The Bill thus became law with no real acceptance from

industry and as continuation schools were a type of partnership with employers some co-operation was essential. The refusal to see a use for continuation schools is indicative of how the employers viewed young labour; they were seen merely as "hands" requiring neither education nor training; in fact in many cases their interest in them ceased when they became eighteen and had to be paid adult wages.

The final measure was a long way from the original aim of breaking the demarcation line between manual and mental labour, but it was still a considerable advance and an Act of some significance. It established "a national system of public education for all persons capable of profiting thereby", which was to be used in the years between the wars by over 90 per cent of all children between the ages of five and fourteen. The State had also accepted responsibility for education other than elementary and to this purpose local authorities now had considerable powers; through the provision of nursery and continuation schools they covered the age groups from three to eighteen. The leaving age was raised to fourteen with the virtual end to exemptions, which was the end of a struggle lasting forty years to abolish half-time work. Alongside this was a statement of a principle which, although at first more ignored than honoured, was to gradually gain more recognition : "Adequate provision shall be made in order to secure that children and young persons shall not be debarred from receiving the benefits of any form of education by which they are capable of profiting through inability to pay fees."[42]

The elementary schools were given a mandate to widen their curriculum to include practical work throughout the school, with advanced instruction for older students either in special classes or central schools. There was authority to keep children in the elementary schools to the age of sixteen and beyond that in certain circumstances. There was provision for the supply of playing fields and school camps. Authorities also assumed a mandatory duty to provide health and welfare services.

On the reverse of the coin, the main defects of the 1902 Act remained : namely the dual system of elementary schools and the small Part III authorities for elementary education. Both were barriers to raising standards but the successful agitation over the 1918 Act against "the threat of central bureaucracy" had if anything strengthened their hand. Although fees had been abolished in the elementary system, the secondary system was untouched. Over the years what had been near bankrupt schools of doubtful quality, had through local-authority subsidies, built up into powerful local institutions, unfortunately too often the strongholds of cultural division.

There was much to find fault with in the Act but given goodwill it could have served to take education forward. The great tragedy was the lack of interest of local industry in the continuation and central schools. These schools had ample scope for the development of graduated sandwich-type courses, but only in one or two cases did anything happen of this nature. Much was expected of the Act and among many optimistic comments the National Society sounded a more sober note with the comment that ". . . the extent of ground staked out is great indeed. The task now before us—and a tremendous one—is to secure its effective occupation".[43]

The impotence of the Liberal administration was further demonstrated by their inability to assist the adolescent. The Royal Commission on the Poor Laws of 1909, a Report on School Attendance and another on Partial Exemption from School Attendance all pointed to the inadequacies of facilities for the adolescent and agreed on measures to correct them; namely raising the school-leaving age, abolition of the half-time system and the provision of day-continuation schools. Public opinion was not generally ready to accept any great extension of compulsory education and the various official reports thought it prudent to leave it to the discretion of local authorities how far to proceed with compulsion after the age of twelve, although continuation classes were thought advisable to the age of seventeen.

To close this period there is a thought-provoking verdict on the educational policy of the Liberals by Lord Haldane, written in 1929 :

Over the reform of education the Liberals were pretty bad. Crewe and I were anxious to begin the work of founding a national system. But from the first it was clear the Nonconformist insistence on getting rid of the church-school system blocked the way. The church schools were indeed very deficient. But they could not be abolished at once, and although we were working through first-rate administrators, such as Sir Robert Morant, we could not get the public or Parliament to agree on any plan of reform. The truth was that, despite the vast importance of the question, too few people were keenly interested in education to afford us the requisite breeze for our sails. I sat on cabinet committees on the subject, and interviewed earnest men like Dr Clifford. But their prejudices I could not break single-handed and I had no keen allies. In this region I failed.[44]

What Happened To The People's Power?
1918–1936

I must pay a tribute to the Fourth Form Room. The first time I made its acquaintance was when I sat for an entrance examination, and I remember so well my disappointment at finding I was among the rejected. I got over it, however, in subsequent years, when I learnt that two of the most distinguished men in public life to-day had shared my fate : one is the First Lord of the Admiralty, and the other—it is the first time I have been classed with first-class brains—no less a person than the late Lord Chancellor, the Earl of Birkenhead. Happy the school whose outcasts and rejected can yet make good in after life.

When the call came to me to form a Government, one of my first thoughts was that it should be a Government of which Harrow should not be ashamed. I remembered how in previous Governments there had been four or perhaps, five Harrovians, and I determined to have six. To make a Cabinet is like making a jigsaw puzzle fit, and I managed to make my six by keeping the post of Chancellor of the Exchequer for myself. I think we have good reason to be content.

Mr Stanley Baldwin addressing the Harrow School Association on 19 July 1923. He neglected to mention that the Cabinet also contained eight Etonians, two representatives of Merchant Taylors and one each from Rugby, Wellington and Winchester.

THE FIRST WORLD WAR was unique both in its size and the sacrifices it demanded from millions of people; and as a result it changed both the social framework and the political map of Europe. The ruling élites blundered into the struggle with little understanding of what they were doing, in the process destroying the structure of blatant control and privilege which had served them so well for centuries and particularly in the last fifty years when the multiple fruits of industrialization had been theirs. Four years of total war made it necessary for the ordinary people to be encouraged to fight by concessions, which in Britain gave the unskilled worker and his wife full voting rights.[1] At a stroke the electorate was nearly trebled so that the political balance was necessarily affected; for the first time the unskilled, underfed, unhealthy, undersized, ill-housed and neglected majority had a political voice. Sheer numbers made them potentially the most powerful section of the community.

There were however complex factors which prevented this political weight from being mobilized. The first was their utter ignorance; for they had passed through an education system designed to impart only the bare elements of literacy and number, which was an indifferent preparation for understanding anything about national affairs especially as the same schools also inculcated a strict discipline and a ready respect for authority. Work conditions of the period translated this into a realistic appreciation of a place at the bottom of the pecking order. Thoughtful members of the upper classes who met working men when sharing the common dangers of war understood their conditions for the first time and realized the lack of justice in the social system. A typical account noted :

> The only trouble is their standard of education is so low. Put the product of the elementary school side by side with the man from overseas, and his mental equipment is pitiful. ... The overseas man, with his freedom from tradition, his wide outlook on life, his intolerance of vested interests, and his contempt for distinction based on birth rather than on worth, has stirred in the minds of many, a comparison between the son of the bondwoman and the son of the free.[2]

Such characteristics help explain why the new voters did not exercise their newly acquired right. The three elections before 1918 had averaged a turnout of over 83 per cent of the total electorate, but the new enlarged electorate of 1918 only managed 58.9 per cent, and although this improved it was not until the 1950s that an 80 per cent vote was recorded again. One reason for this was that the political efforts of the trade unions and the Labour Party were not easily accepted by those they set out to represent. Many were so accustomed to seeking direction in their work it seemed natural to leave political decisions to the managerial classes thus giving rise to the so-called deferential vote. In this pattern an unexplored factor was the conflict of authoritarian husbands and wives, which has persistently alienated some women's votes from working-class candidates, seeing in them an extension of the dominant domestic male.[3] Many older manual workers remained attached to the Liberals, who, as a party, had significance in confusing the issues and thus assisting the Conservatives to retain power. These facts help explain the number of dismal industrial towns which still continued to send Conservative MPs to parliament during the 1930s.

This indifferent mobilization of the working-class vote is all the more surprising because every issue was decided against the background of the one dominating problem of the period between the wars: that of unemployment. There were never less than 1 million unemployed between 1921 and 1938, and for much of the time it was more than double that figure. For the whole period the average proportion of insured males unemployed was 14.2 per cent, but for 1931, 1932 and 1933 it was 21.1 per cent, 21.9 per cent and 19.8 per cent respectively.[4] Children left school often to spend years without a job, even of the transient and dead-end type. In such conditions the Labour Party slowly grew in strength.

Industrial interests had from the start of the century begun to switch their allegiance to the Conservatives. Their financial contribution was significant but to muster numbers of votes they relied on the emerging white-collar workers, mostly minor administrative and clerical workers. From the period 1924 to 1938 wage earners, mainly manual workers, fell from 80 per cent to 74.7 per cent of the work force; in the same period salaried workers increased from 17.8 per cent of the work force to 20 per cent.[5] These emerging lower middle classes, produced by the increasing size of firms and the growing sophistication of industry, were largely products of the grammar schools, jealous of their salaried status and their position as owner-occupiers of semi-detached houses. It was such support which kept the Conservatives in power for all but three years of the inter-war period.

The 1918 election, the first exercise of the working-class vote, was a tragedy. There was the political power with which to begin to solve the neglect of centuries, but, instead of concentrating on housing and social conditions, the leading question at the hustings was what should be done with the Kaiser.[6] Even in slum areas the main interest was not in housing but in clearing former German residents out of the district. The result was a government which the Prime Minister Lloyd George referred to as "the Associated Chambers of Commerce".[7]

The Education Act of 1918 committed the government to having all children in school until the age of fourteen as well as developing "education other than elementary". This was not defined and much of the period between the wars was taken up with trying to do so. The main educational problem was what form of secondary education should be given to the great part of the children in schools, other than traditional secondary establishments.

There were already a number of solutions, some of long standing. There was first the grammar school, which in the Arnold public-school formula centred on a classically-weighted syllabus combined with games and a measure of self government; this was frequently pronounced the acme of successful education. Much of the character of this type of education depended on the schools boarding their pupils, and in fact had been devised to deal with such conditions. Nevertheless the day-secondary-grammar schools, which had by the 1902 Act been given a new lease of life through local-authority financial support, looked to the public schools for their model. They had adopted a mixed curriculum but usually giving preference to the arts for the classics were compulsory for university entrance, and where there was a second language taught it had to be Latin. In a variety of ways they identified with their model, running house systems with prefects; there was also an accent on public school games, which tended to be cricket and rugby football; students wore uniforms while the masters wore gowns. It is an indication of how much this identification was accepted by the children that there was a boom in public-school stories. These had begun in the 1890s but reached new heights with the founding of *The Magnet* in 1908; this weekly pulp magazine, written by Frank Richards (1875–1961), was concerned with a fictional public school, Greyfriars. There was a girls' counterpart, the best of which was written by Angela Brazil (1868–1947).

In financing these schools the State had taken the cheapest

way to provide secondary education, but in doing so had subsidized a series of institutions which already had a cultural character identified with the middle or managerial classes; nothing happened to alter this or to materially alter the type of child attending the school. There was a widespread feeling that this type of education was beyond the abilities of the children of manual workers, except for a few exceptional individuals who would become members of the professions. This was a position which became progressively more difficult to maintain as increases in the number of places were more than matched by the children who came forward able to fill them. The advance was largely due to the improvement in living conditions especially feeding and housing, although these basic requirements were still below an acceptable standard for a large section of the population.

The balance of intake from the elementary schools was 25 per cent and the type of child accepted usually approximated to those already attending, thus ensuring the middle-class cultural style was maintained. Head teachers interviewed children from a group who had "passed the scholarship"; their selection depended on social acceptability and willingness to stop to sixteen, 2 years beyond the minimum leaving age. The latter condition was important because the grant was progressively larger for each of the 4 years of the secondary course. Children who were not accepted could be offered places at local-authority secondary schools or technical schools, which were not usually loaded with middle-class values.

It should be noted there was virtually no contact between the various groups. Teaching staff belonged to different associations and games competitions were among schools of a similar type; thus Eton played Harrow, not the local grammar school and certainly not the nearby public elementary schools.

Elementary education policy was largely controlled by university academics who had little idea what went on in the schools, as this account of the proceedings of a committee convened by the Board of Education in 1920 to report on the teaching of English in England shows. One of the members, "Professor 'X' had no sooner entered the room, than he began to talk about the importance of Anglo-Saxon and when I interjected, 'But we here are mainly concerned, sir, with children, boys and girls in elementary schools; and the lower forms of the secondary schools;

at what age should one begin to learn Anglo-Saxon?' he thumped the table and shouted at me, 'You cannot begin to learn Anglo-Saxon too early!' "[8]

By this it can be seen there was no coherent policy, although there was a tentative movement towards secondary education for all. There were many difficulties, notably a variably qualified staff, makeshift facilities in unsuitable buildings, but most of all little appreciation or interest among the poorer parents who were occupied with procuring the barest necessities of life, such as work, food and housing. To extend the scope of the schools would cost money, and education brought no immediate electoral advantage. So in a period of financial stringency little headway was made; all parties concentrated on more urgent and basic problems.

To extend secondary education two plans could be seen developing. The first was through the continuation schools, the use of which could have been extended in duration and scope, especially if qualifications useful to industry had been produced. Education through co-operation with employers had a long history, most of it not very fruitful. Only a few large and progressive firms were interested, the others used young labour only on menial work and preferred it because it was cheap and trouble free; such firms had no occasion to help train young people. It seems clear continuation schools were before their time for industry needed few skilled experts and these were produced through apprenticeships, usually recruiting from the sons and nephews of long service workpeople.

The second line, already developing, was from the Code for 1904 which authorized special classes and central schools to provide specialized training. These could, it was hoped, build up into secondary schools and take their place alongside the grammar school.

A third line of development had already been tried : channelling all children through the elementary schools in a continuous stream, with diversification at the top of the school to suit individual aptitudes and abilities. With 90 per cent of children in State schools, education together in one institution would have produced a social unity which was not possible when the ablest and more affluent children were hived off to fee-paying schools where there was already a cachet of social superiority. This was the line of development which had been barred by the board's attitude and destroyed by the Cockerton judgment. It would not be revived with any vigour until the 1950s, although this was the pattern of development in most other countries.

A complete theory of post-primary education was advanced by R. H. Tawney in *Secondary Education For All* in 1922, and this was accepted as Labour party policy.[9] There was nothing very original in this, and indeed it was the logical follow-through of the way that the schools were developing. Its importance is in being a statement of a single coherent system in simple language which led to the ideas being widely read and discussed. He denounced the current division of education into elementary and secondary as both wasteful and undemocratic. He advocated a policy both "educationally sound" and democratic, "in which primary and secondary education are organized as two stages in a single continuous process: secondary education being the education of the adolescent and primary education being the education preparatory thereto". The Labour party thus accepted the political objective of developing the schools so that at the age of "eleven plus" every child would pass to secondary education of one type or another, to stay there until the completion of a full secondary course at the age of sixteen. A variety of secondary facilities would be needed, but these could be developed from the central schools, the junior technical schools and similar institutions. All secondary education would be free and maintenance grants would be paid where necessary to the parents who needed the wage support from their children. It outlined a large and rational scheme so that *Free Secondary Education For All* became a powerful and popular slogan.

The key to any educational problem is often the economic situation and this was no exception; already by 1920 the signs of slump were seen and the Committee on National Expenditure was at work.[10] Its report, published in January 1921, scotched the development of day-continuation schools, thus leaving only one way of advance open for universal secondary education. Already there were signs of the inadequacy of the secondary-school provision although it was expanding. In 1920 the departmental committee on the Free Place and Scholarship System found over 20,000 children who had shown they had the ability

TAKING THE EDGE OFF IT.

Sir Eric Geddes. "I DON'T THINK I SHALL LEND MY AXE AGAIN TO THAT COMMITTEE!"
[The Cabinet Committee that is sitting on the Geddes recommendations
is said to be opposed to the suggested economies in education expenditure.]

(*Punch* – 18 January 1922)

suitable for secondary-school education but were excluded through lack of places, or because their parents could not afford to pay for them or, if they were given free places, even keep them at school.[11] The remedy was obviously in more schools, more free places and maintenance grants; but this was not to be.

There was a great campaign over public spending which was shown to have increased five fold between 1914 and 1921–2, followed by a general outcry for cuts which included all the social services. Much of the plans proceeding from the Education Act of 1918 were halted and the number of pupils in secondary education actually declined. The Tawney Plan was not viewed with friendly eyes by the officials of the Board. The Permanent Secretary, Mr Selby-Bigge, faced with the problem familiar to developing countries—of expanding the educational service on an impossibly small budget—sought refuge in the belief that the English, unlike the Scots, did not value education. The term "secondary education" should, in his opinion, be reserved for those schools whose tradition was to train character and intellect, giving "a liberal education unhampered by premature specialisation"; application of this term to other forms of school could only delude the public.[12]

There were other forces pressing for change and not the least of these was the consultative committee, re-established by order in Council on 22 July 1920. Already they had dealt with two questions referred to them by the board; first the differentiation of curriculum for boys and girls in secondary schools, and secondly the possible use of psychological tests in the public system.[13] On 12 June 1923 the standing sub-committee which acted as a pilot body, proposed to investigate "the different types of curriculum suitable to children between the ages of eleven and sixteen and the means by which they could be provided". Selby-Bigge rejected this, alleging that teachers were in general agreement "that the plan of the curriculum" for other than traditional secondary schools "should be a continuation of general education, with a commercial or industrial bias in accordance with the character of the locality". The consultative committee insisted on their interest in "the point of junction" between elementary and secondary education, with the need to investigate some alternative courses for children up to fifteen and sixteen who would not be proceeding to secondary schools. They stated their wish to focus on the children who composed "the multitude who labour with their hands, as opposed to those who entered secondary schools and proceeded to clerical occupations".[14] Although the Permanent Secretary had argued "in particular, the main road to the teaching profession must always pass through the secondary school, and for this reason alone a sound system of secondary schools is essential to a sound system of national education" he considered the committee should not include the secondary-school curriculum on which a number of reports had been issued for this would bring them up against the statutory barrier between elementary and higher education; he also warned that "provision is a matter of money and in existing circumstances money was not forthcoming".[15] It was finally agreed, after some support from the officers of the boards, that the inquiry should cover "the field of advanced elementary, rather than secondary education". The upper limit of age to be investigated was to be fifteen, rather than sixteen, which the board considered would extend the inquiry beyond the bounds of practical politics. The Permanent Secretary drafted the final terms himself, which were :

> The organization, objective and curriculum of courses of study suitable for children who will remain in full-time attendance at school, other than secondary schools, up to the age of fifteen, regard being had, on the one hand, to the requirements of a good, general education and the desirability of providing a reasonable variety of curriculum so far as this is practicable, for the children of varying tastes and abilities, and, on the other, to the probable occupation of the pupils in commerce, industry and agriculture.

It will be seen that the Hadow Committee's terms of reference were not a consequence of the Labour party's assumption of office which did not occur until January 1924.[16]

Meanwhile in 1923 Stanley Baldwin took over as Prime Minister from the dying Bonar Law; he felt he must go to the nation over the free-trade-versus-protection question, but Tawney's pamphlet had also made education an electoral issue. The Conservative party held their annual conference in October 1923, two months before the election. Lady Astor proposed the raising of the school-leaving age to sixteen to assist the unemploy-

ment situation. She pointed out the destructive effects of a young
person being without work; this was bad enough for a man but
five times worse for a child. To allow this to happen was to
waste the nation's capital as well as "making fuel for agitators".
Another woman delegate took a different view claiming child
labour was a very great asset to industry and if the children were
put to work young it came as second nature to them. The resolution was defeated. Baldwin was made alive to public interest, and
a month before the election he addressed a Bristol meeting on
the Conservatives' "genuine and deep interest in the subject of
education", but "I do not say it would be wise, as some suggest,
to give everyone a secondary-school education". He made the
point that in the USA where this was done the standards were
much lower but added "there is a ridiculous myth propagated
by Labour leaders that we are opposed to popular education
because we want to keep the people in a subordinate position".[17]
The election was inconclusive and Labour formed a minority
administration in January 1924.

The newly arrived President of the Board of Education,
Charles Trevelyan, took the view the Hadow terms were too
narrow and considered "the enquiry need not be very elaborate
or complicated". He expected its chief value would be in offering guidance to allay growing concern for unemployed juveniles.
The chairman, Sir Henry Hadow, resisted suggestions to investigate this problem, saying that unemployment was not a problem
below the age of sixteen, and if they were to deal with this then
they must consider the question of raising the school-leaving age
to sixteen, a course the board did not want to sanction. The
problems of finding teachers and accommodation, as well as
combating the opposition of parents were seen as great difficulties,
but also, "the teaching profession has not yet thought out suitable
curricula even for children leaving at fifteen, let alone sixteen".[18]

The Labour government announced an ambitious programme
of educational development with the object of providing free
secondary education for all, in contrast to the previous régime's
standstill order with a third cut in the education budget. The
programme was to be phased over 10 years, but before it could
be launched the Labour party lost office; however, the returned
Conservatives did not revert to their former standstill policy.
The board pointed to the obligations under the 1918 Act to

provide advanced instruction for older pupils, so, although there was a standstill for post-primary development, plans were requested for educational schemes covering three years from 1 April 1927. There was a general acceptance that the dividing line should be eleven, at which elementary education should end and something different and more advanced be provided.

At the end of 1926 the Hadow Report, "The Education of the Adolescent", was presented; it was comprehensive and in effect endorsed the programme drawn up by Tawney who was on the committee. By manipulation of their narrow terms of reference the committee had brought the whole of post-primary education under review and came out for free, universal secondary education. Every child should have an education during childhood, the primary stage, followed by education for adolescence, which should be given as a separate and "secondary" education. They fixed the age of break at eleven, although they acknowledged many educationalists would have preferred thirteen, the usual age in independent education; but from the public administrative point of view eleven was more convenient as it had become the age of entry to grammar schools. As an immediate proposal every child should have a post-primary period of education from eleven to fourteen at least. At the end of five years, in 1932, the school-leaving age should be raised to fifteen to extend the course a further year.

The report clarified the nomenclature of the various types of secondary education. Schools of the existing secondary type where the normal curriculum extended to sixteen were to be known as grammar schools. The term "modern schools" was to be used for central schools whether selective or not. Where no secondary school was available senior pupils were to organize as separate entities known as senior classes. Although junior-technical and trade schools had been expressly excluded from the terms of reference by the board's technical advisers, the committee suggested these might be treated as vocational institutions with an entry age of thirteen, although certain junior-technical schools might be included in their scheme, taking children at eleven, but giving them a non-technical education for the first two years of the course.

Although the courses would vary with the type of school the modern schools, at which most of the children would be receiving their education, were not to be inferior imitations of the grammar schools, but to cater specifically for children of limited academic aptitude, relating their studies to ordinary life, and making manual work and practical instruction important features of their teaching. In certain cases instruction could be given an industrial bias, but it was never to be narrowly vocational. The aim of all the schools was to be to provide "a humane and general education". In the first two years the courses between eleven and thirteen in all types of schools should as far as possible run parallel so that in appropriate cases children could be transferred from one type of school to another without difficulty at the age of thirteen. All establishments providing post-primary education were to have "parity of esteem".

For the first time in an official report it was suggested the two basic types of education—that for the managerial and the other for the manual workers—were brought together in a formula which could lead to them merging into one system. The egalitarian tone hardly commended the report to the Conservative President of the Board, Lord Eustace Percy, especially with a specific date for the raising of the school-leaving age. Moreover the report came some three months after the end of the General Strike, in which working-class militancy had been soundly defeated. His first reaction was to propose a foreword dissociating the board from the recommendations as contrary "to the main lines of a continuous national policy". Calmer counsels prevailed and ways were suggested of blunting the impact of the report. The President in correspondence with Sir Henry Hadow argued that it was national policy to leave the local authorities to decide at their discretion whether, and at what time, the age of compulsory school attendance should be raised in their own areas and that the Labour party had accepted that principle. He quoted his predecessor Trevelyan as saying "as always before, we must prepare for the next advance in the school age by the more progressive authorities showing the way". He claimed the board was committed to this policy under existing arrangements with local authorities through their submission of three-year programmes.[19]

In effect the board agreed in principle with the report, but raising the school-leaving age became a receding ideal.

Nevertheless the board began to make a start with

reorganization of post-primary education along the lines suggested by the Hadow Report which it was believed could be done by existing delegated legislation to alter regulations, but the resulting financial and administrative problems were found to be too complicated. The proposal to make eleven the dividing line between primary and secondary education involved the basic structure of local administration; for, if all education over the age of eleven were to become secondary, the small Part III authorities would be deprived of their rôle in higher elementary education which they had acquired under the 1918 Act. If all higher elementary classes and central schools were to become secondary-modern schools, they would presumably have to be transferred to the county or Part II authorities. Grants for secondary schools were made on a different basis from those to elementary schools, so the transformation of elementary-based development to secondary-type administration would require complicated financial adjustments. Teachers' salaries were also on different scales and needed to be adjusted, which could only be done when the current Burnham Award ran out.

The perennial problem of religious instruction reared its head, for the Cowper-Temple clause which forbade the teaching of distinct religious formulary in elementary schools did not apply to central and higher elementary schools once they were accorded secondary status. Under the Hadow plan voluntary schools with senior classes brought up the whole question of relations of managers and local authorities for, if senior classes were to be transformed into separate secondary schools, new buildings would often be required. The voluntary schools were mostly in financial difficulties, and yet if the local authorities built the schools they would require a greater say in their management.

The principle of "parity of esteem" raised even greater problems, arising from the poor state of existing central-school buildings which would have to be improved to the standards of the grammar schools. The need to bring the schools for the majority up to standards of a minority of superior schools was made all the more difficult by the increase in births in the early 1920s. There were also fewer teachers of secondary quality for the modern schools. Adoption of the Hadow Report in letter and spirit, it was finally realized, required the reconstruction of the whole education system involving great costs. This was aggravated by the question of fees; parity required either the modern schools charged fees or that they were abolished in the secondary-grammar schools.

There seemed little hope of securing agreement among the many interests involved and the national economic condition was not favourable for expensive and far-reaching social measures. In the end the board were driven to abandon any implementation of the Hadow reforms, except a deliberate attempt to educate public and official opinion in the merits of the plan which became known as Hadow reorganization. The board explained their intentions to local authorities in a series of circulars and a pamphlet, "The New Prospect in Education", published in 1928.[20] Elementary schools would break their courses at eleven. Classes would be progressively reduced in size, first to the target of fifty and later to forty. Where practicable, junior and senior classes were to be in separate premises. Some 2,800 schools were placed on a "black list" in 1924 because of their defective and inadequate accommodation; this indicated they were to be radically improved or replaced at an unspecified date. It was at least a statement of intent, but there was much to be done for there were some 20,000 classes with over fifty children with little prospect of reduction because by the 1930s the post-war bulge would have reached the senior classes.

Progress was painfully slow as half the money for school buildings was earmarked for schools on new housing estates. By 1928 some 1,000 schools had been removed from the black list although it was estimated that another seven years would be needed to deal with the other 1,800 condemned schools.[21] The voluntary schools were in great difficulties because there was not the money for reorganization and in many cases older pupils had to be sent to neighbouring provided schools. The Anglican Church agreed to support the board's policy so long as the authorities would permit denominational instruction to be given on the premises.[22] The issue was first raised in a Dorset school in 1928 where a small number of children were allowed religious instruction; this case was used as a precedent and a virulent campaign followed against "the right of entry", as it was called, and the board had to give an assurance that the 1902 settlement was not endangered. Once again the religious question was to complicate educational advance.

In 1929 the question of raising the school-leaving age became a political issue on the publication of a report issued by the First Conference on Industrial Reorganization and Relations. It was the work of Lord Melchett, a Liberal, and Ben Tillet, a leading trade unionist, who recommended the school-leaving age be raised as a means of relieving adult unemployment.[23] The board opposed this as adult unemployment was not related to the amount of juvenile labour available in any area and it was felt most parents would bitterly resent such a step. They pointed out that the great majority of elementary-school pupils left as soon as they legally could, for only 15,000 of the half million who reached the age of fourteen annually stayed on an extra year. Only four local authorities out of the national total of 317 had passed bye-laws raising the school-leaving age to fifteen and they found them impossible to enforce. In the view of the board, if the legislation was passed straight away, it would take at least five years to make preparations to put it into operation by 1935. It was also suggested that legislation should wait until the post-war bulge had passed through the schools, and the Government Actuary had forecast that numbers should begin to fall after 1937. There were serious accommodation and staffing problems which could only be aggravated by raising the school-leaving age without proper preparation.[24]

While this question was being considered, the government fell and Labour returned to office with Charles Trevelyan back as President of the Board of Education. The Labour election manifesto on education was brief and clear, "Equal educational opportunities for every child . . . raise the school-leaving age to fifteen with the requisite maintenance grants and at once develop facilities for free secondary education. Labour will open the road to whoever is able to take it, from the nursery school to the university".[25] The board advised delay but not only was there a pledge to provide opportunity, but also one of reducing unemployment. Discussions with local education authorities convinced Trevelyan that time was not likely to make the measure any easier to carry out.[26] There would always be financial difficulties and in an emergency the central government would have to come to the aid of the local authorities. What was spent on education might well be saved on unemployment and poor relief for, it was argued, by taking 450,000 children out of the labour

force work would be provided for 100,000 men.[27] It was announced in Parliament in July 1929 that a Bill to raise the
school-leaving age, together with the provision of maintenance
grants, would shortly be presented as part of the general policy
for dealing with unemployment.

In framing an acceptable measure it was soon obvious that
all the old barriers to educational change were still as active as
ever. They appeared over two issues. First the provision of maintenance grants, secondly the position of voluntary schools. The
government in their urgency proposed to leave the second and
try to work out a practical way of administering the former
which, in the reduced state of many families, was essential to
make further time at school acceptable. It was usually easy for
a school leaver to find work, although within a year or so he
would be unemployed. This situation was widely appreciated but
poor families looked forward to the time when their older children could be earning, for there was always hope that they
could find permanent employment. Within the cabinet there was
divided opinions on maintenance grants to make up for the
wages the children would not bring home. Working-class MPs
favoured a generous and universal grant to be paid by local
authorities with the provision so framed that the Conservative
interest which dominated many authorities could not interfere.
Government realists feared the Conservative opposition to such
a course would defeat the Bill in parliament.

The issue of maintenance grants was to prove a most serious
obstacle to raising the school-leaving age. Although the payment
of money to help scholars while they studied has a history as
long as education itself, the idea of a general allowance caused
widespread opposition. Help to poor children at secondary
schools was part of many of the endowments schemes of the
nineteenth century. In 1883 the Charity Commissioners reported
that 723 schemes with a total income of £377,881 had already
been framed under the Endowed Schools Acts; it was estimated
schemes were outstanding for another 661 schools involving a
total income of £154,241.[28] This provision had slowly developed
until in 1920 some 128 local education authorities were making
maintenance allowances with annual values up to £40, although
most were under that sum.[29] There was no uniformity about the
schemes and each case was judged on its merits. This was in

accordance with Poor Law practice, which had been translated into the controversial and hated "Means Test" associated with unemployment payments. Although the large civic authorities had been running maintenance schemes for several years to help children stay on at school and complete their education, it can be realized that extension on any terms took the whole question beyond normal educational issues, involving the measure in wider and highly emotional questions.

In the last ten years the material deprivation of many families had been a constant theme in parliamentary business. The Labour party, particularly those MPs with working-class backgrounds, took every opportunity to bring to public notice the wretched existence of the millions in the families of the unemployed and low-paid workers. The plight of children featured prominently in such evidence but, although material was well prepared and documented, without a substantial parliamentary majority nothing could move governments committed to low taxation as the best way of "weathering the recession". One example will suffice to show the situation.

In December 1928 Miss Margaret Bondfield had launched a private measure, the Provision of Children's Footwear Bill, which proposed "to provide footwear for children in distressed areas, the local authority finding 10 per cent of the costs", the Treasury the rest. Supported by six other women MPs the campaign was started on the 4 December, timed to climax at Christmas and also appeal to the women aged twenty-one to thirty, who had just been given the vote. Attention was called to the question of children's clothing "for the express purpose of enabling the minister to give us the government point of view". A week later the question was re-opened with support from all sides of the House. The President of the Board of Education, Lord Eustace Percy, agreed on the gravity of the situation and gave evidence of a "West Riding survey last summer, when 21 per cent of 44,000 children were found to have bad boots", and admitted, "I am afraid that the trouble is that areas which are most acutely distressed could not afford to bear the cost of even 10 per cent of a new service of this kind". Miss Ellen Wilkinson, MP for distressed Jarrow, asked, "Is this a reason for the government doing nothing at all?".[30]

On the 18 December Mr Winston Churchill, the Chancellor

of the Exchequer, gave details of long-standing arrangements to deal with such cases which mainly consisted of help from "recognized local funds". "The government are not satisfied of any sufficient reason for interfering with these arrangements" and there would be no government facilities for the Bill. Prime Minister Baldwin, alert to public interest in the question, spoke of the schemes launched to help such cases, but particularly the government offer to match pound for pound raised by charity through the Lord Mayor's fund. On 20 December there was further evidence given to the House of children "going to school barefoot, others wearing sand shoes, while many have a respectable upper to their boot, but on examining the sole one finds there really is none". The House broke up for the Christmas recess without action being taken.

In 1929 when the Labour government took office much was expected on educational matters and there was understandable impatience to learn the details of proposed changes which seemed long in arriving. On 13 November 1929, the Liberals tabled a motion asking the government to present their Bill. Miss Eleanor Rathbone, newly elected as an independent university MP, took the opportunity to make the case for family allowances irrespective of parental means to all elementary-school children.[31] The truth was that the financial costs of raising the school-leaving age were proving nearly insurmountable. It was estimated that in the early 1930s it would cost about £5.25 million of which £3.75 million would come from the Exchequer, the rest from local rates. This sum only covered increased accommodation, capitation grant, teachers' salaries and some maintenance grants; if this last item was to be extended in any way, then the costs would increase by anything up to £9 million. There would also be increased costs in the secondary schools where about 35 per cent of free-place children received allowances which averaged only 3/– a week to which the Exchequer contributed 40 per cent of the costs.[32] There was also Scotland where it was estimated between 50 per cent and 80 per cent would require allowances. Meanwhile there were no answers to the country's basic economic problems and by January 1930 unemployment was over 1.5 million, the highest since 1923. In the end a grant of 5/– a week was to be given only to cases in need, to which the Exchequer would contribute 60 per cent. Although this was higher than other maintenance allowances paid it was 20 per cent below what had been advocated by the Labour party in opposition.

The Bill, which had been delayed some five months, was presented on 17 December 1929 only to become involved in the voluntary-schools question. The relationship of local authorities and church schools had remained a simmering controversy. In 1921, the President of the Board, Mr Fisher, had been favourable to a private Member's Bill which proposed that all public elementary schools should be placed under the complete control of the local education authorities. Religious instruction of various denominations was to be given during school hours by specialist teachers. A similar system was to obtain in secondary schools and training colleges. Central and local advisory committees were to be set up to advise the local authorities. The non-provided schools were not to change hands but the local authorities were to bear full costs for maintenance and alterations. The Bill met the bitter opposition of the Roman Catholics and was dropped.[33]

The position of the Roman Catholic Church on education allowed no compromise. They held their children must be brought up in an atmosphere which expressed their religious doctrines and values. This was the position taken up by the Anglicans in the nineteenth century, but they had been unable to find the finance to carry it out. In contrast the Catholic community, despite great economic hardship, was adamant in its resolve to maintain control of their schools by making the most of existing government provision. The Roman Catholic congregation in Britain had increased steadily to well over 2 million and it was emerging as politically of some importance, especially to the Labour party for most of its members were manual workers.

However, the scheme had appealed in some areas to the local secular and church authorities, and from 1925 a number of local agreements were sought, chiefly with Church of England schools, by which the schools were to be transferred to the local authorities who were to contribute to the capital cost of maintenance and improvements.[34] Cowper-Temple, that is non-sectarian, religious instruction was to continue in all council schools, but denominational instruction was to be permitted during school hours in transferred schools at the expense of the old managers. Such arrangements were not statutorily permissible so late in 1926 a draft Bill was prepared to make this possible. At this point the Church Assembly published a report which stated that grouping of church and council schools in this way should only be agreed when adequate religious arrangements were made for senior and central schools in the group. The authorities had had enough of religious controversy in the elementary schools and any suggestion that it should intrude into the secondary phase of education was refused. The enabling Bill was therefore dropped.

In 1929 the denominations, particularly the Roman Catholics, approached the Conservatives to promise that if returned at the General Election they would introduce legislation authorizing local authorities to make capital grants to rebuild voluntary schools condemned by the "black list". When Labour was returned it was soon made clear to the President that he could not ignore the problems of the church schools. The demands created by proposals to raise the school-leaving age showed that in many cases the most economic, and indeed often the only way, was to improve voluntary-school accommodation. He therefore dropped his Bill and opened negotiations with both the denominations and the local authorities to try for a nation-wide solution to the problem.

Agreement was achieved between the authorities and all the denominations with the exception of the Roman Catholics. The terms were published in a White Paper and drafted into a Bill in May 1930.[35] In return for financial assistance local authorities were to be given the right to appoint and dismiss all staff in voluntary schools; managers were to be consulted so that a requisite number of teachers was available to give religious instruction in accordance with the trust deeds. To meet Nonconformist objections, where children were required to attend a voluntary school, religious instruction was to be given on an agreed syllabus, or under Cowper-Temple conditions; the right of withdrawal from religious instruction was also conceded.

This second Bill fared no better than the first as it met opposition from the Roman Catholics, to whom the voluntary-school provisions were not acceptable; it was also opposed by certain Labour MPs who objected strongly to the acceptance of the hated principle of showing need by submission to a Means Test. Trevelyan abandoned his Bill and framed a third measure which, as in his first Bill, made no attempt to deal with the problem of the church schools. This new Bill was designed to allay opposition from his own side of the House by grants at a flat rate of 5/- to be paid to parents according to income-tax limits, which thus provided a ceiling qualification which increased with the number of children in the family. He proposed to discuss the problem of voluntary schools at a conference of interested parties.

The new Bill was presented on 31 October 1930 in an atmosphere of economic gloom and mounting unemployment. The estimated costs of the measure were £8 million annually by 1936, of which £6 million would be met from the Exchequer and the rest from rates; maintenance allowances accounted for two-thirds of the expenditure.[36] The Conservatives attacked the proposed "doles" as extravagant and demoralizing. Indeed they attacked any extension of education beyond the age of fourteen, and pointed to the heavy burden which such measures threw on the voluntary schools.

In January 1931 Trevelyan convened the voluntary-school conference. The Church of England, the Free Churches, the Roman Catholic Church, the local education authorities and the teachers were all represented. Trevelyan himself put before them proposals modified from the conditions of his second Bill.[37] It was agreed that in every voluntary school a statutory number of posts should be reserved for teachers qualified to give religious instruction in accordance with the wishes of the managers. An appeal tribunal was framed to settle disputes between authorities and managers. The Nonconformists forced an amendment that voluntary schools in receipt of capital grants should be required to find no less than 25 per cent of the total expenditure. All parties declared themselves satisfied with the final proposals of the conference except the Nonconformists. Their main grievance was that Nonconformists had little chance of being appointed heads of voluntary schools and in view of the large number of such schools this considerably restricted their promotion prospects; they wanted head teachers to be appointed entirely on educational and not religious grounds.

Meanwhile in the Commons the government had suffered a tactical defeat. Roman Catholics did not want to agree to the school-leaving age being raised until the conference proposals had been implemented. A Roman Catholic Labour MP, John

Scurr, therefore moved an amendment to this effect, which the Conservatives enthusiastically supported and the government was obliged to accept it; the Bill received its third reading on 21 January 1931. In the Lords the Conservative peers attacked the Bill on the lines of expense. Only a week before, Labour Chancellor of the Exchequer, Philip Snowden, had warned the House that expensive measures could not be afforded, for any increase in taxation on industry would be the "last straw"; he had urged the need for workers in their own interests to make sacrifices for the present to ensure future progress. With this ammunition the Conservative leader of the Lords, Viscount Hailsham, successfully moved the rejection of the Bill on 17 February. The government were determined to invoke the Parliament Act to force the Bill through, but decided to make a further attempt to reach agreement with the Nonconformists before introducing the measure once more into the Commons. However Mr Trevelyan resigned in March because he considered the financial and political state of the country prevented any further progress towards raising the school-leaving age and free secondary education for all. In August 1931 the administration gave way to a Conservative-dominated National Government which proceeded to slash educational expenditure, including a 5 per cent cut in teachers' salaries. All hope of educational progress was abandoned and a fight to save existing positions from the economy-drive cuts ensued.[38]

Drastic economies in education were recommended by the May Committee which published its report in September 1931. There were some increases in grants to necessitous areas, but the overall effect was to fall mostly on elementary education while secondary education was not as widely hit. A general increase in all fees for higher education was recommended, but the government decided to accept individual proposals to increase fees, where this could be done "without curtailing existing opportunities". The report disguised economies as consolidation, as these two paragraphs illustrate :

We fear that a tendency has developed to regard expenditure on education as good in itself without much consideration of the results that are being obtained from it and of the limits to which it can be carried without danger to other, no less vital, national interests.

Since the standard of education, elementary and secondary, that is being given to the child of poor parents is already in very many cases superior to that which the middle-class parent is providing for his own child, we feel it is time to pause in this policy of expansion, to consolidate the ground gained, to endeavour to reduce the cost of holding it, and to reorganize the existing machine before making a fresh general advance.

The May Committee's recommendations of a 25 per cent increase in secondary-school fees had been rejected by both the Labour and National Governments, but on 31 October 1931, the Treasury again re-opened the question with the Board of Education, suggesting that local authorities adopt "a modified free-place system and a means test for all free places".[39] It was thought that middle-class parents who paid nothing or £7 a year, could be asked to pay £15, or even £25 for fees. The board stressed the incongruities of charging fees in state-aided secondary schools, and feared some of the more gifted children would be sent to free modern or cheap private schools. They enlarged on the haphazard method of levying fees, which had resulted from the initial private nature of the schools. It was pointed out that under existing arrangements many thousands of pupils were in state-aided secondary schools simply because their parents could afford to pay the fees, while their presence excluded abler children whose parents could not afford to pay.

That board noted that secondary schools, at about £100 a place, were costly to provide and at £29 per pupil annually, were expensive to maintain. It was against the national economic interest to fill such high-cost facilities with pupils whose only claim to be there was passing a simple entrance test and their family being able to afford the fees amounting to less than a quarter of the maintenance cost. It was further pointed out that the performance of free pupils, measured by length of school life, success in first examinations, state scholarships and general school placings, was vastly superior to the other children in the schools. If fees were raised this disparity, with its attendant social injustice, would be accentuated, for the field from which fee payers could be drawn would be narrowed and the standard of admissions lowered. Moreover, raising fees would have only a limited financial effect, because they would still represent only a third to a half of the total costs of education provided. It was better business for the State to bear the whole cost of the education of the able, than the major part of the costs of the less able. The board therefore recommended the admission of pupils who had shown themselves by examination most likely to profit by secondary education, and to exact fees in whole or in part from those parents who could afford it, the remainder to be admitted free. This scheme was adopted under Circular No. 1421 of 15 September 1932. Authorities were expected to keep the number of special places about the same as the number of free places. Uniformity of remission procedure was not expected, but between £3 to £4 per week income for a family with one child was the suggested limit for entitlement, with 10/– a week allowed for every extra child. Direct-grant schools were excluded as their fees were already high. The scheme started on 1 April 1933.

The policy of increased fees for secondary education aroused an articulate section of the community and there was a great outcry which created much public interest in what was happening to education under the national economy drive. It became apparent that Hadow reorganization was generally accepted as an immediate and necessary step; there was also widespread discussion about the payment of fees to attend secondary schools but not for central, technical and modern schools.

Meanwhile educationalists, now well established in the universities, and educational officials with experience of a quarter of a century of local-government development, were anxious about the haphazard growth of post-primary education. Numbers in secondary schools had increased greatly, with rather more than 80 per cent leaving at sixteen and only some 5 per cent going on to university. While the older, heavy industries were in recession, newer, light industries, especially those connected with electrical goods, were expanding, thus creating a sharp demand for new technical competence. Meanwhile the secondary schools had retained their academic bias orientated towards their traditional university goals, which were still much influenced by the classicists, so that more taught Latin than physics. There had been no full inquiry into secondary education since the Bryce Commission of 1895; the only other official report had been the

Hadow Report of 1926, which had been mainly concerned with the mass of children who left school at fourteen.

In 1933 the question of a new reference for the consultative committee arose on the completion of their work in primary education.[40] There was support on all sides for an investigation of secondary education in the light of contemporary conditions. The committee was asked to consider, under the chairmanship of Will Spens, "the organization and inter-relation of schools, other than those administered under the Elementary Code, which provided education for pupils beyond the age of eleven plus; regard being had in particular to the framework and content of the education of pupils who do not remain at school beyond the age of about sixteen". As in the case of the Hadow Committee, the terms dictated an empirical rather than a theoretical approach; it was to be concerned with the functions of existing schools rather than the needs of the adolescents. The committee did not report until 1938, but the concept of Hadow reorganization still encouraged those pressing for some increase in the school-leaving age.

Meanwhile the Churches were feeling the effect of the decline in organized religion, which hit them financially and made them readier to accept State support for their schools. The virulence of their antagonisms had faded so that in the 1920s the Church of England and the Free Churches, in various areas, had begun to work out common syllabuses for religious education. By the early 1930s some 200 of the 317 local education authorities had adopted agreed syllabuses for use in their schools. The most popular was one published in Cambridge in 1924 which was used by more than 110 areas. This development went some way to making provided schools acceptable to parents of strong denominational views, but the problem of making the voluntary church schools more acceptable to the Nonconformists remained. An initiative was taken in this direction in 1932 when the Archbishop of Canterbury proposed that agreed syllabuses should be encouraged in voluntary as well as provided schools. He suggested that HM Inspectors should be given powers to inspect religious instruction in both voluntary and provided schools alike; that the timetable clause should be abolished so that religious instruction could be given at any time of the day; finally that better instruction in the teaching of religion should be provided at local-authority training colleges for teachers. These three proposals were later to figure in the famous "five points", the basis of the negotiations between the government and the Church authorities which led to the Education Act of 1944.

The proposals required legislation, but the government was not prepared to become involved in the question of voluntary schools or post-primary education. Such interest as the government had in the education of adolescents was concerned with the setting-up of juvenile employment centres. These had started in 1918 with the object of providing some useful instruction for young people without work, who would otherwise have been left to idle their time away. The problem was to get the youngsters to attend without compulsion. It was thought that if attendance was linked with unemployment benefit by making it a condition of payment, this would be enough; but benefit did not start until sixteen and a half. To solve this the minimum age at which young people might receive benefit was lowered to coincide with the school-leaving age. The Unemployment Act of 1934 required young people to attend a centre in order to qualify for unemployment benefit, and local authorities to provide courses of instruction at the centres. This was the first time a specific duty had been laid on educational authorities to provide instruction to the age of eighteen.

There was some hope that these measures would lead to a sharp increase in the work of the centres with the development of special interests; some government departments even came to see them as an alternative to raising the school-leaving age. It was overlooked that everyone concerned with them considered them a makeshift and so they never developed beyond the original object of bridging the period between school and work. They had no clear educational aim and so as soon as juvenile employment picked up the centres folded. Moreover, towards the end of 1933, raising the school-leaving age became an issue between the parties as the general election due in 1935 approached. In the 1931 election the conditions of financial disaster, which everywhere prevailed, had prevented the denominations from pressing their claims about their schools, but they now began to make it clear they wanted their problems dealt with. As the economic pall left by the depression began to lift the Roman Catholics were particularly militant and, as the largest community after the Church of England, they were a weighty political force. The popularity of the government was waning as they gained a reputation for being reactionary, particularly in educational matters. Although most of the cuts had been restored it was clear only a striking measure could dissipate popular disapproval.

In 1934 the cabinet met to reconsider educational policy.[41] Discussions which had been going on from December had established the necessary link between raising the school-leaving age and providing fresh assistance to the voluntary schools. Local authorities, the teachers and the Nonconformists, all remained opposed to capital grants for church schools; in fact these interests would have liked to see the end of the dual system. The government was advised that the most hopeful course was to bring in a single comprehensive measure which linked the two questions. In this way the opponents of voluntary schools might be persuaded to accept capital grants as a means of achieving educational advance. The cabinet was divided about the desirability of raising the school-leaving age.[42] The Minister of Labour and the Secretary of State for Scotland both thought any money for post-primary education would be better spent on the juvenile employment centres while the costs involved in raising the school-leaving age were not easily accepted by other ministers. In the end the cabinet agreed to raise the age, but with exemptions for any child able to find beneficial employment; children would thus stop at school until they found work. It was estimated this measure could cost only £1 million as against the £7 or £8 million which had been estimated for the Trevelyan proposals, which had included maintenance allowances. The government were aware this measure could have little educational value, but they hoped that it would satisfy the general public, while the educationalists would prefer half a loaf to none.

The board was asked to consider with the Treasury how capital grants to the voluntary schools could best be administered, but they each favoured different policies.[43] The board wanted a lump sum paid direct to the voluntary schools. This method would be acceptable to the Nonconformists since it avoided their objection to denominational teaching being made a charge on the rates, while at the same time it would secure equitable treatment for voluntary schools throughout the country irrespective of the attitudes of particular local authorities. They made the point that if grants to voluntary schools were to be made a charge on rate authorities they would insist on imposing all manner of conditions and there would be little chance of agreeing on the necessary legislation, for this had proved the barrier in previous attempts to assist voluntary schools. The Treasury wanted indirect grants, that is grants to voluntary schools to be made out of loans raised by local authorities on which the authorities themselves would pay half the interest and the Treasury the other half. This procedure was cheaper for the Treasury, for, as against a lump outlay of £1 million over a short period, they would pay interest amounting to some £34,000 a year over 30 years. The Treasury case was, that since education was a local service it was proper that its finances should be administered locally, which in any case would entail much less work for the Board than a system of direct grants. Little headway was made on this fundamental question which was referred back to the cabinet, while the board consulted representatives of the local authorities and the denominations.

Meanwhile in the country as well as the House of Commons there was growing pressure to raise the school-leaving age, stimulated by the fact that unemployment had been running around the two million mark for over four years. In the cabinet there was unease at the prospect of spending more money on education when the country was still in economical difficulties. The Minister of Labour argued that raising the leaving age would increase adult employment since many adult jobs could not be carried on without juvenile labour; he even pressed for a delay of 5 years to allow the juvenile employment centres to become established. The Nonconformists objected to grants for voluntary schools, especially in Wales, where Labour politics were taking over from the Liberals. In the end the cabinet postponed legislation and decided to formulate a policy in readiness for the forthcoming election.

Late in 1934, the Board of Education set up a secret office committee to explore fully the whole question of raising the school-leaving age. Its terms of reference were extensive. "On the assumption that it is desirable that the obligation to attend school should be extended, whether on a whole or part-time basis, beyond the present age of fourteen plus, to consider and report what form such extended education should take, and up to what age it should be continued, regard being had to requirements of trade, commerce and industry and to financial considerations." This wide discussion revealed widely differing views within the board; some did not even think the age should be raised and others did not favour secondary education for all; they wanted a royal commission or similar body to explore the merits of the Hadow policies as against day-continuation classes.[44]

Herwald Ramsbotham, Parliamentary Secretary to the Board, in a minute dated 2 November 1934 argued that the Hadow recommendations on raising the age were incidental to their findings, rather than inherent in them; the recommendation was indeed outside their terms of reference. He described the statements made on page xxii, where the committee envisaged the modern school with good facilities and an ardent, well-trained staff, as "lyric inaccuracy", suggesting it derived "from emotion rather than from any thorough examination of consideration affecting the raising of the age". He advocated a royal commission or similar body to pronounce on the issue authoritatively, as well as its political expediency."

Other opinion regarded an enquiry as a stratagem to delay decision further. By February 1935 the office committee had reached certain conclusions on basic principles. They concluded the age should be raised by one year, but children over fourteen should be exempted for beneficial employment. Despite the unhappy history of exemptions, the committee had finally accepted them in this case as certain industries were likely to be seriously dislocated by the sudden withdrawal of thousands of juvenile workers. Moreover the efficiency and reorganization of the schools could be no less jeopardized by the retention of older pupils. Implementation had better not take place until after 1938 when the post-war bulge had passed through the schools. It was also not forgotten that the rank-and-file Conservatives were obstinately opposed to the school-leaving age being raised at all.

However, the committee wished to make "beneficial employment" have real meaning, and it was proposed that should mean work of a permanent character; so a schedule of blind-alley jobs was to be compiled, which would not merit entitlement to exemption. In order to provide a measure of further education

even for children in beneficial employment, the committee
returned to the idea of continuation classes. All exempted children should be required to attend a vocational course for a stipu-
lated number of hours until they were sixteen. It was thought six
hours a week for 40 weeks in a year would be a satisfactory
guide, but local authorities would be allowed all reasonable lati-
tude in framing schemes to meet local conditions, so that the
interests of agriculture and industry could be safeguarded. The
committee did not favour maintenance grants.[45]

Having produced a report the board began to sound various
interested bodies on the issues raised. Over exemptions all consulted interests—teachers, local authorities, educational reformers,
religious bodies, industrial and agricultural organizations—
opposed them, with the exception of the National Farmers'
Union. Most also favoured maintenance grants. The local
authorities thought exemptions impossible to operate and if
maintenance grants were given they should be borne by the
Exchequer. There was little support for continuation schools,
either as an alternative to raising the leaving age or as a complement to it. The local authorities disliked it because of the
administrative difficulties of making provision for an uncertain
number of youngsters, as well as the disproportionate expense in
sparsely populated districts. The employers considered disorgani-
zation of their work schedules inevitable and that small firms
would find the scheme virtually unworkable. It was universally
acknowledged that continuation schools would be resented by
parents.

At the same time attitudes to making capital grants to voluntary schools were canvassed.[46] It appeared that the understanding
agreed in the Trevelyan discussions were still an acceptable basis
for legislation. The local authorities, the Church of England and
the Roman Catholics were still prepared to stand by the proposals. The Nonconformists, fearful of the spread of these two
faiths, demanded further safeguards. At the 1931 discussions
they had insisted that voluntary schools should be given grants
only for the improvement of existing schools and the amount
should not exceed 75 per cent of the total sum; these conditions
had been reluctantly accepted. The Nonconformists now insisted
such grants should only be given for work carried out within a
specified 3-year period. There were, however, some indications

the Nonconformists might accept the making of grants for the building of new voluntary schools, provided this was done as a once-for-all emergency measure to meet the problems of raising the school-leaving age and not used as a precedent for a continuous process. The Church of England and the Roman Catholics were prepared to accept the time limit, if the provision of grants could be extended to cover new buildings. The Roman Catholics wanted the grants made retrospective to cover the cost of works carried out before the date of authorization. The local authorities welcomed a time limit and were for the most part prepared to help in building voluntary schools, although they were anxious that the Exchequer should bear as much of the costs as possible. The Welsh authorities remained firmly opposed to public money being spent in this way. There were other sharp differences of opinion as to how the grants should be administered, the Nonconformists and the local authorities favouring indirect, and the Roman Catholics direct, grants.[47]

Lord Halifax, President of the Board, met the denominational leaders in confidential talks in an attempt to reach agreement. He sought to persuade the Nonconformists to drop their opposition to the building of new schools and to allow the reorganizaiton to go ahead; he pointed out that since 1931 some considerable progress had been made in replacing black listed schools, but experience had shown that it was not only educationally more satisfactory but in fact more economical to build new schools for senior children rather than patch up old ones. In the new housing areas new schools for senior pupils were a necessity. He offered to accept the time limit if they would accept the provision of grants to voluntary schools, although the actual wording of the formula of agreement would require great care. He also tried to persuade the Roman Catholics that they must ultimately accept indirect grants. No progress had been made when in June 1935 a reshuffle of the Government made Oliver Stanley the new President of the Board of Education.

He surveyed the large measure of agreement and decided the time was ripe for framing a legal measure combining the grants question with raising the school-leaving age, in fact the formula previously discussed in the cabinet.[48] It was agreed therefore to raise the school-leaving age to fifteen, exemptions being allowed for beneficial employment; maintenance grants were rejected by the cabinet, with Ramsay Macdonald's the sole dissenting voice. Proposals for continuation classes were also dropped, as impracticable and likely to arouse parental resentment. Local authorities were to be empowered to make grants to voluntary schools, both to improve and renew their buildings in preparation for the reorganization and provision for the admission of older students staying on at school after the age had been raised. The grants were to cover not less than 50 per cent and not more than 75 per cent of the cost of such work; the money was to be raised by local-authority loans, with the Exchequer bearing half the usual loan charges. The whole arrangement was to cover agreed building programmes which were to be completed within three years.

There were other proposals which were not controversial, among them some which aimed at implementing the increasingly accepted view that secondary education was a level of education for every child rather than a special type of education appropriate to children of a certain class. To this end local authorities were to be encouraged to increase the provision of special places in their secondary schools until every place was a special place, which could only be allocated through a competitive examination. More state scholarships were to be made available for the universities; these were to be open to secondary schools, independent as well as State aided. Other proposals reflected the growing appreciation of the social role of education. Nursery schools were to be encouraged, physical training developed in all schools, the school welfare services were to be extended. There was also to be more provision for technical and adult education. With the general election in the offing the cabinet agreed all these proposals and thus felt justified in the circumstances in presenting its educational programme to the voters under the slogan, "An Advance Along The Whole Educational Front".

By the time the election came in November 1935, Mussolini's invasion of Abyssinia had ousted education from the public mind. Baldwin despite the National government's record collected nearly 54 per cent of the votes cast and well over two-thirds of the seats. The educational programme had been one of the planks of the elecoral programme and its implementation was put in hand with praiseworthy speed. Many of the reforms could be carried out by administrative action, but the two main items raising the school-leaving age and the provision of assistance to voluntary schools—required legislation. The Bill to carry this out was launched within ten weeks of taking office and in spite of the opposition from some education interests, the government's massive majority made it the Education Act of 1936. The main objections to the measure were the provision of exemptions, and less widely, the grants to voluntary schools. No less than 107 local education authorities felt strongly enough about exemptions to protest to the Board.[49]

The Act was brief. It raised the school-leaving age to fifteen, with children in beneficial employment exempted. It permitted the local authorities to make grants to voluntary schools of not less than half and not more than 75 per cent of the sum spent by them on improving the accommodation. In return managers of all schools in receipt of such grants were to surrender to their local authorities the right to appoint and dismiss teachers. A certain number of appointments were to be "reserved", to be made in consultation with the managers as to the fitness and competence of candidates to give denominational religious instruction, the number to be calculated in relation to the amount of building grant received by the schools in question. To meet the needs of the Nonconformists, parents of children attending voluntary schools to which a grant was made were entitled to require that their children should be given "religious instruction in accordance with a syllabus in use in schools provided by the authority" : e.g. an agreed syllabus, on school premises. There was also the right to withdraw children during denominational instructions.[50]

Certain financial concessions were made to assist the local authorities put the new Act into effect. The distribution of expenses for elementary education between the Exchequer and the local authorities was still governed by the recommendations of the Kempe Committee which had operated since 1917 on what was known as the "E" formula. This had been devised to prevent undue expense on this account falling on the local authorities. Expansion of the service with increased costs had brought the need for further revision which had been discussed for two years but had not not yet been finalized. In recognition of this situation the government agreed to raise the minimum grants for educational buildings and equipment to 50 per cent

for work undertaken during the three years starting from
1 January 1936. It was also agreed to bear 40 per cent of transport of children to and from schools to facilitate the reorganization of the rural areas on Hadow lines.

It was clearly underlined at all points that concessions were
for the purpose of this Act only and there was no attempt to
associate these measures with any improvement in the status of
senior schools. The official view was taken that elementary education had been extended one year. The Act was not to come into
effect until 1 September 1939, despite its limited nature. This
delay was considered essential to enable the authorities to provide
the extra accommodation and assemble the necessary staff,
although there were both unemployed teachers and a building
industry that was by no means fully extended. It had been "a
boa constrictor of a struggle to produce a mouse of an Act", which
still did not implement the Education Act of 1918.

A distressing aspect of the Act was the demonstration that two
levels of the community were still firmly fixed in the minds of
many; one was to own and to manage, the other was to get down
to work, the sooner the better. These attitudes were held by
people who had every opportunity to know better, as these two
examples from the Commons debate on the Education Act of
1936 show. Annesley Somerville, formerly on the staff of Eton,
spoke on the needs of country boys, saying:

> Education is not merely book learning. Education is the result of
> every influence that is brought to bear upon the child. It is better
> to have a boy on the land learning farm work, having a number
> of land influences bearing on him, getting a love of the land—all
> making him more likely to stay on the land, as we want boys in
> the country to do. In many cases it is very much better that the
> boy should be working on the land than be in school.[51]

The chairwoman of the Juvenile Advisory Committee to the
Board of Education for 10 years the Duchess of Atholl, MP for
Kinross and Perth, made the claim of the Yorkshire textile indu-
try for young labour, for, she claimed, certain processes . . .
require small hands and "there ought to be kept open a loophole,
provided it is certain that the children will work under beneficial
conditions. Otherwise, we shall be placing a very serious handicap
on one of our most important export industries".[52]

V I

The Act That Never Was
1936–1939

Mr Edward Wood, later Lord Irwin and finally Viscount Halifax, was educated at Eton and Balliol. He was President of the Board of Education from October 1922 to January 1924, part of which time his brother-in-law, the Earl of Onslow, was his Parliamentary Secretary. He held the post again from June 1932 to June 1935, which gave him over four years directing the country's national education system. During his period in office he hunted two days a week and showed little interest in State education. He lived in feudal style on his main family estate at Hickleton in Yorkshire, 150 miles from London to which he returned at weekends. His biographer, the Earl of Birkenhead, commented on his educational stewardship.

"During this period of office, Lord Irwin was an aloof figure at the Board of Education, arriving late in the morning, seeing few civil servants except his immediate staff, chiefly his Private Secretary Sir Griffith Williams, and leaving as early as possible for the weekend in Yorkshire and his congenial duties as Master of Fox Hounds. In this second period at the Board he was so aloof that he became an object of awe in the office.

"The respect of these civil servants was subject to some testing moments when Edward made remarks that seemed to emphasize the gulf between them. Williams sensed what seemed to him a strongly entrenched feudal attitude of mind in Edward, as when he remarked casually on a visit to Hickleton : 'We need a new Church School here. Will the Board agree? We want a school to train them up for servants and butlers.' "

The Earl of Birkenhead, *Halifax—The Life of Lord Halifax,*
Hamish Hamilton, London, 1965, p. 325-6.

THE NEXT YEARS saw little progress for, in an atmosphere of increasing international tension, war became increasingly inevitable. In the spring of 1937 came the first of a series of clashes

between the educational policies agreed in 1935 and the claims
of the rearmament programme which was being anxiously pushed
forward.[1] Competition between government building for defence
purposes and local-authority building for education forced up
the price of both labour and materials. The government gave the
defence programme priority and sought to hold back educational
building. The local authorities were reluctant to pay the inflated
prices and were thus ready to delay their building schemes provided they could do so without financial disadvantage, but the
Act provided a 3-year term on building grants for reorganization.
At the instance of the Board of Education, the Treasury extended
the 3-year period for another year, until the end of 1940.

When the Labour party held their annual conference in
October 1937[2] the international scene was so threatening they
declared themselves ready to accept the government rearmament
programme, although condemning their foreign policy. With
growing fear of war parliament passed the Air Raid Precautions
Act in November laying upon local authorities the responsibilities
for preparing air-raid-precaution schemes. In spite of vigorous
protests, they were required to find half the costs. In May 1938
the Anderson committee was set up to devise evacuation schemes
while the army was allocated £108.5 million for modernization
and reorganization, much of which was to be spent on building
camps and drill halls.

As the defence programme gather momentum, the question
was considered of postponing the day appointed for the Education Act of 1936 coming into force. In spite of a year's extension
to the three-years buiding period continuous competition from
other projects, like housing and slum clearance, added to the
pressures from the defence programme on building costs. As a
result the local authorities were having to increase their rates to
meet higher prices; of the 61 county councils, excluding London,
only eighteen had been able to avoid this unpopular measure.[3]
Growing inflation was going to wipe out the benefits from increased grants under the Act so the County Council's Association
made an appeal for further and substantial extensions under
which the increased grants would be available, and the matter
was raised in the House of Commons. There was concern in
many authorities because preparations to implement the Act
were far from complete; some 25 per cent of urban authorities

and some 75 per cent of rural authorities were seriously behind schedule. The board estimated a further five-year extension would be necessary for total completion. In these circumstances postponement seemed advisable, and this would be popular with other departments although only £8 million of the total of £39 million capital charges had been spent. The board sought for reaction to this policy and found some support from Sir Percival Sharp, the Secretary of the Association of Education Committees; it was expected that the local authorities were already under more pressure than they could bear through their defence commitments and would react favourably. At the invitation of the board Sharp published an article in the periodical *Education* advocating the postponement of the 1936 Act's provisions.[4] He argued that this was necessary as there were not enough schools for the extra children. He proposed that those authorities who were ready for the implementation should be allowed to go ahead, in spite of any general postponement. Although the board denied that any postponement was being considered, the article was recognized as being officially inspired and there was reaction from the teachers, the press and most liberal opinion.[5] The teachers' papers insisted that in educational matters "postponement was the first step to destruction". The 1936 Act had been based on a concordat by which many interests had "swallowed the pill of building grants for non-provided schools" in order to achieve a rise in the school-leaving age; it would be disastrous if now that "the bond of the churches had been honoured" the children did not derive the expected benefit. They appealed to the political good sense of the government not to entertain the "delusive expedient of partial adoption".

The main teachers' body, the National Union of Teachers, led a deputation of other educational associations to urge immediate implementation, and also thought it was time other important educational reforms were made;[6] two million children were taught in classes of over 40 and there were 2,646 classes with over 50 children. The interests of the children were being overlooked for there was little time for backward children; the strain on the teachers was shown by 500 a year retiring annually on breakdown allowances. Teachers wanted a maximum of 30 in a class for modern education was moving away from mass instruction towards "projects" and "activity work" which called for much more individual attention. The President replied that this standard of pupil/teacher ratio would require 25,000 new classrooms costing around £15 million, plus a further 43,000 teachers with a salary bill of over £11 million as well as the cost of training and pensions. The President outlined some of the difficulties facing local authorities; both sides were displeased with the exchanges. A delegation from the London County Council also saw the President in July to obtain authority to reduce the size of classes where practicable, proposing junior classes should have a maximum of 42 and infants of 44, since 30 was not yet practical politics. It was said that since the publication of the Hadow Report attention had centred on secondary education, neglecting the lower sections of the schools, with the result many children who passed on to the senior school were backward; this had to be ended. In reply much was made of London's favourable overall pupil/teacher ratio of 27.23, compared with Birmingham with 33.4, Bradford 31.8 and Manchester 31.2; any defects, it was suggested, lay in maldistribution of staff.

The *Daily Herald,* the main opposition paper, took up the cudgels and denounced postponement as a simple device to maintain a plentiful supply of cheap juvenile labour.[7] The problem of accommodation had been greatly exaggerated for by March 1937 some 61.5 per cent of all senior pupils were already in recognized schools and there was no good reason why the remainder should not be provided for by the time the appointed date arrived. An entire age group was being penalized for the backwardness of a few local authorities. Although the *Herald's* facts were faulty, for only some forty authorities had completed preparation for reorganization, the support of some of the so-called backward authorities plus the denunciation of educational extravagance by the usual sectional interests did not assist the government's case for postponement. Areas with large slum-clearance projects were placed in a particularly awkward position for these were geared to finish in 1938. Liverpool had been badly affected in this way and argued that they could not complete their school programme until 1941 and it would be unfair if they lost their 50 per cent grant because they were overstretched in this way. There was another complication in Liverpool where religious antagonism, influenced by Irish experience, was exceedingly bitter. The Liverpool council had therefore adopted a policy of no grants for voluntary schools, which the Catholic press[8] was quick to point out would paralyse educational development in the city whether the period was extended or not. This situation was only resolved by personal intervention of the board's officials and a separate Act of Parliament.

The issues were put to the test at the annual conference of the Association of Education Committees, when the Parliamentary Secretary, Mr Lindsay, speaking on the subject of secondary education, took the opportunity to suggest the appointed day might be postponed for one year; the result was uproar. Standing orders were suspended to enable the question to be considered; the proposal was put to the vote, and contrary to Sharp's prediction to the President, was defeated. A hastily assembled meeting of the executive of the association affirmed the decision of the assembly. This further alerted public opinion for lengthy reports of what happened appeared in the press and protests poured into the board from teachers' associations. Three days after Mr Lindsay's initiative the education estimates came before the House of Commons. The *Daily Herald*[9] greeted the day with a salvo against the government, promising vigorous opposition to "any attempt to torpedo the school age" measure; the opposition attacked any such move in debate. Mr Lindsay, in winding up gave a categorical denial of any intention of postponement or of ever having had the intention of so doing, but public suspicion remained active.[10]

As the problem remained unresolved the board was driven to grant a further extension of building grants, but the Treasury were once again unhelpful saying they feared such measures would encourage local authorities to extend the scope of their schemes and thus increase Exchequer costs.[11] The board proposed to limit the extension to authorities with special needs enlisting the help of the Ministry of Health, whose slum-clearance and housing projects in some cases were held up through local authorities giving priority to education works.[12] The board proposed an extension until 1943, by which time other services' building programmes would be completed and the competition for labour and materials would have fallen off to minimize additional expense. The Treasury regarded this argument as being "in the nature of a hope rather than an assurance", and before reaching a decision they asked the board if they could "offer any

definite prospect of saving in any other branch of educational
building activity, as for example building of secondary schools".[13]
The board offered to limit expenditure on secondary school building to "the provision of new schools to meet the needs of new
centres of population" and not to improve or replace existing
schools unless some movement of population or the health of the
pupils absolutely required them to do so. They claimed this
would produce a really substantial saving since the ratio of money
spent on building new schools to that spent on improving existing
ones during the previous 3 years had been one to five. In fact
the board was making a virtue of necessity since they expected
that the Spens Report, which was shortly to be published, would
recommend secondary education for all, together with "parity
of esteem" for all types of such education; the board wished,
therefore, to discourage the spending of money on existing
schools of the grammar-school type. In return for this "countervailing economy", as it was called, the Treasury agreed to extend
the period for special building grants to the end of 1943.

Agreement was reached in August 1938, but the arrangement
which resulted was not announced until 14 October.[14] In the
meantime the Munich crisis occurred and war was seen as even
nearer. The issue of gas masks to the general population with a
visible stepping up of preparations for war revealed the realities
of the international situation to everyone. On 1 October the
Treasury circularized all departments of government, urging the
need for economy in civil matters and advising that even the
expenditure already authorized on new services should be subjected to the closest scrutiny. Two days later the Prime Minister,
Neville Chamberlain, announced in parliament the stepping up
of rearmament. The Board of Education made a careful review
of expenditure and took measures which virtually brought educational development to a standstill, excluding only certain services which might be expected to assist the defence effort: e.g.
technical education and the National Fitness Movement. On
27 October the Anderson Report on evacuation was published
and Sir John Anderson was appointed Lord Privy Seal and
Minister of Civilian Defence. Evacuation of large towns was
accepted as official policy in case of war.

On 27 October, the Minister of Health, Walter Elliot,[15]
speaking in a by-election at Dartford, called attention to the

needs of rearmament which might oblige the government to make inroads into the social services. The government record of procrastination in this respect sparked off widespread agitation. The opposition press[16] accused the government of intending to provide defence costs by cutting the social services and pointed out that in London already ten secondary-school schemes had been suspended. The teachers' associations and other educational bodies attacked "countervailing economy" and warned the Government that they would resist cuts in the education service. In the Commons the opposition incorporated protests at proposed cuts in social services in their general denunciation of government. policy.[17] Prime Minister Chamberlain's denials were not convincing, although he said "it was the first he had heard of it" and declared "the whole story is entirely an invention" even when charged with the fact that orders had already gone out for the cutting down of civilian expenditure. It was also pleaded that "countervailing economy" had already been agreed before Munich and therefore was not attributable to the requirements of the national defence programme. The attacks found the board in a difficult position and a memorandum was drawn up by the secretary, Mr Holmes, for the newly appointed President, Earl De La Warr to explain how the situation had arisen and "to dispel the illusion" that the embargo on certain types of secondary school building constituted a curtailment of the school services. This document was used in parliament and also at meetings up and down the country to counter the charge.

The board pressed for a passage in the King's Speech outlining policy for the next session of parliament in November. They could see the need in the light of the international situation to improve the country's technical provision especially in relation to the defence services, as well as allocating more money for facilities under the Physical Training and Recreation Act of 1937.[18] The section "relating to education" contained the statement that the government "will proceed with the development of the educational services". In the debate that followed the government spokesmen drew a distinction between making cuts in the social services and preserving the *status quo;* it was argued that the nation could not be expected to afford the expense of "vast projects of social improvement" and of the "enormous armaments

programme", at the same time claiming that maintenace of the
status quo was very different from cutting the social services.

The opposition denounced the arguments as dishonest because
cuts were already being made.[19] The rearmament argument was
brushed aside, for it was claimed that far from spending less more
should be spent on education; they advocated the introduction of
smaller classes, immediate secondary school education for all, the
immediate opening of nursery schools and a more generous
policy towards the special services supporting the social side of
the education service. If there was not enough money to finance
both education and defence, it was because the government was
the slave of "an outworn system of economy and finance". It was
clear that all the resentments and frustrations of the last 20 years
were having their effect.

In the midst of this situation of mistrust the long awaited
Spens Report on "Secondary Education" was published on 17
November 1938. It was the work of the consultative committee
which had already done much to turn the negative views held in
the prevailing political hierarchy and educate public opinion to
accept liberal policies for the schools. In the sterile period between the wars the importance of the work of the consultative
committee cannot be overemphasized. In two earlier reports,
"The Primary School" in 1931 and "Infant and Nursery Schools"
in 1933, they had already considered the problems of the primary
stage. In their present report the whole range of schools within
the national system catering for children over the age of eleven
was considered for, although their terms of reference had been
limited to "the work of schools other than those administred
under the Elementary Code" which of course specifically excluded the modern schools, they had, as they explained, found it
impossible to discuss the problems with which they were immediately concerned without "some reference" to the modern
schools and other post-primary schools, both vocational and
quasivocational, which were administered under the Elementary
Code.[20] They reaffirmed the principle spelled out in the Hadow
Report of 1926 that education should be divided into two stages,
with the dividing age at eleven.

They rejected as a general solution to the problems of secondary education the bold idea of replacing the existing variety of

secondary schools by multilateral schools designed for the education of the whole of secondary-aged children within comprehensive establishments. The arguments for and against such schools
were carefully considered; the social, educational and administrative grounds were explored but it was finally decided not to
recommend the general creation of multilateral schools as the
goal of long-range policy. The reasons for this were that the
schools would have to be streamed and would be over-large
amounting to at least 800 children. It would be difficult to build
up adequate sixth forms. The influence of the headmaster would
be lost, as well as the special values attaching traditionally to
grammar and other types of school. Nevertheless they advocated
some experimentation with this type of school, especially in new
areas and where only very small grammar schools existed. It was
noted that there had been, in Wales, a combined school project
envisaged in 1929, but the separate salary scales and Codes had
proved administratively impracticable so the plan lapsed, although
the scheme met the local conditions of sparse population. The
report suggested this type of school should be tried out.

When the report was debated in the Commons in February
1939 there was support from Sir Annesley Somerville for the
comprehensive or multilateral solution; he thought nothing of
the Spens objection to the size of the school, pointing out from
his experience as a master at Eton, which had 1,100 boys, that
things could be arranged to provide "the greatest amount of
individualism", and he was all for its gradual introduction into
the national system. The only other support came from Mr W. G.
Cove, formerly president of the National Union of Teachers and
a leader of the National Association of Labour Teachers, who
had pioneered the idea of the comprehensive school as a practical
method to make the nation's schools "a microcosm of real democracy". With the 92.7 per cent of the nation using the primary
schools the way was at least open for a serious consideration of
unity at the secondary stage. Considering the state of public
education in 1938 the Spens Report did at least throw open the
door for the operation of some schools on these lines and the
example of Eton was one frequently called on to combat the
prejudices of the conservative.

The Spens Report outlined a system which reinforced the
division into two streams of education by making its main

recommendation for development of separate grammar, modern and technical secondary schools, providing distinct types of education for children destined on the one hand to work with "tongue and pen"[21] and on the other with their hands. At the same time it emphasized that "the existing arrangements for the whole-time education of boys and girls above the age of eleven plus had ceased to correspond with the actual structure of modern society and with the economic facts of the situation".

The analysis began with the much prized grammar schools and gave official weight to the imbalance of their organization. "Although 85 per cent of the pupils did not remain at school beyond the age of sixteen" the curriculum was "still largely planned in the interests of the pupils who intended to proceed to a university". Much of the work was therefore organized as a foundation for studies which never took place, and to make matters worse much of the instruction was unduly formal. It was recommended the curriculum should be changed, especially as regards the emphasis laid on certain subjects, notably the classics, and also in the content of the subjects taught, so as to provide courses more suitable for the needs of the great majority of pupils whose education would end when they left school, although they should be encouraged to stay on as long as possible. As a consequence of these changes and to assist them the committee also suggested certain changes in the school-certificate examinations, which were largely the measurement of success in the secondary course. The small rural grammar schools presented special problems which in Wales were seen as inviting comprehensive schemes. In general the number of places available should be increased to take 15 per cent of the children in elementary schools.

This still left the vast majority of the children who would pass their adolescent years in the modern schools.[22] Consequently the committee emphasized the importance of ensuring equality of status between modern and grammar schools. In the same vein they considered the vocational post-primary schools, recommending the conversion of certain junior technical schools to become technical high schools, which would be "in every respect equal in status to grammar schools", providing a 5-year course for pupils from eleven to sixteen leading to a certificate examination similar in quality to the national certificate.

The Spens Report laid down a principle which is inherent in universal public education but which had not been stated before, certainly not in such uncompromising language : "The multilateral idea, although it may not be expressed by means of multilateral schools, must be inherent in any truly national system of secondary education." This was a long step forward and was just the conclusion the board had wished to avoid by limiting the consultative committee to the established means of secondary education. Parity of esteem could only be achieved by changes in the structure of educational administration; so it was recommended that all secondary schools should form part of a single administrative system, all with the same minimum leaving age, the same standards of accommodation, the same size of classes and all should be free. Although children were to be allocated to one of the three types of schools all were to run similar courses for the first two years, to facilitate transfer at the end of one or two years from one type of school to another if it was found to be educationally desirable. As a long-term objective the report advocated an educational revolution, for elementary education had not moved far from basic skills and a curriculum which offered little beyond the age of eleven; the prospect now opened up was a 4-year course of secondary education with properly financed and thought-out courses for all, including the non-academic children. It was in effect bringing the 90 per cent who did not have this up to the 10 per cent who did. The magnitude of this task in the provision of facilities has yet to be faced by any political party.

The Spens Committee saw as the first task the clearance of the administrative thicket which kept the two systems separate and for this purpose an official committee was requested to inquire into the position of Part III authorities.[23] As with the Hadow Committee they felt these small authorities complicated consideration of "the inter-relation of schools". In fact the Spens committee contained little that was novel and much of its findings were commonplace discussion in educational circles. Many of its ideas were already being tried out locally by progressive authorities. Its great value was that it provided a coherent and progressive scheme of ideas and practice for the development of secondary education on a national scale; moreover it said much being done was outmoded and the time was right to make changes.

It was unfortunate that it arrived when it did, because in a normal tempo of national business, its simple reasonable tone would have made a big impact and been an effective argument for educational development. In the emergencies of 1939 it had little effect; the whole energies of the country, ministers and officials especially, were all entirely engaged in matters of defence. The war scare of autumn 1938 revealed the extent of unpreparedness to a nation divided over issues of peace and reluctant to face the reality of war which was now imminent. The far-reaching proposals of the report were simply shelved.[24] Only the suggestions about grammar-school curriculum and school certificate examination were acted on; indeed this had been done already by a circular issued in July expanding a 1932 report. Its effect was to loosen the framework of the curriculum required to be covered, encouraging new choices with the aim of giving specialization appropriate to the particular circumstances of the school. One section benefited, for the needs of the defence industries stimulated official interest in technical education which led to eleven new junior technical schools being recognized and the building of some new technical colleges being approved.[25] In contrast to a general shut-down in other building, over a million pounds was spent on sites and buildings in 1938–9 mainly of a technical nature and a further nine projects totalling £0.675 millions were approved.

Within education circles the issues raised by the report were still discussed and out of these there arose various wartime inquiries. Firstly there was concern over finding staff for secondary schools and this gave rise to questioning the training-college curriculum. Secondly the position of the public schools had been the subject of unofficial discusssions with the board for some years, for they were in difficulties; they wanted financial help but wished to retain their exclusiveness and complete independence. The Spens Report had recommended universal inspection of all schools whether in the national system or privately run which included the public schools, targets of increasing suspicion as a main source of social division.

Meanwhile the appointed day for the Education Act of 1936 coming into force approached. Although in June 1938 the

Parliamentary Secretary, Mr Lindsay, had officially denied that postponement was being contemplated, the board had not abandoned the idea. The question came up again in March 1939 when the prospect of war had become more urgent. Discussion within the board had centred on two aspects : the economic and the social. A sharp cut in social-service expenditure could be expected.[26] This was not entirely connected with the war, for a review of social expenses was being made, especially of increases since 1925, following demands for an increase in the old-age pension. This was not the only Treasury attempt at economy, for they were greatly concerned with the sudden expansion of spending on armaments. It was argued, for instance, that the postponement of school building would result, or be helped, by not raising the school-leaving age, with a consequent saving not only in building costs but in the number of teachers employed. The saving on building expenditure would be £10 million, plus £0.5 million loan charges, with a reduction in teaching staff by some 500 teachers worth £100,000 in salaries. Against this it was shown that much of the urgency to prepare had vanished as the school population was already falling. The Act would not be fully effective until September 1940 and, with employment increasing, it was hoped many of the young people would be absorbed into "beneficial employment". The administrative measures to implement the Act would be considerably eased by these factors. It was also pointed out that teachers could not be summarily dismissed in the manner suggested. Another factor of some importance was the likelihood that in some areas the halting of the education building programme would cause severe unemployment, a possibility most unwelcome to the Ministry of Labour.

The social arguments against postponement finally carried the day. In the event of war it was envisaged urban schools would be evacuated to reception areas and at the end of every term difficulties over consulting parents would arise in the complicated procedures of deciding the rights of individual children to exception from school attendance. Raising the school-leaving age seemed the most convenient way of ensuring some degree of orderliness and discipline was maintained among evacuees and at least a year's grace could be obtained in which to establish the exemption procedures and sort things out.

This policy was not well received. Education building, in any case, was already the target of criticism especially from certain local councils and individual MPs, who held that far too much had already been spent on school buildings. From the very inception of the programme complaints on these lines had originated in Southampton and there was support for them from the 1922 Committee of Conservative backbenchers.[27] Now the defence situation and a budget deficit added fuel to these accusations. The Treasury investigated the cost of schools and questioned the need for providing new schools with gymnasia, assembly halls and dining rooms, which it was suggested could be added later when the country could afford such luxuries. The board would not concede that these were unnecessary refinements or that plans were lavish but did agree that it was worth going into the suggestion that schools might be less solidly built, although light buildings raised special financial problems. To this purpose, in May 1939, the board announced new arrangements to meet this difficulty. A longer loan period was allowed for buildings of traditional construction, so the annual charges for light building was actually costlier than a heavier construction as the new arrangements extended the loan period for light buildings from 30 to 40 years. This enabled the board, on announcing the new arrangements in May 1939, to urge local authorities to carry through more modest plans, but in any event not to fall below the prescribed standard of building which it was stressed had been done "not only to raise the level of educational efficiency but also to create a new conception of education".[28] Six weeks later on 31 August, with the war only three days away, the board published a comprehensive circular dealing with the problems which local authorities would have to face in putting the 1936 Act into force once the war had begun. This did not prevent the outbreak of war plunging the whole of the educational system into confusion. In the evacuation and neutral areas schools were closed, while children and teachers were scattered throughout the reception areas with more enthusiasm than order. Administrative staff were depleted by secondment to more essential work and the resulting chaos was left to sort itself out. The main body of the Board of Education, which had been directed to leave London, found itself without even a temporary home, for the lack of direction which had characterized the government during the drift into war was felt in other matters than education. In these circumstances, and the fact that mass air raids on towns were expected hourly, the appointed day for implementing the 1936 Act passed almost unnoticed.

One thing was unchanged for, on 13 September 1939, the Treasury sent a circular to all government departments directing "that in order to reserve the capital resources of the country primarily for such purposes as are essential to the successful prosecution of the war ... capital expenditure by local authorities, whether or not already authorized, should be restricted within the narrowest limits". Building materials were subject to strict controls and a bulk allocation made to the board to cover all educational building. On 26 September the board issued its own circular[29] to local authorities explaining that, "although there was to be no general embargo on school building, the hard facts of the situation would inevitably involve the postponement for a period, which is at present unascertainable, of the great majority of building projects", and the school building programme came virtually to a halt. Buildings in the course of erection, with the exception of a few schools in the reception areas, were left unfinished and sealed off. Plans already submitted were returned to local authorities for re-consideration, and His Majesty's inspectors were instructed to advise that projects could only be accepted in cases of particular urgency. Of £28.5 million of expenditure under consideration between the board and the local authorities only about £7.5 million were allowed to be completed.

In these circumstances the question of implementing the Act of 1936 was clearly out of the question. On 22 September *Education*, anticipating a government announcement urged the authorities to accept whatever proposals were made without suspicion. Many local authorities, and by no means the "backward" and reactionary areas, were already petitioning the board to regularize the situation by postponing the appointed day. Within the board the case for implementing the Act on social grounds had been abandoned; it was clear that the exemption procedure, difficult to operate at any time, would result in the granting of wholesale exemptions which would create bad precedents for the more normal times it was hoped would soon return. It was widely accepted that there was little point in raising the school-leaving age. The Act's intention had been to provide "a wholly reorganized course of instruction organically growing into the final year of elementary education", but in the conditions existing this was clearly impossible.

Accordingly, early in October 1939, a measure was rushed through parliament to postpone the raising of the school-leaving age. The government assured the country that this was a suspension and not a repeal of the Act, and that the whole position would be reviewed after the war.[30] An amendment to enable the government at the end of the war to merely draft an Order to bring back all or any of the six clauses to be suspended was defeated by 91 to 79, and the suspension of the Act passed without serious controversy. Special financial provision was made by the board to compensate voluntary associations which had already incurred expense in buying sites, employing architects and other preliminaries to building.

It was five years before a replacement for the ill-conceived and equally ill-fated Education Act of 1936 arrived, but by that time the smug fatalism of the 1930s had given way to the vibrant, rampant 1940s. Social despair had been replaced not only by hope but even ambition.

The abandonment of the 1936 Act must be reckoned one of the troughs in British education; but it also marks the end of an era. The period between the wars had been a particularly frustrating and negative period, for all the modern developments are in evidence : the use of psychologically-based methods of teaching as against training by rote, a different approach to children and an understanding of the problems of children from poor backgrounds. It is depressing to see this wiser and more liberal approach being widely discussed and accepted in educational circles, only to have implementation of the new ideas prevented by the refusal to make funds available for all but a limited advance.

There is some evidence of progress, but the main barrier to even the moderate Hadow reorganization of a separate department for children over the age of eleven was hampered by the school buildings. The School Boards, inspired by the building grants provided under the 1870 Act and supporting legislation, had provided over 3,330,000 school places;[31] they were mostly housed in formidable buildings which seemed designed to shut the children away from the locality. The windows were so high that for a child to look out it was necessary to climb on to furniture. Most schools built in towns were in a three-storey pattern of factory grimness with the boys on the top floor, the girls on the first floor and children under eight allowed to be educated together in the ground floor "mixed infants" department. Although all three sections shared the same building and often the inadequate playground, great care was taken to stop the over-eights mixing, for the Victorians believed that original sin began to ferment very early. The physical background was a limiting factor on the education carried out. From 1900 to 1918 a further 600,000 places were added in much the same style; but between the wars a million places were built usually on a dispersed plan of classrooms which opened out into wide playgrounds and often flower beds. The early building had been designed to last for ever and so of the total 5 million places, only about a fifth could be considered to offer reasonable facilities for modern education.

In 1924 a survey had shown that of the 5.6 million children, 1.16 million (20.6 per cent) were taught in classes where there was more than one class in the room. At the same time a black list of buildings was made which condemned 2,825 schools outright as unfit for use.[32] Many others were in need of major building works to make them suitable for their purpose. For example in London, one of the better areas, a survey made by the London Teachers' Association of 243 elementary schools found 19 per cent were unsuitable for their purpose, 52 per cent had bad sanitation, 72 per cent had inadequate heating and no hot water.[33]

The failure to face the problems of school accommodation resulted in the reorganization required by the Hadow Report of 1926 to be often more nominal than real although by 1939 some two-thirds of the senior children remaining in the elementary system were in reorganized senior schools. Those on the new housing estates were usually new and spacious, but for the most part the children remained in variations of the old grim setting where the architecture was a barrier against the development of freer and more modern teaching. In such surroundings there could be little real specialization and the handicraft facilities, of which the report had made so much, were usually carried on in makeshift centres shared by several schools. Sports facilities were often largely non-existent.[34] The narrow and unimaginative curriculum which prevailed in many schools caused the 1937 *Handbook of Suggestions* to comment: "The timetable usually shows [the schoolwork] as divided up into a number of subjects and activities. The curriculum thus represented has arisen in a somewhat haphazard way. It has in most cases no philosophical basis and cannot be said to have evolved organically." A third of the children were taught in classes of over 40, and some 100,000 (nearly 2 per cent) were in classes of over 50.

In staffing there had been some small advance made in the years between the wars, as comparison of the qualifications for 1920-1 and 1938 show. For 1920-1 there was a total of 169,314 teachers (37,167 men and 132,147 women) in the elementary schools of England and Wales. Of these 116,069 (69 per cent) were certificated, and of those only 79,526 (47 per cent) were college trained; a further 36,543 (21.6 per cent), made up of 7,682 men and 28,861 women, were untrained and had qualified through attendance at pupil-teacher centres. The unqualified number, 35,457 (21 per cent), was made up of 2,177 men and 33,280 women. There were also 4,248 student teachers (747 men and 3,501 women) and 13,540 women supplementary teachers. The uncertificated were those who had passed a preliminary examination and in theory could be working for a place in college. The supplementaries were a particularly obstinate problem in trying to raise professional standards, for their sole qualifications for appointment were to be over eighteen and to have been vaccinated. Although many were limited to the point of unsuitability, in a period when disposal of spinsters was a problem they tended to hang on to their posts until they reached retiring age. They were usually found in the rural schools[35] where, if they became established local figures accepted by the governors, no matter how inept nothing could be done to replace them.

By 1938, when there were 168,878 teachers in the elementary schools, 79 per cent (131,941) were certificated with 24,058 trained but uncertificated. Among the 17.6 per cent unqualified teachers employed there were still 4,905 supplementary teachers although their recruitment had been discontinued. A new sector in the elementary schools was 11,865 graduates, 7.3 per cent of the total, made up of 6,992 men and 4,873 women most of whom were also educationally qualified. They were mainly employed in the reorganized senior schools.[36]

In the secondary grammar schools the teachers were better qualified, for about 78 per cent of the 25,039 staff were graduates, proportionately more than ten times the elementary sector. This better-educated staff also had smaller classes, for the secondary pupil teacher ratio in 1938 was 19 against 31 in the elementary schools. The average cost of providing a place in a secondary school was £103 against £35.7 in an elementary school; annual maintenance was £33 against £15 for elementary schools.[37] This was the basis of the two-tier system in State schools.

Yet the provision of secondary grammar school places was the main growth point in the educational system for the number of places available without fee had moved from 105,000 in 1920 to 263,000 in 1938, rising from 32 per cent of the total grant-aided secondary school population to 53 per cent. Between a third and a fourth of these were awarded to children who qualified for maintenance, that is children from the poorer homes.[38] The odds of gaining a place from the elementary schools had shortened from 40 to 1 in 1914 to 21 to 1 in 1920, 13 to 1 in 1929 and 10 to 1 in 1939.[39]

The competition for these places was very fierce and an official inquiry, which took three years to complete, found extensive homework[40] and coaching widely developed and seen as an essential part of the selection system. In some cases children began homework at six or seven years of age in schools where "all are expected to do it". The parents had no illusions about what it meant, for they saw "the way to material prosperity lies through homework and a Special Place. In the case of boys, winning a Special Place is the way to avoid going down the pit", or into the factory. The setting of homework was at the instigation of the parents and besides this there was considerable commercial private coaching. A spot check found that of 30 entrants 17 had been professionally coached. Anxious parents also coached their children. "A clever girl in one school said that in addition to three hours homework for the headmaster, she did half an hour more for her father, besides washing the pots."

It had never been intended there should be such fierce competition for the free places for in 1907, at the announcement of the scheme in parliament, the President had made the point that children from the elementary schools "would not be asked to compete with children outside, but would only be asked to pass a qualifying examination".[41] There were great variations in the procedures which usually relied heavily on examinations in mathematics and English. These were the main subjects covered by homework and coaching, so children from a better home background already had an advantage which the support of their parents increased. Early attempts to relieve the strain on the children by introducing intelligence tests brought protests from both teachers and parents, with a demand for "proper examinations papers".[42] The system soon adjusted to the new tests and a battery of commercial coaching books showed the system had been modified but not changed. The general opinion of both teachers and parents was that children had "no chance of gaining a scholarship unless homework is regularly done from an early age".

The next barrier to secondary education was the incidental expense which could be prohibitive to a working-class family.[43] The average 1938 London weekly income of two categories of workers was 77/- (£200 p.a.) for builder's craftsmen, with 57/9 (£150 p.a.) for builder's labourers. These would be typical of amounts earned by skilled and unskilled workers, while unemployment pay for a man and wife was 27/- (£70 p.a.) with 3/- for each child. The sliding scale, widely used for assessing right to educational maintenance allowances, required earning below 88/3 per week (£230 p.a.) to qualify for free fees, usually with a supply of basic books and stationery. There would also be some entitlement for maintenance, usually small before fourteen and somewhat larger afterwards, to encourage children to stay on after the minimum school-leaving age.[44] It averaged £5/15/- a year, which would partially offset the cost of school uniform, gym kit, school society subscriptions, any extra books and stationery such as drawing materials and instruments, together with all the incidentals of grammar-school life. These were estimated at £3/10/- a year for a boy and £4/9/6 for a girl, plus another £1 for sports gear. There was also full or partial travelling expenses, meals and pocket money. There was also a need to meet incidental expenses not usual in working-class life; this could be minimized only by a dropping out of part of the school social life, which if carried to extremes could invoke social penalties. Heavy demands of homework, as well as school rules and social sanctions, prevented a child taking part-time work. An intelligent child would be aware of the costs involved, especially in an area of high unemployment, for in such areas the maintenance allowances tended to be smaller, in some cases even half the national average.

It was not always a happy situation for in the grammar school the child from a labouring background had to adjust to the middle-class environment. In nearly every case selection included an interview with the head teacher, so that although over 80 per cent of the grammar-school pupils had been to the elementary schools, children selected were those who approximated in type to the fee-paying students.[45] Pupils from poor background were the bulk of the 25 per cent who dropped out at the minimum leaving age of fourteen before completing their full secondary course, which deprived the school of the higher rate of grant-aid and naturally added another prejudice against them. The reasons for dropping out were largely economic, often aggravated by the family finances. An intelligent juvenile who had been at grammar school, even if he had not finished his course, could earn 10/- a week and later perhaps even as much as £60 a year. When this income was put against the costs of staying on at grammar school there were great pressures on a child to start earning, especially if the family's main wage earner was unemployed. It was not an easy decision either way, especially as sometimes conflict was caused by the clash of values of home and school.

The running costs of the 47,000 secondary-grammar-school places was £10.8 million, about £23 a year for a place.[46] About half of these places were sold to fee-paying students at £11/11/11d. Some 30 per cent of the places went to children from the elementary schools who had failed to win a scholarship place but could afford the fee. They took these places to the detriment of better qualified children who could not afford the fee.[47] Such students, if they were lucky, could find themselves in one of the new go-ahead reorganized schools where they would have the chance to stay on to sixteen and take school certificate or Royal Society of Arts examinations. Almost certainly they would need to stay on in the elementary school after the age of sixteen to complete their preparation, but this required special individual permission from the Board of Education. A full statement of "the special circumstances" was required and permission was hedged about with reservations. In 1938 only 850 children were staying on in the elementary schools after the age of sixteen. Of these only 285 were taking school-certificate examinations which was the normal completion of the secondary-grammar-school course and in 1938 62,500 were sitting it. The two streams of secondary education were obviously a long way from parity.

The advantage of the two extra years at school were real and immediately of value, for it enabled 20 per cent of the grammar-school students to pass on to higher education or some form of further training with considerable prospects. Fifty-five per cent of the rest went straight to work, but it was employment offering some security and prospects, in contrast to the 90 per cent from the elementary schools, most of whom passed to transient and dead-end employment.[48]

Despite the pressures of custom and finance, there were indications towards the end of the 1930s that more working-class children were making full use of the grammar-school opportunities.[49] From 1934 to 1937, years of economic recovery when there was much demand for juvenile labour, the proportion of girls leaving after 4 years fell from 23.3 per cent to 19.8 per cent; boys also decreased from 20.7 per cent to 18.3 per cent. In the same period the number of girls leaving after 6 years of study rose from 29.1 per cent to 35.4 per cent; the boys' figures moved from 29.9 per cent to 36 per cent. The entries in the school-certificate examination showed the same trends and revealed the large reservoir of undeveloped talent available. Comparing 1924–5 with 1937–8 the total numbers entering for the examinations rose around 50 per cent; boys from 21,962 to 36,449 and girls from 19,485 to 26,099. There was no fall in standards for in 1929, 56 per cent of those who had entered the schools 5 years before sat the examination to gain a 72 per cent pass rate; in 1937 there had been 68.1 per cent entry who scored a 73 per cent pass rate.

In 1938 the same signs were evident in the universities where there was only 1 in 250 children from the elementary schools.[50] The public schools with some 50,000 pupils supplied 54 per cent of the 40,348 undergraduates, the rest came from the State schools which educated over 5 million children. However, children from the elementary schools won 437 of the 798 open scholarships; 67.6 per cent of these went to children from modest-income families who qualified for full remission of fees on the sliding scale of benefits. The elementary-school children were even more successful when they had had the benefit of university life. In 1938 of 293 degrees awarded with first class honours, 258 were to products of the public system, with 156 from grant-aided schools and 102 from local-authority secondary schools. Their superiority in science, mathematics and engineering was even more marked.

It is doubtful if many of these clever undergraduates came from the poorest homes for the economic barriers were hard to surmount even if a scholarship had been won which provided maintenance.[51] The contribution averaged £49/13/9 a year. It varied with the local authority from £30 to £75, yet it was calculated that to enjoy a normal social life at university something like £150 a year must be provided. The family with £600 a year, the usual maximum above which maintenance would not be paid, could find this but the skilled artisan on £200 a year or the labourer with £150 could hardly help their children.

Although the administrative and economic hurdles were formidable, there were others which chiefly prevented children from poor backgrounds taking full advantage of the facilities of the education system.[52] These arose from the widespread poverty which affected from a third to a half of the children, depending where the line of marked deprivation was drawn. The bald truth was that unemployment benefit, and Poor Law payments, as well as the wages of the lower paid, were insufficient to buy food of adequate quality, so that around a third of families were half starved or, expressed in gentler terms, suffering from malnutrition. Although the period was one of steady economic growth the benefits of this were unevenly dispersed for, with taxation kept low, those with regular, well paid work did very well, but low taxation also meant little allocation for the public relief services. The depression mainly affected the older industries, like heavy engineering, textiles and mining; while the newer light industries, especially those connected with electrical components, were among the most prosperous in the world. Geographically the slump was in the northern areas and South Wales, while the South-east and Midlands enjoyed steady development.[53]

Right-wing politicians and senior civil servants thought along lines influenced by the Poor Law which saw poverty and its effects as something which could neither be avoided nor little done to alleviate the distress it caused. Medical officers of health repeatedly included evidence in their reports of shorter life and more illness among the poorer classes. This was ignored, as was evidence of slower and limited development through indifferent feeding, although this was carried out by the Medical Research Council. As early as 1925 it was demonstrated that the addition to an institutional diet of a pint of milk a day or 1¾ ozs. of butter produced marked increase in both weight and height.[54] A year later in a mixed-matched sample it was shown that children with rickets, a disease accepted as a result of malnutrition, had proportionately 2.5 times the number of individuals with intelligence quotients below normal as those who were not so afflicted.

All this type of evidence failed to produce any marked effects.[55] The difficulty was to find a way of objectively defining what was malnutrition and then clearly demonstrating its adverse effects. An article in the *Medical Officer*[56] described the professional dilemma of medical officers of health :

We must find out the clinical signs of malnutrition, for these we do not know. We know that at the present time a very large proportion of the population is imperfectly fed, but we cannot find signs of it. We have districts where the amount spent on food is inadequate to cover the necessities, and we report the observed nutrition of the children—who should be the most sensitive members of the community—90 to 95 per cent good. We know that this is false, and those who quote these results as proof that all is going well, showing that the British people in times of difficulty thrive excellently on bread and margarine ... and are quite happy in doing so, know that it is false also.

The official view was that distress arose "from profound economic change which no medical science, no school feeding and no poor relief, however extensive, can alter or remedy".[57] In consequence of this, after the General Strike of 1926, school feeding was largely stopped throughout the country; it only amounted to about three meals for every child in a year. The

Labour Government of 1929 to 1931 tried to move in this matter but were met by the intransigence of the senior civil servants.[58] Attempts to produce national scales for Poor Law relief were countered by the arguments that it "would contravene the fundamental principle of the Poor Law that the determination of relief is a matter for the local authority"; it would not be worth while compiling data for a national scale because of the many variations for local conditions. Concern for South Wales at the height of the depression, with requests for "food, boots, clothing, bedding" were met by the statement that "it would be useless to approach the Treasury . . . without very definite evidence of need". Accordingly a mass of reports were compiled from the worst depressed areas. The senior officials were unimpressed and one minuted, "the situation generally remains surprisingly normal from the health point of view"; while another countered "the position compared with two years ago seems on the whole to have improved".

The stalemate was broken by the adoption of a new approach to the problem by framing a minimum diet to provide sufficient nourishment for basic health; this was costed and when related to the lower-income groups it was obviously beyond their means.[59] Three separate and independent surveys showed considerable unanimity that the poorest families, who also had more than the average number of children, were considerably affected. Half the children of the working classes were underfed. These findings were repeatedly challenged by the establishment and Sir John Boyd Orr, who was due to publish his findings in 1935 with an election in the offing, was approached by the Minister of Health, Mr Kingsley Wood, who alleged there was no poverty in the country. In the interview it came out that the minister not only knew nothing of research on vitamin and protein requirements, but had never visited the worst affected areas to see things for himself. Pressure was brought to prevent publication and as the work had some official backing there was withdrawal of assistance from the civil service so that the work was published as Orr's personal work and not as an official inquiry. Fearing some further attempt to censor his report Orr gave the key facts in a lecture to the British Association in 1935.

The result of these findings was to provide cheap milk for children in schools by a system of subsidies which, although described by *The Economist* as the "economics of Bedlam", had political significance in reviving British agriculture. By 1937 milk was taken by about half of the children.

This widespread and prolonged poverty had measurable effects in stunted and delayed development, but effects on intelligence and psychological drive still presented unsolved problems of assessment.[60] It seems reasonable to conclude that these deficiencies, affecting the great proportion of working-class children were responsible for the easy acceptance of the development of the two-tier system of education. A lower academic performance from these children was taken for granted, as it was not realized that their backwardness was largely a result of poverty and once this was removed they would be able to tackle intellectual work as well as anyone. Although the Spens Report of 1938 had given a considerable measure of approval for multilateral education this was not taken up by the Labour party with any weight of support until 1951. By that time a period of post-war affluence had considerably improved the health, physique and drive of the children in the community's schools, so that full meaningful secondary education for all became a necessity.

Compiling The New Testament
January 1940–July 1941

Letter from the Right Honourable Hugh Cecil, Provost of Eton to the President of the Board of Education, Earl De La Warr, P.C., an old Etonian, dated 21 March 1940.

The Provost had read newspaper reports that the public schools which were in financial difficulties were looking for assistance from the state and to that end were agitating for a royal commission on their situation. He pronounced it "a foolish proposal", because government subsidy would lead to government control.

"A more amiable desire is to admit children educated in elementary schools into the public schools. I see no existing barrier. The 70 King's scholars at Eton might come from Eton, but what practically hinders them is not so much the fees, for these could be remitted, as the plain circumstance that what Eton College teaches is principally Latin and Greek and that consequently the Entrance Examination is mainly in knowledge of those languages. This obviously shuts out the elementary schoolboy who is never taught Latin or Greek. But is Eton College to give up teaching the ancient languages for the benefit of the few people who wish to learn them, because the elementary schools do not teach those subjects? If it is really desired that boys of very humble origin should come to Eton College, the remedy is to be found in earlier years, when provision should be made for teaching them the subjects in which Eton specializes. But, except in the case of boys of extraordinary ability, who necessarily are very rare, I do not think there is much reality or common sense in the desire that elementary school boys should come to public schools. If the State likes to give large bursaries to boys of extraordinary talent, so that they might be educated in any School that was thought proper, and afterwards in the Universities, I should quite approve of such a measure. It is impossible for the State to spend too much money on the education of boys of exceptional ability."

ALTHOUGH THE MAIN concern of the nation was concentrated on the war, the evacuation of the children from the large towns to the country areas revealed in stark fashion the results of the poverty and squalor in which many of them had passed their lives. Sensational press reporting of the arrival of children from slum areas into families which had not been broken on the industrial wheel was followed by more balanced and scholarly works which both confirmed the picture and looked for the causes. The immediate effect was to add further evidence to growing criticism of the government. Makeshift measures in the evacuation areas, where facilities were barely adequate for the local population, caused the children to be brought back to the towns where the schools were closed or in use for other purposes; it was not an overstatement to say that much of the educational system had broken down. It was not the only area of government in confusion, in fact there was discontent on every side.

St Mark's Schools Violet Hill.
URGENT   N.W.8
23-9-38

To
The Parents or Guardians.

You are earnestly invited to a meeting to hear the L.C.C. plans in the event of a STATE OF NATIONAL EMERGENCY arising
The meeting will be held in
The School.
Violet Hill N.W.8.
on Saturday afternoon. at 3.0 pm.
Do not fail to come please.

J.OE Rogers Headmaster
W.G Cartwright
Headmistress.

Warning notice for parents of school evacuation

The press was full of campaigns on mistakes in high places; but along with this went a great variety of plans for the future, among which were many references to education.[1] The Archbishop of Canterbury[2] voiced a common view when he told the House of Lords in February 1940 that the end of the war was bound to bring far-reaching social changes. Progressive educationalists took the opportunity to press their case that education needed a new orientation. It was to cease to be a factory system processing children to be, at the best, clerks highly trained in certain verbal skills of limited utility, or, more usually, suitably conditioned manual workers. Education must be synonymous with growing up, a series of planned phases which enabled children to reach their full potential and also to give them an appreciation of the world in which they could advance themselves.[3]

The immediate educational condition of the country invited the sharpest criticism and the President of the Board was the main target for attack. Lord Addison from the House of Lords asked why had he allowed himself and his service to be elbowed out of the way by other ministers and hundreds of his staff carried off to work for other departments?[4] Why was his department content to sit at their desks and let local authorities flounder on without assistance or guidance? The board was all the more vulnerable because lack of preparation had been a subject for criticism since 1938. In November 1939 John Morgan[5] had told the Commons about the main school complex in Doncaster catering for around 2,000 children which had been taken over by the army. He accidentally met the unit commander at a Remembrance Day service and asked how he came to take over the schools?

He replied, "Oh, I know Doncaster well. You see, I have been mobilized three times, and as long ago as last July I knew this job was coming on, so I booked the best billet in the town." He walked into it, and the education authorities did not know how he had got there or who had given him authority to get there. The presumption was that he had every right to be there, and so they found 600 or 700 soldiers in their central school, disorganizing the whole educational life of the town and putting 2,000 children, from juniors right up to the evening classes, absolutely at sixes and sevens . . . and there is the colonel sitting in what he regards as the best billet in the town.

In the Commons in a major debate on education[6] the accusation was made that "the general impression . . . is that ever since the war began the Board of Education have lost grip and have not taken the initiative to see that the education services were as little damaged as far as circumstances allowed." The Parliamentary Secretary, Mr Lindsay, who in his account of school reorganization following evacuation had sought to fob off the House by trivia about "howlers" from urban children in their new surroundings, was accused of "impervious complacency" and given a rough ride; but typically the education debate attracted only a small attendance without the support of one cabinet minister. This point was taken up by a number of MPs and one remarked, "It is as if it were relegated from the seat of government as one of those services that has ceased to be vital in the life of the nation". A month later the President, Lord De La Warr, resigned.

In April 1940 the disastrous Norwegian expedition brought matters to a head. The Gallop poll taken in March had a 57 per cent support for Chamberlain as Prime Minister, with only 36 per cent against him. In May 32 per cent were in his favour and 58 per cent against.[7] On the 10 May Winston Churchill became Prime Minister of a coalition government which included some Labour and Liberal ministers, although the main posts were held by Conservatives. One of the last senior appointments to be made was to confirm Herwald Ramsbotham in the appointment of President of the Board of Education which he had taken up on 3 April 1940. He had already served three and a half years in the department as Parliamentary Secretary (November 1931 to June 1935) much of the time virtually running it, for Lord Halifax, the nominal President, had been employed on other duties and had shown little interest in public education. His Parliamentary Secretary was Chuter Ede, Labour, Nonconformist, teacher and local-government expert, an able parliamentarian who was devoted to the cause of public education.

The end of May saw the withdrawal of British troops from the continent followed by the fall of France. This created a feeling of national identity which the new Prime Minister mobilized by a series of challenging broadcasts. Gallup polls on the fall of France showed 3 per cent of Britain believed they might lose the war; by the end of the year this had virtually vanished. Confidence in Churchill stood at 88 per cent in July 1940 and 89 per cent in October. The lowest level of support for him was in July 1942, with the fall of Tobruk and Singapore when it still stood at a formidable 78 per cent; the highest figure for Chamberlain had been 68 per cent.[8] Churchill the man, through the anxieties of war, became a legend. In all large decisions his was the weighty word, so that in many respects for the period of hostilities it was one-man-rule.

It is well to remember that Churchill, although capable of great warmth and generosity, had shown little interest in the creation of the apparatus of social support by which the manual worker was able to climb to full citizenship. He was indeed, remembered with bitterness in many working-class homes for the rôle he had played in the General Strike of 1926.[9] Moreover although he led a coalition government the parliamentary membership on which it was based derived from Baldwin's 1935 election win and the House of Commons was overwhelmingly Conservative, holding 432 seats out of the total of 615. Many of these were, to say the least, tactless in their response to the growing demand from the country for a start to be made on the social reforms which had been postponed for the last twenty years. They saw the end of the war as inevitably a return to the 1930s, for they could conceive of no other social order. There were soon bitter clashes between them and the Labour leaders who had been persuaded into the government on the understanding that they would be able to carry out constructive reform.

Wartime unity however stirred the social conscience of the country. The evidence from the evacuation was proof that something was wrong. The bombing of the East End of London was played up in the newspapers and on the radio, and the message was repeated again and again : these too were British and brothers, a status the unemployed had never had. The picture of Dunkirk as a victory snatched from the jaws of defeat followed by the dramatic success of the Battle of Britain seemed to reveal a nation for whom nothing was impossible. Labour spokesmen were quick to point out that with such national resources why had the evils of poverty, disease and ignorance been tolerated for so long;

something had been very wrong in the old social order. In this vein Ernest Bevin told the Trades Union Congress[10] in October 1940, "if the boys at secondary schools had been able to save us in the Spitfire, their brains could be used to produce the new world" that everyone wanted.

In such a climate of opinion a passion for making social reconstruction plans seized the press, the politicians and the public. Education was much to the fore and schemes were drawn up on all sides, some wildly grandiose and others so liberal they could become reactionary. In this latter character was a plan publicized by the *Times Educational Supplement*. It would have neither school-leaving age nor day-continuation classes, the staple starting point for most reforms of secondary education, but proposed an elastic school-course, "the actual age of release to be determined in the case of each individual pupil, by his or her degree of ability to profit from further education".

The inaction of the government redoubled criticism so that the ministers and officials, who were facing an unrivalled muddle in adverse circumstances, found every utterance seized on with suspicion. For example a reference to part-time day-continuation classes was interpreted as a retreat from pledges given not to abandon the 1936 legal provision to raise the school-leaving age.[11] Inside the board there was the realization that a re-examination of the various educational issues must be carried out as they were likely to become live again before the end of the war. It was seen that the Labour members of the government would insist upon some earnest of the good intentions on reconstruction implicit in the formation of the coalition. It was also seen that the half-hearted measures of the 1930s would not satisfy the reformers with their sights set on a different kind of post-war Britain. It was with this end in view that meetings began within the board to produce a document as a basis for discussion.

The first initiative came from the Deputy Secretary, Robert S. Wood,[12] who felt a note should be taken of views expressed on post-war reconstruction and these should be discussed so that the board's reaction to them could be clarified. The main part of the board had moved to wartime accommodation in Bournemouth, and it was here that a dozen senior officials made "a co-operative and continuous study of educational problems". The informal committee consisted of the six senior administrators, the three chief inspectors with the senior woman inspector, the official in charge of Welsh education, the Accountant General and the Permanent Secretary were ex-officio members. Special sub-committees were set up to consider specific problems.

Meanwhile the first pressures from outside were apparent. The executive committee of the Workers Education Association on 30 November 1940[13] passed resolutions urging that the Education Act of 1936 be put into effect immediately and preparation to be made for raising the school-leaving age to sixteen as part of post-war reconstruction. They urged that the President should be directing the "beginning of building of new foundations". To this end secondary education should not be dependent on the ability to pay, and the principle of 100 per cent special places in secondary schools, founded or aided by the local authorities, should operate forthwith.

On the 21 December 1940 *The Times* carried a letter headed, "Foundations of Peace" signed by the Archbishops of Canterbury and York, the Moderator of the Free Church Council, as well as the Roman Catholic Cardinal-Archbishop of Westminster. It declared that "no permanent peace is possible in Europe unless the principles of the Christian religion are made the foundation of national policy and of all social life". They listed ten principles which they felt confident would be accepted by rulers and statesmen throughout the British Commonwealth of Nations and could be regarded as the true basis on which a lasting peace could be established. The first five of these had previously been formulated by Pope Pius XII as the basis for the ordering of international life. To these were added five "standards by which economic situations and proposals may be tested". They were the abolition of extreme inequality of wealth and possessions, equality of educational opportunity, the safeguarding of the family as a social unit, the restoration of a sense of divine vocation to man's daily work and, finally, the total resources of the earth to be used as God's gifts to the whole human race.

Such similar and high-minded counsels from two widely differing quarters were not without effect. On 20 December the President addressed the annual conference of the Incorporated Association of Preparatory Schools telling them that although discussions were proceeding inside the board on the future of education he saw no likelihood of embarking upon a "new order" until after the war. On 2 January 1941 he told the Incorporated Association of Masters in Secondary Schools of "plans for the future of education when peace returned, and even before" which amounted to implementing the Spens Report of 1938, putting the 1936 Education Act into operation and to restoring the Day Central School Programme for the fifteen- to eighteen-year-olds on the lines of the Education Act of 1918. He was sharply criticized by educationalists for being faint hearted. The *Times Educational Supplement* charged that the proposals contained "nothing more than the statutory enforcement of reforms already enacted but inoperative, together with possibly some improvements which had been authoritatively recommended to the Board of Education two years previously, but had hitherto been officially ignored". A leader in *The Times* of 4 January 1941 sounded a more realistic note, suggesting that the President was being over-optimistic, warning that

> just as he held his present position with over-much complacency, so therefore he was too optimistic about the chances of being able, at one blow, to effect two major reforms, both involving very considerable provision of buildings, staff and equipment, shortly after the conclusion of an exhausing and possibly long war; he would be better advised to begin now to build up reform bit by bit, rather than to wait until after the war in the hope that he could achieve it in a lump.

Matters were accelerated by the government decision to set up a special committee to prepare post-war reconstruction plans. Sir George Chrystal, Permanent Head of the Ministry of Health, was designated as the secretary and on 22 January he informed Sir Maurice Holmes, Permanent Secretary of the board, that as part of the examination of the national scene some suggestions were required for comprehensive post-war reconstruction; he requested early preliminary talks with the board's representatives. Discussions were not to be confined to government circles and on 24 January Labour Leader, Arthur Greenwood, Minister without Portfolio and chairman of the reconstruction committee, received a deputation from the Workers' Education Association to hear their views on educational reform. The two senior civil servants at the Board of Education, Holmes and Wood, were extremely disturbed at this development for it cut across their plans to discuss future plans with official and professional bodies in confidence, thus allowing freedom of discussion but not committing the board to particular lines for reform. It realized that if politicians were to hold public discussions with outside bodies in this fashion then the board would have to produce concrete proposals of its own, otherwise schemes could take root which it would be difficult to eradicate later. To this purpose Holmes told the reconstruction committee secretary that the Board was by no means ready to commit itself to any particular scheme and at the same time pressed his own internal committee to finalize their work and come forward with definite proposals.

In fact as early as 17 January Deputy Secretary Wood had summarized the preliminary conclusions and they had discussed his memorandum. It envisaged public education divided into three stages—primary, secondary and further systems—which followed the lines of the Hadow and Spens Reports. Primary education was to comprise nursery schools from three to five, with infant schools from five to seven and junior schools from seven to eleven. Secondary education was to take place in senior schools, which were to be renamed secondary modern schools; there were also to be grammar schools, junior technical and commercial schools. Secondary education could end at fifteen but might continue to eighteen. Further education would comprise not only adult education but also part-time day-continuation schools for young people up to the age of eighteen, who had not continued their schooling after the minimum leaving age. This last was basically the proposals of the Fisher Act of 1918, which Wood noted had never been given a chance to work. He also expressed the hope that some form of compulsory military training might be continued after the war as a means of instilling discipline. This last was no doubt inspired by the success of the initial conscription scheme for "Militia Boys" which handled with imagination and tact through the direct interest of the War Minister, Leslie Hore-Belisha, had been run on boarding-school lines rather than the bullying training normal for recruits.[14]

The board's committee found the secondary school proposals controversial, for as the system was constituted the great majority of children spent the whole of their school life in public elementary schools, albeit the last three years were sometimes passed in classes which had been distinguished from the main body of the school by the title "Senior Schools" under Hadow reorganization. The proportion of reorganized classes varied between town and country; in urban areas 63 per cent of all senior classes had been reorganized, in rural areas only 16 per cent. About one in ten children went to grammar schools and less than one in thirty to a junior technical school. The Hadow Report of 1926 and the Spens Report of 1938 had accepted this separation of children into different streams, for which they formulated a theoretical basis by distinguishing between the academic, the practical and the general type of child each with different aptitudes. They had insisted on parity of esteem between the different streams as an ultimate aim. Certain members of the committee were opposed to different types of secondary schools. They held that even if fees were abolished in grammar schools and all schools were staffed and housed to the standards of the grammar schools, the very existence of the different types of school would still produce streams of pupils destined for different types of occupation; this would only continue to perpetuate the existing social distinctions between occupations. Only the introduction of multilateral schools, where the future professional and manual workers could be educated side by side, would meet the demands for social equality.

Spokesmen for the technical branch pointed out that the great majority of the children went straight from school into unskilled or semi-skilled work, so there seemed the need for a system which reflected the employment divisions and the ratios of the various sections. They therefore urged secondary education should be defined by the rôle the individuals were to play in the economic life of the country. In 1937–8 of the 570,000 children leaving the elementary schools 450,000 went direct to employment; of the 80,000 secondary school leavers 47,000 entered employment. All but a small section of the 13,000 leaving the junior technical schools went into industry or trades for which they had been prepared and were the only section which the schools had prepared for their employment; they were 2 per cent of the whole.

Most of the committee, while they rejected this strictly vocational bias, felt that whatever system was adopted there would still have to be selection by ability and aptitude. It seemed that conscious of the great material apparatus needed to give all facilities equivalent to the grammar school, which was inherent in accepting the multilateral school, they opted for the existing system as a basis for future development at the same advocating great changes to blunt the social injustice which had marred the educational system to date. Selection would have to be made on natural aptitude and not as in the past, by parents' means and social position. The status of the senior schools must be raised to give them equal esteem in the eyes of the general public. This they thought could be done by bringing the three types of secondary schools under a single Code of Regulations so that all enjoy equal conditions in such matters as size of classes, amenities and staffing. It was felt that the proportion of places in junior technical schools should be increased to produce more and better recruits for industry and commerce and also to provide a more appropriate form of education for many now attending the grammar schools.

With the balance of feeling within the committee favouring gradual improvement of the existing system without radical change it followed that the next consideration was the type of selection procedure to be adopted and at what age it should operate. Both the Hadow and Spens Reports had recommended the age of transfer at eleven, and all the reorganization which had been carried out so far had been based on that principle. Any change would undoubtedly be unpopular and wasteful although it was generally accepted that this, for many children, was too young to determine the most appropriate stream of education for an individual.

Once again the technical representation intervened with some effect.[15] As early as November they had presented a paper to the board's internal committee in which they pronounced it impractical for children to start at junior technical schools before the age of thirteen, because experience had shown that by this age the aptitudes and interests of individual children were reasonably clear. It also reflected a tendency to recruit apprentices for the skilled occupations, which these schools catered for, at a higher age; it was expected that after the war sixteen would be the standard age for starting an apprenticeship, as it was for engineering and the better types of commercial work. It was then recalled that both the Spens and Hadow Reports recommended a general review of all pupils' educational progress at the age of thirteen, so that appropriate transfers from one type of school to another could take place. There were difficulties in making this a reality, for if there was to be mobility between schools in this way then the period from eleven to thirteen would have to be treated as a genuinely preparatory period, with a very similar course being followed in all types of schools. This would call for considerable changes in the curricula of both senior and grammar schools, and the latter were largely autonomous and had nothing to gain from the alteration. It would be very difficult to persuade parents to agree to the transfer of a child from a grammar to a senior school until parity of esteem between the two had been not only established but publicly acknowledged.

The committee were by no means unanimous in the way to meet these difficulties and a number of different policies were energetically canvassed. Chief Inspector Charles proposed that at eleven all children should go to senior schools where they would all be given a general preparatory 2-year course. Suitable children would then be selected upon the basis of their school records and observed aptitudes, supplemented by suitable intelligence tests, for transfer to technical and grammar schools, while the rest would stay on at senior schools. This scheme, he argued, would go a long way to meeting the advocates for the multilateral school and in the committee they supported the proposal, as did the educational theory panel of the committee. The representatives of the secondary branch of the board strongly opposed it, for it would overburden the senior schools and disrupt the education of the majority who would be required to remain there until they were fifteen. It would not provide the gifted minority with suitable groundwork for their grammar school course. They held that grammar school education ought to begin at eleven, and pointed out that the public schools were known to be anxious to reduce their age of entry from thirteen to ten plus; they neglected to add that the reason for this was not unconnected with an attempt to raise more income by having their paying pupils longer at school. If entry was at thirteen for the grammar school, the course would then be only three years which was certainly not long enough for a complete course. To this, Mr Cleary, the chief advocate of multilateral schools, countered that as it was proposed to introduce similar courses for all schools up to the age of thirteen to facilitate transfer, this would occur in any case, so the secondary branch's objection was hardly valid.

A second proposal was to use the lower forms of the grammar schools as the clearing houses by transferring all able children at eleven plus there; at thirteen there would then be a redistribution to the appropriate type of school, with transfers from the senior schools where late development had become apparent. The administrative arguments against this were obvious for the over-loading of the lower part of the grammar schools would change their character, parental anger would probably follow the removal of children from the grammar schools, not to mention staffing problems and the effect on the senior schools as being clearly the residual school in the system.

Once again the technical branch intervened with a scheme of their own, which was designed to ensure that not all the more able children should be snapped up by the grammar schools. They proposed that separate preparatory schools should be created to cater for all able children from the age of eleven to thirteen. At thirteen there should be a sort out, which would not rule out promotion from the senior school. This proposal did not attract much support.

By the end of January 1941 the committee had agreed upon the drafts of several chapters of a lengthy memorandum setting out their views on a wide number of educational developments. Early in February the President, Mr Ramsbotham, referred to the document when addressing representatives of the Workers' Education Association, the Trades Union Congress and the Co-operative Union, describing it as a "New Testament" of education. On 28 February the only serious problem outstanding was how and at what age children should be transferred to secondary schools, and Holmes reported accordingly to the President saying he would support the Hadow and Spens Reports on this point, for any change from eleven would be rash at this stage.

Meanwhile there were signs that educational interests were still restive[16] when late in February, the President of the Association of Directors and Secretaries for Education in his address to the annual meeting claimed a right for educational interests to be consulted on questions of educational reform and that in his view consultations should start at once. He asked when the consultative committee was going to be set up? Holmes saw that the board must make its position clear and on his advice the President of the board took the opportunity of a speech to the

Lancashire branch of the National Union of Teachers on 13 March to announce that as soon as departmental views had been provisionally formulated educational interests would be brought into fullest consultation. Within the board,[17] the President resolved the problem of the age of selection by ruling that the "New Testament" should include a scheme based on selection at eleven, with a review at thirteen. By the middle of May the draft memorandum was completed and in June it was printed and circulated to local education authorities, professional bodies and most of the organizations interested in education. It was not available to the general public and the accompanying covering letter emphasized two points:

(1) The memorandum, as stated in the foreword represents nothing more than the personal views of the officers who compiled it, and does not commit the board in any way.
(2) As a necessary corollary to (1), it is essential that the strictly confidential character of the memorandum should be recognized and observed. Nothing could be more unfortunate than the premature disclosure of suggestions which may be abandoned or radically altered as the result of subsequent discussions.

The memorandum had been bound in green and entitled *Education After The War* and was soon known as the "Green Book".[18] Opinions about its distribution and availability varied. Lester Smith held "it was distributed in such a blaze of secrecy" that its contents became public property, while Kenneth Richmond[19] called it "the famous or notorious Green Book, the choice of adjective depends on whether or not you were one of the select few to be entrusted with a copy". (See page 387.)

Apart from its educational significance, the Green Book is of historic importance in the development of British constitutional practice. The established practice of major public reform was to set up a commission or committee which would examine the existing situation and write up an agreed report. Questions of moment usually have a complicated background of conflicting interests, so that the investigation can become involved in disputes both controversial and heated. The investigation by a body of varied interests not directly connected with the department concerned allows the minister and his officials to remain removed from the area of dispute thus retaining a position of some impartiality. Moreover there is no obligation to act on the report, which can be partially or totally ignored.

On this occasion such a line of investigation was not available to the Board of Education for Churchill recalled the prolonged and heated dissention that had surrounded the Education Act of 1902. He realized that the religious interests were still active and that there was some similarity with the 1902 situation when an overwhelming Conservative majority had imposed a measure which had been desperately fought and bitterly resented by a people who were largely without the franchise. The section who most used the elementary schools had no influence in framing the basis of their operation. The vociferous religious protagonists served to mask the real issue which was over the control of the socialization of the children. On one side was a land-owning aristocracy trying to maintain the type of control they had built up in the villages and an agricultural economy; on the other side was the secular interest fighting for a system more suitable for living in towns and an industrial economy. It was a struggle to break with a social apparatus which had produced forelock-pulling labourers and move towards more informed and independent citizens. Churchill had been made aware of a similar situation developing on the formation of his coalition government, for the Labour leaders had stressed the need for an immediate start on social reforms and made this a condition of their participation. Already there was tension between the more feudal minded Conservative knights of the shires and the Labour trade unionists, two factions diametrically opposed on social questions. In 1902 a small parliamentary force had raised the whole country to protest and the unrepresented majority had vigorously demonstrated their concern with the encouragement of religious leaders. Similarly in 1941 Labour support was running high in the country while they were certainly under-represented at Westminster. There was also great bitterness over social questions which Churchill, as an intransigent Conservative Chancellor of the Exchequer from 1924 to 1929, had reason to appreciate. The left wing of Labour, with little parliamentary strength yet widespread support in the country, would be tempted to mobilize this if it was felt that social reconstruction was not proceeding to their satisfaction. The Prime Minister, therefore wished to minimize the risk of any flare up which could endanger national unity in wartime. Education because of its association with religious dissention, was obviously inflammable political tinder, so that the open display of its issues through a public inquiry were therefore ruled out.

This restriction produced a constitutional innovation in circulating an official brief (the Green Book) as the basis first for written comments and later opportunities for face-to-face exchanges on the points at issue. A similar method was used by the Labour Government 1964–70 when planning the wholesale reorganization of the Health and Welfare services. Significantly the discussion papers were bound in green and called "green papers"; there was however a significant difference in that the Green Book had a controlled circulation, while the later documents are freely available to the public. It is a significant development in the recognition of the pressure-group function of organized interested bodies and there is no doubt that the success of this method of wide consultation played a great part in leading to the inclusion in many of the Acts reorganizing public services of a section setting up an apparatus for continuous consultation.

On 12 June 1941, even before the memorandum had been circulated, the President, Ramsbotham, gave a summary of its contents and purpose to the Association of Education Committees. It seems surprising today that the memorandum was not published or made more widely available for it was largely a summary of official reports made up into a coherent survey of the whole of the educational scene, and various parts of it were freely discussed at public meetings. At this meeting the President explained the purpose of the document as a means of focusing discussion, which was otherwise likely to drag on slowly or to be diverted from the main issue unless the parties had some written material before them to serve as a basis for talking. Such was the purpose of the memorandum. It did not commit the board, for until all considered views had been aired nothing could be decided.

In a personal assessment of the situation he saw two reasons for replanning education at that time; firstly the need for education to keep in step with society, for ideas and conditions had changed with such startling rapidity in the last 30 years that the educational machinery had become old fashioned and after the war would be obsolete. Secondly it was commonplace knowledge that wars and times of political upheaval occasioned educational reform. The war was not distant but affected every man, woman and child, so that something more than mere educational timbering up was needed. He hoped it was the national will to demand for all children their right of "equal opportunity", for such was the expectation of the Prime Minister who, in words which were quoted in the preface of the memorandum, looked forward to, "a state of society where the advantages and privileges, which hitherto had been enjoyed only by the few, shall be far more widely shared by the man and youth of the nation as a whole".

The President saw three main gateways by which children and young people passed between infancy and maturity. At eleven, the prospects before them were the broad highway of the senior elementary school, a small path of traditional secondary-school education for the privileged and a narrow track to the junior technical school. The first task was to make these of equal status and esteem and to remove the artificial barriers that fetter and impede free choice. Alongside this was needed the extension of the period of education for the great majority, which should be passed in conditions alike for all schools as regards buildings and teachers; all should be equally good and efficient. He saw the dual system of education would be a great problem which would face them in achieving the first part of this task; but in time of crisis authorities, teachers and Churches of every denomination had come together in a spirit of solidarity, which might well encourage them to find a new solution to an old problem.

The second gateway was the one that led the majority from school life into earning their living. Public opinion had been concerned for a long time that the bulk of children went into the world at fourteen with no supervision, no guidance or training except such as was given in voluntary clubs and evening classes. A school-leaving age of fifteen would mitigate but not remove the evil. The President said that the age of eighteen must be the age at which State education ceased. Attempts to solve this problem had been made by voluntary organizations and evening classes, but this had touched only a quarter, or at most a third. War had united them in a service of youth. Despite some progress through legislation to ensure decent working conditions in shops and factories the country was still without day-continuation schools which were essential for developing skills, widening interests and providing supervision for the healthy development of the young. Associated with this should be the service of youth in which voluntary bodies and statutory bodies would provide for leisure occupations of young people. It might be possible to move towards a complete system in which all efforts were directed towards the welfare of young people in all aspects, so that their educational, industrial and recreational activities could be combined as the business of one body.

The President's third gateway was the one leading to the higher forms of academic and professional training which should ensure that every well-qualified boy or girl should have the fullest opportunity of university education. There was a need to reshape the system of training the teaching profession. He thought it was also time for the State to make itself wholly responsible for seeing that promising boys and girls were able to go to university regardless of the area in which they lived and the financial position of their parents. He was not suggesting any large increase in university places nor changes in the system of control, but rather to directing those responsible towards the co-ordination and extension of the various forms of assistance. From this he was led on to consider the training of teachers, which was a question of the greatest immediate concern : for upon the supply of well-trained teachers depended the whole structure they were setting out to rebuild. He did not propose to deal with the shortcomings of the existing system, but with the new prospect in view; a form of training would be needed which was not narrow and academic.

He closed by acknowledging that he had left many aspects of education untouched, but the danger in the task of reconstruction was in not seeing the wood for the trees, which then resulted in adding this or that new piece to the old structure without standing aside to see the whole picture. The aim must be not merely to patch and improve but to remould and unify the educational system. All hopes of a better system would come to nothing, unless there were sacrifices of vested interests which stood in the way of progress. The ideal to keep in view in making changes was to secure what was best for the child, irrespective of parental circumstances and place of residence. It was true that opinions would differ as to the best means of reaching this ideal but, as long as they were not distracted by side issues, he believed they would not fail.

This policy speech which contained the gist of both the spirit and contents of the Green Book opened the campaign for a thorough reorganization of the whole educational system. It was the first of a series, for a week later on 19 June, the President addressed a youth rally at Derby in the same spirit when he inaugurated the Service of Youth. He declared he did not want to make a service catering for the leisure of young people something which was merely for wartime, but to establish it as part of the normal educational services conducted by the local authorities. When peace returned it should be considered as part of the educational reconstruction which they were now contemplating; it had an important part to play in catering for the needs of boys and girls up to the age of eighteen in providing further opportunity for the fifteen to eighteen age group to develop new interests and skills.

The following week, 27 June, the President was once again in action at Sheffield where he again expanded on the theme of the educational system after the war to the National Union of Teachers, including in his address much of the material from the two previous speeches. He did however say that he wished to see school dinners become a normal feature of school life. He looked forward to the material difficulties of buildings and staff which would confront the reconstruction of the educational system. On the question of buildings, he thought that just for a few years the schools would have to be content with many makeshift and temporary structures, such as hutments, in fact anything they could get hold of; but the important thing was that the reforms should not wait until permanent buildings could be provided. The next day he made a similar speech to the Nottingham Rural Community Council.

This lively introduction to the period of grass-roots consultation and discussion was cut short by the Prime Minister who, after just over a year in control, had established an unprecedented personal ascendancy which he consolidated by reorganizing his government. Herwald Ramsbotham left the Education Department, to become Chairman of the Assistance Board with the title of Lord Soulbury. He had taken over the Board of Education at a thankless time but had successfully launched the new phase of reconstruction. He had sowed a harvest which his successor, Richard Butler, was to gather in.

Although the complete text of the Green Book can be seen in the appendix (p. 387) comments on its content show how far feelings on education had moved from the days of frustration in the late 1930s. The foreword stressed the need for a new approach which should be on bold and generous lines. The document presented an administrative approach to the educational service, but the criterion for any reform must be to what extent any measure meets the educational requirements of the children. It firmly spelt out the unfairness and indefensible inequalities of education after the age of eleven. The system outlined started with nursery schools from two to five, infant schools to seven plus when the children switched to the junior schools until eleven plus. Secondary education followed the tripartite system of Hadow and Spens. Further education took all who had not had a full course to sixteen with part-time studies to eighteen in day-continuation schools. There were to be more opportunities for continuing education through to the universities. The longest chapter dealt with the situation of teachers and sketched out the need for a complete reformation of the training and conditions of the profession.

This new look at old ideas was promising enough, but central to the reconstruction was the new administrative framework with its attendant financial arrangements, and most important of all the religious settlement. Whatever may be said the quality of the educational service would depend on what was decided on these matters.

The administration of the schools had failed to keep pace with the changes in the service. The State had started in 1870 with a limited rôle which had been gradually widened from the provision of very basic education for the children of the labouring poor to an educational system covering the period from two to eighteen as well as providing help towards university courses for the able. A sketchy service already existed which covered a wide age range and many different matters, but the methods of administration had not advanced to meet these new functions. The legal basis of the service was the 1902 Act which, because of the way it had developed, was full of anomalies especially as regards secondary education. Grammar and junior technical schools were administered by a different authority from that dealing with central and senior schools.

The local-government system on which education was based was itself outmoded for it had not been revised since the 1890s although there had been great changes in population and transport had been revolutionized through the introduction of the petrol engine. It was agreed on all sides that there must be reform of the antiquated machinery but the clash of principles and interests all closely involved with national politics awaited the attention of a Solomon. The main issue was still between greater centralization for efficiency and smaller units for local control. It was this clash between functional needs and democratic control which had largely shaped the compromise structure of the 1870 Act, accounted for the rejection of the 1896 Bill and had caused the small Part III authorities to be created in 1902. The Liberals had maintained that the local authorities were too large and impersonal and had tried to reduce the rôle of the senior authorities without success. It was with some feeling that the board recorded in their annual report for 1908-9 that the fragmentation of authorities, and the need to establish a proper unity in educational organization, was the most intricate single problem in educational administration.

The defects of the existing system were many and complex. With secondary education split between two types of authorities unity of treatment was not possible. In some cases small Part III authorities had grown over the years until they now administered more people than some county-rank Part II authorities; others had remained too small to be able to afford educational expansion or provide efficient administration. These areas were known and avoided by the more able teachers because they offered little scope for progressive work or promotion. Although it was generally agreed that there must be a unified system of authorities of viable size, local pride wished to retain every shred of autonomy although costs of education had grown to three times what they had been in 1902. Wealthy boroughs like Hendon where a penny rate fetched in £7,667 could cope with this although only a Part III authority; in other boroughs where the return could be as little as £160 it was another story.

The original draft of the Fisher Education Act of 1918 had

attempted to tackle this problem but it was part of the controversial material which was abandoned to get the measure through
parliament. The Hadow Report had suggested the creation of
larger provincial authorities in which both the Part II and the
surviving Part III authorities would be merged, but no action had
been taken to give this a legal shape probably because it was
part of a wider problem, for educational administration is
wedded to local government organization.

The Green Book accepted the basic premise that a single
authority must be responsible for both elementary and secondary
education and rehearsed the various ways this could be brought
about. The choice ranged from the elimination of the Part III
authorities to the setting up of large provincial units on the
Hadow pattern. Britain in wartime was administered by a dozen
regional commissioners who controlled the many public services
with singular success. This created a precedent for the larger
authority, but tendencies to destroy the pre-war pattern of local
government were anxiously watched and a pledge had been
given not to keep the regional structure after the war.

To finance education, the Green Book proposed a revised system
of grants. The existing pattern had been a system of percentage
grants from the central exchequer to the local authorities; each
portion of the service attracting a laid down percentage contribution of the total amount the authority proposed to spend. Up to
the outbreak of war these grants had been calculated on a
formula devised by the Kempe Committee in 1914 and this was
freely acknowledged to be unsatisfactory. Under the urgency of
war a system had been introduced of paying the authorities a
percentage of their expenditure in 1937-8 as a grant. Under this
simplified formula the board paid in grants some 50 per cent of
the local education authorities' expenditure, although the proportion paid to individual authorities varied, and in some cases was
as high as 72 per cent. Higher education was governed by one
rule : that the board contributed 50 per cent of the authorities'
expenditure.

The Green Book proposed a reduction of education authorities
with the establishment of a single unified authority, although not
favouring a specific form.[20] However, it pointed out that there
would need to be sufficient financial capacity to undertake all the
forms of education covered. At the same time it was realized

that care must be taken not to cripple the county areas in carving out new Part II authorities by taking away too large a proportion of their income. There was a total of 318 local education authorities if both Part II and III were included. Sixty-three counties and 83 county boroughs made up the 146 Part II authorities. It would not do just to abolish all Part III areas for this would leave unsolved the administration of the small areas. The ideal solution, as the Green Book saw it, was to absorb some of the small areas into the larger ones to make viable units. However, it feared that this solution would not be acceptable and the solution could perhaps lie in retaining all Part II authorities and promoting to their ranks some of the larger Part IIIs, giving around 180 authorities. The Green Book pointed out that a single all-purpose authority would greatly simplify both administration and finance, which could well take the form of a block grant. This would be a sum allocated for a period of years by statutory regulations designed to meet the needs of the area.

The advantages and disadvantages of a block grant as against percentage grants had been argued for many years.[21] Percentage grants were held to encourage extravagance, while block grants which limited the obligation of the State, were not acceptable to local authorities. It is significant that the Geddes, May and Ray committees, which had all been concerned with economies, had favoured block as against percentage grants. A Board of Education memorandum addressed to the departmental committee appointed under Lord Meston in 1922 to consider the balance of this question had argued for the retention of the percentage grant system on the ground that this form was an encouragement to the local authorities to develop their services; at the same time admitting it failed to equalize the rate burden between different authorities and suggesting certain improvements.

In 1926 an attempt had been made to include education in a scheme introduced by Neville Chamberlain the Minister of Health, to reorganize local government. He advocated replacement of grants in aid of the services provided, by a block grant, but this had been successfully resisted. The Green Book now supported this system of financing, which the 1926 scheme embodied in the Local Government Act of 1929, because it was working well and would simplify the administration of education. The major reorganization envisaged should therefore include it.

The Green Book proposed that a proper system of exchequer grants should provide a fair contribution from the central funds to the cost of local services, ensure the local authorities have complete financial interest in their administration by adapting to the needs of the area, allow the greatest freedom to the local administrators thus stimulating their initiative, while at the same time providing sufficient central control and advice to ensure a reasonable standard of service. It considered the Ministry of Health formula met these five cardinal requirements. This could also be followed for the basis of distribution of the block grant, although suitable weighting was considered necessary for the number of children under fifteen in each particular area. It was recognized that the new system was to be introduced in a period of rapid educational change and expansion but it should be able to meet the expanding needs of the service.

No further changes were proposed in the existing system of paying grants for services of a non-local character such as technical education, special schools, adult education, teacher training, nursery schools, play centres and direct-grant secondary schools, although some of these services might be absorbed in time into the public system of education administered by the local authorities.[22]

It was generally recognized that the real obstacle to the reorganization of education was the religious question for, although voluntary schools had been disappearing steadily since 1902, at the outbreak of war there were still 10,533 of them with a population of 1,374,000 children.[23] This compared with 10,363 council schools with an average attendance of 3,151,000. They educated 30 per cent of the children in 1938 as compared to 1901 when they had catered for 52 per cent. In rural areas the church school was often the only one available. The majority of church schools were all-age schools and only 16 per cent had been reorganized on Hadow lines into separate senior and junior departments as opposed to 62 per cent of council schools.

The reason for this difference was the financial situation. Reorganization required substantial alterations and improvements, and many of the voluntary schools were already old. Local education authorities had no general powers to alter or improve voluntary schools, while the voluntary-school managers seldom had the means to meet the costs of reorganization; indeed the sums they could raise barely sufficed to keep existing accommodation in a reasonable state of repair. The Education Act of 1936 had made some special arrangements for the local authorities to spend money on new voluntary senior schools, but these had been largely curtailed under the pressures of defence preparations.[24] Only 519 proposals had been put forward out of which 37 had been put into effect. While the voluntary schools had little prospect of providing education of a genuine secondary character, yet managers would not consent to their senior pupils being removed to schools provided by the local authorities.

Even as primary schools the voluntary schools left a great deal to be desired. Many were housed in old and often unsatisfactory buildings. Of the 753 schools left on the Board of Education's black list of condemned schools, which had been drawn up in 1925, 541 were voluntary schools; an up-to-date list would have revealed a worse situation.[25] It was obvious that the dual system established under the 1870 Act was beginning to break down and if it were allowed to continue an appreciable minority of the country's children would be denied healthy, decent school conditions throughout the whole of their school lives and would be especially disadvantaged in their secondary education.

Moreover presence of the voluntary schools impeded the rationalization of the system by the local education authorities. The unwillingness of managers to let their senior pupils be transferred to council schools, even when they could not afford to provide senior accommodation, led to an uneconomic use of school facilities including employment of staff. The relative smallness of the voluntary schools tended to make them less efficient and uneconomic, although they were often the only schools available to scattered rural communities. The availability of motor transport could facilitate reorganization into larger and better equipped schools, but the local authorities could not close voluntary schools even though the numbers fell below 30, unless there was another school of the same denomination in the locality. No one could be prevented from promoting new voluntary schools. Inevitably there was considerable friction between the local authorities and the voluntary-school managers.

There were those who favoured leaving the voluntary schools to wither away, squeezed out by the poverty of their resources. Although this would have had the advantage of disposing of the dual system and its problems, the pupils would suffer. Moreover the cost of replacing the voluntary schools with provided schools might be very considerable, particularly if it had to be faced over a short time. There was also public opinion to be considered for there was great dedication in some cases to continue the work of the Churches as pioneers of public education. The Green Book therefore rejected the idea of leaving the voluntary schools to their fate and proposed a form of closer integration with the national system. The State would make adequate financial provision while meeting the wishes of the Churches with regard to religious instruction. In return public control would be extended "to ensure the effective and economical organization and development of both primary and secondary education".[26]

It was suggested the primary school buildings should become the responsibility of the local authorities both for repairs, alterations and improvements, in return for power to appoint and dismiss staff. Subject to the Board of Education's supervision, local authorities should have powers to stop maintaining any unnecessary schools, as well as changing the organization and age range of any school; these powers would open the way to complete Hadow reorganization. The Green Book saw the senior voluntary schools ranking equally with other secondary schools, but their finance and administration presented special difficulties. It had always been policy to prevent the problems of the dual system moving into higher education but the position of the voluntary schools under the existing law was so different from the aided grammar schools, it was difficult to see how their position could be reconciled under the same code of rules. This situation had developed out of the growth of primary and secondary education following separate paths.

The local education authorities had a duty to maintain voluntary elementary schools and had control of their secular education with the right to veto appointments and dismiss staff. This situation would obviously continue when they became secondary modern schools. This created a precedent so that public opinion would object to other modern schools maintained at public expense over which the local authorities had no control. In the case of the grammar schools the power of the local authorities to give financial assistance was discretionary, while the control of

secular instruction and staff appointments were entirely the concern of the governors. The Green Book therefore advocated a
separate provision for non-provided modern schools.

It was proposed that the local authorities' position as regards
non-provided secondary modern schools should remain unchanged with responsibility to maintain and keep them efficient,
but not to carry out repairs, alterations or improvements. This
gave the right to control secular education and veto the appointment or dismissal of staff on educational grounds. If the governors were unable or unwilling to carry out their part of the contract then the system applicable to primary schools should operate, which meant the local authority assumed the duties of the
governors as regards the school buildings and control of staff.
It was proposed these provisions should apply to new modern
schools as well as existing ones, although it was not envisaged
that many would be promoted because the cost of building new
schools to secondary standards was likely to be prohibitive. As
in the case of primary schools there was to be the right, subject
to the board's consent, to stop maintaining unnecessary schools.

These changes called for a revision of the 1902 settlement as
regards religious instruction. The Churches had been pressing for
some time for a more positive attitude to religion in the nation's
schools and there was evidence of support from the public, for
the country was at war with a pagan ideology and religion had
acquired a certain flavour of patriotism. The dangers of war,
which were not less real at home, had quickened religious
interest.

Religious instruction in schools had been the subject of bitter
wrangling which had repeatedly barred the way to educational
advance. Any compromise was hard to maintain and condemned
by at least one section of the interested parties. Between the wars
denominational feeling had declined as the growing indifference
of the people to religious matters forced the Churches to think of
other faiths as potential allies rather than rivals. This was given
striking form in a letter published in *The Times* on 12 February
1941 under the signatures of the Archbishops of Canterbury,
York and Wales as well as the Free Church Leaders which urged
that all children should be given instruction in the Christian
religion by teachers competent and willing to act as instructors.
There should be exemption for the children of parents who

objected. It was foreseen that there would probably be few teachers in some schools for this work, so it was proposed that the timetable conscience clause should be abolished so that the specialists in religious instruction could take classes at any period in the day. It was hoped that the use of agreed syllabuses which were being widely used, in spite of the Cowper-Temple clause, would also be universally adopted in church schools. Moreover it was proposed to start the day in all schools with an act of worship. The Church leaders also suggested that religious instruction should be inspected "in respect of its methods by HM Inspectors or some other duly authorized persons". To meet the teaching requirements of this proposed change there was agreement on changes in the training of teachers so that religious knowledge should count towards the professional qualification. It was also suggested local authorities should develop their post-certificate training in the subject and actively encourage teachers to use such facilities.

The Green Book went a long way towards meeting these proposals by accepting that religious observance and instruction should become by statute part of the curriculum of both primary and secondary education, according to agreed syllabuses. To facilitate this, in non-provided modern schools, the Cowper-Temple clause should no longer apply and denominational instruction should be permitted. Agreed syllabus instruction should be available for those children whose parents wanted them to receive it. The local authorities should be responsible for seeing there were sufficient suitable teachers to give denominational instruction in non-provided primary schools, using a system of reserving a number of staff appointments on the lines already agreed in the 1936 Act.[27] In the provided secondary modern schools the ending of the Cowper-Temple clause should go a long way to meet the situation. In the non-provided secondary modern schools the continued power of the governors to appoint their own teachers should go a long way to compensate the Churches for the increased public control over their primary schools. To safeguard the interests of staff no teacher was to be worse or better off by reason of giving or not giving religious instruction.

There was so much which was balanced and reasonable in the Green Book, *Education After The War*, that it is difficult to see why it was not published, for it was the first official survey of the whole educational system (in one cover). This attempt at secrecy was nullified in any case by the minister giving summaries of the memorandum to large meetings of interested bodies, who then continued their deliberations more or less openly, and, when replying to the Board's suggestions, frequently gave their replies to the press. A singular lesson emerged from the circulation of this review of educational problems in that the many voluble interested groups ceased attacking the board in their zeal to publicize their own points of view.

Herwald Ramsbotham's part in the national presentation of the Green Book deserves comment. He came from a well-established Lancashire family with a long tradition of public service. Association with banking interests, through his marriage, and a profitable 10 years in the City had made him wealthy, so he decided to fulfil an undergraduate ambition and became MP for Lancaster. Stanley Baldwin, attracted by his classical scholarship, saw his potential as "an honest broker" type of politician and used him to support ministers with an indifferent grasp of their departments. He inspired trust and even affection like several others on the intellectual left of the Conservative Party such as Harold Macmillan, Walter Elliot and Oliver Stanley, all men influenced by their service in the 1914-18 war. Like them he did not always feel happy with the more ruthless aspects of party policy but they responded to the Whips and supported what was done. Men like this, as well as others from well-established backgrounds did not easily accept Churchill's leadership. Recent research shows something of the unanswered questions in his political and social background. He had been 35 years on the political scene and by many his career was seen with some justification, as revealing more flair for self-interest and publicity than integrity and public utility. Yet in a world of tarnished politicians he emerged as the only well-known figure who could command a hearing for at least he had spoken out against Hitler; but he was by no means universally accepted when he became the Prime Minister in May 1940.[28]

In April 1940 Herwald Ramsbotham had been asked to go to the Education Board which had caused much concern by its ineffectiveness. He was fifty-three, with 10 years' successful ministerial experience, well respected in Conservative party circles and set fair for a political career which could have taken him to high

Mr Herwald Ramsbotham—President of the Board of
Education
(*By permission of Sir Peter Ramsbotham*)

office. He had already served some four years in the department
(1931-5) and so appreciated the neglected and low state of the
service. He must have been given some assurances of support for
putting matters right, otherwise to accept would have been
political suicide. When Churchill confirmed his appointment he
must have renewed those assurances for the public concern over
schools had been well ventilated in parliament. On taking over
Churchill, intent on securing his leadership, also gave assurances
to the Labour leaders that social reconstruction would go ahead,
appointing one of them, Arthur Greenwood, as minister for
reconstruction in all but name with a seat in the cabinet. As
Churchill's journalistic skills aided him to use radio talks to
establish himself as the nation's leader, his ready acceptance of

social reforms hardened. As soon as this was realized a row developed which threatened to break the uneasy Labour and Conservative coalition. Herwald Ramsbotham wished to resign but it was urged that it was better to let the situation cool off, so he agreed to wait. Instead of just clearing out his desk he quietly took steps to ensure that, despite the attitude of the Prime Minister, educational reform would go ahead. He had the civil service brief, *Education After The War,* both printed and bound to give it an added authority. This was no mean feat in wartime and no similar document was given the same treatment. These volumes were circulated to all local authorities, interested pressure groups including the Trades Union Congress, the National Union of Teachers as well as many influential and interested individuals. All were asked for their comments in writing, thus ensuring the brief was widely discussed. To cap everything he held a series of public meetings in which he gave the gist of the document showing it to be a means of meeting the widespread demands for educational reform. It is inescapable to conclude that the President was doing his best to ensure that the whole educational establishment was talking about reform of the system in an informed and constructive manner, thus making certain that whatever the Prime Minister might say, some form of reconstruction would be necessary if only to satisfy the ground-swell of public opinion which had been started. This was the solid foundation on which the Education Act of 1944 was built for, with the many and varied interests discussing not only the general ideas of reform but the details of possible plans, here was groundwork for the compromises which were later reached. Even if the new President had obeyed Churchill's veto on preparing a new Act, he would have been faced with a first-rate revolt of grass-root interests which had been inspired to actively seek educational reform.

In September 1941, six weeks after leaving the Board of Education, Mr Ramsbotham, now Lord Soulbury and Chairman of the National Assistance Board, addressed a youth rally in the Lancaster constituency he had represented for twelve years. He had seen Churchill's impregnable political position and had decided to leave politics, although continuing in a variety of public offices for another thirteen years. He had always shunned the limelight, but the Prime Minister's change of ground on the question of educational reform had prompted him to a series of untypical actions. He crowned it with a speech in which he gave his verdict on the Conservative policies which had prevailed between the wars, speaking with unusual freedom of the work of the department which he knew so well .

In a long and thoughtful speech he surveyed the problems of youth and pointed out the co-relation of unemployment and lack of education :[29]

No child could be considered to be properly trained and equipped to take his place in the workaday world if his school days ended at fourteen. It is far too young to be thrust into the strain and stress of modern industrial civilization. The late Mr H. A. L. Fisher succeeded in putting on the statute book over twenty years ago an Act of Parliament, which, if it had been put into full operation, would have solved many of the problems which now beset the training and the development of boys and girls between the age of leaving school and manhood and woman-hood. Had the Act been carried out most of the boys and girls in the land would have attended from the ages of fourteen or six-teen, to eighteen, day-continuation schools for seven or eight hours a week in their employers' time. That would have meant an enormous gain in national skill, intelligence and efficiency. Unhappily, after the Act was passed the attractions of a short-sighted, ill-conceived economy made it of no effect, and twenty precious years have been wasted. It is impossible to correct that mistake at the present moment ... but when the war is over they must not make the same mistake again and they must realize that never more can they permit any of their young people between the ages of fourteen and eighteen to be completely divorced, as so many of them were today, from all contact with education after they were fourteen years old. It was neither fair to them nor to the community.

He spoke of the "many boys and girls who, on reaching the school-leaving age of fourteen, felt themselves impelled to earn something for the family budget as soon as they possibly could, and entered jobs in which they had no opportunity to acquire any skills or aptitude of lasting value : and when they got to eighteen they found themselves stranded without any industrial proficiency, and having forgotten much of what they had learned at school." He concluded that unless the community "substituted more responsible methods of employment and provided better technical training during adolescence, the process of manufacturing applicants prepared to rest on the Assistance Board in their early twenties, would continue unchecked. . . . It was a problem for which youth had a right to demand an answer."

Mr Ramsbotham's avoidance of personal publicity should not prevent his contribution being noted, for his Green Book went forward as the educational basis of the new Bill and survived largely intact, leaving his successor in office free to concentrate on the tangled religious issues. Besides this, in his efforts to evade the intransigence of the Prime Minister, he developed a new method for the public debate of wide issues of concern to many interests which is now established as part of the machinery of open debate; significantly such public discussion documents are called green papers. Lastly, as one of very few who have resigned from high office in the cause of education he deserves a special mention in the history of the public system.

VIII

The New Broom
July 1941–June 1943

On 3 October 1941, H. G. Wells called on the President of the Board of Education and had a long conversation discussing his educational reform plans. Mr Butler minuted the meeting in his files.

"The most intriguing thought that emerged was that in a period of convulsion, any plan which was ready and thought out, was apt to be accepted and put into force by the rulers of the day. He instanced the fact that in many of the most interesting periods of the world's history, calculated reforms had been introduced by the chief of the state. This was because those responsible for an abstruse study of this nature had quietly perfected their plans; they had only to put them before the ruler at the critical moment."

THE CIRCULATION OF the Green Book had started all interested parties discussing reform and the arrival on 20 July 1941 of Richard Austen Butler[1] as the new President of the Board of Education was construed as further evidence that something would happen, for he was accepted on both sides of the House as a moderate and constructive politician. His background and the circumstances surrounding his appointment reveal a great deal, especially when associated with his subsequent career.

His family had had active and influential connections both with Cambridge and the Conservative party over several generations. He had obtained a first-class degree, been President of the Cambridge Union and secured a fellowship at Corpus Christi College. In a time of industrial stagnation, unemployment and widespread distress culminating in the General Strike of 1926 he had been steadfastly right wing. He was just too young to have served in the 1914–18 war which had influenced many of his type, no matter what their background or scholastic discipline, to be critical of the established order of affairs, for which they blamed the ruling Conservative party. Butler, however, followed the family tradition and while on the staff of the university became active in the Conservative cause, serving as an assistant to Samuel Hoare, then Secretary of State for Air. He buttressed his party allegiance in 1926 by marrying the only daughter of Samuel Courtauld, head of the textile firm of that name.

In 1929 he abandoned his academic career for politics when he was elected Member of Parliament for the safe agricultural seat of Saffron Walden, which he retained until his retirement from politics in 1964. Although only twenty-six the family precedents and connections guided him through the "green-eyed jungle of Westminster" to his first ministerial appointment three years later in 1932 at the India Office. In starting his career he had contacts through his uncle, Geoffrey Butler, MP for Cambridge University, which allied him with Neville Chamberlain, Samuel Hoare and Halifax. This association with a powerful in-group gave him a flying start to ministerial appointments, but it also associated his fortunes with theirs. Under Hoare at the India Office he assumed increasing responsibility for the preparation of the reform of the government of India. It was an involved task in which he made his mark as a patient but firm negotiator whose moderation led him to clash with Winston Churchill, an encounter which was to have long-term effects.

In 1929, when Butler arrived in Parliament, Churchill's fortunes were very low. After some success under the Liberal colours in the first world war, he had contrived to be a Conservative Chancellor of the Exchequer for the period 1924–9.[2] It was a disastrous period both for him personally and for the country, for against the advice of Maynard Keynes he had insisted in keeping Britain on the Gold Standard.[3] As the economist had forecast, depression and an embittered industrial scene followed which drove the Conservatives from office, with Churchill largely blamed for the economic and electoral débâcle. New member Butler had occasion to remind Churchill of the lack of success of his economic policies.

Churchill, who had never been strong on party affiliation, sought to keep himself in front of the public by carefully selected interventions which caught the mood of the right wingers who felt themselves threatened by the spread of progressive ideas. The issues he selected and the manner of putting them over were very similar to Enoch Powell's interventions in recent years. For the ten years, 1929–39, he followed an independent political line in which he consistently challenged the Conservative leadership under Baldwin, and later under Chamberlain. After 1931 Labour were too divided and weak to provide an effective opposition, so Churchill for much of the period took over that rôle. It was a situation which suited his colourful style and he chose his targets for maximum effect: it is said taking as his pattern Disraeli's attacks on Peel over the repeal of the Corn Laws in the 1840s. He seized on the reform of the government of India as a suitable issue to further his cause and opposed "any surrender to Ghandi", the Indian leader, making an appeal to latent jingoism. He forecast that "India will fall back, quite rapidly through the centuries, into the barbarism and privations of the Middle Ages", as the result of granting Dominion status with a modest measure of self-government. The main architect of the successful India Act was Butler who, during its passage through Parliament, took part in a number of bitter exchanges with Churchill, whose intemperate outbursts on racial issues only served to add to his isolation. Butler's patient handling of the measure won him considerable respect from all sides of the House.

Churchill's one-man campaign was widened to castigate the Conservative government for their general inaction, particularly their policies of "drift and surrender" towards the European leaders, Hitler and Mussolini. On the question of appeasement of these two dictators he was able to score repeatedly in the Commons, and the exchanges attracted increasing support for him in the country. In February 1938 the Foreign Secretary, Anthony Eden, and his undersecretary, Lord Cranborne, resigned to align themselves with Churchill; their posts were taken by Lord Halifax with Butler as his junior minister. This left Butler as the spokesman in the Commons for Foreign Affairs, facing Churchill and Eden. He was thus thoroughly identified with Chamberlain and Halifax as one of the appeasers of the dictators which culminated in the final humiliation of the Prime Minister's visit to Munich and the claim to have brought "Peace in our time". Therefore, when Churchill took over as Prime Minister on 10 May 1940 Butler was well aware that he was not one of those likely to be advanced by the change. Apart from previous antagonisms, his style of politics, cautious and meticulous, was in direct contrast to the colourful showmanship of the wartime leader.

Butler's personal situation was not improved by an incident, which he mentions briefly in his autobiography, which occurred as the international situation deteriorated rapidly.[4] By 2 June the British expeditionary force had embarked from Dunkirk leaving most of their equipment behind. By the 14 June the Germans were in Paris and on 22 June Pétain signed the French capitulation. On this latter date Butler had an interview with the Swedish Minister, Bjoorn Prytz, at the Foreign Office. According to an account given wide circulation on the continent, it was alleged Butler said negotiations were still possible with Hitler, for British foreign policy would be decided by "commonsense not bravado", such as could be expected from "diehards like Churchill". The suggestion was that this statement was made with his chief's authority. On 26 June Churchill wrote to Halifax taxing him with what he had learnt of the talk, the burden of his displeasure falling on Butler who had actually spoken to Mr. Prytz. Even so, as late as 27 May Halifax had been urging a similar policy in the War Cabinet, giving Churchill reasonable grounds for suspecting that the Foreign Office had not responded to the new hand on the tiller. A week later a document signed by Churchill was circulated to all departments of the government warning that "the Prime Minister expects all His Majesty's subjects in high places to set an example of steadfastness and resolution". In a broadcast speech he declared, "What has happened to France makes no difference to our actions and purpose . . . we shall fight on". Butler was soon aware of the intention to replace those concerned with Munich policies.

As soon as Churchill began to establish his hold on the country he brought in his own people. In March 1941 Eden returned to the Foreign Office; Halifax was sent as ambassador to the United States and Hoare went to a similar post in Madrid. Much can be claimed for these appointments, but they were exile from the domestic political scene. Chamberlain was edged into a political backwater before he retired to die late in 1940. Butler had no illusions about his future and had consultations with his political sponsors including Stanley Baldwin. He heard that Ramsbotham wanted to leave the education department and obtained a copy of the Green Book on the grounds that he would "be able to serve a useful purpose as a link between the central committee of the [Conservative] Party to consider reconstruction and government policy".

In July 1941 he was sent for by the Prime Minister. Butler has given two different accounts of the interview, the first in a television interview in 1966 and the second in his autobiography.[5] In the earlier account Churchill opened by offering an unspecified "fowin post" and was surprised when Butler countered with a wish to "go to the Ministry of Education". "I said my family had always been interested in education and also I had great hopes of making some reform there during the war. He said then that if I wanted to go he'd be glad to send me, but that he wouldn't like to wipe the children's noses and smack their behinds during the war: he didn't know what I'd be doing—so I said I would keep very busy and let him know."

In the second account Churchill opened with comment on his political experience and suggested "it is time you were promoted", following with, "I now want you to go to the Board of Education. I think that you can leave your mark there. You will be independent. Besides you will be in the war. You will move poor children from here to here", and lifted up and evacuated imaginary children from one side of his blotting pad to the other; "this will be very difficult".

There is little doubt that Churchill's aim was to break up the group of politicians who had dominated Conservative policy to minimize any challenge to his authority. Neither Halifax nor Hoare went willingly. Butler as a junior minister with no personal following could be safely allowed to remain in the country. Churchill at that time was preoccupied with winning the war which had four years to run. He had never had much time for the social services for, when offered the Local Government Board at the outset of his career, he had refused saying he did not want to be shut up in a soup kitchen with Beatrice Webb. He was at least consistent for, in 1951, when he formed his first peace-time cabinet he initially excluded his Minister of Education. Like many politicians of the old school he considered the education department a dead one, and as such suitable for Butler at that time. Typical of comment in political circles was Sir Henry Channon's entry in his diary noting the appointment as a career set-back because politically it was "a backwater".

The reason for this valuation of the education post lay in the twenty years between the wars which had been almost entirely dominated by Conservative policies seeking to minimize public expenditure. This had resulted in a consistent resistance to the extension of educational facilities so that nothing had been achieved in the department and it had come to be considered by that party as a political limbo suitable for parking those for whom a post must be found. Incumbents were naturally anxious to move on so, significantly, in the ten years since the formation of the National Government in 1931 to Butler taking up the appointment in July 1941 there had been six ministers in the office averaging a stay of eighteen months, and the running of the department had fallen into the control of the permanent officials.

Butler was well aware of this, but having backed the wrong political horse he saw the need to lie low and the Presidency of the Board of Education suited him admirably. He knew something of its shortcomings because he had consulted Lord Halifax, his former chief, who had held the post for some four years. Although an unfashionable post it put him outside the orbit of the restless and energetic premier so he could expect an undisturbed tenure in a position which he realized had great political potential. His only instruction from Churchill was a scribble telling him "to introduce a note of patriotism into the schools".[6] Unlike his chief Butler was interested in the problems of the post-war period and he foresaw the urgency with which reconstruction plans would be required. Moreover it gave him a government department at the age of 38, especially as it had come to him as a windfall when his political career had looked to be disrupted. Any doubts he had about the shrewdness of his choice must have been removed by the growing interest in post-war problems dramatically demonstrated by the reception accorded to the publication of the Beveridge Report on the reform of the social services in December 1942. The sales broke all records and caused a queue literally a mile long outside the government bookshop in Kingsway, providentially across the road from the wartime London office of the Education Board.[7]

Another reason he wished to avoid being sent overseas to the spurious glamour of a foreign post was that he had already started to rebuild his political future by taking a leading part in drawing up the reconstruction plans of the Conservative party. Unlike many of his political colour he realized that when peace came there would be a different social climate, with less easy acceptance of the privation which had been the lot of many between the wars. Already he was trying to recruit suitable people to counter the growing weight of Labour-influenced literature which was circulating on post-war reforms.[8] On the 26 June 1941 he wrote to Geoffrey Faber, chairman of the publishing house of that name, offering him the chairmanship of the Conservative party educational sub-committee considering the post-war situation. Butler wrote, "I am keen to secure people to run these committees who are of the Conservative faith, but are yet outside the party machine. Those who would be most valuable to help would be controversialists who are known and can break lances with the leading Knights of the Left." All the while he was at the Education Board supervising the reconstruction plans for the educational system he was carrying out a similar service for the Conservative Party. Neither programme was an easy one, for most of the people not committed to active participation in the war tended to be older and seemed only able to think in terms of the past and not a future which was going to be radically altered. Among the general public left-wing plans for wholesale social reconstruction for long ignored were being widely discussed, building up considerable political capital for the Labour Party. The more farsighted Conservative leaders became alarmed as they sought to change their party image from being widely considered "as interested in nothing but money bags" to something more progressive; but the groups assembled for this purpose proved to be thoroughly reactionary.[9]

The new President was faced with a formidable task caused by thirty years of neglect through financial stringency, yet the circulation of the Green Book had set all interested parties hoping for a renaissance which was felt to be long overdue, for since the start of the war there had been dozens of books and pamphlets published on the educational situation, nearly all critical.

In British public education there is a striking contrast between the high status accorded to academics, especially from the older universities who have in no way been contaminated with the State system, and the low regard in which the practitioners in the schools are held. As a consequence Butler's first-class degree at Cambridge and three years as a lecturer at the same university gave him some authority among educationalists. It was bolstered by accounts that he was the fourth generation of his family to obtain this distinction and references were made to the group of public school headmasters and university dons his family had produced in the last 150 years. He was at least a change from the succession of disinterested grand seigneurs, and his quick intelligence in mastering background briefs consolidated his authority as a reforming minister.

He also found a staunch and valuable ally in his Parliamentary Secretary, Chuter Ede, who was a teachers' leader, a prominent Nonconformist and widely experienced in local government. Not least of his connections was his friendship with Ernest Bevin, perhaps after Churchill, through his trade union dominance, the most powerful figure in the wartime coalition government. He was to give stalwart backing in the cabinet for educational reform. Ede was dedicated to the reconstruction of the educational system and refused promotion to see the negotiations brought to a successful conclusion. He knew the educational scene thoroughly both as a teacher and as his party's spokesman in this sector.

The pressure groups were not long in moving [10] and on 15 August Butler and Ede received a deputation of church leaders. Archbishop Lang of Canterbury and Archbishop Temple of York represented the Anglicans; the Free Church spokesmen were Dr. Alfred Garvie the Congregationalist and Dr Scott Lidgett the Methodist, both of whom had played a leading part in fighting the Education Act of 1902 and were trusted by their respective denominations not to surrender cherished principles. The deputation pressed for the acceptance of the Five Points which aimed at making religious instruction and communal acts of worship in the schools more real and effective, so that education would "preserve those elements in human civilization and in our national tradition which owe their origin to Christian faith". The meeting was courteously conducted and Butler closed with a gracious speech in which he stressed his agreement with their purpose but made the point that the "issues raised were far above the run of ordinary politics" and must await the outcome of consultation with the many other interests involved. He invited the

Archbishop of Canterbury to close the meeting with a prayer. This show of ecclesiastical strength warned of difficulties ahead.

Meanwhile replies from Green Book discussions were accumulating, requiring 61 files for minor respondents as well as the 24 for the major pressure groups. Other departments were asking for information for their own policy guidance. The field was wide with many varied and contradictory viewpoints. The President wrote to the Prime Minister on 12 September 1941 for guidance, pointing out that the circulation of the Green Book required action on problems long ignored.

He listed the three main topics before the board: firstly, individual and technical education, linking the work of the schools with employment; secondly the necessity of finding a settlement with the Churches on the questions of their schools and religious instruction; lastly the future of the public schools which he saw "may easily raise widespread controversy".[11]

Butler noted that "as regards the first, this country has clearly lagged behind the practice on the continent and elsewhere. The apprentice system is in decline, and something is needed in its place if we are to keep in the forefront of industrial production". Over the Church settlement:

> neither the Anglican nor Roman Catholic Church can find the necessary funds to discharge their statutory duties, and children in voluntary schools are in general at a serious disadvantage as compared with those in council schools. Any hope of improvement in education will be frustrated unless a desirable settlement of this long-standing controversy is reached, though there is no disguising the danger of old antagonisms being raised on this issue.
>
> Apart from these specific points, the machinery of education becomes increasingly ill-adapted to present-day requirements, and there are different views about raising the school-leaving age. The arrangements for the local adminisration of education call for early review, although this cannot be apart from the general consideration of local government organization, which is now in hand.

He mentioned the circulation of the Green Book and forecast that "out of all this, unless I am mistaken, there will come a demand for some public statement of the government's plans for the future of education". It was in his opinion "unwise to rush into legislation" and "some practical method of ventilating the specific and general issues" was needed to prepare for a Bill in due course. A departmental enquiry would not be wide enough because the wider national interest should be represented, but a joint select committee "would be a forum worthy of the issues involved, though its membership [would] need to be carefully chosen. By adopting this course, the government would not be involved in a dogfight in Parliament itself, and get into 1902–1908 difficulties." It would also allow "the government to choose the best moment for introducing a Bill".

In a tactfully worded closing passage Butler noted, "the procedure suggested is designed to avoid trespassing too far on the ground of political or sectarian antagonisms just now, while yet providing a method of harnessing the spirit of the times to the cause of social reform. We should be showing the world that we have the urge and vitality, not only to save ourselves and civilization but also to build for the future."

The next day the Prime Minister replied revealing a much more limited approach to the board's work :

> It would be the greatest mistake to raise the 1902 controversy during the war, and I certainly cannot contemplate a new education Bill. I think it would be a great mistake to stir up the public schools question at the present time. No one can possibly tell what the financial and economic state of the country will be when the war is over.
>
> Your main task at present is to get the schools working as well as possible under all the difficulties of air attack and evacuation etc. If you can add to this industrial and technical training, enabling men not required for the army to take their places promptly in munitions industry or radio work, this would be most useful. We cannot have any party politics in wartime, and both your second and third points raise these in a most acute and dangerous form. Meanwhile you have a good scope as an administrator.[12]

"The Prime Minister's frigid reception" of the proposals was all the more galling because a fortnight before Butler had worked out with the Permanent Secretary, Sir Maurice Holmes, a timetable for their educational reforms leading up to a Bill in Parliament. Despite this setback he decided to disregard the Prime Minister's comments and go ahead with his plans. He was able to virtually complete his work within the timetable drawn up on the 1 and 2 September 1941. In any case with the whole educational world aroused by the Green Book he had little option but to see the major groups to discuss their reactions to the proposals.

The reason he was able to do this was because Churchill, absorbed with his plans for the war, saw his place as in the map room and at the conference table. He did not want to be bothered by schemes for reconstruction which he saw largely as a means of ensuring the people accepted the constant hardships of the war, such as stringent food rationing and virtual universal conscription of both sexes. Two aims characterized his wartime policies : first to maintain national unity with high morale, which was but a means to his second and main preoccupation—the determined prosecution of the war. To achieve the first he took into his government selected leaders of the 166 Labour MPs, the price of their co-operation being, as we have seen, the implementation of policies of reconstruction which they had waited years to introduce.

The government split into two working parties, one under Churchill concerned with the active prosecution of the war, the second under Attlee occupied with the domestic scene and reconstruction plans. As a generalization, the first was largely made up of Conservatives, but at times included Morrison (Home Office) and Bevin (Labour); while the second was mainly Labour in composition, but included Butler in charge of education. For the most part the day-to-day business of the Commons went on without the Prime Minister, except for a weekly session of questions.

It was possible in such a situation for a minister to go along on his own, each body thinking some direction was being given by the other. Butler described how this exceptional wartime situation allowed him to bypass the cabinet.[13] The preliminary deliberations "used to go before a body called the Lord President's Committee, but I must tell you that the greater part of the negotiations and preparation for this huge measure, which is still largely unimplemented—this shows the size of it—today, was done outside the cabinet, and outside the Lord President's Committee." He was thus able to have his draft for a Bill endorsed by the reconstruction group in the government, so that when he presented it to the war cabinet, particularly in the light of growing disappointment over the Beveridge proposals on reform of the social services, it had to be accepted and proceeded with.

Once the initial decision was taken to proceed there was the need to eliminate as many controversial subjects as possible to simplify negotiations over the main problem of the schools. The President initiated various bodies to investigate and report on the curriculum and examination system for secondary schools, the recruitment and training of teachers and youth leaders, the situation as regards the public schools and the State system of education, the organization and content of compulsory continuation education, the relationship of the universities and technical colleges, as well as establishing the Youth Advisory Council and a study group on school buildings.

This left the field for the investigation of school reform somewhat simplified and proceedings less likely to be disrupted by other contentious matters. There still remained plenty of highly charged issues to be clarified, for reform of the dual system of administering the schools was inextricably bound up with the completion of Hadow reorganization, the unsatisfactory state of the buildings, raising the school-leaving age and the provision of a legal code to remove the statutory muddle existing for the provision of higher education.

The main parties with an interest in the reshaping of the educational system show the confusion of competing pressures which could build up. First in size, because of its many schools, was the Church of England which wished to keep its schools but wanted assistance with its financial burdens, and was prepared to compromise to obtain this. There was a vocal extreme section of the Church which did not want to see their situation in any way weakened, but as they had no answer to the financial question they carried little weight in the final analysis. The Roman Catholic church wanted to keep their schools and were not prepared to compromise on this question. However they planned to obtain a more generous financial support for their schools from the central exchequer. The Free Churches hoped to end the church schools, but they felt most strongly about the areas where there was only a single school and that an Anglican one.

The professional interests, the National Union of Teachers and the administration bodies, preferred the end of the dual system because of its adverse effects on their professional work. The Trades Union Congress was all for the end of the dual system and a thorough rationalization of the educational system but they had many other problems which they considered more important. Naturally these views were reflected in the Labour party which, however, was sensitive to the fact that it relied on the large Roman Catholic vote. Neither the TUC nor the Labour party had a worked-out educational scheme and this was a neglect which was to cost them dear.

The power in the situation was with the Conservative Party with its traditional links with the Anglican Church and at that period it was still difficult to see one without the other. Thus in the last resort the Anglican interest would command the weight of the Conservative majority in the Commons, although of its 365 MPs 263 (72 per cent) had been educated at public schools, 29 (8 per cent) had passed through the grammar schools and none admitted to a mere elementary education. This educational bias probably accounted for the Conservative tendency to stress, in their discussions on education, moral training rather than the imparting of knowledge.

Meanwhile analysis of the comments received on the Green Book showed the various positions the main interested parties had taken up which allowed the President to see where he had to move to achieve a compromise. It revealed an area full of conflicting and emotionally charged interests, although the commitment to a written statement cleared much of the prejudice of its rhetoric.

First in order of importance, was the Church of England. The Archbishop of Canterbury, Dr Lang, wrote to Butler saying that he favoured the Green Book solution, especially for its provision for reserved teachers for denominational instruction. He was prepared to negotiate on the policies put forward. It was realized that he had to carry his Church leaders with him and they were by no means united in their position. A very different view was taken by a group led by the Bishops of Oxford and Gloucester, who saw the church schools as "a sacred trust" which should not be given up. They were against any relaxation of ecclesiastical control which would result from more State assistance, but they had no realistic suggestions as regards finance. There does not seem to have been any suggestion of reallocating funds to meet the needs of the schools. There was even a section of the clergy who proposed to hand over the schools to the State system and concentrate their limited finance on the training of teachers.

A different position was taken up by the Roman Catholic Church who also wanted to keep their schools, but were prepared to go to great lengths to pay for them. Its dedicated and disciplined clergy made fund raising part of the social life of their people which had enabled them to build churches and schools to transform an itinerant, drunken and violent peasantry into useful citizens.[14] The Church's teaching orders of nuns and brothers had staffed the schools and they were paid at full professional rates by the local authorities. Communal living with personal vows of poverty ensured these teaching orders could make a considerable financial contribution towards the upkeep of the schools. The Catholic aim was to obtain as generous a contribution as possible from the State towards the building and upkeep of their schools. Consequently in their reply to the Green Book they pleaded financial difficulties and made what was considered a "plea for further measures of public aid to non-provided schools without loss of facilities for denominational instruction".[15] They offered two solutions; the first an extension of the 1936 Act which provided 75 per cent of school building costs; second, the adoption of the Scottish settlement by which the State provided the schools and virtually all the running costs, handing them over to the Church to manage.

They knew they were in a strong position because they were prepared to finance their schools, so a realistic and unified campaign was mounted to win the largest contribution towards educational costs. Unmentioned but not forgotten were the tactics surrounding the Scurr amendment which in 1929 had wrecked the Labour government's education Bill and showed that the Church was not without resolute friends in Parliament. The Catholic system of deficit financing, by which each parish took on large mortgages and worked to pay them off, does not seem to have been appreciated by the board. A succession of senior clergy paraded their financial difficulties before the President in a series of meetings, the gist of which was that the Green Book solution was not generous enough and that the Roman Catholic church possessed "no hidden coffers". It had been anticipated that the Catholics would use the grants provided under the Education Act of 1936 as a precedent, but both Nonconformist Chuter Ede and the Permanent Secretary, Sir Maurice Holmes, opposed a temporary emergency being made the basis for a permanent solution. Butler was puzzled by the Roman Catholic intransigence and in his own personal notes made 21–25 November 1941 thought they were acting against their best interest in not accepting the Green Book solution. He considered the later settlement which they accepted was worse and this conclusion was to some extent confirmed by the Bishop of Pella at a meeting on 5 September 1942, although this is not universally accepted.

The third main religious interest was the Nonconformist Church. Its strength was based on communities often of great local importance and dedication, but being a federation of several interests it lacked unified leadership. During the nineteenth century it had been prominent in many progressive causes but with the development of working-class politics through the Labour party it had lost its place as the main organization for protest and action against repressive policies. Although it had lost the power to tear the country apart as it had done in 1902, its many links with the leadership of the trade unions and the Labour party made it an important pressure group. It would have liked to see the end of church schools and denominational teaching within the educational system. This was a view it shared with many secular bodies and sensing that it had a large backing in the country it was reluctant to agree to any extension of support for the Churches' educational efforts. Many Nonconformists had a traditional aversion to the Roman Catholics, although both faiths tended to appeal to the working classes and had many members active in Labour politics. On one matter they both felt very strongly and that was the existence of areas where there was only one school and that a church school, for these were usually Anglican schools in rural areas of some isolation. Although the resentment surrounding these situations was embroidered with longstanding local grievances, it was hardly a national issue.

The Green Book proposals promised continuation of the voluntary system and the bitterness which had surrounded the 1902 Act was recalled. Butler was warned that although the proposed solution was "most ingenious, [it] could not but lead to a head-on collision with the Free Churches". The Free Church Federal Council wrote to Sir Maurice Holmes[16] repudiating the Green Book settlement as they had always been "opposed to the continuation of the dual system and that therefore the committee cannot concur in its perpetuation". They also charged that "under the dual system it is impossible to attain complete equality". The Free Church leaders concentrated on destructive criticism showing a preference to leave the voluntary schools to their fate. As some 1,300,000 pupils were involved and there was already an outcry about the state of their education this was hardly a practical proposition.

A commanding figure in educational thinking on the Left was Professor R. H. Tawney, who was influential through his work in building up the Workers' Educational Association as well as his position in the Labour Party. Although he had been prominent in framing the Hadow Report on secondary education in 1926, which had then appeared very revolutionary, he does not appear to have moved from that position although there was already a small section in Labour circles advocating comprehensive or multilateral schools. By this time he was in his sixties and his dominance largely accounted for the unadventurous nature of Labour Party educational claims.

On the 5 September 1941, just before leaving for the USA on a teaching contract, he called on Butler at the education department to give his views on the Green Book.[17] He seems to have spent quite a large part of the interview in a harangue against the public schools, a topic on which Labour spokesmen spent much parliamentary and other time, without formulating any scheme to remove them. Tawney, who had been at Rugby, said he looked forward to public schools being absorbed into the grammar schools. He considered it essential the public school question should be tackled as he was "greatly impressed by class divisions in England which existed despite the war". He considered that "we were only continuing to fabricate, through our own educational system, the class struggle". In his note on the interview Butler wrote, "He glowered at me, and said I was responsible for doing this. He thought his proposal would avoid a clash which might otherwise occur."

Tawney was pleased with provisions to raise the school-leaving age but thought it should be sixteen, not fifteen. To

Butler's delight he considered Chapter I of the Green Book, which deals with reform of the school system as "good" and that "on the whole the Green Book was tolerably benign". He considered the percentage grant better than the block grant, as it led to increased effort on the part of the recipient. He saw "no fundamental objection to Day Continuation" which created "a great opportunity in education", and declared " 'I might for the first time be able to support the board,' which he had rejoiced in attacking". Butler noted, "I think it myself a pity that he is leaving us since, despite some of his observations, it would be intriguing to obtain his views from time to time". It was obviously a relief to find one potentially powerful critic disarmed.

Not only was the Left without a forceful lead on educational matters, they were faced with a dilemma over the dual system. Following the Nonconformist lead they were unconditionally opposed to the Anglican church schools with their historical association with the squirearchy and the right-wing interest. On the other hand, making use of the legal provision to develop their own schools in working-class areas were the powerful and well-organized Jewish and Roman Catholic communities, many of whose members were prominent in progressive left-wing movements. The rapidly growing Roman Catholic interest was particularly strong. The problem to be faced was how to preserve a traditional attitude to the Anglican schools while leaving the Catholic establishments not only intact but well supported.

The Workers' Educational Association was the institution through which many working people acquired an informed background which enabled them to assume political leadership of their own folk. WEA status in the pre-war left-wing movement was considerable. Among other things it offered a bridge between the intellectual and working-class divisions of the Labour movement.[18] The Association was early in the field attacking the dual system for its continued use of obsolete buildings. Most of these would be Anglican, for the Catholic schools were of later construction. They also felt the board's views were "inspired by too great a tenderness to the vested interests concerned, and too great attention to a small but vocal body of opinion which is not necessarily that of the parents and of the general public". Later in the meeting they compromised somewhat by suggesting a case could be made out for "one separate settlement with the Church of England" which could be led to "give up its schools without any question of 'compensation' of reserved teachers or otherwise". A different settlement should be reached with the Roman Catholics. The Association closed by repeating that they preferred to see the compulsion applied to both, if necessary, to achieve a settlement.

The powerful Trades Union Congress published its views on the Green Book under the title, "Memorandum on Education", in August 1942. It was a weighty document and had a wide circulation. In format it followed the arrangement of the Green Book and was moderate in its demands. On multilateral schools it urged the board to "undertake really substantial experiments in the way of multilateral schools", which would "greatly facilitate the transfer of children at thirteen plus". It dealt at length with the shortcomings of the dual system and pronounced that "however worthy it is in origins, it can no longer meet modern needs, [and] must not be allowed to hold up educational advance". It declared :

> denominational instruction of any kind should not be allowed in the State schools. All religious instruction should be in accordance with an agreed syllabus. The present system in the local authorities' schools, based on the Cowper-Temple clause, appears to have worked satisfactorily, and there is no apparent reason for departing from it. If the doors of the post-primary schools are thrown open to denominational teaching much confusion and friction will arise. The public school is not the place for denominational teaching. Let that rather be done in the home, in the Sunday school and in the Church.

To facilitate withdrawal, religious instruction should be given at the beginning or end of the school day.

Denominational schools should be placed on the same basis as private schools who would be subject to the ability of the denominations being "able and willing to bear the whole cost of their separate institutions". They wanted an end to the existing State policy of "You provide the school and we will keep it running", for they did not see why church schools "should be placed in any different category".

This was almost a statement of the Nonconformist line and

obviously made no concessions to the many Catholic trade unionists, who were not slow in raising their voices.

Another influential voice in educational reconstruction was the main professional association, the National Union of Teachers which, through the effect of wartime on the schools, was somewhat tardy in revealing its reaction to the Green Book. The teachers were understandably wary of government promises. They had borne the brunt of the recent débâcle of the evacuation of children and schools. The older representatives recalled too vividly the twenty years of government inaction over the Fisher Act of 1918 and several years of resented pay cuts. It took time to win their confidence. Basically the teachers found their professional area obstructed by religious issues; and their resentment over this was aggravated by "the all too frequent indiscretions of individual members of the cloth in references to council schools" and other educational matters.[19] They objected to the religious interests discussing the schools and planning without proper reference to the profession that operated them. The teaching profession was not concerned with the religious settlement but with what it saw as "the stake, being an educational advance for the children of the country", and it "writhe[d] when ignorant critics talked of the 'Godless Council School' ".

The National Union of Teachers' solution to the religious problem was a nationally agreed syllabus.[20] This was seen as clearing the way for accelerated re-organization of the schools. They realized the strength of the dual system and although they disliked it they were prepared to assist the formulation of a solid measure of reform which must be secured by legislation. The comprehensive nature of the Green Book proposals, especially when expressed later as a White Paper, attracted the teachers, for it promised them a considerable measure of freedom within their own sphere with a reduction in interference from outsiders. To win this they finally accepted a less complete dismantling of the dual system than they at first envisaged.

Sir Frederick Mander, the General Secretary of the union, considered the Church of England could be persuaded to accept an agreed syllabus of religious instruction,[21] but warned that "the real crux of the problem lay in the Roman Catholic schools" recalling "the tortuous course of the proceedings in the Trevelyan Conference of 1931," of which he had been a member. He drew attention to "John Scurr's subsequent triumph over the government in the House of Commons" with its inference that the Roman Catholic claims "cannot be sidestepped or evaded".

The union published their views in a pamphlet, "Educational Reconstruction", prepared for their Easter conference in 1942. It was generally anti-clerical in tone. They opposed the right of clergy to enter the schools, the abolition of the Cowper-Temple clause and considered religious instruction should be based on a nationally agreed syllabus which should be treated in schools like any other subject. Although this idea of a national syllabus intrigued the Prime Minister—he called it the "County Council Creed" and in a more florid moment "Zoroastrianism"—Butler considered it would savour too much of a State religion and nothing came of it. The teachers considered the local education authorities should assume the control exercised by the school managers so that non-provided schools would be in the same position as council schools. The sole exception should be that managers should have control of denominational instruction. Managers should be re-allocated, with four appointed by the foundation interest against six appointed in accordance with the Education Act of 1921. "Managers as a body should have the status not of principals, but as agents of the local education authority."

The various associations of local government came up with variations on the solutions put forward by the main pressure groups.[22] The Association of Directors and Secretaries of Education together with the Association of Education Committees recommended the end of "administrative dualism and all its harmful results", with the transfer of non-provided schools to the local authority. In discussion it was soon feared that the Roman Catholics would require to have full control of the staff while the Free Churches would oppose it because it would relieve the church schools of costs, for which they would have given up no material part of the control.

The County Councils Association advocated an extension of the Act of 1936, with the proviso that managers unable to raise 25 per cent of school costs should have to transfer the schools to the local authority.[23] The board were not anxious to encourage this solution as a measure to this effect had been defeated in the Commons. The education committee of the Association of

Municipal Corporations considered the Green Book solution inadequate to secure equality of opportunity. There should be more generous provision for both provided and non-provided schools. Moreover "if religious freedom is to be upheld, schools with a denominational 'atmosphere' must continue to exist alongside schools which are not attached to a particular denomination", and to make this existence possible a version of the Scottish system was advocated, by which the local authorities were responsible for the provision of schools which were run by denominational managers. Both these solutions, especially the latter, were welcomed by the Roman Catholic interest.

The most influential contribution from the local government bodies came from the meeting at the board with the deputation from the Association of Education Committees on 19 March 1942, in which two types of school were envisaged: the council schools and the "transferred schools" which were under local authority control.[24] The second type would have compensating rights to give denominational teaching to some or all the children. It was proposed that schools would not be able to contract out of the proposed transfer. Out of this meeting Chuter Ede developed an idea which became the basis of the proposals subsequently adopted in the 1943 White Paper. Briefly he proposed that there should be two options open to non-provided schools: the option to make themselves available for use as council schools, that is handing themselves over to the local authority; or, alternatively, they could accept a method of financing and control which was to be agreed and the same for all voluntary schools. The deputation was numerous and experienced, it found in the proposals much to be discussed with scope to finalize the details and advance towards agreement. The seeds of compromise had fallen on fertile soil.

The Department of Education had sounded all quarters of opinion by circulating the Green Book; and the book had served its purpose in making the main interests define their position, so it was then possible to see exactly the different view-points which had to be reconciled. The situation was no longer confused, although much involved. On the one hand the Trades Union Congress and the National Union of Teachers was supported by most of the local government associations in a wish to end the dual system. The Anglican leaders, perhaps prompted by the impending loss of their schools, were agitating for religious teaching extended to all schools. A demand which wartime uncertainties caused to be much supported. The Roman Catholics wanted an increase in State aid for their schools without sacrifice of control. The board also had certain guiding principles which it felt it must not contravene and they centred on the restriction of the religious controversy. This was not to be allowed to extend beyond the primary schools and even in that sector any increase of State aid was to be accompanied by further State control. There were also two measures which were seen to be necessary to obtain the co-operation of major interest groups. The Nonconformists required a realistic solution to the single school area situation and the teachers wanted an end to religious tests. The solution which was framed to meet this involved a situation which gave rise to what was known as the White Memorandum to differentiate it from the Green Book.

The plan in brief was for the local education authority to have overall control of the whole framework of schools with power to make decisions on organization, age range and closure of redundant schools under the supervision of the board. The council schools were no problem but the voluntary schools were given a choice. The first alternative was to transfer the school to the local authority, who would take over the running, and denominational religious teaching would cease. The owners would be entitled to use the school on Sunday or weekdays when not required for educational purposes. The second alternative was for managers to find 50 per cent towards required alterations and improvements, the remainder to be supplied by the State. Such managing bodies would then retain control of staff under local authority supervision as to suitability on educational grounds. Religious instruction would continue under the control of the managers.

In single school areas there was to be no choice; the school was to become local authority controlled. The Archbishop's Five Points were incorporated in the system with the extension of the Cowper-Temple clause to secondary schools. It was thought that the first alternative would be acceptable to the Anglicans, although they had perhaps hoped for more. The uncompromising terms for single school areas were particularly resented. The second alternative was designed to meet the needs of the Roman

Catholic situation and was also available for other interests, notably those Anglican congregations who wished to retain their schools.

At the first public discussion with the Association of Education Committees it was thought the plan had the basis of a national agreement.[25] The 50 per cent offer in the second alternative was seen as within the Roman Catholics' ability for fund raising, although probably too much for most Anglican congregations. The Association gave the White Memorandum its support. The Nonconformists were delighted with the proposed end of single-school areas and were prepared to compromise on the 50 per cent support for Roman Catholic schools. Chuter Ede considered this was because in most areas where there were Catholic schools there was a choice, so Nonconformist conscience was not involved. The National Union of Teachers relaxed their intransigent attitude to church schools as negotiations proceeded and they realized that there was in fact going to be a thorough reorganization of education.

The stumbling block to further agreement was the lack of Anglican acceptance for they regretted the loss of the Green Book offer.[26] As Lord Selborne put it, "the Church has only got five mingy points and was being made to give up all their schools". While the single-school-area proposals were attacked for applying "compulsion for the sake of unification would be neither equitable nor in accordance with our national heritage".

On the other hand the White Memorandum made many Church leaders see that they could no longer find the money for their schools and they were anxious to find acceptable terms on which they could be relieved of the financial burden.[27] A variety of solutions were proposed. The Bishop of Derby gave "whole hearted approval" to the memorandum, seeing the 50 per cent contribution as the chance to get rid of the worst of the church schools while the rest were retained; which was in fact what finally happened. He emphasized the importance of religious teaching in State schools where the bulk of the Anglican children were to be found. Instruction there should be "constructive" and "enlightened". Pursuing the same line the Bishop of London put forward a compromise suggestion by which church schools handed over to the local authorities should teach from an agreed syllabus to all the school, with certain days reserved for denominational teaching. Ardent Anglican advocates for school retention, through the Bishop of Woolwich, came up with a version of the Scottish solution by which the State paid school running costs and left the administration to the managers. It does not appear that this group made common ground with the Roman Catholics, although it would have strengthened their hand. It was the more active of these Anglican congregations which elected to operate the independent alternative primarily designed for the Roman Catholic situation.

In April 1942, William Temple, Archbishop of York, was appointed to the See of Canterbury, making him the leader of the Anglican church. His career had been a stormy one for he had dedicated himself to bringing his Church into the twentieth century.[28] Through a series of twelve memorable conferences in the 1920s concerned with Christian politics, economics and citizenship, he had widely publicized the application of Christian principles to all manner of problems ranging from the treatment of crime to international relations. His contribution to the modernization of British social policies is immense, for he had led a campaign to move the Anglican Church from its close identification with property and privilege to concern for the conditions of the people. It is doubtful if any other Anglican leader had the same status and vision. His appointment at this time was indeed fortunate for those working for an educational settlement, for it was rumoured another much fancied candidate had not been acceptable to the Prime Minister, leaving the selection open for Temple. On initially entering the negotiations he was not fully briefed and so allowed himself to be guided by his staff but, as he grasped that the vehemence of the Anglican rhetoric only served to mask an inability to provide for the schools on which they set such store, his attitude changed.

On the 3 June 1942 Archbishop Temple gave his maiden speech to the influential National Society, which from 1811 had provided Anglican schools.[29] In his own words he realized he faced a difficult task for he had on the one hand "to meet the Board of Education demands on educational reconstruction" but also he must "carry the diehards" of the society with him who objected to the White Memorandum. He carefully pointed out the weakness of their position and the need for tact in dealing with "the growing professionalism among teachers", which "is not only all to the good, but is something indispensable to education . . ." He spoke of the better understanding with Free Churchmen and "the astonishing approximation which has been growing among the theologians of all Christian communions". Over the single school area question he urged Anglicans to see the other point of view, saying, "I think a devoted Methodist, or Baptist, resident in a parish where there is only one, and that a Church of England school, has some grounds for complaint . . . for he must send the child to that school". In more belligerent mood, he would not have the Five Points balanced against the fate of the church schools; they had been drawn up for improving religious instruction in provided schools, on the assumption that church schools would remain. There was no question of a national syllabus, for that would inhibit development of the existing syllabuses, which were admirable in their way. In essence he stood by the dual system as it existed and he saw that based on three principles: "One is the content of the teaching itself, the syllabus, or Church Catechism; the second is the appointment of teachers; the third is the living association between the school and the Church." Of the last he said, "I do not see how that is to be provided in any way at all except through the maintenance of a body of managers constituted substantially as the managers are constituted now." The *Church Times* reported it as a fighting speech under a headline calling it "a trumpet call".

Its uncompromising tone prompted Butler to change his tactics.[30] Two days later, on 5 June, he met the Archbishop when he led a deputation from the National Society to the board's headquarters. The deputation included the Bishop of Oxford, the leading champion for the Church retaining its stake in the schools. Butler dwelt on the indifferent state of many Anglican schools, stressing the disparity of condition between the educational provision in provided and voluntary schools, rounding off his case with some damaging statistics. There were 10,553 voluntary schools, of which only 582 had been built since 1902. A further 288 had been rebuilt since that date, leaving 9,683 schools which were at least 40 years old. As regards the Hadow reorganization which dated from 1926, 62 per cent of provided schools had been reorganized, against 16 per cent voluntary schools. The black list of condemned schools drawn up in 1925 showed 731 were still in use nineteen years later; 543 of these, virtually 75 per cent, were church schools.

It was the turning point in the negotiations. Temple had not been unaware of a situation which did little credit to the Anglican support of their schools, for he had written to a friend about his speech to the National Society, "I was doing a rather elaborate egg dance, and some of the eggs are such that it was most important not to break, because the smell would be awful". Butler in a personal note on the meeting revealed that the Archbishop later admitted to him that the production of the damaging statistics made him realize for the first time "that the government were in earnest about educational reconstruction, and that he would have to do his best to wean his flock from their distaste at the White Memorandum and the alleged threat to their schools". Butler had successfully called the bluff without actually breaking the eggs in public, but it was very difficult to bring the import of the situation home to old-style church worthies often living comfortable sheltered lives in rural areas. The changing industrial scene with its concomitant need for educational advance was difficult for them to grasp.

Throughout the summer negotiations went on to persuade the National Society to come to terms. Archbishop Temple was several times in contact with Butler to try to work out arrangements which would make the two-choice basic settlement offered by the White Memorandum acceptable. Luckily both he and the President were men who understood the conservative Anglican element so they found they could work together, ministerial concession matching the Archbishop's conference difficulties. It was perhaps inevitable that there should be charges of a "backstage concordat" but both were reasonable men facing the facts of their situation. Butler knew that if only for the number of their schools he had to have Anglican agreement. If he failed to win their co-operation the resulting dissention would alert the ponderous Conservative parliamentary majority which would mean an end to any hope of legislation. Temple realized the sorry state of the church schools and the implications; with little prospect of doing anything about them without State assistance, unless a settlement was reached, they could only deteriorate still further.

The National Society, as the institution concerned with the

church schools, was the redoubt of reaction which had to be won over. By 4 September a further meeting with them at the board's headquarters reduced the unresolved difference to the matter of Anglican anxiety over relinquishing the right to appoint head teachers. This was left to the President and the Archbishop to devise a formula of consultation and the way was clear for the third offer for an agreed settlement.

This cleared the way for the circulation of the revised version of the White Memorandum, widely known as Plan III. It commenced with a statement that the aim was to modernize the whole national education system. It followed that the provision in voluntary schools must be in no way inferior to that in council schools. There would be a full completion of the Hadow reorganization, so that all education over the age of eleven would become genuinely secondary.

To achieve this voluntary schools were to be offered two alternative options: alternative one, handing the school over to the local authority to finance and administer; or alternative two where the managers could find 50 per cent of the costs of modernizing the schools, they could retain control on existing terms.

In alternative one, the local authority took over all financial costs both for alteration and improvements, as well as running costs. They assumed control of staff appointments, but would consult with the school managers before appointing head teachers. Religious instruction was to be given in accordance with an agreed syllabus, but two weekly periods were also available for denominational instruction for those children whose parents desired it. This would be given by "reserved" teachers appointed under the terms of the 1936 Act; no other teachers could be obliged to give religious instruction. The position of managers was to be worked out to put the foundation managers in a minority to the representative managers, the reversal of the existing situation. These concessions, made to make handing over schools to the local authority more acceptable especially taken in local context, gave the religious interests considerable residual say in the running of the school. It was this fact that enabled the board to weather the inevitable criticism which followed.

The autumn of 1942 brought a blossoming of claim and

counterclaim. It began with the public discussion on the Trades Union Congress's publication, "Memorandum on Education", which had already been presented to the board as the TUC statement of its position on educational matters. The annual congress at Blackpool passed a motion condemning the dual system outright despite Roman Catholic protests which continued up and down the country. The TUC saw "an overwhelmingly urgent necessity that young people should be fitted to be useful citizens in a free democracy" together with a need to expand technical education and "to throw open the doors of the universities as widely as possible".

In the same period the Conservative Party sub-committee on education issued its first report, called "Looking Ahead— Educational Aims", about half of which was concerned with religious teaching in schools, described as "in stern need of correction : that it must be a primary duty of national education to develop a strong sense of national obligation in the individual citizen, to encourage in him an ardent understanding of the State's needs, and to render him capable of serving these needs". There "must be the teaching of a national purpose, transcending all party interests". They presented a national ideal, not for "conquest or self profit", but "the ideal of the nation, as a leader among the nations—with which every child can identify in his own future, is the necessary first task of the national education in the United Kingdom". The quasi-fascist tone was even more noticeable in a second report dealing with the fourteen-to-eighteen age group.

These two opposing view points from different ends of the political spectrum gave plenty of cause for argument. The Church of England was in some turmoil and Temple had to work hard to make the agreement on Plan III a practical proposition; but the publication of Butler's damaging statistics on church schools finally won the day. A casualty of the settlement was the summary end of single area schools which once more caused Free Church protest which threatened to flare up with all its old lack of reason. In late September Butler started negotiations with the Roman Catholics who were to prove elusive but dogged opponents.

The scene was further activated by the issue of Plan III, which caused the main contestants to make a last flurry to try to improve their final position, all of which ploys Butler parried with great patience. The National Union of Teachers tried to force their case for a national syllabus for religious education in their wish to have the clergy finally out of the schools, but they were pacified with guarantees of no religious tests and safeguards that the agreed syllabuses should not in the future be "packed full of doctrine". The Welsh section of the Free Churches made a last threat of strenuous resistance and called for a separate settlement for Wales, which was firmly resisted on the grounds that the whole settlement was based on equality of treatment for all. The Anglo-Catholic Anglicans revived a claim for the Scottish system for church schools using the church press to good effect to publicize their case. Besides this there were many articles in the newspapers arguing for or against some portion of the proposed educational settlement.

In the midst of the splutterings of prolonged negotiation, Butler, with an assurance from Temple of the Anglican agreement to Plan III, felt he could ride out the storm and reach an agreement with the Roman Catholics. There was further encouragement when on 2 December the Beveridge Report on the wholesale reform of the social services was published and received with nationwide enthusiasm, which found response throughout the world. Butler on 18 December, with a nice sense of timing, reported his progress to the cabinet as "substantial approval of his scheme by all negotiating bodies, except the Roman Catholics; here the objection was not on doctrine or threatened liberties but on the financial implications". He was given authority to go ahead with drafting his Bill. In the changed political atmosphere his work was welcome because despite much talk on the future there were still no other plans for reconstruction ready for legislation, and there was growing concern among Labour MPs as well as in the country generally. The *Daily Mirror* cartoonist Zec exploited this with hard-hitting drawings which taunted the government and delighted millions of readers constantly, by referring to the lack of firm commitments to reform. (See page 308.)

Meanwhile Butler busied himself in the first half of 1943 with attempts to reach an understanding with the Roman Catholic hierarchy. In the early 1940s the Roman Catholic Church had a population estimated as between 2.5 and 3.5

millions, with 1,800 places of public worship. Although religious statistics are notoriously difficult to interpret, Catholicism, after the Anglican church, was the second largest single denomination in Britain. More important still, while the influence of most other faiths had been declining since the start of the century, Catholicism could point to substantial gains in its congregations and schools. These latter were central to their community and a Pastoral letter circulated in 1942 put the uncompromising Catholic view point: "We shall have our Catholic schools where our Catholic children shall be educated in a Catholic atmosphere by Catholic teachers approved by a Catholic authority. We cannot surrender our schools."[31]

There could be no acceptance of an agreed syllabus of religious instruction and so as a result the Catholic community saw itself "saddled with extra and crushing financial burdens" when they had already paid for education in their taxes.[32] The negotiations therefore centred on how much the Roman Catholic hierarchy could persuade the central authority to contribute to their educational expenditure. The board tried to find an authoritative negotiating body but only succeeded in seeing a succession of vigorously vocal bishops, who paraded their financial difficulties before the President in a series of meetings, the gist of which was that the offered solution was not generous enough.

Although there was considerable exchange of views in a cordial atmosphere, there was no confrontation of positions followed by haggling and a bargain made, as with the other interests. This was not for want of trying for, although, unlike the Anglicans with traditional links with the establishment and the backing of the parliamentary majority, the Catholics had no great institutional support, Butler would certainly have liked to seal the last major loophole in his agreement if only to ensure there would be no wild-cat tactics of the John Scurr type to overturn his carefully balanced bargain. He went to some length to investigate small increases in the grant and also to look into the possibility of a Scots-type administration for church schools. What he could offer was not enough and what was asked, if granted, would have resulted in the whole weight of the objections, which he had overcome in two years of negotiation, returning with renewed force with no prospect of being pacified a second time. So there were fair words but no binding agreement. It is likely that this was how the Catholic interest preferred it. For this way they secured at least the terms applicable to the Anglican schools, while still free to use whatever guerrilla tactics they could devise, and yet were able to claim, as Cardinal Hinsley said on the publication of the White Paper, that his Church had "at no stage agreed to the financial conditions now made public". So on 27 April 1943, when Butler reported the general acceptance to the War Cabinet with the Roman Catholic assent was noticeably absent.[33]

In view of the radical temper of the times the mildness of the progressives is remarkable. It was only in the latter stages of the negotiations that the Council for Educational Advance representing the Trades Union Congress, the Co-operative Union Education Committee, the National Union of Teachers and the Workers Educational Committee began to be heard advocating "a unified system of administration to replace the dual control of schools". But it was too late, for the bargain was already made to ensure continuation of church schools; although all that had happened was but the opening exchanges in a long debate.

The Bill The Whips Liked
July 1943–August 1944

Mr Gresham, a wealthy landowner, considerably influential in his own county, controlled the nomination of the local Parliamentary candidate. At a time when calls for reform were widespread and must be met, he mused on the choice of candidate :

"The Fletchers had always been good Conservatives, and were proper people to be in Parliament. A Conservative in Parliament is, of course, obliged to promote a great many things which he does not really approve. Mr Gresham quite understood that. You can't have tests and qualifications, rotten boroughs, and the Divine Right of Kings back again. But as the glorious institutions of the country are made to perish, one after another, it is better that they should receive the coup de grace tenderly from loving hands, than be throttled by Radicals.

"Mr Gresham would thank his stars that he could still preserve foxes down in his own country, instead of doing any dirty work —for let the best be made of such work, still it was dirty—and was willing, now as always to give his assistance, and if necessary to spend a little money, to put a Fletcher in Parliament and to keep a Lopez out."

Anthony Trollope *The Prime Minister,* 1875, Ch. 34.

RICHARD BUTLER MAY have thought he had his share of conflict in his negotiations, but all was not sweetness and light elsewhere in the government : in the Commons the strains of the uneasy coalition were obvious and increasing. For some 25 years there had been a demand for better social support facilities to ease the lot of the wage earners, but this had been consistently evaded or, where the issue had been forced, minimized, as in the case of the Education Act of 1936. The total mobilization of the 1940s called on all to make great efforts, accept hardships, shortages and dangers. This was widely accepted with astonishing cheerfulness, but at the same time there was ample evidence of rising concern for the future.

The situation was clearly demonstrated in the House of Commons which had been elected in 1935 when Baldwin had used his considerable charismatic and political skills to obtain 431 out of the 615 seats. It was estimated that half of the majority group were from aristocratic families, and no less than 127 directly held or were closely connected with hereditary titles. Over 70 per cent of the Conservative MPs had been educated at major public schools.[1] This unrepresentative section of the national community had been elected by some 11.8 million votes, 54 per cent of the vote giving 70 per cent of the seats. Against this Labour had polled 8.5 million votes (38.6 per cent) to win 158 seats, while the Liberals gained 1.4 million votes (6.4 per cent) to take 21 seats. This meant the main opposition parties had 45 per cent of the poll but occupied only 29 per cent of the parliamentary seats. It was this situation which led political wits to point out the aptitude of a government poster issued at the start of the war. It read: "YOUR courage, YOUR cheerfulness, YOUR resolution, will bring US victory." Up to the early stages of the war the Conservatives were able to show a 50 per cent support on Gallop polls, but in December 1943 this had shrunk to only 27 per cent of the electorate, while Labour claimed a 40 per cent support. This situation remained until the election of 1945 gave the opportunity to change the government. It is against this background that concern for reconstruction must be seen as the growing issue in domestic politics even while the war continued.

The interwar years had been notable for bitter social conflict between the opposing interests which was clearly apparent in the MPs each side returned. It was even easily visible for the Conservatives were noticeably taller and Labour members sometimes fainted from underfeeding.[2] Many of the latter came from manual working backgrounds and had spent much of their lives in poverty. Their education was for the most part confined to the State system. Although the average age of all MPs was nearly sixty in 1943, in contrast to a national average of forty-five, the Labour representatives were older than their Conservative opponents. This was because their passage into parliament

had often been through several years of union activities, demanding some dedication and personal sacrifice. An interest in social
reconstruction was central to Labour's political philosophy.[3]

By their anecdotal evidence Labour MPs were of limited
education. They seemed to accept without question that there
should be a two-tier system of secondary education and this
probably stemmed from the widespread malnutrition and poor
cultural background of many families of manual workers. Those
associated with religious, trade union and political interests had
some access to a wider culture and such families formed a
working class élite, which because of their own hard won success,
tended to back selection systems. Many Labour MPs were from
such backgrounds.

Working-class views on education were conditioned by personal experience and ran on lines which saw the need for
the basic skills of letter and number, such as the primary
schools provided. Secondary education had to be utilitarian
and in this thinking was conditioned by long-standing unemployment. They saw the woman's place as in the home which
meant little support for nursery schools. They favoured training
in domestic skills for girls. Further or higher education meant
several years without contribution to the family budget. The
main college-type education they knew about was teacher-
training and that entailed a grant which had to be repaid.
Assistance for university places did not cover maintenance and
required considerable support from the family, even if the
student could live at home. As a consequence of these economic facts they saw suitable secondary education for an able
boy from a manual working background not as Latin and the
arts subjects but as a grounding in technical drawing and
experience with workshop tools. The realistic objective was
apprenticeship to a well-paid and valued craft. A few brighter
boys and girls looked for typing, short-hand and book keeping,
which some schools covered but were generally available in
evening classes. Certificate success in these subjects would enable
a youngster to obtain the coveted security of an "office job".
Coming from such backgrounds the views of Labour MPs on
education tended to be limited.

In contrast the Conservatives, many with influential family
connections, had mainly been educated outside the State system

at the major public schools and the older universities. Their arrival in Parliament had often been eased by their ability to pay all their election expenses amounting to between £400 and £1,200, as well as subscribing annually between £500 and £1,000 to the local party association. This would ensure the employment of a competent agent, so such affluent candidates were usually quickly accepted by safe seats. In this way through long association many seats were virtually the pocket boroughs of certain well-placed families. In Parliament such Members were interested in the departmental work of the Foreign Office, the Treasury, agriculture and the armed services. Their only interest in the social services was in keeping costs low. Understandably in debates on social matters the feelings of the two major parties were markedly different and exchanges were often bitter. Some Labour MPs found it difficult not to make reference to the favoured background and education of their opponents.

At the start of the war an uneasy political truce was made and the opposition agreed to an extension of the existing electorate's rule rather than accept the division of an election which was due in 1940. After an uneasy start a coalition government emerged under the leadership of Winston Churchill. This was not a national choice but at the instigation of senior members of the Conservative Party. Indeed Churchill was much disliked in some quarters for his political tactics when out of office, but most of all for his ruthless suppression of the General Strike in 1926. The war had given him a new lease of life and, on the resignation of Neville Chamberlain on 10 May 1940 with the Labour Party pledge to serve under a new Prime Minister, Churchill emerged as the wartime leader. He consolidated his government by nominating Labour leaders to head key departments. This removed any focus for opposition; and by the inclusion of Bevin to mobilize labour and Morrison to run the Home Office, ensured the co-operation of the trade unions and the lower-paid workers.

In return for Labour's co-operation there was the promise that reconstruction should go ahead, and as an earnest of this Arthur Greenwood was included in the cabinet as minister without portfolio with special responsibility for reconstruction. Through the extension of hire purchase in the late 1930s radio had become generally available, and Churchill discovered that his peculiar style of oratory "came over" to such good effect that in a short time he had established himself as the supreme figure in the country. For years he had been in the political wilderness and he could see that if the precedents of the Boer and 1914–18 wars meant anything he would be able to hold an election at the end of the war to return him as the post-war premier. Economics had defeated him when he had been the Conservative Chancellor of the Exchequer 1924 to 1929 and this had been the cause of his political isolation. As his position became more secure his attitudes to reconstruction plans hardened for he did not want to commit the post-war government to specific policies and great expenditure. Reconstruction plans began to materialize with the Scott, the Uthwatt and Barlow reports which pointed to the need to envisage planning on a large scale. This would involve sweeping controls for demolition and the redevelopment of large areas with the construction of a large number of houses and factories. Nationalization of land was discussed. Such a challenge to property rights was not acceptable to the Conservatives and finally, as a protest at the lack of progress he had been able to make, Arthur Greenwood resigned in February 1942. The uneasy coalition government was badly strained, for there had been no lack of voices which had denounced it, warning it was but a device to prolong the control of an unpopular governing interest.

Meanwhile, both in Parliament and in the country, there was growing frustration at the slowness of the development of reconstruction plans and the absence of firm pledges for the future. The publication of the Beveridge report in December 1942 brought the matter to a head. On every side the idea of personal security "from the cradle to the grave" was being seriously discussed, while the government remained noticeably silent. This focused the unrest on this topic so that reaction to the report "became the test of allegiance to the future or the past, and those who were 'for' were in no mood to listen to qualification or doubts'.[4]

Churchill pointedly ignored the report and the Labour party became more critical at the delay in reform. A few days later Butler, with a nice sense of timing, on 18 December had presented his proposals for an Education Bill which, with the backing of Ernest Bevin and the support of the Labour party, was allowed to go forward. In February 1943 Bevin put his Catering Wages Bill before the Commons in an attempt to give some measure of protection to an industry largely run on casual labour. When he had been brought into the government to mobilize the labour of Britain Bevin had been given powers which were virtually dictatorial; but in this modest reform he found the Conservative majority blocking his progress and questioning his integrity. In a magnificent moment he rounded on his critics, reminding them, "You have trusted me since 1940 with powers and never questioned my exercise of them. If you have never questioned me in ordering millions of people about the country, why do you question my integrity in appointing a commission now for this purpose? Am I good only for one purpose and not another?"[5]

These exchanges involving the man who, through his trade union leadership, was after Churchill the most influential man in the country, showed the coalition threatened by open rupture. The Prime Minister could no longer ignore public opinion. Early in March he gathered his material, assembling departmental drafts as the basis of a radio script, which he dictated in his car while motoring from Chequers to Dytchley Park and back.[6] The broadcast on 21 March 1943 was a masterly performance in which he admitted his purpose was to stifle party controversy in order to concentrate the nation's energies on winning the war, but at the same time he sketched out a four-year plan for economic recovery and social reform. It was a cleverly designed soporific to appeal to middle opinion and avoid committing the government to anything more than preparatory work on plans which would only become effective after the war was over.

The calm did not last long and it became apparent that if the government coalition was to continue there would have to be at least one measure of reconstruction put into effect. There were three main areas where widely discussed reform plans required legislation. The first was concerned with urban replanning and the provision of a large amount of housing which involved sweeping powers over sites and property with obvious application in many towns. The opposition of propertied interests was understandable. The second was the implementation of the

Beveridge report which implied a complete restructuring of the
health and welfare services, including the abolition of the Poor
Law based policies. It was obviously expensive and far reaching
in its extension of the social services. The third area was covered
by the Butler Education Bill, which commanded much popular
support. It was a carefully defined limited measure formulated
by an experienced Conservative minister which followed well-
known patterns. Its costs had been kept as low as possible. It
avoided controversial subjects like the public schools and the
extension of the social services for children, the case for which
had been established by the Women's Group On Public Welfare
report, "Our Towns—A Close up". It could be counted on to
involve the greater part of the community, for it concerned
religious and local authority interests. There was reason to
believe that these interests, through patient consultation and
compromise, were at least reconciled to the measure. It was a
comprehensive piece of reconstruction and the Labour interest
wanted it.[7]

The government whips, who had begun to despair of their
task of preserving at least a show of unity, saw it as a measure
commanding a wide range of moderate support from both
sides of the House whilst still providing much material for
discussion. It was just the topic to keep Parliament occupied in
the tricky period following the Beveridge report and obviously
worth a lavish allocation of parliamentary time.

Consequently the government Chief Whip, the Hon. James
Stuart, the architect of Churchill's control of Parliament, was
delighted with the length and complexity of the proposed Education Bill. To make the most of the single reconstruction measure
which the government agreed to back it was decided to take the
whole of the discussion to the floor of the House, which threw
the debate open to all MPs and protracted the proceedings over
a year. The more usual practice with such a measure would be
to take the Bill "upstairs" to a committee of about 60 Members.
This would have shortened the procedure so that the Bill could
have been processed in a month or six weeks; but Churchill
wished to have some reconstruction measure occupying Parliament so that he could silence his critics.

Despite the wide discussions that had taken place the war
cabinet decided not to go ahead with framing legislation, but

first to issue a White Paper to further test public reaction and hold full-scale debates on the issues involved. No doubt there was some apprehension about religious differences, but the issue of a White Paper just before the summer recess with full two-day debates in both Commons and Lords, ensured that a reconstruction measure could be discussed throughout the country during the parliamentary recess. When Parliament reassembled in the autumn the text of the resulting Bill would again attract attention and this would be followed by protracted discussion of its many clauses. Butler, conscious of the frailty of his agreements, would have preferred an early Bill.

Accordingly "Educational Reconstruction" was published in July 1943 and allocated two days for debate, the 29 and 30 July, an unusually liberal allowance of parliamentary time for a White Paper, which ensured the issues raised were kept simmering until October. In the text two styles of writing are blended, the technical survey of education side by side with appeals to advocates for reform to accept its possibilities. Above all it attempts to suit all interests. This is apparent in the Janus style of the opening passage which declares the aim of the reorganization is :

> to secure for children a happier childhood and a better start in life : to ensure a fuller measure of education and opportunity for young people and to provide means for all of developing the various talents with which they are endowed and so enriching the inheritance of the country whose citizens they are. The new educational opportunities must not, therefore, be of a single pattern. It is just as important to achieve diversity as it is to ensure equality of educational opportunity. But such diversity must not impair the social unity within the educational system which will open the way to a more closely knit society and give us strength to face the tasks ahead.

Although the proposals were largely a reorganization of the existing facilities it was announced that "the government propose to recast the national education system. The new layout is based on the recognition of the principle that education is a continuous process conducted in successive stages." This began with an adequate provision of nursery schools for children before the age of five wherever they were needed. The school-leaving age was to be raised to fifteen without exceptions as soon as possible after the war, with a subsequent extension to sixteen as circumstances permitted. The completion of Hadow reorganization was to be carried out to provide "well designed and equipped primary schools" for all children up to the age of eleven. This stage was to be followed by true secondary education, "of diversified types but of equal standing" for all children. Two sentences condemned the policies of the interwar years and endorsed the progressive movement. "At the primary stage the large classes and bad conditions, which at present are a reproach to many elementary schools, will be systematically eliminated; at the secondary stage the standard of accommodation and amenities will be raised to the level of the best examples. The provision of school meals and milk will be made obligatory."

Religious instruction was to become an essential element of education. The voluntary schools were to be brought up to standard, so that they could play a full part in the national development of education. After full-time education there was to be compulsory part-time education in working hours for all up to the age of eighteen, together with proper facilities for technical and adult education. A considerable extension of the services for the health and physical well-being of children and young people would be provided. A system of inspection and control of all independent schools would raise standards. Local educational administration would be reorganized to accord with the new arrangements. As part of plans to improve conditions and raise standards there was to be a gradual decrease in the size of classes. In the secondary schools there was to be an end of the special-place system and entry would be by merit only. Beyond the secondary schools there was to be an expanded youth service together with an improvement in facilities to enable poor students to attend universities. There was to be reform in the recruitment and training of teachers.

This bold sketch of wholesale educational reform attracted little adverse criticism and much praise, although it was noted to be "regrettably inexplicit". Only in left-wing publications was there a tendency to question what was implied. Many recalled that the Fisher Education Act of 1918 had covered much the same ground and Harold Laski voiced these doubts when he said, "I fought, the Prime Minister can say, to give you victory over your enemies : I made no pledge that I would lay my hand to the construction of a new social order."[8] He noted Mr Butler's fine claims for his White Paper adding, "it is not cynicism but, in the light of history, no more than a wise precaution to remember how little was left of the Fisher Act after the Geddes Axe had hacked at its clauses". The *New Statesman*[9] noted that in "judging Mr Butler's plan we have to bear in mind that he puts it forward as a leading Conservative, in very close touch with his party machine, as a minister of a coalition government which is trying to avoid controversial issues, and as an 'old school-tie' Christian gentleman" who still has "plenty of scope for doing new things without antagonizing the bulk of his party—provided he lets the vested interest in class education pretty much alone". But even this critic granted that when he judged the proposals against what he would like to see they came out "pretty well".

The parliamentary discussion on the White Paper produced evidence of the handicaps the children of the manual workers suffered in their education. Anecdotal evidence, mainly from Labour MPs, made a graphic case for reform. One teacher Member told of an old man going into the school "and pointing to a long desk, said, 'I sat there sixty-five years ago, and my grandchild is sitting there today' ". He recalled "when the education of the country children had been openly sneered at".[10]

Another revealed he was "one of five survivors of a family of 21. The five of us have had children who had won scholarships in the County of London. But the tragedy has been that each one of us has been compelled through economic circumstances to take away our children from further education and put them to work on the labour market in order to bring some measure of support and income to the family to keep the home going."[11] There was one suggestion which, if taken up, could have changed the whole face of British education, when Sir Harold Webbe recommended attention to the Cambridgeshire village colleges where "all the social and educational activities of the whole area are concentrated in one spot"[12] with all the community sharing the facilities, swimming pools, playing fields, library and class rooms, both for day and evening courses. It was thirty years later before this formula was widely advocated.

As the discussion progressed the three main areas of dispute —none of them educational—became apparent. First was the dual system, the difficulties of which the President outlined with some frankness in his opening speech.[13] He described how he had hoped to find a formula to end the dual system, but denominational opinion of more than one faith had insisted that their children should be at school among " 'Church members'; that the whole staff should be practising members of the body of the Church, so that children passing from class to class should never leave the atmosphere of the faith". Although he had the greatest respect for their attitudes as a minister responsible to Parliament he had to meet all interests, and the best he could offer them was a second alternative for their schools which was "more generous . . . than had ever been put forward before". If he went beyond this he would not only have perpetuated the dual system, but also "have alienated beyond recall certain partners in the field of education who are indispensable, namely the authorities, the Free Churches and the teachers. Therefore I have not been able to concede the full demand of those who desire complete liberty of conscience." This speech was much reported and commented on in the religious press, not always with the fairness it deserved.[14]

Roman Catholic spokesmen in both Houses urged their cases with well-reasoned arguments for the adoption of the Scottish system. The Anglo-Catholic interest followed the same line of argument. A surprise turn to the religious pressure groups' campaign came when the Archbishop of Canterbury speaking in the Lords[15] asked for the 75 per cent grant made in 1936 to be renewed, and in those areas where 80 per cent of the local population signified a wish for denominational schools these should be provided. These were suprising proposals in view of his general good-will towards educational reform. However he wished to see if concessions were possible on the first point and in the latter was forestalling a more disastrous amendment by one of the extreme Anglicans in the Lords.

The second area of dispute—the abolition of the Part III areas, the minor educational authorities—was the subject of much vocal support for individual Part III areas, invariably the speaker's own constituency. The tone was set by a Member in the opening exchanges of this general discussion who claimed:

"A place like Barry must have its full control of elementary, and indeed higher education".[16] At that period Barry had less than 40,000 inhabitants. But, as with the third topic which attracted much questioning—the alleged inadequacy of financial help from the Exchequer—the impression is speakers were on the feet with their constituencies in mind. They wanted an account of their speech in the local paper, perhaps with a column of editorial endorsement. The House was well aware it had been sitting for eight years and an election could take place at any lull in hostilities.

The mild temper of the exchanges, which were nearly always accompanied by endorsement of the general line of reconstruction, was a far cry from Bevin's tigerish anger. As the education question involved the two insoluble issues of local government and religious rivalry in a context which promised to be constructive the Whips were delighted. Senior Labour Members, Creech Jones and Arthur Greenwood, were full of praise for the White Paper. The latter said :

> This discussion is of great significance because I think it is the first time in the history of education that we have had a two days' debate on the subject, in which everybody could think aloud and where the government might be expected to listen to what has been said. I would hope that after the debate closes today, the government will bear in mind what has been said. The advantage of this new technique, this procedure of a White Paper committing nobody to anything to be followed, if the Government are wise, by legislation which takes account of what has been said in the House, is considerable.[17]

The success of the first tactical moves by which the Conservative majority conceded an Education Act in order to hold up radical reform in other sectors could hardly have been more complete. It was to be the only measure of major reconstruction achieved by the wartime coalition government.

Although the White Paper gave peace to the Government it sparked off antagonisms among the religious interest groups. The intemperate outbursts, although they reflected the wishes of the sections they claimed to represent, were mainly the work of extremists who did not comprehend the overall situation, nor realize the strength of the forces which had made compromise possible.[18] While most of the exchanges took place in the religious press with a limited circulation, the general press reported the more explosive passages, which did not further the public image of the Churches. Nevertheless the articles must have caused some distress to leaders who had struggled with their consciences and worked hard to make the best settlement they could for their denominations.

The Archbishop of Canterbury as the instigator of the Anglican agreement to the settlement had been a target of attack, especially since his address in October 1942 calling on the Church Assembly to accept some variation of the Butler offer. After the publication of the White Paper he went out of his way to rally moderate opinion to appreciate the vision and generosity of the settlement, with evident success. There were signs of Anglican willingness to hand over their schools on the terms offered, and the Bishop of Chelmsford warned against sectarian strife because the main issue was "not whether the people of England will be Anglicans or Nonconformists, but whether they will be Christians or nothing at all".[19]

The Anglo-Catholics led by the Bishops of Oxford, Gloucester and St Albans made common ground with the Roman Catholics in condemning the retention of the Cowper-Temple clause against denominational teaching in State schools and the use of agreed syllabuses. This last was seen as "disembodied Christianity" made up into "a synthetic article" which was but "an artificial product of politicians". The Anglo-Catholic movement centred its attacks on Archbishop Temple and the National Society. It invited support for a newly-formed body, the Church Education League, described as "a spontaneous movement of unofficial Church people who are profoundly dissatisfied with the leadership of the educational mandarins, officially recognized by an ecclesiastical bureaucracy", which aimed at securing denominational instruction for Anglican children attending county schools and to obtain a higher exchequer grant towards the reconstruction of existing church schools.[20] They continued to be vocal but as the official Church leadership had accepted the settlement there was little they could do.

There were other rumblings which warned of the precarious nature of the settlement.[21] The National Union of Teachers did not like the paragraph relating to denominational instruction in some local authority schools. The Trades Union Congress declared its intention to press for a satisfactory solution of the single school areas, but added that unless the final compromise was quite unacceptable there would be no question of using its influence to defeat the whole Bill. This generous proviso made in a letter to *The Times* on 7 September had sedative effects, stimulating no doubt a letter in the same paper on 25 November in which the two archbishops and the Free Church leaders made a similar declaration that any modifications they may urge would be suggestions only subject to the overriding condition that they did not imperil the settlement. This expression of confidence was of great value to Butler by strengthening his hand in dealing with the Roman Catholics and also countering the lack of support which he was receiving from his own party.[22]

The only major denomination outside the national educational settlement, the vigorous Roman Catholic community, was united in its opposition to the offers open to their schools. They were alone in their fight as neither of the major parties could accommodate this position within their policies. The Conservatives largely followed the Anglican lead, while Labour approximated to the Nonconformist line. The Catholics had a few spokesmen in the Lords, a handful of able speakers in the Commons and their own press, but their greatest asset was the singlemindedness of their community. From the hierarchy through the parish priests to the members of the congregation : they had a clearly defined objective : the control of the education of their children from first to last. In contrast to the Anglo-Catholics who were defending nineteenth-century schools and trust deeds, the Catholics saw themselves fighting for a living community. At one stage the offer was made to hand over to the State virtually everything only insisting that, although the local authority selected the staff, all appointments were filled by practising Catholics.

Many of the congregation had their origins as Irish peasantry or as labourers in industrial England or Scotland, with ample justification for distrust of English politicians. A few days after the White Paper parliamentary debates on 6 August an article by Archbishop Amigo expressed this feeling by saying,

"They speak very nicely, but I fear we shall get precious little out of them".[23] On the 24 August the Catholic hierarchy issued a statement enumerating the constructive proposals put to the Board of Education and concluded with: "Our people will stand united and determined in what to them is a matter of life and death. They must use every available means to make the justice of their claims widely known and completely understood."[24] The Apostolic Delegate Monsignor Godrey, passed on to the hierarchy of bishops a message from His Holiness the Pope congratulating them on the firm stand they had taken, and encouraged them to regard the issue of the church schools as a vital one.[25]

The campaign already being waged escalated[26] as all members of the Roman Catholic Church, clergy and parents, both at home and overseas, bombarded their MPs and the appropriate government departments with letters. Catholic trade unionists were vocal in their cause among their fellows. Catholic organizations and press carried on a crusade in support of their schools. In the main industrial cities mass meetings and demonstrations were held, while all over the country Roman Catholics made a point of raising the question at all meetings where the White Paper or other educational matters were being discussed. The laity formed the Catholic Parents Association. The campaign was organized through district councils which coincided with parliamentary boundaries so that pressure was brought to bear on individual MPs through letters, leaflets and personal visits. The impact on MPs was considerable, especially as some of the material they received was not couched in the usual diplomatic terms and even included some threatening letters. Some Members were concerned in claiming justice for a large minority, which was also a considerable political force in a number of constituencies. Others were irritated by various aspects of the campaign and one spoke disparagingly of "all these pathetic stories about collecting halfpennies from little school children".[27]

There were other signs of reaction especially from Nonconformist spokesmen who threatened to react in kind to what was considered an unjustified and intemperate campaign. Sir Frederick Manders, the General Secretary of the National Union of Teachers, speaking at a stormy Essex meeting warned the campaign was causing "such a wave of feeling . . . that all

your non-provided schools may be swept away altogether!"[28]
On the eve of the publication of the Education Bill *The Times*
of 10 December urged moderation so that the government
would continue with its plans for reconstruction, for difficulties
could cause abandonment with the result that "not only are the
non-provided schools unlikely to survive long, owing to financial
difficulties, but the public will have been so alienated that the
result will be secularism in the schools of this country as in most
of the Dominions and the United States. The time for a settlement is now or never."

The administrative unity of the Catholic hierarchy was disrupted by the illness and death of their leader, Cardinal Hinsley.
This hiatus left the bishops with divided counsels. In 1936 the
then acting leader, Archbishop Downey of Liverpool, had won a
long fight against the Protestant dominated Liverpool council's
refusal to finance his schools. To compensate for the long years
of neglect caused by this discrimination he had received a preferential settlement allowing grants up to 75 per cent of school
costs. He was unconvinced that these terms could not be
extended to Catholic schools throughout the land. As the President could not move beyond 50 per cent without upsetting his
agreements with those interests that wished to see all church
schools closed, attempts at compromise led nowhere.

Meanwhile Butler still tried to locate some negotiating body
to find out what could be the basis of an agreement.[29] Eventually, early in September, he had a more fruitful meeting with
Archbishop Williams of Birmingham, who confirmed a belief he
had made from previous meetings that there was considerable
anxiety over the provision of new schools. This was of importance to the Catholic community because the large local authority rehousing plans between the wars had cleared many of their
congregation out of the central slum areas to new housing estates
on the outskirts of the towns. They were thus faced with a massive rebuilding programme to provide new schools in these
areas. This had been vigorously commenced with a foresight no
other religious denomination had shown. It had been a great
drain on their funds and they felt justified in demanding more
help from the State. Butler was able to convince the archbishop
that the Education Bill based on the White Paper would
become law, no doubt describing the political facts surrounding

the measure, and ended with a warning on the dangers of anti-Catholic feeling resulting from their agitation. In Butler's own minute of the meeting, "I said that I was quite certain that the Bill would be passed and that his agitations would then be left high and dry".

This produced later in September, a meeting with the seven northern bishops at Ushaw College near Durham, at which Butler, by now aware of the Catholic psychological use of pageantry, brought along for support Chuter Ede and Sir Maurice Holmes.[30] He sketched in the historical background to the situation to the bishops and expressed a personal opinion that if they could accept this settlement they could achieve more advantageous terms "within another generation". The alternative was to stay outside the present negotiations and if the existing agitation continued much harm could accumulate to their cause. Despite a calm exchange of views there was no let-up in the Roman Catholic campaign which Butler no doubt feared could spark off the whole religious controversy he had worked so patiently to damp down.

The next month the President met the hierarchy and discussed their financial worries.[31] Bishop Marshall of Salford proposed a ceiling to their costs as a means of allaying fears of increasing prices, the exchequer meeting expenses over the ceiling. A figure of £15 per place was suggested which Butler rejected as too low, and although this was further investigated nothing came of the suggestion. The possibility of the transfer of concessions from an existing school place to a new school built as the result of official planning was also discussed; this was later accommodated in the final Act. The President looked for further means of assisting the Catholic interest so that they could be included in the settlement, thus removing the major danger of a breakdown before the measure could be made law.

The Education Bill was presented to the House of Commons on the 15 December 1943 and although it followed the White Paper closely it included calculated concessions to the religious interests. Among these the Bill contained an authorization to transfer school places from an old to a new school, as requested by the Roman Catholics. There was also a provision to allow agreed syllabus teaching in single area schools to please the Nonconformists. In similar vein, denominational teaching could be provided to aid small church schools accept "controlled" status under the local education authority, so assisting Anglicans to accept the hand-over of schools they could not afford.

The Times of 17 December gave the Bill high praise "as a masterpiece of compromise and an inspiring embodiment of educational advance".[32] There was general support from both the Anglican and Nonconformist leaders, who having travelled so far were now determined that the settlement they had achieved should not be lost. They set about reassuring their followers by public meetings in which they shared platforms to explain the benefits of the Education Bill.

The Bill was a long and involved measure. The original draft of 111 sections attracted over 1,000 amendments, of which 340 were debated. About a third of these, 114 motions, were accepted into the framework of the final Act lengthening it to 122 sections. Although many of these were important to some section of the educational interest none of them materially altered the basic line of the Bill which was one of careful concession so framed that expenditure should be moderate and the timing of the advances should remain with the government. Butler resisted all attempts to tie down promise of improvements by including dates for commencement or detailed items of equipment to be provided or similar binding clauses which a number of MPs sought to have included in the Act.

It was inevitable that such a wide measure affected a large variety of interests, so Butler and Chuter Ede agreed when each should carry the brunt of the argument. In general the President handled the Anglican and Conservative interest with bland but firm tact, yet always appearing somehow when pressed to find a small concession; but on the basic principles of the Bill, on the few occasions when forced to stand firm, he did so. The Parliamentary Secretary, secure in his party's backing of the Bill, dealt with the more awkward Labour spokesmen, as well as the Nonconformists, besides handling the educational issues. Both were experienced House of Commons men well respected by all parties, Butler for his stand on the India Act and Chuter Ede for his personal sincerity. They were both able speakers, Butler perhaps pedestrian in style, but his logic was always formidable; while Chuter Ede had a pert turn of phrase which could drive home a telling point without causing resentment. Despite their combined skills the debate was not an easy one, although, as it turned out, the realities of political power meant the Bill was never vulnerable; indeed it was this fact which made difficulties.

By this time Winston Churchill had established an unprecedented domination over the country and Parliament. His radio broadcasts created a persona which the mass media built up into a shrewd, colourful, swashbuckling character, who, after the colourless figure who had recently occupied the leadership, caught the imagination of the people, so that he became a legend in his own lifetime. By the start of 1944 the war was beginning to swing against the Axis powers and Churchill was deeply involved in the preparation of the Second Front which finally took place in the first week of June. Except for a weekly session of questions, the Prime Minister did not usually take part in parliamentary business and his cursory treatment of some matters, especially where reconstruction was concerned, caused resentment, and he was accused of arrogance as well as flouting the authority of Parliament. There were repeated promptings for action on the several shelved reports which showed the results of years of neglect.

Early in the war it had been deemed politic to create the impression of a vigorous and lively democracy, although the massive government majority, the Defence Regulations and virtual universal conscription made this something of an illusion. A number of MPs were on the reserve list of the services and were given leave of absence from the House of Commons. This was then extended for other duties until some 200 Members were absent. This removed certain obstinate reactionaries and evened the numbers with the opposition somewhat, although a Conservative majority still remained in the House. On occasion the so-called "ticket of leave backwoodsmen" could be recalled to support the Government. Each case was apparently judged on its merits before leave of absence was given by the government chief whip, the Honourable J. G. Stuart, and he operated the system shrewdly so that the political realities of the wartime coalition were largely lost on the man in the street. The aim was for the Conservatives to lose their reactionary reputation built up since 1931, although nothing can be understood of the period's politics without appreciating the overwhelming parliamentary majority of the Conservatives. The device of granting large numbers of MPs indefinite leave was attacked as a form of patronage for the Member had to obey the Whip if recalled, and thus was not performing his proper function in the House. It was a device which had to be used with much caution because if the public realized what was happening and resentment against the dictatorial methods of the Conservative party grew, an election could be forced before Churchill was ready for it, with danger to his war strategy.

Meanwhile although pressure for action on postwar domestic problems built up, Churchill would not budge from his preoccupation with the grand strategy of the war. Paradoxically, while his reputation remained high that of his party slumped, but this was a period before Gallop polls commanded respect. Sensing the mood of the public, the newspapers and magazines focused attention on the future and there were scores of pamphlets published on reconstruction. The armed services were given periodic literature explaining the content of parliamentary reports on domestic problems, and as part of routine training discussion on these matters took place.

In a Commons with an average age of 60 there were naturally a large number of old-style Tories who found the agitation for reconstruction most disturbing. The Member for Croydon, Sir Herbert Williams, even protested publicly when the ladies of the London Conservative Party invited Beveridge to talk on his welfare plans. Such people wanted no truck with measures which they dubbed "socialist nonsense". This faction alleged "there was not a true Conservative in the war cabinet", and saw every discussion on reform as a threat to their way of life. Their traditional opponents, the Labour Members, watched their tactics, both open and indirect, as they blocked social reconstruction, with mounting wrath. Herbert Morrison at the Home Office concluded that "constructive planning of a kind which was bound to be controversial was almost impossible", but made an exception for Butler's work at the education department.[32]

This was very true, for Butler was alive to the new currents of public opinion and realized the threat they posed to Conservative influence. Both in his work as a minister and as an organizer within his party he consistently advocated Bismarckian Socialist

PRIORITY PLANS

(*Punch* – 12 April 1944)

principles, trying to explain that if satisfactory moderate schemes were not provided to meet popular demand, more ambitious and expensive solutions would prevail. This was too subtle for the old-style Tories who suspected any deviation from time worn policies and, as one of them put it, they "wished to eschew the pinkish slop which was cluttering up Tory principles".[33] They saw grave dangers that the drive of the private individual to look after himself and family, would be sapped by community organized support.

Such attitudes were to trouble Butler a great deal, for it was necessary that he should have a show of backing from his party for his Education Bill but, even though he had organized the Conservative education sub-committee himself, this was difficult to muster.[34] Their forward-looking policies seemed to remain grounded in the Education Act of 1936 and unable to move from the limited approach to raising the school-leaving age from 14 to 15. Moreover, by surrounding the authorization with exemptions they showed they considered the youngster better occupied at work than at school. Their draft report was initially so reactionary that it was not circulated to the public until considerably modified by Butler, to be published after the Bill had been launched in January 1944 under the title, "Looking Ahead—The Third Report". The committee's true colours were shown in their remarks on the Bill, which they saw as mainly concerned with mass education. They pointed out that "mass education does not solve the other half of our educational problem—how to make the best use of our best material". It was then suggested that "to make things too easy" for all children was to hinder this second important process, and they directed their attention towards the detection of the able few thrown up by the mass educational process, prophetically indicating the selection issue which was to dominate the educational scene for the next quarter of a century.

Not all Conservatives were of the same mind and some forty younger MPs could see where such intransigence was leading. Under the leadership of Lord Hinchingbrooke and Quentin Hogg, they formed the Tory Reform Committee which included several names later notable in politics such as Peter Thorneycroft, Henry Brooke, David Eccles, Hugh Molden, Lady Astor and last but not least Thelma Cazalet Keir, daughter of a wealthy financier. This group saw their political progress blocked by the diehards of their own party, while the Labour Party trade unionists advocated progressive policies from within the government. Expression of their own brand of politics was barred, and to do something about this they arranged a series of gestures, aligning themselves with suitable measures and causes in a way which called attention to themselves yet did not endanger their political prospects.

The parliamentary processing of the Education Bill was subject to all these opposing influences, and there was the feeling that such a long measure could meet disaster at any time. Butler knew that the political might was with the Conservative Party, but he also knew that in a free vote it was doubtful if they would have accepted the Bill. Moreover the brutal use of the majority vote had to be used sparingly for, in the political climate of the time, all the pent up resentment could break up the government and force an election before the Prime Minister was ready for it. Moreover he also knew the Bill had, at the best, only lukewarm support from Churchill and many old-style Tories, so, although as a Conservative minister he appeared to stand with the potential protection of the majority vote, it was only political expediency which had allowed the measure to proceed against Churchill's declared policy of no complete social reconstruction until after the war.

As a consequence the reforms were kept within well-defined limits and there was minimal involvement in social controversy, especially over such an emotionally charged subject as the public schools. It also meant ignoring the growing lobby to frame policies to deal with the situation revealed by the evacuation of children from the towns at the start of the war. There had been shattering evidence of the inadequacy of existing arrangements. This had been colourfully exploited by the newspapers so as to become common knowledge and even a public scandal. A more comprehensive and sober account by the Women's Group on Public Welfare under the title "Our Towns—A Close Up" had been published in March 1943, and in two years ran to six printings. Out of this had developed a feeling that social services to deal with children's problems should be built up within the local education services. Most education committees had a care sub-committee and it was proposed to build on this to provide properly financed and staffed facilities to cater for the manifestly large number of children adversely affected by poverty and family breakdown. The resulting lobby pressed for more boarding school facilities within the education department to act as short-stay accommodation. It was obviously inexpedient to include such an ill-defined area within the present Act, so this acute social situation was largely ignored until the Curtis Report of 1946 and the Children's Act of 1948 set up separate departments outside the educational system, thereby removing children in difficulties from the normal line of treatment. The situation had first come to public notice in 1939 but effective action would not be taken until some ten years later, demonstrating once again official indifference to the nation's children. Attempts in the debate to widen the social purpose of the Bill were evaded by pointing to the outline powers it contained for this purpose, although their use remained largely permissive and not mandatory, despite the history of the last 25 years showing the failure of certain local authorities to act in this direction.

The Labour Party had been battering its head against the Conservative majority since 1931 and were grateful for any measure which held a promise of real reform. They had no clear education programme of their own and the Bill was along lines which they found acceptable, so, although they would have preferred either of the other measures—e.g. on rehousing or reform of the social services, they made it their limited aim to see that Butler's Education Bill was successful. This meant they accepted the restricted nature of the measure and did not dwell unduly on the agreements which had been reached outside the House. This still left them free to achieve some suitable modifications to the terms, although they realized they were in no position to force a major change. The most prolonged tussle was the attempt to keep education in the control of the community it was serving. There were several interests involved, not the least being the local pride of the community, for as one MP noted, "It is an extraordinary thing that local authorities are always complaining of the burden Parliament imposes upon them : yet whenever one suggests that the burden should be lightened, there is tremendous opposition".[35] The proposal to remove the small borough-size authorities, the Part III authorities, from educational administration and concentrate the power in the county councils and county boroughs caused "tremendous concern in the country". Member after Member spoke against the removal of control from a "vigorous authority" to an impersonal body, often many miles away. Several cases were quoted of the difficulties of travelling to the county towns. One told of a three-hour train journey of 160 miles. As a consequence there were dire warnings that "the professional man, the shopkeeper, and the working man, who are members of the local authority at present, with full powers, will not be able to participate in full administration. An ordinary working man can attend a committee meeting in the evening. He cannot spend the whole day going and coming back." It was also pointed out that while borough elections were hotly contested, county council elections were largely ignored. It was alleged that as all important decisions woud be made at county level, the lower authorities would become merely a rubber stamp for their policies and the best men and women would no longer be interested in local government.

Much was made of the anomalies of the proposed changes. In one case "a county borough was a population of 24,000 next door to an area with 60,000 with the county borough having complete control while the other with the bigger population having no control".[36] It was noted there were twelve county borough with a population of under 60,000. Although there was reluctance to "support the mandarins of the parish pump" there was a general cry of "Hands off our local councils".[37]

Professor Gruffydd, representing the University of Wales, pointed out the dangers of parochialism, illustrating his point from the Rhondda Education Authority which was well known as a good Part III education authority. There too much local control meant the children who went to the local secondary school had to go to a college in Cardiff. Returning home each night to the Rhondda, they never had the opportunity to mix with other students. The graduate could then end up on the staff of one of the four secondary schools in the Rhondda valley with the result, "the whole Part III authority is inbred from top to bottom . . . throughout the country". This was very true, but living at home and attending the local red-brick institution was a great help for the children of poorer families obtaining higher education.

This was a struggle which was doomed to failure from the start because of the larger issues involved. It was long acknowledged that local government was due for a radical reorganization but it was too lively a political issue to tackle. Wartime administration had been carried out on the basis of regional units and this gave a unique chance to cut out the smaller units when the time came for restoring normal local government. The academic solution was to retain about a dozen regions covering the whole country and hand them wide powers, but this was considered politically damaging, so a compromise policy was adopted to build up the county councils at the expense of the small borough-size community administrations. Unfortunately, as the debate revealed, the county areas in many cases had no economic or even geographic unity and were by no means a rational solution. They had, moreover, because of their remoteness from lively working communities, largely been run by the leisured and educated middle classes, whose interest in social services largely centred on keeping the provision cheap. Conservative governments between the wars had discovered that social services granted on a permissive basis and controlled from the county councils were successfully limited to minimum expenditure. This was the basis of the educational provision of the 1944 Act.

There were compensating advantages which came from the insistence that the service should be professionally run and this was ensured by the appointment of the head of the service, the education officer, being subject to departmental veto.

As a result of the change in local-authority control there was an inevitable build up of the central authority which was expressed by the department being upgraded to ministerial rank on a Labour amendment, which was widely backed by the House, although it was a change resisted by the cabinet.[38]

There was no doubt that the authority given to the Minister by the Act was considerably more than in any other measure, for the central government was given statutory rights to compel the local authorities to act. He was also actively charged with the duty to "promote the education of the people of England and Wales, and the progressive development of institutions devoted to that purpose, and to secure the effective execution of the local authorities under his control and direction, of the national policy for providing a varied and comprehensive educational service in every area". To ensure this the Minister was given explicit powers to override local education authorities, school governors or managers of any controlled or State-aided school, if he believed they were acting "unreasonably".

These powers were the subject of several attacks mainly from the Conservatives. In the upper house, Lord Rankeillour opposed the powers proposed for the Minister as "undemocratic". In the Commons, Sir Joseph Lamb argued the powers were excessive and should be reduced in the interests of democracy, and moved an amendment to remove the term "control" for which he had some support; but when it was seen that Mr Butler was firm on the point he withdrew without forcing a division. David Eccles asked for reassurance on this point as "control" implied a master-servant relationship rather than a partnership. The President's assurance of partnership between the central and local authorities did not entirely satisfy the group of Conservative MPs who saw the powers as "a challenge to the quality of our local government".

Later in the debate Sir Joseph Lamb raised the point again, alleging that effective political power was being taken out of the hands of the House and vested in government departments. Moreover he felt that the wide powers the executive had been granted in wartime would be retained in peace. He saw the development of over-centralization in the Bill in the reduction in the number of authorities. This was denied by the President, who claimed that by reducing the number of units to be dealt with administrative efficiency would be achieved.

The second round of the battle to control the education service was equally abortive for it centred on the control of the schools. This was a long and passionate debate in which all manner of suggestions were put forward to link the schools with the community they served through the appointment of governors with local affiliation and interest. The most radical suggestion came from Kenneth Lindsay, the former Conservative Parliamentary Secretary of Education who claimed "if we are to have wider areas, counties and county boroughs, we must associate in some way the local people who are interested in education, with the individual schools".[39] This "direct democracy" should be so designed to give parents representation on the governing body. He mentioned the success elsewhere for, "this principle is being practised in Moscow, both in relation to housing and education. It is not a question of putting people on a local authority and then into contact with the schools. It is associating them directly with a housing estate or a school. It is a very remarkable development . . ." He pointed out the advantages of this system for "there are a large number of people who cannot afford the time or the money to sit on a local authority . . . who wish to be associated with schools . . . willing to sit one day or two days a month and to be associated with a particular school".

Mr Butler was unimpressed with these arguments, as also with suggestions that the assistant teachers should be associated with decisions on school management. He pointed out that the Bill gave the head teacher standing for the first time, and in doing this he thought it had gone far enough. Nevertheless the lobby to link schools with their neighbourhood and to have representative governors forced him to rewrite the clause relating to appointing governors. The new sections carefully placed the writing of the constitution of schools and the appointment of governors with the county authority. Governors had no security of tenure and could be removed by the authority which appointed them at any time. The only right which the Act secured for them was that of resigning the appointment.

It can be seen that the debate did not reflect the realities of the political situation, but the views of moderate and progressive MPs of all parties with an interest in education. Their many representations and suggestions achieved little. This was all the more disappointing because many MPs saw the governors as the guarantors of the quality of the school's service and the only way that parity of esteem and facilities could be secured. This was seen as particularly applicable to the secondary schools, and much of the indifferent development in that sector was correctly forecast. Lindsay was brutally frank, saying :

. . . there is a great deal of humbug going on at this time. Sooner or later there will come a clash. Anybody who says to me that the children attending the 450 old unreorganized departments in London, with some 40,000 children, are attending the same type of school as the grammar schools which have existed for many years, with a sixth form producing classical and other scholars who have gone on to Oxford and Cambridge for the last 200 years, is talking nonsense. The two things have no relation to each other. Yet in this comprehensive way we say that these are all secondary schools.[40]

Professor Gruffydd forecast that the Act would implement the slogan "Secondary education for all" with some accuracy, explaining it would:

> . . . do that . . . merely by using the word "secondary" in a new connotation and not by creating a really new system of secondary education. The secondary schools of England and Wales in future will not only be secondary schools of the grammar school type, but they will also contain all the residue, the children who failed to pass the examination to go into the grammar schools, the children in the modern and technical schools, which necessarily must, if education is to be compulsory, contain a large proportion of the unteachable, who must by law go to these so-called "secondary" schools.

His concern was for the existing secondary grammar schools and he wished to know if "the very excellent start in secondary education . . . is not going to be stultified by degrading the standard of the secondary schools we have already got".[41]

The President replied that the country was "entering a new secondary school world under this Bill" and that "pupils will be encouraged to go to whatever type of secondary school suits them best, grammar, modern, or technical. And they will not go by rigid examination tests. There is, thus, one secondary school world and not two or three". This was an acknowledgement of the unity of the education system, at least at secondary level. He also mentioned a suggestion that grouping of schools should take place, where convenient, namely "to group different types of secondary schools so as to include pupils in the different types of the secondary world". He noted that although it did not command general approval it was favoured in certain areas. He saw it as evidence for "the need to preserve variety in the method of governing or arranging our secondary schools". He indicated the difficulties in framing the general principles on which schools ought to be managed.[42]

After being foiled on control of the schools, the educationalists sought to have provisions as to the quality of the service written into the Act. As drafted it was largely an outline framework with a number of general proposals for reforms and changes. It was obviously an advantage if these could be more specifically defined so that the government would be tied to undertake implementation by a certain date or in a certain way. There were naturally a number of attempts to do this but practically all failed. The main sectors of these attacks were concerned with trying to improve the quality of the education by decreasing the size of classes and there was a determined and prolonged campaign to have a statutory limit of 30 pupils in a class, as "a maximum, and by no means a minimum". Chuter Ede came into action to beat off determined support for an amendment on the question of overlarge classes. He recalled, "I was taught in a class of 90. The first class I had when I left college was 73, and the smallest class I ever taught before I left the teaching profession, for its own good, in 1914, was 55 in number." He made the case that the government was conscious of the "problem of the size of classes, with its necessarily correlated subjects, the supply of teachers, which goes to the root of this Bill. It is quite clear that unless we can get an adequate supply of teachers this measure will not give the country the results for which we all hope." He pointed out that such figures were a matter of history and it would be better to leave the service free to work towards "something like the figure" mentioned.[43] There were attempts to enlist the backing of the Tory reform committee but as this was not forthcoming the matter passed without a division.

There was an outline provision for nursery schools in the Bill, but it was foreseen that unless they were incorporated in the school system proper, it would remain, as it had between the wars, a dead letter. Proposals were therefore made to extend the infant school to cover children from two to seven years of age, with attendance voluntary under the age of five. This was obviously full of opportunities to develop nursery-school classes. The President pointed out that there was a division of educational opinion about the length of stay in the infant or first school and to rule on this "in a statute of all places . . . would really be madness", and the government felt "it will be necessary to keep elasticity in the general system . . . and that to lay down a rigid rule would be impossible".[44]

Moves to require a timetable for completing the re-organization of schools on Hadow Report lines were similarly blocked, although these measures had first been discussed in 1926. On the other hand both sides of a largely male House rallied strongly to call for specific requirements for physical education and sports facilities. It was related how many children only had the streets to play in, but when, as a result of evacuation, some facilities had been found, the teachers had quickly responded by organizing games. Much was made of children's road accidents, many caused through playing in the streets.[45] In the six years, 1937–43, there had been no less than 5,000 dead and 15,000 injured as a result of road casualties. Against this sorry picture was shown what could happen. Portsmouth had "no playing grounds belonging to the schools", but teachers during the last year had borrowed grounds from the services to run six football leagues for their forty-six teams, six cricket divisions for thirty-seven teams, and their swimming competitions had attracted 1,000 entries. The whole of the training, the umpiring and the organization was carried out by teachers out of school hours, mostly on Saturdays. There was much support from MPs that better sports facilities were essential, but the introduction of a clause on the equipping of schools with "adequate playing grounds and fields" was not allowed by Mr Butler who insisted that this would be taken care of in a proviso to the effect that ministry regulations would require local education authorities to maintain all school premises "to such standards as may be prescribed", which would be taken to include playing facilities.

Similarly attempts to insist on named items of audio-visual equipment to be universally provided was held to be included in a general provision. This was a forward-looking suggestion because school equipment of the period tended to be primitive with little technical apparatus. Mention was made of the excellent pioneer work of the British Broadcasting Corporation's schools service which had been tried in something like half the schools, and there was even a suggestion of the introduction of television for educational purposes.

There were several attempts to have the general lines of the Bill framed in more specific terms, e.g. to include named items to be completed by a certain date, but there was not the voting power to force any of the issues raised. However, this line of attack attracted the attention of the Tory reform committee who, when their votes were added to the dissident Labour vote, could not be easily brushed aside.

In contrast to the educational debate of 1902 it was the social issues which generated the most heat. This was aggravated by claims made in the Bill that it was promoting educational equality, although it also included provision for the continuation of the controversial fee-paying schools, which were seen as perpetuating the class division in society. Fuel to this dispute was added by the publication in August 1943 of an interim report of the Fleming Committee set up to investigate means whereby the public schools could be associated with the general educational system. Eleven of the eighteen members recommended complete abolition of fees in all grant-aided schools and published a majority report to that effect. The other seven members signed a minority report favouring the retention of fees. Conservative MPs were nearly all products of the fee-paying schools, not one admitting to attending an elementary school. Even if Richard Butler had been in sympathy with the recommendation abolishing fees, the weight and intensity of the support for this issue among his own party forced him to follow the minority report which was more in keeping with fundamental Conservative philosophy.

In the second reading of the Education Bill in January 1944 Mr Parker of Romford put the commonly held Labour point of view, explaining:

Educationally, today, this country is a country of three nations. If you take the adult population, only 2 per cent have been to so called "public" schools. What proportion of this present House of Commons have had the privilege of this type of education? 56 per cent . . . State aided secondary schools form 5 per cent of the population, but in this House $21\frac{1}{2}$ per cent have been to that type of school. If you take people who have only been to elementary schools, they form 92 per cent of our people, and in this House 22 per cent. Can you say from these figures that we have an educational system at the present time which is a proper national system trying to make the best of the talents of the whole nation?

He called attention to the Fleming Report and called for the end of fee paying. Mr Silkin, the Labour MP for Peckham, was one of many who taxed the government over fee paying and the advantages it was bound to give those who could afford them. Many agreed with his challenge that, "if there had been a genuine wish to abolish privilege in education and to secure an equal opportunity for all I would have hoped that fees in all types of secondary schools could be abolished". One MP even called it one of the "two great blots" on the Bill and also mentioned the direct grant schools which survived only by public aid yet were not responsive to public policy.[46]

Conservative spokesmen defended their own schools.[47] One pointed to the State schools where "there are literally thousands of classes in this country which are of an unmanageable size and the task of the teacher is not teaching, but really that of a drill sergeant, trying to get a little discipline and to keep the noise down". He asked, "How can it be wrong to send a boy to a school where he might learn something more and better; perhaps than is given by current State education?" Captain Cobb put it another way, "Generally speaking, our education system is the kind of mass production", and he welcomed proposals to set up local-authority boarding schools and saw them as developing for an élite, for "it is essential to make every possible effort to pick out the most promising children and give them the best possible educational advantages". At the same time he gave support to fee paying, saying :

> I feel that the abolition of fees in council schools may have the effect of depriving parents of a right to which they are entitled. . . . My view is that parents should have the right to send a child to whatever kind of school they desire, against the wishes of the education authority, provided they are prepared to pay the fees. I cannot understand this idea which appears to prevail in progressive and left-wing circles that there is something indecent about parents paying for a child's education. To my mind this instinct which parents possess ought to receive encouragement from the government.

He added "I regard money spent on education as very largely an investment which will return handsome dividends".

At the committee stage of the Bill the opposing views were

once more debated when W. G. Cove supported a Labour amendment calling for the abolition of fees in all State-assisted schools, contending that a democratic system of education was impossible as long as fee paying was retained. He claimed, "You cannot divorce a school from its social implications . . . Hence, I say quite definitely that, as a matter of educational policy and practice, as a matter of national policy, and in order to get social integration and national unity, we ought to break down every barrier within our educational system that even smells of class privilege."[48]

Mr Butler was aware of the feeling which speech after speech from both sides had demonstrated. His reply was moderation itself, but he was firm in his resolve to retain fee paying. He stressed the fact that in

> . . . planning this Bill we were considering the principles which would govern the new secondary world [so] we decided in framing this measure that children should receive whatever type of education would suit them best, and that the children should be able to transfer from one type to another. It is therefore of the greatest importance, to use the words of the Spens Report . . . that there should be "an equivalence between the types", or "parity of esteem" . . Therefore we had to decide whether to reimpose fees on the vast range of the modern schools, or free the whole of the secondary range of education coming within the purview of the local authority."

The latter course was taken and as a result "the education in all county and auxiliary schools maintained by the local authority shall be free; that is a very large proportion of the secondary world . . . The percentage able to charge fees is only four per cent." In answer to pleas that this would make it impossible to have democracy unless there was a complete sweeping away of fees, he replied "education cannot, by itself, create the social structure of a country. It can have considerable influence on it." He added that "One of the fundamental principles on which the Bill was built was "that there shall be a variety of schools. One of the varieties, which I think is quite legitimate, is that there shall be schools in which it is possible for parents to contribute towards the education of their children."

The amendment was defeated by 183 votes to 97, but of the

Labour backbenchers only two voted with the government and those of the Tory reform committee who voted, supported the government. The impotence of the opposition was fully exposed.

The second aspect of the social implications of the Bill was the reverse of the coin of privilege, that is the attempt to find ways to alleviate the lot of the many deprived children whose condition had become graphically apparent through evacuation. To tackle such distress was basic to Labour's political philosophy, but once again try as they might they were able to achieve little expansion of the Bill's provisions in this direction, although there were precedents. The education service had been used to supply some medical, feeding and welfare services for over 100 years, first on a voluntary and later on a statutory basis, so it seemed reasonable to extend these provisions. Hansard of the period is scattered with questions on these topics relating to the employment of children, the treatment of delinquents and other associated problems which could have been dealt with by widening the social provisions of the Bill and placing a duty on local education authorities to operate them. Many of the provisions were already operating in a small way but only the school health and meals services were placed on an obligatory basis.

Although a permissive authority to finance a school meals service from local authority funds had been won as long ago as 1906, the extent to which this had been used was not great. The urgencies of wartime rationing forced a new appraisal of this obstinately contested problem and in November 1941 a national meals service was inaugurated.[49] The consumption jumped from a pre-war consumption of 3.9 per cent to 23.5 per cent in February 1943. The debate revealed twelve local authorities out of the 315 made no provision for children at all. No local authority provided for over 65 per cent, while only seven local authorities provided for 50 per cent. Mr Cove, a teacher, made the case that there should be proper facilities where "the eating of a common meal by the children is a great co-operative experience. It is training in good manners and coming together, as it were, in a great co-operative act—almost an act of worship." The feeding of children had been the first effective measure the Labour Party had accomplished and, in the context of the time, not to include this in the Bill as a universal service to be continued after the war would have been political folly.

The promptness with which an amendment to this purpose was included in the measure suggests this was a carefully planned area for concessions. Similarly the extension of the school medical service to include facilities for handicapped children suggests the same parliamentary tactics.

Covering the other parts of the service which had a heavy weighting towards social assistance, e.g. nursery schools, boarding schools etc., there were wide permissive powers included in the Bill, which in many cases were merely an extension of measures in force between the wars. There was in fact a complete child-support service in embryo, which if it had been put into operation could have done a great deal for the situations revealed by evacuation of the children from the towns. The extent to which these were neglected became apparent when the Children Act of 1948 began to operate.

It might be thought that all the drawn-out discussions which had taken place on the religious aspects of the Bill had exhausted these issues,[50] but the compromises arrived at outside the House served only to damp down the heat of the clashes, for having reached agreement both the Anglicans and Nonconformists were anxious to see the Act on the statute book. It was also pointed out that church attendance was only 15 per cent to 20 per cent of the population, which accounted for the lack of sympathy in the country for religious rivalries.

The sensitive question for the Nonconformists was the area with a single school. This was one of the few examples of mishandling in the negotiations, for the initial agreement had been reached on the understanding that in all such areas the school should be taken over by the local education authority. It was perhaps not appreciated that there were 4,000 such areas served by voluntary schools, most of which were under Church of England control. When it came to be seen in this light it was inconceivable that a Parliament with 430 Conservative MPs, mostly around the age of 60, could agree to such a handover, no matter the justice of the cause. Mr Butler was equal to the occasion, explaining that such action was against the general spirit of the discussions on which the Bill had been built. He would not have "coercion from the centre" which would lead to a continuation of bitter feeling in the 4,000 affected villages. It says much for the accord reached between the two religious interests that this question was settled without open rupture, by a ruling which required that in all schools agreed syllabus teaching should be available.[51]

The introduction of compulsory religious instruction and collective worship was of universal interest, not all favourable. The clause that every school day should start with a collective act of worship attracted a lively debate in which it was suggested that it would lead to "organized blasphemy" because many children were irreligious; but when carried to a division the clause stayed in the Bill by 121 votes to 20.

The dissatisfaction of the Roman Catholics with the financial terms available to them was well presented on several occasions through the debate on the Bill. Mr J. J. Tinker, the Roman Catholic MP for Leigh, gave the House formidable facts of his community's educational efforts.[52]

> There are 2,400,000 Catholics in this country, with 370,000 between the ages of eleven and fourteen attending elementary schools. During the last 25 years, to try to keep our schools intact, we have collected £3,500,000 to meet our end of the burden ... Under the new arrangements, it is estimated that the cost to the community will rise to £9,850,000, that is taking the 1936 agreement with the present requirements of the new Act ... When I meet my people they say, "Right and justice demand that we should have 100 per cent".

These were cautiously-framed figures, for there were about 3.5 million Catholics in Britain, which out of a population of 48 million rated some 40 MPs in a fully representative Commons. The Catholic community was largely manual and with only eight Members fully reflected the general bias of the wartime parliament.

While the campaign for recognition of the Catholic position continued in the country, the small band of Catholic MPs assisted by a few friends, mostly Scottish Members, staged a well-argued campaign in the Commons. They rested their case on the social justice of their position. They were mainly a working-class community of no great wealth, but with a great record of self help which had contributed much to national society. As Mr Stokes told parliament, "Every penny spent on education in the Catholic Church comes out of the pockets of the workers, by and large. There is no great fund; people have told me they are sick and tired of getting up whist drives to pay for their children's education. They pay through the rates and are provided with a form of education to which they cannot, conscientiously, submit their children." The Catholics saw themselves fighting "the possibility that because we cannot find funds sufficient to come up to the standard . . . no one has as yet defined . . . we shall be closed down".[53] The extra costs too were difficult to define because of wartime inflation but every indication was that they would be beyond Catholic resources.

The estimated costs were not disputed and their case for hardship was obvious. Once this was acknowledged, despite their light parliamentary weight, Butler who had first counselled patient acceptance of the terms offered, found he had to move. The alternative was not only to have 1,200 Catholic schools remain permanently educationally sub-standard, but to earn the enduring political enmity of the second largest single religious denomination in the country. The balance of agreements with other interests ruled out more direct financial assistance, but the offer of long-term loans at reasonable interest went some way to meet the Catholic case without causing abrogation of the agreements on which the religious settlement had been built. This was naturally open to all Churches and encouraged more Anglican schools to remain independent, so that some 50 per cent continued with independent status. Although not entirely satisfactory to the Catholics, they had demonstrated what a minority could achieve by a determined campaign. Although only partially successful, they had made their point, so that when post-war inflation made their position intolerable, there were sympathetic reactions from the governments of the day and further increases of support, so that by the Education Acts of 1959 and 1967 the situation was brought to a final solution without further bitterness.

The debate on religious questions was noteworthy for its lack of bitterness. Speech after speech reflects passionate beliefs but for the most part arguments were rational and tempers were kept in check. This was undoubtedly due to the discussions which had taken place to reconcile denominational differences. Where spokesmen seemed to be going too far, both Butler and Ede did not hesitate to draw attention to the precariousness of the agreements reached and the mutual benefits which would result. In a typical incident Chuter Ede put the matter squarely on the line when speaking on an amendment dealing with controlled schools and the religious education which would be available in them. He replied in the impish vein which was his trademark, "I am afraid that, in happier times, this would have been described as a wrecking amendment. Quite clearly if this amendment were to be carried the whole balance so carefully built up by my right honourable friend would disappear." A mutual friend remarked to him, "You have built up such a balance that you make Blondin look like a blundering fool". This amendment would "give such a shove in one direction, that my right honourable friend would . . . be plunged into Niagara at once".[54] The amendment was withdrawn.

As part of the religious lobby there was considerable pressure to further agreed syllabus teaching. The National Union of Teachers were prominent in this because teachers favoured an ethical rather than a ritual approach to religious instruction. Agreed syllabuses meant different things to different interests and the teachers saw them as an updated and extended version of the Cowper-Temple clause which they had operated successfully since 1870. A national agreed syllabus was discussed and attracted much attention including that of the Prime Minister. It appeared to offer a simple direct solution to the sectarian squabbles and the NUT would have liked something of this nature to assist them withstand the clerical interest in these matters.[55] Butler resisted any involvement of the central authority, leaving the framing of syllabuses to the theologians and educationalists. Although some of these had wide acceptance they varied according to the regional compromises reached, but there was always the feeling that by calling another conference of interested parties they could be redrafted, which assisted in their general acceptance. Butler, feeling that the framing of a new State religion was not part of the duties of an educational minister, resisted NUT pressure to publish examples of agreed syllabuses under a government imprint, so that his department remained aloof from theological doctrine.

There was no direct opposition to the Bill, but the continuing theme of Aneurin Bevan's attack on the government was what he referred to as "Mr Churchill's morbid preoccupation with his own ascendancy" and the way decisions were being taken without reference to parliament. He saw the education debate as a means of furthering this campaign and, with a number of other MPs, he complained that owing to agreements made outside parliament with religious and other pressure groups real debate on the issues raised by the Education Bill was prejudiced. Moreover, as the measure progressed through parliament so the relationship between the political parties worsened. A number of by-elections, in which continuation of the political truce was demanded by Churchill, added more grievances. This was especially so in West Derbyshire where the poll was carried out in indecent haste in an unsuccessful attempt to retain the seat for a scion of the Duke of Devonshire, himself Under Secretary to the Colonial Office.

As the political temperature of the Commons hotted up, Churchill remained absorbed in war planning coming only to the Commons to answer questions in a weekly session. Some of these, especially if concerned with reconstruction, he dealt with in cavalier fashion. His remoteness and arrogance led to growing references to "one-man rule" and disregard of parliament. March 1944 produced a series of debates which showed the coalition to be near breaking point. The topics discussed—Civil Aviation (14 March), Housing (15 March) and a National Health Service (16 March)—all brought out the differing view points of the Left and the Right. There were many small clashes mainly concerned with attempts to prod the government into action on reconstruction. Even a War Medals Bill on 22 March produced a long rambling discussion in which feeling against Churchill ran high because it was alleged the decisions had already been made by him without reference to parliament.

These troubled waters attracted the attention of the Tory reform committee who hoped by championing liberal policies which they had little chance of implementing they would enhance their own reputations as progressives and help remove the old-style reactionary image of their party. They had had some success and chose certain aspects of the Education Bill as suitable for their purpose. On 21 March they forced a division on an amendment to include a firm date for raising the school-leaving age to sixteen. With the support of the Labour backbenchers they mustered the largest vote against any part of the

Bill, only to be defeated, with 137 votes to the government's
172. This was a considerable tactical achievement.

A week later, on 28 March, they put up another amendment
to include in the Bill a clause requiring equal pay for men and
women teachers. This was an issue with repercussions beyond
the bounds of the Education Bill and the debate was protracted. A number of MPs left the chamber for lunch thinking
that there would not be a division and, in any case the previous
week had shown there was ample government support to ensure
a victory. The result being that the amending clause was carried
by 117 to 116. What had started as a gesture to identify progressive Conservatism with women's rights had ended by
threatening the Education Bill, and because of the political climate of the previous month, there was danger of the breakup
of the wartime coalition.

Churchill descended on the House in wrath and "dismissed
them for the afternoon like naughty school boys". Although the
manner of defeat was accidental and really had little political
significance, he saw the matter as it would appear to occupied
Europe and elsewhere in the world. The invasion of France
was only ten weeks away and any political weakness in Britain
could be used to comfort the enemy and depress the occupied
peoples from whom considerable co-operation was expected in
the invasion. So Churchill treated the whole matter with theatrical severity by requiring a sweeping vote of confidence and to
ensure this he recalled the 200 "backwoodsmen". This was not
popular, nor was his insistence that the defeated clause should
be reversed.[56]

The whole matter showed how out of touch Churchill had
become with the backbenchers, and was something of a personal
débâcle. The confidence debate was delayed until the 30 March
to ensure full attendance. Churchill had prepared a rhetorical
speech which was addressed to a world-wide audience, but as
he had required that the debate be confined to the particular
clause, Bevan on a point of order had such an address ruled
inadmissible. He was then reminded that he knew nothing of
the intricacies of the case for equal pay. In a statement the
Prime Minister had insisted that the offending clause be ex-
punged from the Bill and the original government wording be
replaced. Member after Member of all parties urged him to

be satisfied with a mere vote of confidence and not to devalue the parliamentary process of a legal measure in this way. The sulking Prime Minister refused to budge, and became involved with Earl Winterton over his parliamentary manners.

A reference was made to the backwoodsmen who had turned up to support the Prime Minister, who replied tartly that they were "doing public work, and are often in the services". Bevan scenting a sensitive area, referred to the beneficial results of bringing to the House many Members who I did not know were Members. "I am very glad to see them," adding impishly, "I am disappointed that the Prime Minister was unable to speak." Churchill in the most clumsy way possible achieved his vote of confidence with 425 supporting the government and only 23 against, which was sufficiently decisive to flash round the world as conclusive evidence of support for his government. In the circumstances the 150 abstentions was another telling figure.[57]

The rest of the Bill went through without further trouble, although there was feeling over financing, as well as the changes caused by the disappearance of the small authorities. Such was the dominance of Churchill that no one would risk pushing any matter to the limit. The Bill finally passed on to the statute book on 3 August. Butler was the hero of the hour and he acquired a prestige he had not previously enjoyed either in his own party or in the country; his political future was assured.

The 1944 Act was basically a measure repairing a run-down system and it is difficult to find one area of innovation in its many clauses. It originated in a civil service study group which above all aimed at being safe, so the educational aspects of the schools system were probably the least considered. Policies were framed to suit the administrators and not for the benefit of the majority of children. The result is that although it rendered "obsolete every work of law relating to education which had been written", it merely reconstructed the system built up on the 1902 Act, and put into effect the Hadow report of 1926.

It is therefore an ideal administrator's measure with the initiative and control with central government. The exchequer has always tended to see the education service, along with other family support services, as a luxury which is the first area to be cut in times of financial stringency. The 1944 Act, drawn up in vast general sections, is ideal for this and successive ministers

UNDER THE COUNTER

(*Daily Mirror* – May 1945)

have not scrupled to operate it in this fashion, so that whole areas of education have never been properly developed, notably nursery schools and further education, not to mention the ill-fated secondary modern schools.

Nevertheless the Butler Act was the greatest advance which could have been achieved in the time and circumstances. It is in effect a vast enabling Act drawn so wide its limitation lie not in its terms but their interpretation and operation. The Act was conceived in an era redolent with resounding phrases about equality and greater opportunity. It was discussed at a time when, although the nation was consciously fighting for its life, the air was full of plans for the future. There was a general feeling that this time the better future, promised after 1918, should not be lost and such feelings were frequently expressed in popular articles and cartoons. Such democratic sentiments were written into the 1944 Act, and although they are dulled by being overlooked, they deserve fresh scrutiny, for it seems the only people who have interpreted the Act are administrators anxious to keep the provision within a tight budget. A fresh look at the measure shows the whole question of the two-tier secondary provision lies not in its clauses, but in the way they have been implemented. There has never been enough money allocated to operate this vast measure to the full, yet in the Act the local authorities have firm commitments to supply specific facilities to clearly defined standards. It would therefore appear that an appeal to the courts in the manner used in the USA to break segregation in schools could usefully have been tried. There seems ample grounds for action against authorities who have not provided schools to ministry standards in over 25 years. The local authority has a clearly expressed duty to provide "efficient education" and other loosely phrased clauses which lie open to liberal interpretation by experts, for if learned witnesses can pronounce on the extent of damage or injury, the quality of literature, and other difficult questions, expert evidence can surely be assembled on the standard of schools and other educational matters. In many cases the mere assembling of the evidence would make the case obvious. Britain can hardly plead poverty to the extent that many of her schools should be sub-standard a quarter of a century after a statutory duty has been imposed to put the matter right.

There is not one word in the Act about selection and the whole process is based on a very shaky legal and educational foundation as many legally-minded parents have discovered. The key is in an amendment by the Lords which laid down that local authorities would "have regard to the general principle that, so far as is compatible with the provision of efficient instruction and training and the avoidance of unreasonable expense, pupils are to be educated in accordance with the wishes of their parents". This statement of parental rights, which became Section 76 of the 1944 Act, was prompted on religious grounds, but together with Sections 7 to 10 and 37(3), as well as the "obiter dicta" in the parliamentary debate referring to "parity of esteem" and "equality of schools", it has been widely used by certain parents to insist on secondary grammar education for their children. Authorities when firmly challenged, have frequently found it politic to agree to provide suitable places, rather than risk their ruling being challenged in the courts. A few well-publicized cases could drive the proverbial legal coach and horses through the selection procedures, making a comprehensive system inevitable.

One of the features of the debate was how accurately the educational experts among the MPs forecast the future of the school system. It was also foreseen there would be a lack of interest in county-authority government, which largely handed this level of government over to councillors who were scarcely representative of the people, with a continuation of restrictive policies especially as regards education. One of the results of this has been the reduction of school governors to functional nonentities, for they largely became the nominees of the professional officials who ensured that they should be the type who would be no more than nominally interested and thus create no trouble for the administration. The development of local pressure groups with an interest in the schools is a movement which will probably grow. The professional associations are slow to insist that they should be represented on governing bodies in more than a nominal way, largely because of the domination of such bodies by head teachers who are not anxious to see their control of schools in any way diminished.

It is paradoxical that the Education Act came about through an able politician wishing for a quiet post whilst his political star was in eclipse. Richard Butler then built up his personal standing using the despised department to redress the neglect of two decades with a pantechnicon of a Bill which, in defiance of the Prime Minister's express order, was smuggled by the back stairs into the cabinet in circumstances which necessitated its acceptance. Churchill's consistent intransigence towards social reform resulted in the Bill having a rarity value both

from the point of view of propaganda and parliamentary tactics. The defeat of the Conservatives in 1945 added to its
reputation as the pattern for future right-wing policy.

It is also worth noting this reform took place during the
virtual absolute rule of a Prime Minister who had little time
for schools or educationalists. Of his own Harrow school days
he wrote, "It was an unending spell of worries that did not then
seem petty, and of toil uncheered by fruition, a time of dis-
couragement, restriction and purposeless monotony".[58] He had
been offered the Board of Education in 1905 but refused it, for
he conceived the department to consist of "smacking children's
bottoms and blowing their noses". He could not even bring
himself to give a few words of thanks to the teachers who had
borne the brunt of the evacuation muddle. His wry sense of
humour probably demonstrated something of his true feelings
for the Education Act of 1944. In May 1945, the wartime coalition was finally dissolved, leaving Churchill as Prime Minister
to run the country with a caretaker government. These interim
ministers were his nominees and as the Under Secretary of the
education ministry, he chose back bencher Thelma Cazalet Keir,
the very person who had proposed the amendment which had
defeated the Bill in the previous year. She certainly thought it
wry, for in her memoirs she related how he telephoned her well
after midnight to offer her the post which she accepted, stating,
"I can only think the pixie side of his nature made him enjoy
the thought of putting me in charge of education in the House
of Commons, when I had been a good deal of a nuisance
during the Education Bill a year before.... He must have
liked the idea of forcing Satan to reprove sin."[59]

Great Expectations; The Education Act of 1944 Applied 1945-1972

The child on the way to school is the man on the way to work—at the age of eleven or so, he will know which part of the factory canteen is his, and which part belongs to the others. Education and employment have gradually become even more closely related with the growth and complexity of managerial problems on the one side, and the simple automatic tasks on the other, both of which are features of modern industry. Any inequalities in the educational system begin to take on an added sharpness ... [yet] ... few will deny that such inequalities exist and our schools are writ large in all schemes for social reform, where every proposal involves a genuine overhaul of the educational system, or falls victim to its inadequacies.

Dennis Potter, *The Glittering Coffin*, Gollancz, London, 1960.

ON EASTER SUNDAY, I April 1945, Part II of the Education Act of 1944, the more substantial part of the Measure, came into force and set up the new parts of the basic educational system. It was already seen as a milestone in social progress, for the Churches held public services to ask a blessing for the workings of the Act and for the ministers responsible for placing the Measure on the statute book. To Chuter Ede it was a memorable occasion for he recorded in his diary, "I stayed awake until midnight in order that I might know the moment at which the elementary education system expired". *The Times,* in a leading article, headlined "A Landmark in Education", heralded the new era, but also pointed out the snags it involved saying, "by passing the Education Act, the government and the people have committed themselves to shouldering the task of turning policy into practice". The trouble was that the old system was in much disarray for it had never been lavishly pro-

THE NEW BOY

Mr. R. A. Butler: "It may not be very easy at first, but you'll soon settle down."

[The new Education Act came into force on April 1st.]

(*Punch* – 4 April 1945)

vided, and under the stresses of war it had begun to fall apart. This was not only in those areas most affected by the hostilities, but also in parts untouched by bombing or evacuation and their consequent aftermath of confusion. There was a shortage of teachers; most of the younger men were away in the forces, and a proportion of them would never return but move on to other prospects. Some school buildings had been bombed and others commandeered; all had been neglected, for stringent regulations allowed only running repairs. New construction had remained at a standstill. School supplies were hard hit by six years of extreme shortages which necessitated total control of all materials. The old system which had grown out of the Education Act of 1902 was run down to the point of collapse. Only in one respect had it improved. The physical condition of the children, despite food rationing, was better than it had ever been. There were several reasons for this. Once again wartime enlistment in the forces or work in the factories had provided practically all families with a regular income for the first time since the 1914–18 war. Moreover, because of the shortages of essential food stuffs, the whole nation had become nutrition conscious; and concern for the condition of children led to the introduction of universal school meals which were now part of the normal education service. This continuous benefit was soon apparent for each generation of school children was physically well ahead of its pre-war counterparts. It was soon impossible to find any school athletics record which dated from before the war. Such physical well-being reflected in the children's academic work; there was a need for more activity and study which required more concentration and taxed intellectual abilities. The child of the 1950s was a very different pupil from his predecessor of the 1930s.

On 8 May 1945, barely a month after the new education system had come into being, the war in Europe ended, which brought about a break-up of the coalition government and a general election. The election of July 1945 produced the unusually high turn out of 73 per cent of the voters. It returned 393 Labour MPs, giving the party for the first time a clear majority; the Conservatives mustered 213 while the Liberals were reduced to 12 seats and a variety of minor groups returned 22 MPs. Labour with a majority of 146 over all other parties had effective political power for the first time. After six long years of exhausting effort they took over a country faced with enormous problems of reconstruction. As a party they were dedicated to the establishment of social justice and pledged to the removal of poverty and privilege.

The greater number of the Labour MPs were new to the Commons and generally of a different type to the old activists who had founded and built up the party. They were better educated than the old guard whose formative years had been marked by bitter poverty and a political experience never far from physical confrontation. The Prime Minister, Clement Attlee, an able administrator, was aware that the political dynamism of his movement came from these older members, who in many cases held wartime office. Therefore he allocated his appointments to them while supporting them with junior ministers of the new type. Of the thirty-seven members of the cabinet, eight were former miners and eleven had been active trade unionists.

This was the pattern in the education department. As soon as it was obvious the poll was turning Labour's way, the MP for Jarrow, the diminutive Ellen Wilkinson, took the overnight train to London in order to petition Attlee for the post of Minister of Education, to which he agreed. She was a Labour stalwart and, as Ernest Bevin said, well known as "a great fighter for the common man". She had waged an imaginative campaign for her depressed constituency before the war, so that the tiny figure of "Red Ellen" was widely known through newsreels and photographs showing her speaking with great passion or at the head of the hunger marchers from the northeast as they trudged on their way to put their case to the government in Whitehall. It proved to be not altogether a fortunate appointment because the tremendous backlog of neglect alone called for great administrative skill and tactful coaxing of officials, which were hardly Miss Wilkinson's forte. There were other problems mainly concerned with limited national resources which made her task even more immense especially as she knew little of the development of the State education system and the intricacies surrounding it. Her Parliamentary Secretary, Mr. David Hardman, a Cambridge man whose strengths lay in his links with the older universities, could not help in this respect.

Miss Wilkinson sought to solve problems of resources by frontal assault, made all the more exhausting by the terminal illness which affected her during her year and a half in office. This was a double tragedy, for such was the confusion caused by the war, the change of administration and the large amount of administrative direction needed, that the bold expression of an imaginative forceful leadership could have been accepted without too many questions being asked; but the chance to direct educational policy into a new channel slipped away. In default of such a lead, the initiative stayed with the local authorities who merely picked up the system as they had operated it between the wars and renewed it, thus reinforcing the tripartite system of secondary education. Elsewhere new radical social developments were being worked out, while in the schools the results were rather confined to a change of nomenclature. The new local authorities in the preparation of their development plans which the Act required them to present to the Ministry of Education deemed all the children between the age of five and eleven to be in primary schools, while those over eleven were similarly considered to be in secondary schools. Even *The Times* noted that this was "largely a paper transaction" of limited meaning "until manpower and materials became freely available".

From the outset the question which dominated the educational situation was whether or not to raise the school-leaving age to fifteen or postpone it. The implementation of this clause would add to the demands on staff and accommodation which were already posing unanswerable problems for the administrators. Initially the 1944 Act had set the date for this at three years hence, which was 1 April 1947; it only required a Ministerial Order to postpone this date. To the bulk of the children this was the most important clause, especially as it was linked with later raising the age to sixteen and the provision of a full term of secondary education for all children. The local authorities, on whom fell the burden of provision of facilities, were conscious of the effects of implementing this part of the Act.[1] They were already faced with frightening post-war difficulties, and they naturally pressed for an immediate decision on whether or not the fifteen-year-olds were to be retained in school; for this meant not only added accommodation for the numbers concerned but also some all-round improvement in facilities to meet the needs of older students.

In this respect education services had to compete with other needs for a share of the available national supplies to the building industry. Not only were demands being made to repair the extensive war damage but the chronic housing shortage plus the call for new factories were added to the call for hospitals and other buildings to meet the needs of the newly created welfare services; all this meant calls on every side for building labour and resources. There was no alternative but to continue wartime controls; and even a handyman, requiring a bag of cement and a few lengths of timber, could only obtain materials by submitting details to obtain a licence to purchase.

Even within the education service the claims of schools had to be balanced against other departmental needs, the chief of which were the provision of a school meals service, the extension of teacher training facilities, and the calls of further education, especially where concerned with the training of apprentices. In all directions there was not only the backlog of the war to make up but the provision of new services.[2] By Circular 48 of May 1945 the Minister of Education virtually confined all educational building to the erection of prefabricated huts which could be put up quickly using little skilled labour.

In August, following the dropping of atom bombs, Japan surrendered and hostilities ended abruptly, sooner than had been anticipated. There was an almost immediate withdrawal of lend-lease facilities by the USA which complicated the problems of providing for the occupation of vast areas until civil government could be re-established. At the same time the need to take decisions and go ahead with domestic reconstruction took on a new urgency.

Education officials had assembled figures on which national priorities could be worked out. It was apparent that facilities for raising the school-leaving age would require an all-out effort but scrutiny of the amount of hutted accommodation available added to repairs to old and damaged buildings showed it was possible. Shortage of staff could be overcome by retaining the services of married women and retired teachers, who were already in the schools to meet wartime needs. Armed with this data, Miss Wilkinson went to the cabinet for a decision on whether or not she could go ahead with raising the school-leaving age to fifteen for the school year which started in 1947. She had enlisted the support of the Secretary of State for Scotland who controlled Scottish schools, and they urged that the educational position should have recovered sufficiently to make the planned implementation date of 1 April 1947 possible. This would add a further 390,000 children to the school population in England and Wales, with 65,000 to 70,000 in Scotland. It was noted the full consequences of the Act would not be felt until September 1948, thus allowing three full years for preparation. Basing teachers' demands on a staff/student ratio of 30 for seniors and 40 for juniors, it was forecast that 13,000 additional teachers would be needed for the year after the school-leaving age was raised. Scotland was seen as requiring a further 1,800 teachers.

The main part of the requirements was to be met by the emergency training scheme. There were already some twenty extra colleges in England and Wales catering for 3,500 students by February 1946. The normal two years' training had been halved to enable the scheme to provide over 8,000 new teachers by September 1948. A further twenty colleges were to be opened, but it was realized the scheme would not meet all needs for extra staff created by the increased numbers wanted in the schools, as well as fill the gaps left by the departure of elderly and married teachers who had continued to teach in war time. Although it was felt some of the deficiencies would be made up by teachers returning from the forces and women teachers who, when married, were no longer required to resign, it was accepted as inevitable that the decision to raise the school-leaving age would halt progress in the reduction of class sizes; in fact it was expected that the size of classes would increase for a time.

The accommodation situation was somewhat similar, for there were resources available for only 7,000 classrooms, which would house some 200,000 children. The remaining 200,000 staying on for a further year in school were to be fitted into existing buildings. Educational requirements from building resources were wide and varied so that they made up a formidable total, even when all items had been pared to the minimum. For the three years 1945 to 1948 building works amounted to £20 million for England and Wales with a further £3 million for

Scotland. This heavy expenditure needed to implement the Education Act of 1944 should not be taken as an indication of great advance but rather as the extent of the neglect of the service between the wars. Even this sum did not make provision for the extra new schools needed on the new housing estates, which were being planned in every area to meet the chronic shortage of homes.

These departmental demands were immediately in conflict with the ceiling of available national resources. The total work allocated to education for the year starting in August 1945 was valued at £5 million, which represented a labour force of 8,300 men, but only about 4,000 were immediately available. If the target was to be met in the initial year the labour force required increasing to 12,500. It was not altogether hopeless for as the run down of the armed forces proceeded the building industry was expected to mobilize a million men, although the nation's number one priority of housing would claim the major share of this force.

The education department therefore made their bid for an increase in labour, pointing out the smallness of their demands when considered against the national mammoth total, and also drawing attention to the fact that three quarters of their accommodation was to be prefabricated building which did not require skilled building workers. This was coupled with a demand for some priority for educational reconstruction now that the hostilities had completely finished. It was felt that there should be more generous treatment as regards the allocation of labour and materials, as well as the early release of teachers from the armed forces. These concessions were necessary if the school age was to be raised in 1947, for even if the original minimal plan which stretched all resources was completed satisfactorily, approximately 40 per cent of the children required to remain an extra year in school would spend it in unreorganized all-age schools while much of the overall accommodation was makeshift and temporary. Moreover class sizes already swollen were bound to increase and the whole school system would suffer.

The Minister of Education argued that these unpalatable facts must be faced for, if the cabinet wished to wait for more ideal conditions this would amount to postponing the measure indefinitely which would shake confidence in the 1944 Act and in the government. This was not the only pressure that was being put on the cabinet, and in fact since the end of the war in the Far East it had been forced to consider demands for favouring the civil authorities, in favour of the supply and defence departments, which, although no longer geared to an all out war effort, still had large residual commitments. The cabinet was in the process of switching the priority of national effort to meet the needs of housing, industrial building, and the demands of the newly created health and welfare services, as well as those of education. The problems were immense but housing was easily the first priority and at this stage 60 per cent of labour was allocated to this task. Although the case for educational building was acknowledged, there was only marginal assistance possible. Various expedients were proposed such as taking over disused service hutting and building new school of special light construction to save building steel. In London one of the worst hit areas, the ban on educational building was to be relaxed. Such was the temper of the times that, despite all difficulties, the cabinet could see no barrier to effectively raising the school-leaving age on 1 April 1947.

On the second key question, that of staff, the first pessimistic figures were being revised and the situation appeared altogether more hopeful. Ministerial calculations had called for 58,000 new teachers for England and Wales. These had been allocated as 13,000 for raising the school-leaving age, 25,000 for replacing normal wastage, with a further 20,000 to reduce the size of classes to 30 for seniors and 40 for juniors. With only 12,250 expected from the emergency training scheme, a short fall of 45,750 teachers had been foreseen. It had been decided to abandon the reduction of classes as an ideal which could not yet be realized and to carry out a revision of the wastage situation. Many married women and a number of teachers over the retiring age chose to stay on, which cut the wastage figure to about 10,000. On this new data it was estimated that in September 1948 the shortage of teachers would amount to approximately 10,000, only 5 per cent of the national total which although not desirable, was not a serious risk to the breakdown of the educational system.

The decision to go ahead was published in Ministry of Edu

cation Circular No. 64 dated 27 September 1945, which proclaimed 1 April 1947 as the date from which the school-leaving age of fifteen would be operative, together with a promise of help from the ministry by the provision of hutted classrooms. These were, if possible, to be erected within the boundaries of the school or on land controlled by the school authorities. In all cases the approval of His Majesty's Inspectors of Schools was required, especially if new sites were needed. Where it could be shown that provision for raising the school-leaving age could be more economically made by completing a building left unfinished at the outbreak of war, or new housing schemes necessitated a complete new school, the case was to be put forward to the ministry without delay, so that such requirements could be fitted into the overall allocation of building materials and labour.

The government was thus fully committed to a measure which strained the available educational resources to the limit. It was only one of several similar bold plans by which national reconstruction was being pushed forward despite the many material shortages on every side. The nation, united in a determination to build a new and better Britain, accepted the effort and hardships in the way they had accepted the needs of war. Labour's period of office was in many ways a continuation of war time; but now the enemy was seen as Beveridge's giants of poverty and ignorance. Difficulties were inevitable in such gigantic endeavours, and education had its share. The first came over the supply of teachers, for by the end of 1945 only 6,195 had been released from the armed forces under the normal procedure which was known as Scheme A, based on the length of service and age. Early in 1946 to accelerate the process the profession was allocated 10,000 places for early or class B release; this was later increased to 13,000. The same scheme provided the occasion for the early release of certain specialists needed in educational reconstruction. However it was soon apparent that teachers, by the nature of their training and education, had been appointed to positions of responsibility or specialist duties, so that there were difficulties in releasing them. The Royal Air Force meteorological service was found to rely heavily on teachers whose sudden withdrawal threatened routine operational efficiency. Many others were in the Royal Army Education

Corps which was fully committed to educational and vocational training schemes as part of the demobilization programme. Class B release entailed some loss of terminal leave which, in the case where a man was a well-paid specialist meant a financial loss, so some teachers elected to wait for demobilization in the normal way. Nevertheless by April 1946 nearly 13,500 teachers had returned from war service and by the beginning of 1947 some 20,000 were back in the schools. At the same time other specialists released from the services accelerated educational reconstruction as the stream of national effort began to flow towards the causes of peace. The emergency training scheme also functioned satisfactorily, so that the teaching force in England and Wales which had been 150,000 in the autumn of 1944 had risen by the end of 1946 to 188,000, with the expectation of 200,000 by the end of 1948.

Accommodation occupied by the services amounted to 1,345 educational establishments at the start of 1945; by the end of that year 844 had been released for school use and a further 366 were freed in 1946. The remainder presented no great problem. However elsewhere the provision of school accommodation soon ran into difficulties and before the end of 1946 there were moves to re-open the whole question with the cabinet because of difficulties in Scotland. Miss Wilkinson, however, took a different view, although her difficulties were every bit as great. By the autumn of 1945 it was already apparent that the amount of new accommodation required by the authorities for raising the school-leaving age had been greatly underestimated; even the agreed building programme was proving difficult to accomplish. Inside the ministry it was openly expressed it would be "next door to a miracle" if even the inadequate programme was completed on time. Nevertheless the ministry were anxious their problems should not be raised with the cabinet at this stage for fear emphasis on their difficulties should be interpreted as a plea for postponement of the date for raising the school-leaving age. It was therefore thought wiser to strike a confident note, for already some local authorities had begun to despair of being able to complete their share of the task and needed encouragement. It was also felt that once other departments gained the impression the task was hopeless, it would no longer be possible to carry on the struggle at local level to secure priorities for educational buildings which were necessary for even limited success. Other departments were similarly stretched in carrying out their reconstruction plans and in order to jump the queue would make the most of any suggestion at cabinet level that the educational scheme was impossible to complete in the specified time. Once the credibility of the programme was shattered it could collapse, so an appeal for further help, which anyway had little chance of producing considerable material help, could well have precisely the opposite effect to that intended.

Even postponement would not solve the situation, for it raised new problems, not least of which was the employment of emergency trained teachers, many of whom had been specially released from the armed forces. Once this situation was appreciated, the ministry and the Scottish Office made reports, in December 1946, to the Lord President's Committee which played down their problems. However it was reckoned that the addition of available hutted classrooms to existing premises would only accommodate 86 per cent of the extra age group, a smaller proportion than had originally been estimated. It had also been realized that difficult sites had slowed down the erection of huts so that only 5,500 had been installed in place of a projected 7,000. It was still hoped that extra assistance from the Ministry of Works would enable the full programme of hutted classrooms to be completed on time. A solution was also sought for the deficiency by increasing the number of new schools to be completed to a light-weight specification for permanent constructions.

The unaccommodated 14 per cent represented some 55,000 students, 29,000 of which required places by September 1947. This number, added to the needs of new housing estates, called for fourteen new primary schools to free classrooms for secondary use, plus 40 new secondary schools together with the extension or completion of 38 existing schools. To achieve this, procedures were streamlined and local authorities instructed to build by stages, initially erecting only essential classrooms, leaving craft workrooms and even sanitary facilities to be added later. The Materials Allocation Committee meeting on 9 December 1946 treated educational requirements with some generosity although only granting an allocation of 7,000 tons of steel for building purposes against a demand for 9,000 tons. The ministry pronounced grants for furniture and equipment to be inadequate and proposed to take this item up with the cabinet. In their situation report the ministry sounded guardedly optimistic of success provided there were no holdups and the programme was given the required priorities.

Ministry fears that rumours of difficulties would revive the issue of postponement were soon seen to be well founded, for late in December 1946 the Ministerial Committee on Economic Planning proposed to include in its draft economic survey for 1947 which it was submitting to the cabinet a recommendation that raising the school-leaving age should be postponed from 1 April to 1 September 1947. By this time Miss Wilkinson was nearing the end of her life and under great stress, but a fighter to the last she rallied her failing strength to resist any cabinet decision to delay or modify the implementation of the 1944 Act. In a memorable appeal she pointed out that the education service had too often been the first casualty of economy campaigns and a Labour government should be the last to resort to encouraging child labour as a means of meeting a forecast of economic trouble. In an analysis of the results, she pointed out that in July 1947 the maximum child labour which postponement could produce would be 150,000 youngsters aged fourteen, many of whom would be employed in posts of little productive value. For example only 1 per cent would be in coal mining, one of the industries chronically short of workers; 24 per cent would enter the distributive trades, usually in blind-alley jobs; the largest group of 50 per cent would be in manufacturing industries, but all the evidence was they added little to productivity through the capacities in which they were employed. If the school-leaving age was kept at fourteen, it would amount to making another 150,000 wage earners adding only a small contribution to the country's economic production, but boosting consumer demand by the amount of their earnings. It would also deny the children a whole year of education and they would not be able to benefit from the county colleges which were to be established later for day release. Moreover the children of manual workers would be those most affected, while the children of better-off parents would still be kept at school. Postponement would throw staffing arrangements into confusion, especially as the emergency training scheme had been particularly geared to take men and women from the war services and train them as teachers. Postponement would mean unemployment for people who had been given special release and promised a new career. It would adversely effect the confidence in the government's planning, and local authorities would not respond to a call to complete plans by a set date.

The cabinet finally accepted the arguments that the country's over-burdened economy would benefit little from postponement, and would produce social and educational hardship. It was recognized that the withdrawal of the fourteen-year-old from the labour market had already stimulated the best employers to move towards starting employing labour at sixteen, realizing that increased demands for skill required more basic education, which was now linked with higher output. The government was also moved by the political disadvantages which would result from breaking definite pledges given in parliament.

The axe however fell on further education, although the preparation for county colleges was already well advanced to the extent of sketching out a five year plan requiring some £80 million, with £50 million earmarked for the reorganization of technical colleges and the rest for setting up county colleges. There were some who believed the expansion of the further education service should have been effected before the school-leaving age was raised, in order to cover the period between leaving schools and reaching maturity; a period which was seen as formless and lacking discipline, especially where youngsters were in blind-alley employment. This defect had been highlighted when training in preparation for compulsory national service had been instituted. The proposed extension of further education covering the period from fourteen to eighteen was designed to be covered by one-day-a-week school attendance with suitable training to bridge the difficult years of adolescence. It was pointed out that one school place in a day-release scheme served no less than five students and was also available for other technical and commercial education. Reform of education starting in the further education sector had the advantage of cheapness and avoided the charge that the Minister was forcing a higher school-leaving age on a run-down and largely unprepared school system.

Ellen Wilkinson true to her policy of providing working-class opportunity risked everything, for she had realized the acuteness of the situation and plumped for the total measure—an extra year and secondary education for all—as the one which her party would find most difficult to refuse. If she had placed the priority on providing further education first it would have invited disaster when the pressure to make cuts came, with the loss of further education as well as the extra year in school. She considered that in any case the schools had to be provided, so it was more economic to exert all pressure on obtaining whatever was available for them rather than spreading the expenditure over a wider area. Moreover industrial and business interests were already moving to make the case for the provision of further education, especially as agitation grew for the training of more scientists, so there was much support for the county colleges which were planned for 1952–53. However a proposed circular which was intended to begin the expansion of further education was modified to invite local-authority plans for that date without committing either them or the ministry to plans that far ahead. There was legal provision in the 1944 Act for the development of adolescent education in this way.

These matters had scarcely been decided when the country was hit by the most severe winter in Europe since 1880–81. It interfered with transport and production in Britain so that the loss was estimated by Stafford Cripps, the Chancellor of the Exchequer, as £200 million in exports alone. For two months bad weather crippled the country just as an all-out effort had been launched to speed reconstruction and recover from the war. A series of restrictive measures followed and with much of the world in similar economic straits there was the danger that the stagnation of the 1920s could be repeated, but the Marshall Plan provided a pump priming which led to two years of dramatic advance, although every major part of the economy, in both the public and private sectors, was rigorously controlled on lines which were a continuation of wartime measures. Further economic difficulties led to devaluation of the £ sterling in September 1949 by 30 per cent. To the growing financial and right-wing criticism of the government was added the protests of the left wing against growing dependence on the financial interests of the United States as well as the expenditure on armaments. An aging and tired administration facing these grave national problems still managed to carry out ambitious programmes of social reconstruction to improve the lot of the common man and his family. Although continuous sacrifice was required of the population this was generally accepted as benefiting the whole community. However as basic conditions began to improve there was a feeling the advance towards more material well being was too slow. There was also a growing tiredness with wartime austerity which had been carried over to peace time.

It is against this background that education's progress must be viewed. At the height of the extreme winter, on 6 February 1947, Ellen Wilkinson died; her last effective act as Minister was her appeal in the cabinet to stop the postponement of raising the school-leaving age. In the light of the overall economic situation the county colleges were dropped from the immediate development plans, day-release and similar training being fitted into the existing facilities. Although this was not intended as a permanent dismissal of this part of the 1944 Act this is what happened, for the county colleges have never been established and their rôle has been gradually taken over by the expansion of technical colleges.

It had not been a fortunate period of office for Ellen Wilkinson who had wanted the appointment, seeing it as a "unique opportunity to strike a resounding blow for the under-privileged children of England and Wales", the section of the community to whom she had dedicated her life.[4] Very early in her reign she had been accused by the teachers' MPs of not getting to grips with her department. Her lack of initiative and enterprise was a great disappointment to the educational world who had expected more than was possible. She lost much prestige over her lack of understanding of the ministry pamphlet, "The Nation's Schools", which had been prepared by the previous Conservative régime and had a reactionary tone which disturbed many Labour educationalists. At a time when many adventurous ideas were being talked about and the comprehensive school lobby was beginning to attract widespread attention, Miss Wilkinson refused to give it official support, although the idea was in keeping with her own philosophy of providing an open system of education. There were service camps on offer and there is no suggestion these were taken up, for at least there could have been some experiments with the least adventurous of the comprehensive proposals; that of establishing a school base, with a grouping of all manner of facilities for common use by several schools. She had also taken over the emergency scheme for training teachers, although it was a blatant dilution which must have long-term effects on standards already very low. The training of teachers was already based on many small, low-quality colleges often isolated, not only geographically, from the communities which they served. Their defects were so obvious that money spent should have been pumped into them, rather than reproducing more, and even worse, temporary colleges. Although the need for graduate teachers had been apparent with the adoption of Hadow re organization, there had been few moves to bring the colleges closer to the universities. A chance was missed to build up some of the colleges into larger and better staffed institutions with opportunities of working towards degree courses despite the promptings from the McNair Committee Report, "Teacher and Youth Leaders", published in 1943 : it was twenty years before this was taken up.

Most of all there was the chance to seize the national education system as it emerged from the war, confused by the change of administration, deficient in every department, ripe to respond to a bold, imaginative initiative from the top. Instead of enlisting the teachers to her cause much energy was expended in fighting for an acceptance of the school meals service. In default of central leadership the officials took over and they merely picked up the threads as they had been in the 1930s. The malleable moment was lost. Much can be explained by the weight of the economic forces, but it is not easy to see why she allowed the existing pattern of nursery schools built up during the war to be closed down, especially as they were linked with women working in factories, and the country was still hungry for labour. Perhaps the truth was revealed in her obituary notice, when one of her senior civil service advisers saw fit to mention that for the last year her health had been so poor she had been unable to cope with her department. Nevertheless, it was not a stewardship without honour, for her dying effort to maintain her schemes for raising the school-leaving age had a lasting effect on her male colleagues whom "Red Ellen" reminded of their socialist principles; her memory guarded education from too drastic cuts during the remaining life of the hard-pressed government.

Up to this time the shaping of the ambitious social reformation had proceeded rather like the erection of a tent in a storm of wind, but the tempo changed to a howling gale. The new Minister was George Tomlinson,[5] a former weaver and trade union organizer who had left school at the age of twelve to work as a half-timer earning half a crown a week. Attlee had great respect for his commonsense yet describing him as one of "a certain number of solid people whom no one would think particularly brilliant". He had been a local government councillor with a special interest in education since 1925. In the spring of 1939 he had been a member of the Labour Party's education advisory committee which had been called on to consider the multilateral schools for possible official party backing in the implementation of secondary education for all. The committee had favoured a few purpose-built schools which could show the value of the approach to secondary education, but did not back the idea as the sole or ideal method of organizing secondary education. Tomlinson continued this attitude when he became Minister and advocated large purpose-built schools with six or seven stream entry with all types of school within a single integrated unit. However, in a circular dated 16 June 1947, he directed that selective schools should not share catchment areas with comprehensive schools. From this ruling there developed the practice of a family whose child "failed the eleven plus" and did not win a place in a grammar school moving to areas where comprehensive education was available.

It is significant that both these working-class Labour stalwarts saw the traditional grammar school as the acme of secondary education.[6] Miss Wilkinson claimed "I was born into a working-class home and I had to fight my own way through to the university" and her own experience was translated into an acceptance of élitism in education, so that the important thing was not full secondary provision for all but for those who were able. Tomlinson declared himself "thrilled at the prospect of helping to make a reality of the slogan 'Secondary Education for All'", but the declared policy of his department was "to maintain the highest possible academic traditions" so that the nation could benefit from "the finest trained brains it possesses, from whichever class of society those brains come". There was some concern for early selection of able children, as well as to prevent early leaving from the grammar school. The same concern was not shown for their less able brethren. It was a virtual adoption of Conservative secondary education policies. At the same time whatever public belief there had been in the quality of the secondary modern schools was rapidly eroding. These were the schools where the reluctant child stayed on an extra year. They were the recipients of the emergency trained teachers. Too often as part of Hadow-style reorganization they were housed in buildings which had been known as elementary and board schools, with teachers still present from the older period. Many of the facilities were obviously makeshift with too small playgrounds further limited by the erection of huts. A story current in several parts of the country told of a newly appointed head teacher eager to establish the school's new identity noticed the school's former name carved on a board nailed over the main entrance. It read "Firshill Senior School". The newly appointed woodwork master was keen to carve their new title on the reverse of the board: "Firshill Secondary Modern School". The help of the caretaker was enlisted to take the board down so the operation could begin. Returning sometime later, the head saw the board had been removed to reveal on its reverse face deeply carved in gothic lettering, "Firshill Elementary School". Even more revealing, it was now clear the board had been originally designed to hide the inscription carved in the stone lintel over the doorway, "Firshill Board School".

Tomlinson was a most popular minister with a genius for public relations and he was no doubt appointed to paper over the cracks in an educational programme which could only move slowly towards the more suitable system. Funds were not available to fulfil all expectations for a system so long neglected. Unlike his abrasive predecessor, he toured the country displaying his genius for smoothing over difficulties with hard-pressed local authorities. He summed up his own term in office in July 1949 when he said, "I am waging an economy campaign. It is not the old sort of economy campaign to reduce expenditure on school building. It is a campaign to get more schools built for the same sum of money." He knew he was fighting a rear-guard action against economic stringency, but he shrewdly illustrated his approach to the task, saying, "I try to convince the Chancellor of the Exchequer that the money he provides for other ministers is spent, but that which he provides for me isn't spent—it is just invested". Equally to the point was his appreciation of the work in the classroom. "I realize that it is not economical or commonsense to train a teacher and then put him in charge of such a large class that all he can do is prevent the children from breaking the furniture."

In the adverse conditions the struggle to improve the basic conditions in the schools went on. The annual reports of the Ministry of Education were virtually a catalogue of deficiencies and the 1948 report deals at length with the deficiencies in buildings, at the same time showing the effects of modern facilities. It reveals a limping service trying hard to stabilize conditions before moving forward. On every page there is a frank confession of inadequacy with a promise to do better, which is even stated in considering local-authority development plans; alongside notices of all manner of makeshifts in the service is the statement, "The material framework of education will look very different when the plans have been put into effect".

In a period of great expectations, which were not realized, there was a singular renaissance in educational thinking and practice which is still working in the schools. Its force is by no means spent and indeed it is part of the revolution in contemporary social attitudes, if not the source of the change. The Ministry of Education produced a series of pamphlets which, apart from the initial one, were essays on educational policy written simply with sincerity. They put over the liberal ideas which had been around in educational circles since the start of the century, although with only limited acceptance. These booklets were cheap, well produced and brief, consequently they were widely used for initial and inservice training of educationalists. The most successful, *Story of a school*, published in 1949, showed what was possible with an archaic building in the introduction of liberal methods. Lively illustrations carried the message to even the casual reader. It is still in print and there must be few teachers who have not been affected by it. The result of these pamphlets was a change in the atmosphere in the schools. Within a decade the authoritarian relationship between teachers and children had changed to one of leadership with the teachers harnessing the energies and interests of the children. This movement had first been launched in Britain at the start of the century through the teaching of the Macmillan sisters relating to nursery schools, but it had moved slowly up the school, via the infant classes, until in the 1950s it had greatly affected primary school teaching. Its effects on secondary education, especially the traditional grammar schools, is hampered by the demands of certificate work which are often met by the development of an intensive cramming course. It is an area where the generation gap becomes apparent, for many parents recall their own regimented school days and view with suspicion their children's new found interest in school. They see methods used which puzzle them, so they are torn between doubting if they are educationally effective, while amazed at the spirit of inquiry and somewhat unco-ordinated knowledge they produce. It is on these doubts that the Black Papers relied for their effect.

At this time there began another educational influence which soon reached into every home. At the end of 1950 there were half a million television licences which fifteen years later became 14 million, approaching one set per household. Unlike radio, television quickly became available to wage earners through easy access to hire-purchase facilities, which had only existed for such purposes from the late 1930s. The first generation of children with television experience were watching annually something approaching the hours spent in school. This daily window gazing on the wider world gave contact with vocal skills and the exploration of all manner of questions by knowledgeable commentators. The resulting sophistication and experience of the world provided a further stimulus for more demanding education.

In a mixed national economy Labour's restrictions to achieve social reform were an open flank for political attack. Business interests were eager to exploit the demand for goods which ten years of rationing and shortages had created and with a largely right-wing press there was a persistent campaign to show up government incompetence. The General Election of 1950 saw a turn out of 84 per cent, the highest since 1910, with Labour collecting 13.3 million votes for 315 seats against Conservative 12.5 million for 298 seats, with nine Liberals and three others. Labour felt their hold on power was precarious and seemed to lose confidence, for many of their leading ministers were old and tired after over a decade in office. In opposition a new wave of younger Conservative businessmen MPs, sensing the government's uncertainty, introduced a campaign of harrying tactics to force an election in October 1951, much to the disgust of the younger Labour Members.

The Conservatives with 13.7 million votes obtained 321 seats against Labour's 13.95 million votes for 295 seats, with only six Liberals remaining in the House. Churchill at the age of 76 led his first peacetime government. His aging and failing figure was used as a figurehead for a government of business interests, which saw the solution to reconstruction in releasing all controls on land, commodities and trade as quickly as possible, at the same time slashing the newly constructed welfare provisions under the pretext of avoiding prodigal administration and waste. The result was an uncontrolled boom with the start of a spiral of inflation of prices and wages which has never since been checked. While entrepreneurs made fortunes, the expansion of investment in the state social apparatus proceded at a snail's pace.[7] The construction of schools, hospitals and other public-service building faltered, while no less than 110 people became millionaires in the building industry alone, largely through the ending of building controls in November 1954, leading to property speculation. Under the leadership of the Edwardian figure of Winston Churchill a new era began. It was the end of the Puritan ethic as the altruism and community concern of the war period dissolved in the development of consumer society whose first watch word was the political slogan, "A little bit of what you fancy does you good!", used to advocate the end of meat rationing.

Churchill in a broadcast said the country had regained "the freedom, initiative and opportunity of British life" as he unleashed the forces of the market. He had scant use for State education and it was the last senior appointment made when he nominated sixty-year-old Florence Horsburgh to the department. She was not initially included in the cabinet, despite widespread protest at her omission. Her brief was simply to cut down on educational spending which she proceeded to do with so little tact that within a month of taking office the whole educational establishment was in uproar. After six years of cautious expansion with the defects of the provision publicly discussed and acknowledged by the ministry, Miss Horsburgh called for cuts of 5 per cent in all educational planning. The circular announcing instructions for the cuts was cynically sent out on the day parliament broke up for the Christmas recess. The teachers' unions and other pressure groups fulminated in vain. It was the old story of politicians educated outside the State system not appreciating the need for social support through the schools. Two months later, with the storm over the cuts still continuing, Churchill told the Commons the date of the issue of the circular ordering the cuts coinciding with the date of the House's adjournment was accidental and not by design; he was greeted by laughter. Miss Horsburgh was three years Minister of Education, during which time she never seems to have established herself as being interested in educational issues; she merely reproduced the pattern of Conservative educational chiefs between the wars : a Treasury representative to watch expenditure. The restricted targets which Labour had adopted in the period of financial stringency remained despite the gradual return of peacetime conditions and even affluence.

The inadequacies of the schools was shown in a parliamentary exchange of 21 October 1952. National Service for all men of eighteen continued to meet occupation and similar commitments, and the tests given to such recruits provided a check on educational efficiency. A parliamentary question revealed that after eliminating the obviously mentally and physically unfit about one in five men were semi-illiterate, with the implication that about a quarter of all who passed through the State system in their teens were barely able to read or write. This damaging evidence of the defects of the State schools caused no great concern in the government, although the case for a decrease in the size of classes was evident.

Professional educationalists pointed out the unsatisfactory nature of the system particularly in the secondary modern schools. There was growing concern at the unsatisfactory nature of selection tests for grammar school education and the uneven provision of places throughout the country. On 29 June 1953 the National Union of Teachers, alarmed at the effects of growing inflation on education coupled with the lack of progress in implementing the 1944 Act, sent an open letter to all Members of Parliament pointing out the deficiencies in the schools and claiming "the fundamental cause of the present educational difficulties is that no government has allocated sufficient money, labour and materials to meet the needs of the schools and the child population". They also dwelt on the different provisions which were available from "good" and "bad" local education authorities. This sober appeal had little effective response from government circles.

In October 1954 David Eccles took over as Minister.[8] He was a wealthy businessman, a product of Winchester and New College, Oxford, whose previous political appointments had been mainly concerned with economic matters. His writings in 1967 reveal him as a nineteenth-century Tory with a wish to contain the growth of the social services and encourage "more voluntary and private provision" so that society "will become more human the more we practice putting ourselves in our neighbour's place". His educational beliefs still held that the three types of secondary school could be imaginatively built up to give parity of esteem and correspond with children's abilities and aptitudes. He did however see this ideal as unlikely because people "feel safer with uniformity", so "politicians turn to comprehensive secondary schools, hoping to please the voters". While he did not like the Labour suggestion that there must be a revolution in the schools to ensure every child is taught social responsibility, he saw this as not a matter for politicians but for "religion with a new insight and a new model of the truth", as a means of preventing Communism or any one-party system of government. As Minister of Education he followed the same restrictionist line but with more tact, to earn himself the nickname of "Smarty Boots". There was growing agitation over teachers' pay but perhaps his greatest omission was his refusal to prepare for the reduction in the size of classes by increasing the intake of teachers in training. He preferred to wait for a drop in the school population, although the large number of children born in the years 1946 and after, known as "The Bulge", were to be in the schools for at least the next ten years.

In 1955 the post-war boom gathered momentum, employment was high, the balance of payments was in hand and the government had added a million houses to the nation's stock in the last three years. At this favourable moment Churchill handed over the leadership of the Conservative Party and the premiership to Eden, who promptly called an election to increase his parliamentary majority to a comfortable 60-seat margin over all other parties, besides claiming the support of nearly half the votes cast. In December Attlee resigned from the leadership of the Labour Party leaving an unresolved feud between the moderate leadership of Gaitskell and the colourful, left-wing Bevan, which bedevilled the party until the latter's death in 1960. The opposition was not only in disarray but its organization was so poor that no less than $1\frac{1}{2}$ million of its supporters failed to vote in the 1955 election. It is the tradition of the two main parties to treat internal rivalry differently. So Conservative jostling for position was discreetly hidden. On the other hand, Labour's internecine strife, if not actually shouted from the roof tops, was trumpeted across conference and meeting halls. The difference gave a mainly right-wing press much scope for scoring points in commentary.

Eden preached a participating democracy, advocating "partnership in industry" with "joint consultation" in management. This was an imaginative approach, especially to the younger affluent worker and the Labour Party had no effective counter to this new right-wing line. With all set fair for his term of government in the autumn of 1956 Eden became involved in the Egyptian campaign to regain control of the Suez Canal. He forgot Britain's dependence on the United States, both economically and strategically; pressure was soon brought to bear and having launched a campaign which was on the point of success, Eden had to face the humiliation of having to call it off. In January 1957, he resigned to be succeeded by Harold Macmillan. Labour was so disunited that even with this major set back they could not force an election, although opinion polls showed considerable loss of confidence in the government. No one was more aware of the precariousness of their position than the government, for 8.4 million working days lost by industrial disputes in 1957 underlined the dissatisfaction in the country.

The Conservatives, fearful of handing control to an extreme left-wing government, invested considerable sums to introduce commercial marketing methods into politics. Among other spendings was one public-relations campaign costing £468,000 to create an acceptable image of the 63-year-old, Edwardian-style Prime Minister, associating his aristocratic and avuncular figure with a secure and prosperous community. A similar process was applied to the Conservative Party to free it of association with "privilege". With an eye on an election in 1959 there was a careful overhaul of government appointments to give the administration a new look. Education was to stress technical advancement while basic facilities received no increased support. Consequently in September 1957, Geoffrey Lloyd, a Baldwin protégé and a leading figure in Midland Tory circles, took over the Ministry of Education with the announcement that for the first time there was a science graduate in the office. He was supported as Parliamentary Secretary by Edward Boyle, one of few leading Conservatives with an informed interest in the State system of education. The new minister's first major speech was at the opening of Brunel College of Technology at Acton, where he dwelt on the social effects of technical education. He claimed :

"The Butler Act was the most fundamental social reform of the twentieth century. All the barriers to opportunity must come down, whether this is done by providing financial help sufficient to enable students to stay on at school or go to technical college or university, or by ensuring a way forward for those whose talents develop late. As the general standard of education rose and new leaders streamed into the active life of the nation, one might, if one thought in old-fashioned terms, say that a new governing class was being born. But this was to put it wrongly, for although they were bound to be leading men in the broadest sense, by virtue of their ability, they did not spring from any one class but from the nation as a whole. Few people now remember the extreme class bitterness between the aristocracy and the rising middle class in the nineteenth century, because almost in a generation the public schools merged the two contestants to form what became known as the governing class. The educational reforms under the Butler Act, in my belief, will

similarly forge an even wider alliance, in fact embracing the
whole of the nation. As I see it, the old class issues are dying
and we should help them to die quickly."

He added significantly that, "today and for at least a generation
ahead, the country will have to direct its energies and its ablest
men towards the decisive strengthening of the economic sector".

Such a switch of public interest did not take place without
attempts to try to cause the government to pay more attention
to the basic provision. Sir Ronald Gould at the North of England educational conference of the National Union of Teachers
told the delegates that "the great illusion of our time is that 'the
stumbling block' to equal opportunity is the eleven plus examination. It is not. The stumbling block is an inadequate education system." He proceeded to list some of the defects, which
included 150,000 children, 8.4 per cent of those of school age,
still being taught in all-standard schools. Speaking of the general
conditions, he said, "If my diagnosis is correct, then the real
problem is not the examination but the lack of facilities. At best
the solution must take years, and certainly longer than the lifetime of the next parliament, for the task is colossal." It had to
be tackled eventually and it required first "the end of dilapi-
dated and unsatisfactory primary school buildings, and overcrowded classes, with the recruitment of some 100,000 more
teachers".

Meanwhile teachers were protesting about their conditions
and pay, for it was becoming obvious that the quality of male
recruits was falling off and there was a tendency, once qualified to seek employment elsewhere. There was the start of a
campaign for teacher participation in both local and national
policy formation. The Labour Party also had an eye on the
impending election and promised all classes would be reduced
to 40 for primary schools and 30 for secondary schools, with a
reduction to an all-round maximum of 30 as quickly as possible. Sir Edward Boyle defending his government's position,
pointed out this latter measure would require 116,000 teachers
to be added to the present force of 260,000.

A parliamentary debate in January 1959 on the government
White Paper, "Secondary Education For All", produced the
assurance that the Minister Mr Lloyd was "a zealot" and par-

ticularly enthusiastic about "secondary re-organization". It was pointed out that the Parliamentary Secretary, Sir Edward Boyle, had made much of the 10,000 children in secondary modern schools who took the General Certificate of Education, but in the grammar schools with a quarter of the numbers in the modern schools, ten times that number took it, an adverse ratio of 40 to 1. Exploring this situation Labour MP, Edward Short, formerly a headmaster, attacked the White Paper and the policies coming out of it.

> It was as though a doctor diagnosed appendicitis and then treated the patient for indigestion. Everything in the diagnosis pointed to the need for bigger schools which would have a full range of courses. Then they were told that they wanted smaller schools maintaining the distinction between the capacity ranges for which they catered, i.e. schools with a restricted range of courses. The building programme also was a pre-election confidence trick. The general grant was fixed some time ago. The local education authorities, some weeks later, were given a programme of educational expansion and told that the general grant included provision for it. Many just did not believe it. Even if it was true it was absurd. The programme was focused on specific defects which did not occur uniformly; unless the local education authorities were given finance according to the size of the defects in their areas, there could be little hope of the programme being carried through.

The government had also introduced an order increasing the period for teacher training from two to three years, the normal time taken for a degree course. There was great disappointment that little was done to link the teaching qualification with a degree, although this had been discussed since the start of the century and strongly recommended by the McNair Report of 1943 on the training of teachers. This was not lost on Edward Short who told the Commons that in not having implemented policies of this nature when they had introduced the three year course "the government were missing a great opportunity to raise the status of teaching". He asked, "Why not concentrate on the training colleges near universities, integrate them with the universities, and terminate the three year course with a degree in education?"

The 1959 manifestos of the two main parties were very similar as regards what they promised in the educational field, although the Conservative text reflected the punchy style of advertising copywriters: "During the next five years we shall concentrate on producing a massive enlargement of educational opportunity at every level. The necessary work is already in hand. Four programmes, each the biggest of its kind ever undertaken in Britain, are already gathering momentum." As in 1955 both parties promised to replace old school buildings and reduce the size of classes; Labour even pledged themselves to reduce all classes to 30. One noteworthy thing was the growing importance of education in elections, for whereas it rated little mention in the party manifestos of 1945, 1950 and 1951, in 1955 both parties admitted obligations to improve the educational service generally, and secondary education emerged as a party issue. The Conservatives claimed "we need all three kinds of secondary school, grammar, modern and technical, and we must see that each provides a full and distinctive education. We shall not permit the grammar schools to be swallowed up in comprehensive schools. It is vital to build up secondary modern schools, and to develop in them special vocational courses, so that they and the technical schools offer a choice of education that matches the demands of our expanding economy." Labour, as part of their party reconstruction after their electoral defeat in 1951, had adopted the comprehensive school as the form of secondary education which they supported and had issued a pamphlet, "A Policy for secondary education", in June 1951 which identified the comprehensive style of education with the party's political philosophy. Labour wished to do away with selection at eleven, while the Conservatives advocated bringing the modern schools up to the standard of the grammar schools. This whole question was a lively issue in 1955, but in 1959 in a society dedicated to affluence and individual progress, it had become even more important.

The overall political strategy of the Conservatives in October 1959 was so successful that in a 78.8 per cent poll, the party scored a landslide victory when their 13.75 million votes secured 365 seats, against the Labour vote of 12.2 million which rated only 258 seats. In the reformed government David Eccles returned to take over the education department; but even in the moment of triumph there were already signs of stress in the schools. The professional educationalists had repeatedly warned that the basic provision of the education system was inadequate, calling attention to the too large classes and the many inadequate buildings. There was also concern over the numbers and standard of teaching staff. Although the effects were felt throughout the system it was in the adolescent sector where a series of adverse reports revealed much cause for anxiety. Attention was focused on the problems of the adolescent, whereas in many cases, especially where the social background was adverse, the origins of the trouble were much earlier, and the introduction of nursery schools could have tackled many of the problems at their source.

As early as 1954 a report on "Early Leaving" revealed some of the ways the schools were not meeting the needs of the older children, but in December 1959, the Crowther Report, "15 to 18", gave the press materials for some sensational commentary: the *Daily Sketch* prophesied it will "shake every parent", while the *Daily Herald* said it showed "our poverty stricken education must be revolutionized". The report was a lengthy one of 500 pages supported by another 200 pages of statistical data compiled by the Central Advisory Committee for Education. It had been presented to the government in July but was not ready for publication until after the election. Its theme can be illustrated in one brief passage on the case for raising the school-leaving age immediately to sixteen: "The country is a long way from tapping all available supply of talent by present methods. Half the national service recruits to the army who were rated in the two highest ability groups had left school at fifteen."[9]

This damning report of the neglect of the young people of Britain was not alone, but backed by some dozen others all supporting the same picture[10] and confirming the truth of the teachers' unions in their appeals for more financial support to build an educational system suitable for an industrial society. Already in 1958 Robert Carr, a Conservative industrialist, later a leading Minister in the 1970s, had investigated the conditions surrounding the training of young industrial workers. A shortage of even elementary statistics complicated his task, but the situation he found was not complimentary to the employers or the facilities available. In his report he urged that an organization be set up "keeping apprenticeship and training arrangements under review". His sensible appeal to industry to put its house in order met with little response as Andrew Shonfield, a leading economist revealed some three years later in an article in *The Observer* in June 1961, when he found conditions had not materially changed. This situation was all the more deplorable because the year before, in 1957, there had been an inquiry into the training and qualifications of teachers in technical colleges which revealed that only about a third were trained. The report showed a need to seriously re-think the recruitment of skilled staff for which it was forecast there would be an increased demand. Technical education appeared to interest neither educationalists nor industrialists for the report caused little comment, not even rating a leading article in *The Times Educational Supplement*. The Coldstream Report of 1960 which inquired into art training showed another facet of the general neglect of further education. The McMeeking Report of 1959 on commercial education suggested this had moved little from teaching elementary office skills such as typing and book keeping, when modern languages and a deep understanding of business conditions with their associated problems was required. It pronounced that "sustained action must be taken to overhaul and re-invigorate the existing system of commercial education".

The need to give the 80 per cent of youngsters attending non-selective schools a recognized qualification occupied the attention of the Secondary Schools Examinations Council. This was important because of the failure of local-education-authority leaving certificates to establish themselves and the limited suitability of other existing examinations. The Beloe Report published in 1960[11] recommended an "examination below the General Certificate of Education 'O' Level standard", although there were reservations that its development should be watched so that it did not dominate the modern school curriculum. Sir David Eccles already under public pressure for his failure to act on the accumulation of reports, pronounced the examination recommendation "not a very sound proposal", although the main plank in his party's educational policy was to raise the modern schools to parity with other secondary schools. *The Times Educational Supplement*, usually gentle in comment, fumed at his attitude, saying, "First Crowther and now Beloe! Will there be no end to his *laissez-faire*?"

Investigation of the social factors surrounding the lives of youngsters showed much to be desired and an almost total community neglect of the pressures of contemporary life, especially on adolescents. Wartime needs to prepare young people for national service had taught the nation the need for youth clubs; money and support had been forthcoming as well as a pledge for a continuation of the interest in peace time. The Albemarle Report[12] issued in February 1960 showed this had not been honoured, for with the rest of the education system it had been starved of funds. A few dedicated people were striving against odds so that only a minority of young folk were reached by the service. The report in allocating blame for this state of affairs singled out the Ministry of Education for "the lack of an effective lead, which has contributed largely to the weakness of the existing service". It recommended a ten year programme be adopted which included training for staff, together with better pay and conditions. The outlay initially was only £3 million which ensured prompt attention from the ministry, but as Stanley Rowe, the secretary of the National Association of Youth Leaders and Organizers, pointed out, "the report is, it seems, rapidly coming to be regarded as gospel by those concerned with the youth service. This is dangerous, for the more one examines the report, the more one realizes that, in fact, all that is being recommended is a rather incomplete salvage operation."

Allied with this was the Wolfenden Report, "Sport and the Community"[13] of September 1960, which listed the national deficiencies in sports centres, not only for the popular games like football, hockey and tennis, but also for athletics. Finland with a population about a tenth of Britain's had 730 cinder tracks while Britain had around 200. There were few swimming baths and only a handful of international competition standard. The most serious want was in facilities for indoor sport, but the dearth of coaching facilities was nearly as bad. The report recommended the setting up of a sports development council to distribute an annual Treasury grant to worthwhile projects concerned with physical education. The press gave the report a universally enthusiastic reception, but a decade later there is little evidence in international competition that its application has been ample enough to produce noticeable results.

The report, "Our Towns—A Close Up" of 1943, and the Curtis Report of 1946 had shown widespread adverse conditions affecting the lives of many children, as well as the need for continuous concern on this account.[14] The Children Act of 1948 had therefore set up the children's service. Out of these investigations had emerged the need for properly trained and qualified staff, employed under suitable conditions to provide a professional service. A decade later the Younghusband Report[15] of May 1959, investigating the social work in local authority health and welfare services, showed how indifferently the call for proper standards had been followed. Its 400 pages were a plea for basic conditions to establish professionalism, starting with the need for accurate information, the coordination of resources and facilities for research. There was a need for better working conditions, improved training and a supervisory professional body. It is revealing that despite the impact of Freudian doctrines on medicine, nursing, teaching and social work, as well as its effect on the law relating to children, the annual general meeting of the Association of Child Care Officers when discussing this report felt there was much misunderstanding, not only on the part of the general public but also local councillors and MPs, for people were "still apt to believe that the service could be carried on effectively by any sort of person with no more qualification than an awareness that the child existed".

The Committee appointed by the Home Office to enquire into the law as it affected juveniles before the courts, reported its findings in the Ingleby Report on 27 October 1960.[16] It was felt that juvenile procedures should move away from the criminal court and its practices, so that methods could be developed to encourage the co-operation of parents with the local-authority services and the police. Once again the need for training was recommended, this time for the panel of juvenile magistrates so that they should be more aware of the constructional aspects of their work.

This summary of official reports demonstrates the failure of a successsion of Conservative governments in a decade of undoubted national prosperity to show concern for the welfare of the younger generation, especially those with little social advantage. In this period practically every family had acquired a television set costing the best part of £100, there had been a big increase in car owning; yet all the public services dealing with children and young people had been kept starved of money. The neglect was all the more noticeable because the strains of war together with the social concern of the Labour government of 1945–51 had produced pioneer reports which indicated the need to take action, especially in those areas affected by the poverty and neglect of the inter-war years. Sir David Eccles, the minister in charge of education for the greater part of the period of Conservative administration, revealed that he had difficulty in making the cabinet understand the State education system because so few of the members had been involved with "maintained schools".[17] In the five years he was responsible for State education only one subject was discussed in cabinet and that was the proposed Oxford ring road which threatened a cherished university open space.

There was even more to come when in October 1963 the Newsom Report, "Half Our Future" investigated the education of children between the ages of thirteen and sixteen[18], of average or less than average ability, that is the pupils of the secondary modern schools. The report made the glib assumption that there was a clear division into two types of children from birth: the secondary modern school child suitable to be a manual worker, and the grammar school child destined for a managerial position. Despite this obvious gaffe, there was a frank acknowledgement of the inadequacy of the educational service available to the non-academic child. It dwelt on the slum schools where "teachers came and went like water", the complacency of staff with the indifferent facilities, and conveyed the hopeless atmosphere to which many youngsters were subjected in their early adolescence. It was clear many schools had completely lost touch with their children, and neither offered what they required nor what they wanted. It was felt those affected "will eventually become half the citizens of this country, half the workers, half the mothers and fathers and half the consumers". That the country owed them a better deal than the one they were getting, was inescapable.

There was another radical change in the machinery by which

government traditionally managed the people, has escaped notice, although the long term results are accumulative. In the nineteenth century teachers were seen as part of the machinery of control. Teachers are by nature conservative in their views and because of their occupation they tend to support established authority, values and customs with little questioning. With the failure of the Churches to communicate with the mass of people, the teaching profession has become the keepers of the nation's conscience. This is recognized in law by securing for the teacher a unique position in administering corporal punishment. Up to the 1940s the status of teachers was high. They were acknowledged to be better educated, better dressed, secure in regular employment which involved clean work indoors. The pay was high by working-class standards, the holidays unbelievably long and the pension was the hallmark of the quality of its worth. Recruitment was from the lower middle classes and the more able children of the manual workers.

The improved conditions of the 1950s eroded these advantages fast and especially for men,—there were many more materially lucrative openings; soon even the pension scheme did not compare to terms offered by most large firms to long-term employees. Teachers between the wars had supported the central authority even to the extent of accepting a pay cut to help the national economy with little protest. Disillusionment came with the muddle over evacuation, the dilution of the profession and the failure to rebuild the education system after the disruption of the war; all these events began to produce a change in attitude to government. They began to move from their apolitical stance and their unquestioned acceptance of government decisions; and this was furthered by a growing dissatisfaction and questioning, especially among younger teachers. The breakdown of the Burnham machinery in pay negotiations in the early 1960s was the culmination of brushes over pay settlements in 1954 and 1959.[19] Teachers began demonstrating and striking in industrial style with the support of many of the older members of the profession, which was indicative of the new atmosphere. Recent affiliation with the Trades Union Congress and acceptance of their guidance on the Industrial Relations Act of 1972 show a profession traditionally recruited from the working classes now tending to remain identified with its origins rather than transfer allegiance elsewhere. Such attitudes cannot help but rub off on the youngsters they teach, especially as a result of the spread of child-centred education, when there is a radical change in the relationship between teachers and children. Teachers are no longer taskmasters but are tending to be leaders, more like older brothers and sisters to their pupils.

Meanwhile in July 1962 Harold Macmillan, aware of the increasing unpopularity of his government, sacked seven of his cabinet, and in this shake up Edward Boyle became Minister of Education. Although typically educated at Eton and Oxford he had already made his mark as Parliamentary Secretary to the department from January 1957 to October 1959. There was the inevitable flurry of economic trouble but, with less than two years before the next general election, this was not to be allowed to interfere with revamping the social services which were seen as one of the causes for dissatisfaction with the administration. The indifferent state of education being well established, current expenditure was allowed to exceed £1,000 million for the first time. The school building programme was stepped up and some £7 million authorized for training college expansion to meet a shortage of teachers. A £21 million salary increase was granted to teachers. Research funds were trebled to £70,000, still a ridiculously small sum for a service with an annual budget of £1,000 million and no scientific evidence for many of its practices which had evolved from tradition. Middle schools were allowed to go forward and there was an investigation into streaming in primary schools. The Central Advisory Council for Education was reconstituted and asked "to consider primary education in all its aspects, and the transition to secondary education"; their report was published in January 1967 as the Plowden Report "Children and their Primary Schools". Comprehensive-style secondary education had been gaining ground especially in middle-class areas, the typical Conservative strongholds, so the Minister withdrew his party's opposition and in a major speech encouraged experimentation to break away from one national form for secondary education.

Such a large expenditure was welcome, but the education system, like much else of the infrastructure of Britain, had never recovered from the neglect between the wars, aggravated by wartime attrition and the low expenditure of the 1950s. To make an overall impression on the situation there has to be carefully planned lavish expenditure for a decade or more.

Even this renaissance of interest did not fully benefit the basic system because another priority had emerged which had a greater political significance. In 1962 the Anderson Committee had reported on the need for review of the financial backing of students in higher education, followed the next year by the Robbins Report on higher education. This latter is a formidable document fully supported by statistical research and the government with their eyes on the impending election accepted it without reservation. It was however widely attacked for its projections of student numbers, yet it was soon realized that they were usually too modest and a decade later nearly 50 per cent under the actual figure. Nevertheless the permanent officials accepted the need to take action in this costly area, for it was recognized that British education had fallen behind most countries of similar development, and this was linked with a danger to national economic and technical efficiency. As an earnest of this realignment in March 1964 there was established a new Department of Education and Science consisting of four units, to cater respectively for higher education, science, schools and planning. The government went into the election claiming that

> ... the thirteen years of Conservative Government between 1951 and 1964, were a period of unprecedented educational advance in which the proportion of the gross national product, which had itself doubled during those years, devoted to education rose from 3 per cent to over 5 per cent. The main features of educational progress ... were the virtual elimination of all-age schools, which had numbered 5,300 in 1951, a revolution in technical education, a trebling of teacher training places, an increase of 50 per cent in the number of university students and the founding of eight new universities.[20]

For several years there had been growing unrest at the paternalism of British society, and young people were particularly affected by widespread satirical attacks on the existing order. This feeling suddenly flowered into surging hope and youthful expectancy that there could be a new start. The Labour Party offered this with the promise of an end of economic stop-go policies while modern technology would provide an age of affluence. The general election of October 1964 gave them a majority of six. They were home by a whisker only to find a concealed deficit of some £800 million in the balance of payments. The prime minister, Harold Wilson, was forced to choose between two unsatisfactory courses. If he made political capital of the situation he would damage confidence in the £ sterling. The advice of the classical economists in such a situation was to devalue, but that was to be avoided as the only other devaluation had been effected by the previous Labour government. On the other hand he was pledged to finance the increased social services out of increased productivity, only to find that in the circumstances he dare not re-inflate the economy. He decided with his tiny majority to sit tight and bluff it out, waiting for a suitable moment to improve his electoral margin. A damaging dock strike plus the failure of some of his senior ministers to cope with their departments further complicated the position. It was not until October 1966 that he dare go to the country when he secured a resounding majority and he was in a position to act on the economy. The situation gave little option but to devalue, and in the light of hindsight he would have fared better if he had done this immediately on taking office, for the economy was further affected by the world recession following arms cuts by the USA. In brief, recurrent economic difficulties never allowed the Wilson government to expand the economy to provide the ambitious public spending which had been promised. However, although the overall economic plan never materialized, a great deal was achieved by facing the realities of foreign defence commitments and also by administrative adjustments in the tax system designed to make the wealthy pay more. In education this was used to improve basic standards in the schools such as cutting the teacher/pupil ratio, improving buildings and providing more equipment especially to improve associated welfare services. Moreover Labour assumed control at the moment the post-war bulge hit higher education. The expansion of secondary education had been sufficient to increase the demand for university standard courses by 25 per cent in 1964–65. Prince Charles whose two "A" levels took him to Cambridge set up much resentment among youngsters who were having difficulties in finding university places. The impending enfranchisement of eighteen-year-olds, foreshadowed by the Latey

Committee report on the age of majority published in 1967, gave this sector of education added political importance and great weight was put on colleges to take more students. Student unrest was not unconnected with overcrowding.

The atmosphere of continuing crisis caused frequent ministerial changes so that ministers were never long enough in their posts to master their part of an intricate department, which had been once again securely in the control of its permanent officials for probably twenty years. There is usually good reason for such changes and a brief survey of the Labour period in office is useful. The Premier was not insensitive to the importance of education and he initially appointed the able Michael Stewart as Minister only to find that he needed him at the Foreign Office. Time showed that his second choice, Anthony Crosland, although he had a big reputation, was unable to cope with an entrenched civil service, the intricacies of the system and the need to manage the lumbering local government machinery. When it was found necessary to appoint a new team it was also discovered that there would have to be cuts in expenditure. Mr Gordon Walker's fading political star suited the situation, for he could then depart scapegoat like, taking the obloquy with him, leaving the way open for the very man for the job, Edward Short, who would never have accepted the cuts. Mr Short saw the need for consolidating positions claimed but only half won. Against the resistance of the permanent officials he insisted on framing a new Act to preserve liberal advances in the statute book. At the start of his reign in April 1968 it looked possible to collect many disparate recently enacted small measures and add other progressive material to make a new Act by 1970, the centenary of the start of the State system; a creditable ambition for a dedicated former head teacher. He underestimated the power of the officials, and the decision to hold the election in the spring of 1970 rather than the autumn pipped him at the post.

In surveying the period in more detail it will be realized there was no effective Minister of Education until January 1965, three months after the election owing to the rapid promotion of Michael Stewart. The longest incumbent was Anthony Crosland who held the post until August 1967, a two and a half years which were both crisis ridden and economically austere; but the failure of the Labour education programme was largely his responsibility. He had been educated at Highgate School and Oxford where he returned to lecture in economics from 1947 to 1950. As a leading member of the academic wing of the Labour Party in 1956 he wrote *The Future of Socialism*. This was revised in 1964 to become the Bible of moderate left-wing intellectuals. In the revised edition of 360 pages eighteen are devoted to education, seven dealing with public schools and six with comprehensive education. Intellectuals have a habit of underestimating educational situations assuming that attendance at school gives a thorough understanding of the processes involved. However the State system, which depends on co-operation between the central authority and many local authorities over whom there is only indirect control, is full of pitfalls. It requires more than an instant solution. This energetic minister with no understanding of the pedestrian depths of provincial administration and the problems of the lower levels of the schools, sought the advice of academics for the most part similarly handicapped. As happens the pressure groups moved in immediately to try the new man out. The civil servants were waiting with their version of the "bum's rush" over the question of higher education. They had already tried the same tactics successfully with Mr Stewart leading him to negate significant links between the universities and the colleges of education although the situation is well explained in the short McNair Report of 1943 as well as the voluminous Robbins Report of 1963. In this case the Minister was led to espouse a binary policy for higher education by being pushed to make a policy speech on polytechnics, which, although he rated it "an appalling blunder", he did not reverse. The permanent officials aimed at having a publicly announced policy by which the pressures for higher educational places could be met in the cheapest way, which obviously made life easier in a department always dependent on allocation of funds for decisions on how far educational policies can be implemented.

Mr Crosland must also bear the responsibility for the failure to make the most of opportunities to reorganize teacher education, which was in the end cobbled in the worst tradition of British gradualism. The training colleges had been repeatedly condemned as indifferent. The source of this was easy to see; they were too small, geographically and intellectually isolated with mediocre staff. In some hundred years of development they had produced no educational research, developed no applications of psychology and sociology to the work in the schools, there was no body of theory or knowledge about education based on field work, and no scholars of standing had emerged from the colleges. Every investigation showed them to be generally reactionary and indifferent in quality. Their worst failure was in not involving their students in the problems of the children, in contrast to the social workers who evolved their training much later. The chance was presented to both radically reorganize these colleges, virtually the sole source of teachers in the unselected part of the system, and at the same time use their sites, which were often extensive, as the base for expansion on polytechnic lines. What happened was a perpetuation of the binary system of teacher education as to meet the teacher shortage, other small colleges were founded, and worse still small colleges expanded but solely for teacher training. The result was that their faults were writ large as the poorly qualified instructors of one subject were promoted to take over newly created departments, and progress was hampered by lack of experience in any other form of education. The renaissance of State education was put back at least a quarter of a century.

This omission was compounded in April 1965 when Mr Crosland made a speech in which he claimed to expound fourteen ways of producing and utilizing teacher manpower more efficiently. In practically every instance they involved dilution of training and education. It was a cynical disregard of those egalitarian principles Mr Crosland had expounded so ably in his writing. There was the refusal to see the importance of the nursery, infant and primary sector, especially to children from indifferent background. As a result the issue of Circular 10/65, declaring the government intention to end selection at eleven and back comprehensive secondary education, meant many children were unable to benefit from the new opportunities, as the Plowden Report of 1967 showed. The announcement of a programme to set up some 30 polytechnics can be similarly faulted. He was hardly the man to pluck the nettle of the public school which worried many Labour MPs, so a commission to investigate their integration into the national system was set up. This two and a half years was one of deep disappointment to many educationalists who had looked for so much. It was not altogether his fault for there was no Labour plan for education and the economic situation was never easy, but much more could have been done if the grass-root situations had been understood. There was *ad hoc* treatment of problems as they were presented and the evidence suggests an acceptance of existing departmental policy leading to indifferent and wasteful development.

There was a change of team in August 1967, but the winter of 1968 saw the global economic situation affected as the USA began at last to feel the effects of long entanglement in Asian wars. Traditionally cuts in social expenditure were called for. On the 16 January 1969 the Education Minister, Mr Gordon Walker, flanked by Alice Bacon and Shirley Williams, explained to a special press conference the necessity and nature of cuts in educational expenditure. The main item was to postpone raising the school-leaving age to sixteen for two years in order to save £70 millions. Someone with Ellen Wilkinson's dedication was sadly missed!

After three gifted amateurs a professional was engaged to take over the department in Edward Short. In some intellectual circles he is not highly considered, but he has the advantage of spanning several political strands of the Labour Party where he commands much respect in trade-union circles. He is an ex-headmaster who came to Westminster through local government in Newcastle. After his week in Parliament he flies home for the weekend with his wife, a primary school headmistress. He is a product of the State education system, not the bright boy who escaped to Oxbridge and lost touch, but the one who stayed with his own folk. Only Chuter Ede before him had the same understanding and dedication to the State schools. The academics can enthuse about education as the main vehicle for social mobility, but to practitioners like Short and Ede the power of the school to help children, many of indifferent ability, was part of their way of life. He had the practitioner's suspicion of the theoretician and administrator, so time-honoured tactics of trying to rush him into policies did not get very far. He looked round for professional advice, only to discover that he was the only educationalist in decision-forming circles, for the department was dominated by the

administrators while the specialists, the members of Her Majesty's Inspectorate of Schools, were relegated to an advisory capacity. There is a long history of uneasy relationship between the administration and the educationalists, which is seen in the relations between the executive and the Educational Advisory Council. Professional representative groups, like the National Union of Teachers, have traditionally much to say to the executive but they are not noticeably effective. Situations are dealt with on administrative and not educational grounds, indeed the ruling seems to be often contrary to professional advice which is brushed aside. All but a handful of the ministers in charge of education have been educated outside the State system and consequently have little understanding or sympathy with a department which by the nature of its work can show few dramatic triumphs. To such people the part played by local authorities and the attitudes of professional bodies are hard to understand. The department has been used patently and repeatedly as a parking place for politicians between posts. In such conditions the permanent officials have worked out their own course which they will try to follow, adding on the way gestures of the appropriate political flavour. Such officials are not educationalists and have no reason to understand or be sympathetic to the problems of non-selective education. Bureaucracy, no matter how enlightened, favours the known routine and the unruffled cycle of the administrative year, which means acceptance of the guidance of the senior department, the officials of the Treasury. The record is not a good one and much of the indifferent quality of British education comes from this lack of leadership at the centre. The department had not bothered to arm itself with a research department until Crosland introduced one in 1966, although the muddle over teacher supply must have prompted a search for guidance machinery. The Fulton Committee investigating the working of the civil service found

---

"Edward Short, the weathered headmaster from the north, who after four dissipated years of Labour administration was left to pick up the pieces in the Department of Education and Science"
—Brian Jackson

(*New Statesman* – 12 November 1971)

much to ponder on the workings of the education department. The root of the matter is that education is not given full professional status as a department, as those involving law and medicine; the professional head of the department is not therefore an educationalist.

On taking over the department Mr Short refused to accept the official current attitudes to education issues and sought for professional advice to help realign departmental policy. The solidarity of the civil service moved quickly to block the introduction of outsiders in the same way that the introduction of independent economists had been discouraged from working for the Ministry of Economic Affairs. After a survey of the situation in the face of departmental passive resistance, Mr Short maintained the need for a new Education Act to introduce social justice into the administration of the service. He considered this was necessary to pronounce on half-won principles, such as comprehensive education, and to widen the horizons of higher education as well as consolidating numerous small measures in the one enactment. He set in progress a review of the whole educational scene. This started in 1968 shortly after he took office so it seemed reasonable to plan to launch the Bill in 1970, the centenary year of the first Education Act, but this underrated the delaying power of the permanent officials. Nevertheless he went doggedly ahead sketching out the ground plan of a truly national education system to be embodied in the first major Education Act of the Labour Party. The planning followed the lines of the preparatory work for the 1944 Act. Some sixty organizations were circularized for their suggestions and reactions to gather the feelings of the main interested bodies especially the teachers and local authorities. It was a carefully planned review covering the pre-school age to higher education, with especial thought for the largely forgotten non-academic youngsters. The consultations went on for over a year when the first drafts of a Green Paper were prepared to act as a focus for the national debate which was to precede the next Act. Early in the planning it was realized that impending local-authority reorganization complicated even draft schemes.

Meanwhile something was done to piece together the fragments of his party's educational promise even though the economic climate was difficult. Not the least of his worries was the inheritance of the culmination of teachers' dissatisfaction with pay settlements which had grown out of the actions of two previous Conservative ministers, Sir David Eccles and Sir Edward Boyle, who had both rejected or sought to alter pay agreements arrived at after Burnham Committee consultations. A strike resulted which was particularly embarrassing because the government had declared a wages freeze, while a variety of newspaper articles showed graphically how poorly teachers were paid. There was no doubt where public sympathy lay and there were even demonstrations by older children supporting their teachers. It was pointed out that the profession was short of 4,000 members and there were still some 700,000 children being taught in classes of over 40. Mr Short managed to meet the claims of his own profession more or less in full, although as it was belated he gained little credit for it. He set about rebuilding the machinery for salary negotiations and re-establishing trust between the central department and the profession. However his proposals for a selfgoverning profession were viewed with some suspicion.

The patently unsatisfactory state of the schools enabled him, even in a period of severe economic restraint, to secure an historic departmental allocation of £2,500 million, against £1,418 million in 1964, the first time that national spending on education had surpassed defence. Even this sum did not allow for much other than the reduction of class sizes and repairing the cuts of 1968. Realizing that the funds were not there for nursery schools as required by the Plowden Committee of 1967 on the primary schools and the Seebohm Committee of 1968 on the reorganization of the social services, Short encouraged playgroups. He saw this as one way of building up a voluntary movement which would facilitate political acceptance of universal provision when the occasion allowed. Deadlines were given to the local authorities to end the employment of unqualified teachers and overlarge classes. Middle schools began to appear with the growth of independent infant schools. To assist him in his planning the Minister arranged quarterly meetings of the inspectorate which gave a new feeling of solidarity to that body.

All the time the great fulfilment was frustrated by lack of

funds but no sector was worse hit than secondary education. Labour were committed to ending eleven-plus testing and the furtherance of comprehensive schools. The result was a series of inadequate policies based on Circular 10/65 of 12 July 1965 which listed six types of comprehensive schemes, including two which did not provide full opportunity for secondary education for all children. These were to be regarded as interim measures until suitable buildings for a full comprehensive scheme were available. The crux of the matter is the need to have a school for about 1,000 children in order to be able to offer the full scope of courses. Without such buildings there was the need to fall back on buildings designed for around 500 places. Such makeshift arrangements gave ammunition to those opposed to the comprehensive principle. Conservative local authorities had every opportunity to procrastinate or to evade the principle of equal provision by a variety of ingenious schemes which protected grammar school interests. Without funds to provide the buildings, successive ministers went through the ritual exhortation of reactionary authorities to take action. Mr Short had the misfortune to see a small Bill framed to do away with eleven-plus selection defeated on a technicality in committee.

Such frustrations in a department which cried out for radical reform made the new education Bill all the more important for it would at least give the principle of equal educational opportunity the support of the statute book, as well as ironing out the unequal provision between the progressive and indifferent local authorities. All was set for publication of the Green Paper in the spring of 1970, but the preface supplied by the departmental draftsmen did not suit the Minister, who insisted on considerable revision. It was a fatal delay. The Conservative opposition had singled out the Prime Minister as the most effective speaker on the political scene both in the House and, more important electorally, on television. They resolved to concentrate their resources on damaging "his credibility". In this respect they had two advantages. Firstly Mr Wilson, committed to ambitious schemes of social reform, and unable to give more than token fulfilment because of the economic situation which prevailed, was particularly vulnerable. Secondly, with the Conservative interest having almost complete control of the press, a campaign was launched which could not be effectively answered in kind or in volume. The success of this campaign caused him to decide to hold the impending election in the summer of 1970, rather than the autumn. Ministers were planning for this latter date and Mr Short was caught with his work completed but unpublished. His Green Paper would certainly have been useful in the election, but the year and a half's work went into the departmental pigeon hole for the election was lost.

It is nevertheless an important educational document because for the first time the Labour Party had a carefully thought out educational programme which could eventually be the basis of a fresh revision of the basic legislation. There have been several versions of the programme circulated, the most widely known embodied in the planning document, "Labour's Programme for Britain", published in July 1972. Its author has since been promoted to the deputy leadership of his party but will be reluctant to see his plan abandoned. It provides that the education department should take over the responsibility of education for the under fives, with complete comprehensive provision from that age to sixteen. The standards of this service were to be secured by requiring local authorities to meet standards laid down by the central authority, thus ending the wide disparity in the opportunities available in different parts of the country. Selection was to be abolished for all school places up to the age of eighteen. To make the control of schools more democratic, local institutions, older pupils, parents and staff were to have some say in the running of their schools. Parents and senior pupils were to have the right to elect for religious education, which must be provided in all schools. Continued education was to become a condition of employment for young people between the age of sixteen and eighteen. All education and training in industry was to be under the supervision of the education inspectorate. The long-term aim is to do away with all fee-paying schools of which there are some 2,700 in England and Wales, only half of which are recognized as efficient. These schools cater for seven per cent of the nation's children largely depending on the parent's ability to pay fees. A system of licencing was to be introduced and these would only be renewed when the schools satisfy standards laid down by the central authority. This would deal with the indifferent institutions while the public schools would be restricted by the end of their valuable financial privileges. Their advantages of small pupil teacher ratio, influential connections and specially provided linked scholarship to the status universities have long worried the Labour Party as strongholds of class privilege. The realization that some of their financing is treated as charitable, thus avoiding tax on the basis of foundation documents which purport to provide for the education of needy children, has stimulated this resentment. The 176 direct-grant schools were to end, so that they will have to opt either to become part of the State system or be entirely dependent on fees.

The several versions contain some thought-provoking variations. For example in the document for political discussion at the popular level a more cavalier treatment of public schools is advocated than in other versions. It is also noteworthy that out of deference to the manual workers' dislike for prolonging education, in the popular version no mention is made of proposals to raise the school leaving age to seventeen and eighteen towards the end of the 1970s, which is included in other versions.

In April and May 1970 the opinion polls gave Labour a consistent lead so Prime Minister Wilson's decision to go to the country seemed a good one, but when the election was held in late June it was the Conservatives who were returned. They attracted over 13 million votes (46.4 per cent of the total cast) to secure 330 seats, while Labour with nearly a million less votes (43 per cent) captured only 287 seats.

The chief reason for Labour's failure to win re-election arose from the great expectations their 1964 victory had aroused as regards reconstruction, reform and social advance, which had not been dramatically fulfilled. Labour's failure to find the finance for their plans had caused first disappointment and then resentment. The plight of the Prime Minister first balancing on a precarious majority of six, as he angled for his electoral win in 1966, followed by his mask of calm as he faced economic difficulties leading to devaluation in 1968 was not understood; for a politician in difficulties often increases them if he brings them into the open and much of the time Harold Wilson had little space for economic and political manoeuvre. This seeming inaction discouraged traditional Labour supporters so that they refused to vote in local elections for their representatives. It also encouraged another and far-reaching reaction in a revolt against paternalism by which, instead of accepting passively, people demonstrated their dislike, demanding to be consulted and to have a share in the deliberations before decisions were made. Although this trend had flowered in the 1960s it was not entirely new. It can be seen as a logical extension of the nineteenth-century utilitarians with their dedication to the happiness of the greatest number. It had been given popular expression in the growth of trade unions from the 1890s, but the movement had been submerged in the interwar period, only to blossom again in the urgencies of the 1939–45 war. It had been expressed in the widespread adoption of shopfloor representation which had developed into the post-war shop-steward movement, an expression of the individual worker's feeling of helplessness against the impersonal management of larger and larger industrial units. This desire to be a party to more and more community decisions had been taken up by the post-war generations, who were better educated than their parents thanks to the extended facilities available under the Education Act of 1944, the affluence of the 1950s, the widening experience of television and foreign travel. These informed, energetic younger people were impatient with the passivity of their elders. They had expected much of the 1964 government and were impatient with its difficulties. The Labour Party were not entirely unsympathetic with activities which reflected the early political careers of many of its members, and indeed most of the measures of reconstruction shaped by the 1945–51 government and since had included machinery for consultation. In fact Edward Short's lost education measure included a reorganization of the governing bodies of schools and colleges to introduce elected representatives of local interests, parents and older pupils to replace the unsatisfactory, nominated and remote bodies set up by the 1944 Act.

On the other hand the older and more authoritarian sections of society looked on the resulting rash of demands and demonstrations this movement produced as signs of the decline of the long-held Protestant ethic and morality based on hard work, thrift and obedience. They were inclined to blame the increasing freedom which was evident in the schools for this. There was a demand for reassurance that the old ways and values were still valid, and a wish for firm government which would stand no nonsense. The Conservative Party, with a promise of a return to the old and trusted ways where everyone had a place and knew it, rallied such people to its support, especially the older generations and those who felt challenged by the vigour of the youthful movement.

The world of education found itself part of the battle ground between the old and the new. There were many attacks on the liberalized education system and these were finally focused through the publication of a series of so-called Black Papers on education, the first of which appeared early in 1969. They were collections of right-wing writings, for the most part brief and easily read. Complaint was made about freeplay methods in the infant classes, project teaching in primary schools, comprehensive secondary education, the rapid expansion of higher education and experimental courses in some of the new universities. Unease was expressed that the teachers were no longer the fountain of true knowledge expounding on the glories of past civilizations. It was feared Communism or worse lurked in every academic corner, with anarchy the fashion of the day. The evidence of a changing pattern of staff/student relationships with a demand from the students for a say in the running of their courses appeared to herald the abrogation of scholastic control. These tracts were widely commented on and educationalists realized how far they had travelled from the ideas of school and college entertained by parents with only the narrow and formal experience of their childhood to guide them. At the same time there were demands from students for radical changes in teaching methods and administration.

Even before the 1970 election Conservative spokesmen on education had repeatedly made the point that education costs were soaring beyond the limit which the country could support and ways must be found to prune them. This was urgent because the voting age had been lowered to eighteen so it would be difficult to openly curtail further education costs which were considerably higher than other forms of education. There was much "kite flying" to see public reaction to cutting the social assistance side of the schools service such as school meals and milk. There was even discussion of fee paying for all schools.

'. . . and, due entirely to my foresight, the throwing of school milk bottles has virtually been eliminated.'

Margaret Thatcher and School Violence
(*The Observer* – 9 April 1972)

The Conservative government of 1970 was led by a cabinet made up almost entirely of bankers and businessmen. Of the 330 Conservative MPs, 189 had clearly defined business interests, mostly with major companies, many holding several directorships. The social service section of government was the subject of special attention, the Department of Education and Science being put in the charge of two able financial lawyers with no commitment to the educational service. The senior minister, Mrs. Margaret Thatcher,[21] was the archetypal Tory lady married to the director of an oil company. Her twin children went to public schools; the boy to Harrow, the girl to St Paul's. Like Prime Minister Edward Heath, she came from a small tradesman's family, and passed via the local grammar school to Oxford. As a barrister who specialized in tax cases and had been in a Conservative team specializing in Treasury matters, she was the typical exchequer watch-dog in the educational chair. There was no evidence of interest in education or children's problems before she became shadow Education Minister

in November 1969; indeed she had supported a backbench
attempt to restore the use of corporal punishment for young
offenders. When taxed by the National Union of Teachers for
not consulting them on major policy decisions as had long been
the practice, she made her position plain with the reply. "I
believe consultation is only meaningful if you enter it in a state
of mind where you intend to be influenced by the representations." Lord Butler may have thought this but would never have
made such a remark. In a year she achieved the distinction of
becoming a legend in her own life time, as a figure of crass
reaction in an area where liberal ideas about the treatment of
children and their problems had been common currency for
years. Attacks on her were so bitter that on one occasion an
opposition spokesman appealed for moderation.

Her educational philosophy, as far as one can be seen, was
concerned only to preserve an area of parental choice, which to
most families meant very little. As the popular *Daily Mirror*,[22]
put it in one of its rare educational pronouncements, "Mrs
Thatcher's talk of educational choice is moonshine unless she
can solve the grievious overcrowding in some schools". To a
minority of the middle classes who are paying for the education
of their children it has significance, but there was little evidence
of her concern for the large majority of children. This was
probably an advantage because the task which faced her was
not an easy one. As a minister in a government dominated by
commercial interest, anxious to negotiate entry into the
European Market but bedevilled by unemployment, bad industrial relations, costly peace keeping in Ulster as well as brisk
inflation, she could expect little help from her colleagues. The
problems which faced her were many. There was a growing
middle-class lobby of traditional Tory supporters for nursery
schools; the Plowden Report had underlined the parlous state
of many primary schools, local pressures were gathering from
areas of all political colours for full comprehensive facilities
while raising the school-leaving age in 1972 to sixteen showed
up the inadequacies of many non-selective secondary schools
and also the indifferent provision for further education. The
same measure stimulated more students to take "A" level courses
leading to an increase in the demand for higher education, the
notoriously expensive sector of education. The demands for

"I've put his name down for Holland Park Comprehensive
of course."

(*The Times Educational Supplement* – 2 July 1971)

funds to maintain the development of the thirty polytechnics
had caused university growth to be halted, with neither section
happy with their share of the cake. There had also been a
notable increase in the demand for higher education from girls.
These accumulated pressures, many from traditional Tory sections of the community as well as the newly enfranchised
eighteen-year-olds, had no small political significance.

Faced with this situation Mrs Thatcher had above all else to
conserve her funds and yet give an appearance of progress.
Everything which would allow a charge was reviewed as a
possible source of income, so up went the cost of school meals
and there were cuts in the supply of free milk for the over

sevens.[23] When these increased costs caused some children to bring sandwiches for their midday meal, there was even an attempt to charge for the use of the school facilities, which ceased when a public outcry resulted. Not all the cheese paring was so clumsily managed, for by study of the previous government's economies, ways were found to extend them; the mere extension of a precedent which the opposition has set made effective criticism difficult, as Labour found when they attacked over the school milk and meals issue. The botched comprehensive schemes, those with several smaller units on different sites suddenly found favour, for by a process of name changing and some minor additions, secondary modern schools could be designated as supplying comprehensive education. As a consequence, the larger schools were discovered to be confusing to the children and educationally undesirable, while the smaller units were given ministerial blessing. The Labour Party, conscious that they had allowed the dilution of the comprehensive formula, found difficulty in attacking this further distortion of the principle.

Similarly, expanding higher education through the polytechnics had pointed the way to a cheaper system, but these institutions have already shown themselves politically sophisticated through their links with local industry and other interests. Consequently there were soon signs of a powerful lobby for comprehensive higher education, while some colleges make no secret of their intention of pressing for university status. In view of their brief history it is interesting to contrast this advance with the slow development of the colleges of education. One of the educational successes of the Labour government, the Open University, was exploited to provide an even cheaper form of higher education for youngsters who have just completed a secondary school course. Higher education for more people moved further and further from the original pattern of the older universities, but as two Labour ministers had encouraged the start of a binary system for Higher Education the party in opposition were limited to quibbling on details, always a position of weakness.

Somewhat disturbing is the popular image of students of higher education resulting from their agitation for better conditions and allowances. This has been played up by the press to represent them as extreme and idle, a view only too readily accepted by some sections of the public, which is regrettable as more children of manual workers take higher education courses.

This survey of the development of the public education system ends in a moment of hiatus in 1974. At the start of his period in office in 1970, the Premier, Edward Heath, had promised his party "a quiet revolution" which would "permanently change the outlook of the British nation". What he intended was the establishment of a right-wing régime which would stand firm in dealing with the trade unions and allow the forces of the Market to decide the stabilization of the economy following entry into the European Common Market. Such a nineteenth-century approach to both labour and management was publicized by slogans about everyone standing on their own two feet and denying any help for "lame ducks". Confrontation with the unions was inevitable and despite repeated defeats the government persisted with a widely unpopular Industrial Relations Act which united organized labour more strongly than at any time since 1926. With social security allowances and back payment of income tax, the strikers still knew hardship, but "the whip of starvation" was no longer available to break strikes. Confrontation showed there had been a swing in the balance of power between labour and management. Unions were better organized, strategy and tactics had become sophisticated, leaders more adroit in negotiation. Moreover communication is in many ways instant because television takes the issues into every home. Use of government force is limited, for after years of military intervention in Ulster, no government could lightly use troops in civil disputes. The Conservative government enmeshed in union struggles, slid into ordering a three-day working week which lasted over ten weeks, to fall in 1974.

The result was a minority Labour government who could do little in a period of world uncertainty aggravated by rising prices in many important primary commodities especially oil, which caused a dramatic change in the negotiations between suppliers and consumers. Disagreement in the Common Market, loss of confidence in the USA through the Nixon scandals leading to his fall in August 1974, and threats of nationalization saw the stock market plunge to its lowest point in 50 years. A succession of financial débâcles showed "the unacceptable face of capital-

ism" and completed the managerial party's discomfort. Indicative of this were discussions on coalition and national governments, retired senior officers of the armed services setting up
embryo Fascist groups while a flurry of newspaper articles
scouted the idea of a take-over by the army if inflation could
not be halted. Timely concessions, such as worker directors, were
widely proposed but not by workers. The Conservative manifesto
for the election in October 1974 followed this approach. The
education offering put forward by the shadow Minister, Mr St
John Stevas, promoted parental rights through local representation on school governing bodies, with a call for educational
opportunity for all through a system of improved quality. This
sounded like a summary of Mr Short's draft Green Paper which
had gathered dust for four years during Mrs Thatcher's rule,
when Mr St John Stevas was a junior minister in the same
department.

The moment of balance between the parties illustrates the
recurring dilemma in the development of popular educational
facilities. The Right see these as a social privilege which can be
extended in scope and quality as public demand requires. The
Left consider them a social service, along with others relating to
health and welfare, all needing a uniform provision to improve
the quality of life, first attention being given to the more fundamental needs of mankind. This repeatedly banishes education to
a position of secondary priority, especially as the Left seems only
to acquire power in times of economic set back. The Right,
unencumbered by any ideology, sees the situation in terms of
winning and retaining power, and to this end when under pressure there is always the quick concession; unfortunately the
mass of people have little commitment to education, so any
demand tends to be selective, even élitest and of a middle-class
pattern. The advance of public education is therefore always
haltered; when the Right are in power they supply restrictive
facilities to meet the wishes of their supporters. When the Left
are in power they have grandiose plans but fail to find the means
of fulfilling them. Great expectations are raised which faced
with the realities of government they cannot satisfy. When they
lose momentum and falter, the more politically astute Right are
ready to move in.

XI

The Promised Land

"Only the educated are free"—Epitectus.
"There is no wealth but life"—Ruskin.

ONE CONCLUSION WHICH should be clear from this study
of the development of State education is the consistent social
process to minimize the provision of more educational opportunities for the children of manual workers.

The causes for this are elaborately involved. The early realization that schools were expensive and an ignorant working class
was more amenable than an informed one, are only two factors
in a log jam of obstacles blocking the extension of State education. Although the techniques of modern public relations obscure
the contemporary situation, very little has changed in the basic
positions; indeed as the same interests advance the same arguments used 150 years ago to counter each extension of educational provision, they are virtually predictable. The outburst of
arguments against actually raising the school-leaving age to
sixteen, over a half century after it was promised in the Education Act of 1918, have a distinct similarity to those advanced
in the nineteenth century over curtailing the employment of
children in factories or raising the school-leaving age as an
extension of the 1870 Act.

Historical resistance to change is always surprisingly durable
and especially so in Britain where the invocation of tradition
will create an instant halo of excellence. This is successful in
education, although little of quality in the system predates the
1902 Act. At the present the biggest obstacle to overhauling the
system is the reverence of the grammar schools, although educationally they are often dated in approach, being little more
than cramming establishments. Their long histories have little
significance and it is time their limitations were exposed, for

they are possibly the worst part of the system, and certainly a socially divisive force.

A quick run through the development of the national education system illustrates most of these points. It starts with the initial setting up of two distinct systems to serve the sharp divisions in the caste structure of British society. Charitable bequests which could have blunted these differences tended to be used to preserve the divisions, by being interpreted so that instead of bringing in the labourer's children, they were diverted to help the poor of the middle classes. Although the two main systems of schools started to take institutional shape in the sixteenth century, there remained a variety of establishments, especially among the non-grammar schools. In nearly all financing was effected by charity and fees, giving a variable income at the best barely adequate for maintaining efficient standards. Early in the nineteenth century Arnold revitalized the ailing residential grammar school system thereby establishing anew the model for secondary education. At the same time the development of the monitorial system gave a pattern for the schools for the lower orders; its main teaching technique, learning by rote, influenced the methods of instruction for more than a century. The reports of the 1860s officially defined the school categories and tended to persuade existing institutions to accept themselves as one of the two types. If a school had a good measure of financial support from an endowment, social pressures prompted moving towards becoming a grammar school. This was a continuing trend and, in some cases, even the necessity for an Act of Parliament to authorize the change, proved no barrier.

The 1870 Education Act and its supporting legislation gave a firm foundation for the State education system by adequately financing school places for all children and making attendance compulsory. In a decade the new board schools began to challenge the grammar schools, many of which were inadequately financed and consequently deficient of quality. The threat to the grammar schools came from the addition of extra classes at the top of the school as more children stayed on and the curriculum was extended. These "higher tops" as they were called, and developments of technical education appeared to be setting the educational pace; a facility catering for the lower orders was becoming more successful than the private schools used by the monied classes. Morant, the evil genius of British education, found a way of cutting off the advance to the "higher tops" and reasserting the traditional supremacy of the grammar schools. He destroyed the embryo comprehensive schools and built up the ailing system of private secondary schools by regular financing and inspection. He obtained some of the money for the renewal of the schools used by the managerial classes by cutting off support for the under fives. This was particularly detrimental to the poorer families because such early schooling allowed women to work. It also cut down a flourishing development when about half the children between the ages of two and five attended school, a rate of attendance not yet re-established. This was at the time when the nursery school movement was demonstrating its potential for helping poor families raise their standards. This saving used to finance the new secondary grammar schools, set a pattern of expenditure which was not modified until the 1944 Act. The teachers for the elementary schools were the products of the same system and they had been pointedly shut out from any measure of training or education which would improve their academic background or considerably raise their status. The establishment of municipal universities gave opportunities to do something about this but Morant, the creator of secondary education in the public system, appears to have written off the whole of the labouring classes and the schools they attended. This unsatisfactory situation defied successive Liberal governments from 1905 up to the 1914–18 war; attempt after attempt failed in the larger issues of constitutional reform and the Irish question, leaving the unsuccessful Bill of 1912 as evidence of their efforts.

It is noteworthy that the concessions made to involve the lower orders in the 1914–18 war included a revision of the education system. Even with that advantage the 1918 and 1920 Education Acts were but part of the proposals planned in 1912. The granting of nearly full franchise in 1918 proved a big disappointment because the working-class vote divided between the Labour and Liberal parties, so that the political skill of the Conservative leader, Baldwin, ensured that although only commanding a minority allegiance, the other parties never made common cause and the Conservatives dominated the interwar period. The post-1918 legislation was quickly frozen so there was little educational advance for a quarter of a century, except the secondary grammar schools slowly expanded and improved in quality. Nevertheless this was a new period of social development because, up to 1918, politics had gone on over the heads of the bulk of the population for they had no vote. The Franchise Acts of 1918 and 1928 changed all that and completely altered the character of the electorate bringing in two hitherto neglected but major interests, namely the poorer paid, mostly manual workers, and all women. Although both sections were unprepared for the franchise and were led to support all manner of policies which ignored their interests this could not continue indefinitely and, almost imperceptibly, policy-making took more and more account of the poorer families, although appeals to international politics could still affect the nation; even so imperialism was harder to sell. Yet this broadening of the franchise worked against the advance of education for the emerging working-class movement concentrated its resources on winning material benefits such as unemployment allowances, better housing, and modest extensions to the embryo health service. The failure of the General Strike of 1926 and the division of the Labour party on the formation of the National Government in 1931 ensured that the speed of social reform remained safely in Conservative hands. The device of permissive implementation, and the concentration of control in the county councils were the main techniques used to ensure the public services were run at minimal level. In education the demands of expanding industry for more professional and technical skills were met by the steady increase of students from the grammar schools, few of whom went to universities. Where further qualifications were required they were acquired by evening study after work at little financial cost to the community. This ensured an increasing number of children were taken from the elementary schools to be processed through the grammar schools. The system disguised the subsidizing of fee-paying places and had other advantages for managerial interests. It fed this section with a steady reinforcement of able children, at the same time keeping secondary education cheap for the less able children who could afford to pay for a place after they had failed the scholarship test for a free place. Most important from a parental point of view was that the manual workers' children, although the majority in the community, remained a minority in the grammar schools, so the middle-class style cultural ethos was not swamped, for only those children who conformed to the accepted attitudes of the grammar school were likely to settle down and make full use of their opportunities. This also led to the estrangement and re-orientation of able children from the working classes, if they accepted employment in the managerial establishment, they were alienated from their own people. At the same time higher education with its entry to the posts of control required both fees and maintenance, which successfully sealed off most of the senior sector from children of working-class origin.

Teacher training was the main educational means of social mobility open to the children of families of small means because grants were made to cover expenses and, although these had to be repaid, they were easily obtainable and training had a declared link with a known, secure, comparatively well-paid profession, which qualified for employment in the elementary schools. Those who wished for more than this could try for employment in the London area where there were some further opportunities for obtaining graduate qualification through evening study. It should be also noted that a university degree could be widely used and was something of a general entry ticket to the managerial section of society; a teacher's certificate was of little use except to work in schools.

In the interwar years Morant's policies continued to hold sway and their class bias was marked. Nursery schools were kept at a prototype stage catering for about a tenth of a per cent of the age groups eligible. Money for modernization of elementary schools was minimal and the black list of schools declared by the department of education itself in the late 1920s remained to mock the national effort to renew the primary schools and those catering for over 80 per cent of the children between the ages of eleven and fourteen. Although the school meals service had been authorized at the start of the century only three per cent of the children at any one time were benefiting from the scheme despite its depressingly low standard of service designed to keep costs down. There was virtually little advance in meeting the needs of children, about a third of whom were deprived in one or more ways. It was not until the second year of the war that school meals became universal and that following an official report on the poor physical condition of school children. Although it was widely recognized that many families depended on the earnings of their children to make ends meet, attempts to provide for a universal educational maintenance allowance for children in their later years at school were blocked in the House of Lords, while children attending grammar or technical schools were able to claim allowances for being at school and these continued until the child was eighteen. The selection for grammar school places even when intelligence tests were included was highly subjective as the Hadow Report was at some pains to make clear. In cases where there were two schools available, the older, higher status grammar school took the children who were more middle class in appearance and outlook; the others were sent to the more recent local authority secondary schools or to technical schools.

Although it was not openly stated the working-class child, unless able to modify his approach to life considerably, was not wanted in secondary education, because of indifferent performance. This was because of the strains of meeting costs of uniform, sports gear, special equipment, travel and other extras which required more than the allowance for staying on at school, if one was given. Moreover because of parental financial strains such children tended to leave before their course was completed, that is crowned by the university controlled certificate examinations taken at sixteen, with advanced subjects taken at eighteen. Even fewer went on to university. In an age of "conform or go under" there was no great concern about why the secondary and higher educational facilities were so weightily class biased, even though the evidence suggested that those students from poorer homes who were able to persevere with their courses did outstandingly well. In the universities some four in every 1,000 students had attended elementary schools catering for over 90 per cent of the children, so in effect the undergraduates were virtually exclusively drawn from managerial and professional homes. Throughout the system the social sanctions were reinforced by varied forms of "ragging", or more clearly, bullying. Whatever was the intention, the higher positions in employment were well protected from the intrusion of the lower orders.

The Education Act of 1944 did away with much of this class

discrimination but there was surprising life in the rearguard action of the old régime. It was not until the 1960s that education for the under fives became an effective lobby, although it is noteworthy that it is the middle-class voice which leads this campaign, and development is uneven. Despite the earlier maturity of young children, official education has hardened its decision so that school attendance starts in the term at which the child is five. With smaller families the custom, many children have no others on hand to play with and because of better feeding, backed by the influence of radio and television, the young child is not only ready for school, but actually needs the extra-family contacts and competition from its peers.

The infant and junior schools have built up into an exciting system of learning which has only recently begun to develop. It is in the hands of minimally qualified teachers who are proceeding pragmatically with very little research to guide them. A much more important deficiency is the lack of support workers, for here the child is malleable and much could be done if background disabilities were discovered and approached with remedial programmes, where possible enlisting the parents. If the last vestiges of the scholarship or eleven-plus pressures could be removed, a relatively small expenditure on modernization and support could bring about a big advance.

It is in the secondary sphere that all the doubts remain. The tyranny of the general certificate of education examinations blights the whole system. There is also the need to devise a sound educational approach to the non-academic children; the teaching profession have been faced with this problem for over a hundred years and are no nearer finding a solution. This is a fundamental problem which should command great resources to solve. Education is basically an indoctrination of the individual to fit into the community. In modern circumstances that also means that the young person should also accept the rôle for which he is prepared; if this is not so then society must accept the price of casualties. This non-academic majority have been cheated again and again largely because they are inarticulate and express themselves in action or inaction. The solution to their problems may lie in some of the work the youth service is developing. This service should certainly be extended and properly financed as was promised over 30 years ago. There is a

"Eventually, I suppose, it'll be Bucks Comprehensive versus Middlesex Secondary Modern". The Eton *v* Harrow cricket match held annually at Lord's is a great social occasion.
(*Daily Mail* – 30 June 1967)

need to link the school with the home and leisure scenes of the adolescent, as well as demonstrating the use of the curriculum in their future life. For example, the school-leaving age is only two years away from the legal age of maturity with the right of franchise, but for the most part the education system sends the young person into the world with very little knowledge of the society he is to live in or the interests which will control his community; the teaching of modern history or current affairs are conspicuously absent from most schools. Similarly there is little done to prepare for marriage, although the age of puberty and sexual experience has dramatically advanced in recent years. Even more evident is the absence of any help to cope with problems of tax, personal welfare, housing and the complex system of social benefits. Little too is done to meet the widespread antagonism many young people of all ages feel towards the police and legal authority. The attempts to meet the needs of the sixteen-year-old in the non-academic secondary schools has shown up the poverty of what has been going on for years in many schools. The alienation of a large part of the school population from the educational system is an indictment of the teaching profession and the community.

The results have erupted several times on the public scene to cause momentary concern with calls for bringing back the birch and then nothing. Race riots at Notting Hill, scuffles involving Mods and Rockers along the south coast in the 1960s, have been more recently followed by football club hooliganism across the country. It is a version of tribal warfare which finds no legitimate outlet; it is a series of symptoms which will be neglected only to erupt again. Speaking about the recent outbreak of soccer spectator violence, football league referee, Mr Gordon Hill, who is also headmaster of a high school in Hinkley, said:

> The crux of the problem is that for something like 80 per cent of school children in this country between the ages of thirteen and eighteen, the curriculum is totally irrelevant. We are creating an education system for an élite and are denying an adequate education for the rest, a situation which is encouraged by the parents. The attitude in many schools seems to be—"Well, 20 per cent of you will be measured by 'O' levels and the like, while the rest go to the wall". Thus in a society which labels "winners" as "successes" and "losers" as "failures", a number of "failures" are going to rebel, to become anti-social.

These young people are casualties of the last rearguard action against the extension of meaningful secondary education for all. The barricade at which this is being fought is over the extension of proper comprehensive schools for all children. The rearguard is largely middle class, well entrenched in local politics, voluble on concern for the local rates, emotionally charged with prejudice. But they are equipped with alternative schemes, all capable of carrying the comprehensive label, yet containing an an element of bias in their sponsor's direction. This formidable defence is backed with claims for parental choice, sparing the public purse and accusations that comprehensive education is untried; all of which amount to little more than politician's rhetoric designed for the consumption of the party faithful. Three decades of virtually full employment, with high earnings, coupled with many industry-based schemes to select and train suitable staff for shopfloor leadership, have not markedly increased the demand from manual workers for higher or even further education for their children. There could be a change in this situation as comprehensive schools establish themselves in working-class areas, but the class cultural gap is such that the educated element tend to be alienated from their own folk, both in way of life and geographically. Those few who find work among communities similar to where they came from, are remarkably effective and find their work doubly rewarding. Such posts tend to be in the public sector, e.g. concerned with the education, welfare or health services; there are few openings for company secretaries, lawyers or arts graduates in coal mining and heavy industrial areas.

There are however fundamental changes taking place. Modern teaching methods stress an investigating and questioning approach, but this mode of thought established in the formative years seems to carry over to later life when long established practices are challenged with some effect. Such action can be disturbing to older work mates who have accepted the well-established routine over many years. There is further reinforcement of this by the change in teacher/student relationships. In the nineteenth century, the teacher in the schools for the working classes was clearly seen as a member of the establishment, a figure of authority, a kind of children's police who would ensure the young obeyed and conformed to society's rules. There are many references to this rôle for school teachers and it still survives in the legal authority vesting the right to use corporal punishment in the profession. The teacher as the agent of indoctrination and authority was the enemy of the children, one of "them" against "us", but in recent years this has begun to change. Child-centred teaching has led to the children and teacher becoming allies. Children who are aware of what can be earned in industry are often critical of the conditions and pay of their teachers and there have been demonstrations by pupils in this cause. These new types of teachers who identify with their children often find themselves in conflict with colleagues of the old style, but on the whole this revolutionary re-identification is spreading smoothly and quietly. School is no longer a place children detest, much to the puzzlement of their parents who know nothing of activity methods and suspect what goes on; for as far as they can find out the lower forms only play while the older children discuss. It seems that "nobody tells them or makes them do" and the rarity of corporal punishment confirms this. It was such feelings which were appealed to by the Black Papers and reaction is still a force to be reckoned with in the schools as the pronouncements from head teachers' organizations give periodic proof. Meanwhile the new alliance between children and teachers, both feeling that the community has treated them indifferently, breeds a deep feeling that there is much to be put right in society, along with a growth of confidence and resourcefulness. The change-over of one of the national bulldogs from the automatic support of the establishment to challenge its authority must have far-reaching effects especially as most television news programmes give lessons in the art of protest.

The 1944 Act entrusted further education to the county colleges but these never materialized. In their place, as part of the general development of this sector, a large number of new colleges have been built to provide basic technical education and other local needs. Day-release facilities have also been provided but despite the efforts of the colleges such instruction has doubtful value for a large part of the students, mainly because of their alienation by secondary education experience. One of the biggest contributions of this section is in providing another way to obtain general certificate qualifications, for those who have rejected being treated as children and found secondary school unbearable.

Overall there has been an increase in the quantity and quality of secondary education, with consequently a much larger number of students gaining two "A" level certificates, the usual passport to higher education. Meanwhile student grants have opened up higher education to working-class children. The evidence is that comparatively few from the families of manual workers or labourers succeed in securing a place in the universities, for if they arrived on a *pro-rata* ratio they would swamp such institutions, and this is clearly not happening. The polytechnics developed to provide cheap higher education by absorbing and developing existing facilities, provide further opportunities, only to be faced by an unprecedented demand largely from the middle classes. The reason for this is not far to seek. Middle-class status is bound up with obtaining more education and training than the manual workers. Raising the school-leaving age to sixteen has led more middle-class children to stay on to eighteen, which means completing an advanced level course and provides an opportunity to follow a degree course. The chance of three or more years away from parental control in a stimulating environment, largely self-regulated with a modest personal income, is something of a status symbol and is especially acceptable to girls. The middle-class child can see the advantages of such an opportunity, particularly now degrees are becoming more pointedly directed to entry to management and the professions. To the children from a manual worker's background three years for intellectual growth and self-development is breaking new ground, too often seen as a prolongation of school. There are signs that this attitude is changing but it is a slow process and it will be some time yet before the family of the unskilled worker understand what is available for their children.

There has however been sufficient new blood entering the universities to change the atmosphere in some parts of higher education. Other parts are still untouched, notably the science and medical faculties. In the General Strike of 1926 university students were active in strike-breaking by helping to keep essential services going. Today in a similar situation this could hardly happen, and it appears likely that any help given would be for the strikers. Demonstrations in the 1960s by the first students whose education had been completely under the 1944 Act occurred notably in the more liberal institutions. These were written up in the press with more emotion than understanding to appeal to the reactionary older section of society. Their success on their own campuses, often very liberal and open, have been marginal; their real victories have been in other institutions where, alerted by the over-publicized protests elsewhere, staff were ready with concessions and staff/student consultative committees have brought about improvements in teaching methods relaxing the unnecessary restraints and a new attitude to students to replace discarded paternalism.

The educational situation can also be approached from the wider context of what is developing in the community. One of the aims of this work is to bring into perspective a diverse mass of historical material. It is therefore useful to identify the main themes of general social progress over the last 150 years as the background to the educational advance in the same period. Overall there has been a gradual, but uneven elevation of the lower orders of society. This is evidently, as one writer has remarked, a magnificent journey, but every advantage captured in stubborn fight can be made to sound like the ruin of society; it is merely a different point of view. Recently this process has accelerated as Britain since the 1940s has moved from an economy where labour was cheap and politically weak, towards a situation where labour has strength and is demanding better conditions. Managerial skills at all levels seem unable to comprehend what has happened and cannot deal with the changed balance of power. Nationally there is a tradition of describing work situations in terms of conflict, which is destructve. It should be noted that it was in the English context that Marx drew up his theory of class, based on work situations in nineteeenth-century Britain. It was at the same period that the State school system was forged, expressing a point of imbalance of social power. The retention of the resulting two-tier system perpetuates the antagonisms of the period of origin. Elsewhere the work divisions are not frozen in antagonism to one another. It is significant that advanced and harmonious industrial conditions seem to go with an open and unified system of schools. The USA, the leading country in this respect, in the period of its development was short of labour and had a unified comprehensive system of education. The result was a feeling of unity to achieve high output efficiently for the benefit of all sections of the community. This has become the basis of a partnership which, in a century of starting from nothing, has built up standards of productivity unsurpassed in history; there is no sign of any other formula competing with this achievement. In contrast Britain's industrial position has slumped and as technological change accelerates, both management and unions see these new opportunities not as new wealth to be shared, but as further cause for conflict.

It is frequently said that public education should be outside politics and the decisions made on professional judgments, but this can hardly be allowed. Firstly, the content, philosophy and operation of the schools run by the community for its children are closely wrapped up with two of the main ingredients of politics : namely public finance and changing people's point of view. This is not only in the narrow sense, but in the very broadest context, on both counts.

For example decisions on the spending of public money occur right down the line, starting from the intial cabinet decision of allocation for education, to a ministerial decision to spend more or less on the under fives or some other particular aspect of education. This goes on down to the grass roots, where the head teacher lays out the sum allocated to the school, making each class or subject teacher an allowance to spend as they see their work developing. The flexibility of the system is limited because, once established on the public educational menu, no service can be completely deprived of funds, so the choices are really those of accent; but nevertheless they exist and are subject to hard debate all along the line. The number and variety of pressure groups concerned with education has never been greater and as more educated women arrive on the scene as a result of expansion of higher education these will increase and become more effective.

Even more important is the long-term, delayed action of State education. What happens in the schools today is reflected in the national community in perhaps twenty years. There is ample evidence of this; for example, the development of a literate working class following the 1870 Act with its consolidating legislation produced a cheap mass press, large trade unions for the unskilled workers and working-class political groupings which resulted in the foundation of the Labour Party. The 1902 Act was responsible for the growth of the middle classes by providing secondary schools to act as a reinforcement agency, which served the country well both in peace and war. It also was responsible for the spread of women's education which resulted in the demand for the franchise and once this was granted produced a major shift in the emphasis of party politics from imperialism to matters relating to the nuclear family. Similarly the Cowper-Temple clause in the 1870 Act, which embodied the compromise on religious teaching in the schools, created the concept of a non-denominational religious philosophy which has played a considerable part in the national acceptance of the social justice of the Christian ethic with little regard for the religious institutions; the modern result is the welfare state.

The 1944 Act has radically changed the face of Britain by opening up opportunity largely for the lower-middle class and skilled manual workers' children. It has also brought many more girls into higher education, especially from the better-off families who formerly did not bother to make the effort of providing full education for their daughters on the grounds that they would marry and not need it. The first crop of young people whose lives had been fully influenced by the Act became adults in the 1960s and erupted with new ideas into every facet of life, from the Beatles in pop music to Mary Quant in fashion and Arnold Weinstock, the tycoon of the electrical industry. For the scores of this age group who became household words, there were thousands of others who followed the trends they set. It was the first expression of a lively grass-roots culture since the music halls at the turn of the century.

Both popular opinion and careful research see education as the main hope for social change, as well as personal advancement. For the children from poor backgrounds it is the main hope for avoiding a similar deprivation throughout their lives and also for their children. Education is a community responsibility so it is worth looking at what the two main parties say on this obligation; they represent the two class divisions in the country. The Conservative 1970 manifesto saw that; ". . . in education above all the problem of resources is crucial. The number of children in the schools is rising. More and more are qualifying to go on to colleges, polytechnics and universities. That they should be able to develop their abilities to the full is not only right in itself but a vital national investment in the future." The Labour Green Paper saw "the growth of education services and the extension of educational opportunities have always been seen by Socialists as a means of extending the horizons and freedom of every individual and promoting an egalitarian society".

With differing emphasis both sides see educational provision as a worthy activity. This takes much of the sting out of any

debate because any argument is about detail, not about principles; it is hard to whip up enthusiasm on matters of minor reform. As a result educational provision is in a difficult period, for on every side high aims relating to equal and full opportunity are conceded. The service is now faced with the long haul to make these reality. Every week facts are reported which reveal the inadequacies which are widespread even after some thirty years of general advance. They are easy to come by. In September 1973 at the general meeting of the Trades Union Congress, the Agricultural Union's delegate reported that despite the Plowden and Giffin Reports one school in Norfolk has passed no child to full secondary education in seventeen years. A month later a widely reported survey, "Born To Fail", showed that one child in sixteen, about six per cent, is heavily handicapped by its inadequate milieu. People working nearer the problem know how conservative this figure is.

There is still a great deal to be done to make true the promise of democracy.

THE GREEN BOOK
"EDUCATION AFTER THE WAR"
JUNE 1941

CONTENTS

FOREWORD

The progress of educational development in this country is marked by some notable milestones—1870, 1889, 1902 and 1918. Apart from the memorable advances associated with those dates, there have been many forward steps of a less spectacular character, some the fruit of legislation and others of administrative action.

But when all credit has been given, as it should be given, to those who planned and carried into effect those reforms which within living memory have changed the face of our educational system beyond recognition, we are still far from having attained in the field of education the social ideal which the Prime Minister has set before us of "establishing a state of society where the advantages and privileges, which hitherto have been enjoyed only by the few, shall be far more widely shared by the men and youth of the nation as a whole". The proposals outlined in the following memorandum have been informed by this ideal : they are so framed that the better system of education which they envisage would be equally available to all, irrespective of their means.

It is believed that the nation will expect the planning of education for the post-war world to be conceived on bold and generous lines, and will look not simply for developments within the existing framework of the educational system, but for such reconstruction of the framework itself as may be essential to progress. It may be necessary, therefore, to modify, or even to abandon, some conceptions which have long been held and to think in new terms for new times.

The Memorandum must not be taken as embodying the Board's considered conclusions. Before reaching such conclusions, the Board would need to consult the views of Local Education Authorities, teachers and others on the many issues which the problem of educational reconstruction must raise. In order, however, to ascertain their views, there are obvious advantages in putting before those who can speak for them a document which may serve as a basis for discussion. It is with this object that the present Memorandum has been prepared by some officers of the Board. It represents nothing more than their personal views of the directions in which the educational system stands in need of reform and their suggestions as to ways in which such reform might be effected. These suggestions are intended to apply generally to the whole area over which the Board's superintendence of matters relating to education extends. But in their application full account will need to be taken of the special conditions of Wales, which have their origin in the history and character of the Welsh people and country, and which have given to Welsh education a character and problems of its own.

The Memorandum is concerned primarily to offer an administrative approach to the problem of planning and to indicate the legislative and administrative changes that appear to be required; it does not attempt to enter into the detailed consideration of pedagogical issues. At the same time it has throughout been borne in mind that the criterion for determining whether any piece of our existing educational machinery should be retained, remodelled or scrapped, must be the extent to which it meets, or fails to meet, the educational requirements of the children and students for whose service it exists.

A word is needed on the nomenclature of schools as used in this Memorandum. As indicated in Chapter 1, it is proposed that in the suggested educational lay-out all full-time education up to 11 should be termed "Primary" and all full-time education from 11 upwards, within the range of school life, should be termed "Secondary." Secondary education will be conducted in three types of Secondary School. For the purpose of this Memorandum these three types will be referred to as :—

(i) The Modern School, corresponding with the present Senior School;

(ii) The Grammar School, corresponding with the present Secondary School;

(iii) The Technical School, corresponding with the present Junior Technical School.

In a document which deals partly with the past, partly with the present, and partly with the future, consistency in the matter of nomenclature is impossible. But it is hoped that the type of school referred to will, in all cases, be clear from the context.

M. G. HOLMES

June, 1941

CHAPTER 1.—FULL-TIME SCHOOLING

Introduction

1. This chapter is concerned with the "great staple" of the public system of education, the full-time schooling of children in Elemen-

tary, Secondary and Junior Technical Schools, covering in all approximately 5½ million pupils.

The purpose of the education so given may be broadly defined as :—

(a) to provide a school environment and training that will enable every child to develop his capacities to the best advantage as an individual;

(b) to prepare him to take his place in the life of the community as a useful citizen. In this connection the importance of equipping him to earn a livelihood must always be kept in mind;

(c) generally so to assist the development of body, mind, and spirit as to enable him to lead a healthy and happy life.

2. It may be desirable to indicate the meaning that is attached in this memorandum to phrases which have passed into the common currency of educational discussion, such as "equality of opportunity" and "secondary education for all."

"Equality of opportunity" does not mean that all children should receive the same form of education. At the primary stage i.e., to the age of 11, education should be the same for all, but thereafter at the secondary stage there must be ample variety of educational opportunity to meet the very varying requirements and capacities of the children. Indeed, in the educational sphere, much more than in the dietetic, one child's meat may be another child's poison. The provision for all children at the secondary stage of the same type of education would not connote equality of opportunity but rather the reverse, as it would involve large numbers of children receiving an education that could not possibly fulfil the purposes indicated in the opening paragraph. Equality of opportunity means, therefore, acceptance of the principle that the accidents of parental circumstances or place of residence shall not preclude any child from receiving the education from which he is best capable of profiting.

It will be clear from what has been said that by "secondary education for all" is meant not the provision of the same type of education for all at the secondary stage, but that all types of full-time education at this stage should be regarded as on a parity and should receive equal treatment in such matters as accommodation, staffing, size of classes, etc.

The Present Position

3. Compulsory education in this country begins at the age of 5, though a certain number of children enter Nursery Schools or Nursery Classes at an earlier age on a voluntary basis. The infant

stage normally lasts for about three years from 5 to between 7 and 8, when the child passes into the Junior School, where he stays until about 11. At that age occurs the main break in the child's educational life; all children eligible by age and standard can sit for the Special Place Examination, on the results of which selection is made for Secondary and, in some cases, Elementary Central Schools. Children so selected enter the Secondary School on payment of a fee graduated from the full approved fee to nothing, according to a local income scale, and, if the parents' income so justifies, they receive in addition a maintenance allowance. At the Secondary School they prepare for the School Certificate at about 16, and are bound under agreement not to leave school before that age. A proportion, about one-tenth, remain at the Secondary School after 16 in order to pursue advanced courses directed to entry to Universities, Training Colleges, etc. Notwithstanding what has been said, it should be noted that in practice some 25 per cent of the pupils, including a substantial proportion of those entering from Elementary Schools, leave before the age of 16 and that some 40 per cent do not even take the School Certificate Examination, the passing of which is regarded as within the capacity of pupils of normal intelligence. It is not suggested that such children do not derive benefit from their education, but it may well be that some other form of education after 11 would prove more suitable to their aptitude and capacity.

The remainder of the children not selected for Secondary Schools, apart from those who still continue in unreorganised all-age Elementary Schools, pass into the Senior Elementary School or department. There, unless they are selected at 13 for Junior Technical, Junior Commercial, or Junior Art Schools (which provide a two or three-year course) or for late transfer to a Secondary School, they remain until at least the age at which the compulsory period of education ends. For the time being that age is 14, the provisions of the Education Act, 1936, which raised the age to 15, having been suspended by the Education (Emergency) Act, 1939. A considerable number, however, stay on voluntarily to 15 or even 16.

The number of children of 11 and upwards in Elementary Schools is now more than 1½ million, of whom 828,000 are in Senior Schools reorganised on the Hadow Plan. 440,000 children of this age are in grant-aided Secondary Schools, of whom three-quarters have entered from Elementary Schools and nearly one-half enjoy total exemption from fees. The number of children in Junior Technical and similar schools is about 27,000. It will be seen that of the two million children receiving education after the primary stage, some three-quarters are in schools which, for purposes of statute and regulation, are classified as elementary and one-quarter are in schools which are recognised as being in the sphere of higher education.

Objections to the Present System

4. It has long been a cardinal weakness of the system outlined above that the statutory and administrative distinction between elementary and higher education corresponds with no educational distinction, and this lack of correspondence becomes progressively greater with each raising of the school leaving age. The content of the education given in Elementary Schools could reasonably be said to be elementary at a time when it was recognised that an intelligent child of 10 had derived from it all that it had to offer, but to apply the term elementary to the education given in a school, all the pupils of which remain in attendance until 15, is a misuse of language. It is suggested, therefore, that the time has come when statutory and administrative distinctions which do not rest on educational distinctions should disappear, and that post-war educational development should not be confused and retarded by conceptions and definitions which may have been appropriate enough 70 years ago.

Moreover, quite apart from any question of administrative inconvenience, the present distinction between elementary and higher education perpetuates a caste system which should find no place in a national scheme of education. Equality between the three types of post-primary education (the Senior School, the Secondary School, and the Junior Technical School) can never be secured either in fact or in the public mind until the same administrative machinery is made applicable to all alike. At the present time, disparity is emphasised in a number of ways—differences in standards of accommodation and amenities generally, in the size of classes, in the salaries of teachers, in the units of local administrative control, and not least in the matter of charging fees. In the Senior School, fees are prohibited by statute, whereas in Secondary and Junior Technical Schools fees are charged according to the means of the parents.

In the result, Secondary Schools now enjoy a measure of esteem in the minds of parents which has a damaging effect on the life and work of the Junior Schools. The Special Place Examination has become a matter of keen competition, on the results of which it is felt that a child's whole future may depend, and preparation for this examination tends to distort the training of the Junior School and often imposes a strain on children at a time of their lives when their mental and physical growth should be left free and unfettered.

Proposals for Reform

5. The basic aim of measures of reform should, it is suggested, be to secure a greater unification of the educational system. The educational life of the child would, of course, have its breaks and stages, but each stage is a preparation for the next which together should form a coherent whole.

The two major educational developments which may be expected after the war are already embodied in statute, viz., the raising of the age for compulsory school attendance to 15 in the Act of 1936, and the keeping of young people after that age who leave school under some measure of educational supervision until the age of 18 in the Day Continuation Schools of the Fisher Act. The former Act will require modifying by the omission of the exemption clauses, and the precise content of Day Continuation Schools will need to be determined in the light of post-war conditions. On this basis, a plan for education might be sketched in three stages, as follows :—

I. *Primary Education.*
　　(a) Nursery Schools, age 2–5, or Nursery Classes, age 3–5.
　　(b) Infant Schools, age 5–7 +.
　　(c) Junior Schools, age 7 + to 11 +.
II. *Secondary Education.*
　　(a) Secondary Schools, with a leaving age of 15 + (Modern Schools).
　　(b) Secondary Schools, with a leaving age of 16–18 (Grammar Schools).
　　(c) Secondary Schools, with a leaving age of 15 + or 16, with a Technical or Commercial bias (Technical Schools).
*III. *Further Education.*
　　(a) Part-time Day Continuation Schools up to 18.
　　(b) Full-time education in Technical and Commercial Colleges.
　　(c) Part-time Technical and Commercial education, whethei in the day or evening.
　　(d) Adult education.

[*Note.—There are, in addition, the Universities and Training Colleges. With the Universities, apart from the University Training Departments, the Board are not directly concerned, but they are concerned with the avenue to the University from the Secondary School, a matter which is dealt with in Chapter 5. Training

Colleges, which in one sense are a form of further education, are dealt with in Chapter 7 from the angle of recruitment and supply for the teaching profession.]

6. If the general principles already enunciated and the educational lay-out indicated above, are accepted, certain consequences follow, some of a general and some of a particular character, and some involving legislative and others administrative changes.

(a) Distinction between Elementary and Higher Education

As has been indicated in paragraph 4, the present distinction which places some three-quarters of the children over 11 in the sphere of "elementary" education has no educational justification. What is now termed elementary education and which, it has been suggested, should be termed primary education, should in future cease at 11 +. Modern Schools would accordingly take their place as Secondary Schools and, as such, fall within the sphere of higher education, and would be subject to the conditions applicable to schools of higher education. Some of the legal and administrative consequences of such a change, particularly as regards provision for religious instruction, are considered in Chapter 9.

(b) Units of Local Administration

Both the essential unity of education, to which reference has been made, and the limitation now proposed of elementary or primary education to the stage ending at 11, alike point to the need for the abolition of separate Authorities for elementary education. This matter is dealt with in Chapter 8.

(c) Duty of Authorities to provide Secondary Education

The duty now resting upon Local Education Authorities under Section 17 (1) of the Education Act, 1921, to provide for the elementary education of children in their areas for whom sufficient and suitable provision is not otherwise made will need to be extended so as to embrace secondary education.

(d) A single body of regulations for Secondary Schools

Modern Schools should be aligned with Grammar and Technical Schools under a single code of regulations providing for equality of treatment in such matters as accommodation, size of classes, etc.

(e) Abolition of Fees in Secondary Schools

There would seem to be an unanswerable case for making Secondary Schools of all three types free up to the age of 16 or the end of the school year in which that age is reached. If the State is to compel children to undergo full-time education up to the age of 15, it must also shoulder the responsibility for providing them with appropriate education. If, therefore, the appropriate education is of a kind which necessitates staying at school until 16 to complete the course, or a defined stage of what might be extended into a longer course, then it must be prepared to see the child through up to that point, *i.e.*, up to 16 or 16+. But it would surely be uneconomical to abide strictly by the logic of this argument. It is precisely at the age of 16 that the economic pressure to withdraw a boy or girl from school becomes most insistent, and unless that pressure can be countered by continuing free education, a number of those pupils whose extended education might be of the greatest benefit not only to themselves but to the State, are likely to be withdrawn. It is suggested, therefore, that free secondary education should continue throughout Secondary School life. This will necessitate the abolition of fees in all Secondary Schools provided or maintained by, or which receive their grants from, Local Education Authorities. The Grammar Schools in receipt of direct grant from the Board present a special problem. To deprive them of their fee income would mean their disappearance, and it is suggested, therefore, that the present arrangement should continue whereby in recognition of State aid they offer an appropriate percentage of free or special places.

(f) *Transfer from the Primary to the Secondary School*

It is inherent in these proposals that the age of transfer should remain as at present 11. In order to relieve Junior Schools of the incubus of the Special Place Examination it is proposed that children should be selected for transfer at this age to the different types of Secondary School on the basis of their school record, supplemented by suitable intelligence tests. It would, however, run counter to educational opinion to regard 11 as the appropriate age at which a final and irrevocable choice should be made of the particular type of secondary education which any given child should pursue. Indeed, there is a substantial volume of opinion that the right course to adopt would be to transfer all children at 11 to Modern Schools, the age for transfer to Grammar and Technical Schools being fixed at 13. Such an organisation will, if thought desirable, become possible as new school accommodation comes into being. In the meantime arrangements will need to be made for a genuine review at 13 and transfer as between all three types of Secondary School in whichever direction may be found appropriate.

In order to facilitate this interchange at 13, it is contemplated that the content of the education given in the first two years 11-13, though differentiated in detail, should in general be the same in all types of Secondary School.

7. It is realised that no scheme of this kind could be put into

effect immediately on the passing of the requisite legislation. A very large building programme, much of which would in any case have had to be faced in order to complete Hadow reorganisation, will need to be carried out before all the children over 11 could be accommodated in Secondary Schools. Rather less than one-half of the children over 11 now in Elementary Schools are not in separate Senior Schools or departments but are in all-age schools. Until appropriate secondary accommodation has been provided, these children must of necessity remain in such schools which, for statutory and administrative purposes, must continue to be regarded as in the elementary sphere.

8. The proposals put forward in this Chapter involve some fundamental changes. It has, however, to be remembered that vested ideas, perhaps more than vested interests, are liable to stand in the way of educational replanning. The truth of the matter is that successive changes in the law of school attendance, by taking the line of least resistance and amending existing statutory provisions to the minimum extent strictly necessary for the purpose, have inevitably led to a blurring, if not indeed a distortion, of the meaning of elementary education. There is thus today a conflict between the statutory and administrative conception and the educational conception of the term. In such a conflict it is submitted that educational considerations must prevail and that the statutory and administrative machinery should be remodelled to meet educational needs.

CHAPTER 2.—DAY CONTINUATION SCHOOLS

9. The Education Act, 1918, commonly known as the "Fisher Act", made provision for a comprehensive system of Day Continuation Schools for all young persons, subject to certain exceptions, between 14 and 18, the lower age being established by the Act as the school leaving age. The relevant sections of this Act, with some minor modifications, have been incorporated in Sections 75 to 79 of the Education Act, 1921.

10. The following provisions of the Fisher Act may be specially mentioned :—

(a) The prescribed hours of attendance were 320 in the year, or, if a Local Education Authority so desired, 280 hours during the first seven years for which the Act operated in the area. The hours might be distributed over the year as best suited local circumstances, but it was assumed that, normally, attendance would be for 8 (or 7) hours per week, either one full day or two half-days, for 40 weeks in the year.

(b) For the first seven years the obligation to attend the schools ceased at 16.

11. As is well known, the Continuation School scheme was put into force in only a few areas. Within a very short time the difficulties in the way of carrying on even in those areas became more and more formidable, and compulsory attendance was abandoned in all of them, with the exception of Rugby, in the years 1921 and 1922. The Rugby school survived owing to a fortunate combination of support from local industry and of the initiative and resource of teachers and administrators; even here attendance ends at the age of 16.

12. The main cause of the failure of the scheme was the severe financial crisis of 1920–21, but there were other adverse factors. It is now easy to see that it was a mistake to start the schools in a particular place without regard to what was happening in neighbouring and industrially related areas. This meant that boys and girls in London, for example, were not available for full-time employment whereas those in Middlesex or Surrey, were. Thus a sense of grievance was created not only among London employers but also among the young people who saw that they were at a disadvantage in finding jobs as compared with those coming from outside the London County Council boundaries. There was, again, too much of improvisation about the arrangements, particularly in the matter of buildings, largely because of a natural desire to get the scheme going before public sympathy had waned.

The Need for Day Continuation Schools

13. It is unnecessary to argue at length the case for Day Continuation Schools. At the present time the great mass of pupils leaving the Elementary Schools do not pursue their education in any form. As a result, much of the work of full-time schooling runs to waste. A certain proportion who possess the necessary energy and foresight do carry on their education in Evening Institutes and Technical Schools, but the total enrolment of evening pupils between 15 and 18 is under 400,000, and something like two-thirds of the young people in that age range cease to be under any educational influence after they leave the Elementary Schools so far as the public system of education is concerned.

14. A number of these may, of course, be associated with one or other of the various voluntary organisations which endeavour to provide for the social and recreative interests of adolescents in their leisure hours. But it is well known that, admirable as the work of

these organisations is, they do not in fact touch half of the total age group. When every allowance has been made for home influence and for the work of the voluntary bodies, it is true to say that hundreds of thousands of girls and boys are left without the supervision and help that they need in the formation of character and the training of mind and body during these critical years.

15. The view that a responsibility must continue to rest on the State for the welfare of these young people in the broadest sense of the term "continued education" will not be disputed. The supervision of their health, the encouragement, and the provision of opportunity, to develop their interests and capacities are alike essential to securing that the nation's youth shall be alive and alert. From the point of view of the country's industry and commerce the training which would be afforded by attendance at Day Continuation Schools in conjunction with employment is long overdue.

The Framework of a New Scheme

16. Though the Fisher Act will naturally be the background of the new scheme, conditions have changed in the last 20 years and it would be unwise to follow its provisions slavishly or to interpret them in precisely the same way as in the past. In particular the new Continuation School system will follow on a school leaving age of 15 instead of 14, and this fact coupled with the educational developments since 1918 must influence the organisation and content of continued education.

17. So far as the structure of the system is concerned the following should, it is suggested, be the main features :—

(a) The scheme should apply with a strictly limited number of exceptions to all boys and girls between the ages of 15, when obligatory full-time schooling will cease, and 18. Partial exemption at least will probably have to be granted to those who are over 15 when the Act comes into force, the majority of whom will have entered employment, but if possible the machinery of the Act should be used to secure the attendance of these young people for some form of physical training. Those who are receiving approved full-time education will, of course, be exempted, but no other major category of exemptions should be admitted.

(b) As in the case of the Fisher Act, special arrangements should be made for young people serving at sea, but it will be easier now than it was 20 years ago to secure the co-operation of the shipping industry in evolving a satisfactory scheme. The operation of the Act in sparsely populated rural areas will present difficulty and will have to be adjusted to the seasonal conditions of agriculture with consequent concentration of the periods of attendance. Advantage should be taken of the increased number of school camps which may be looked for after the war; in the late autumn and winter months, these could be used as centres for periods of full-time attendance of a month or more. The details of a scheme for rural areas must be investigated jointly by the Board and the Ministry of Agriculture.

(c) The hours of attendance should be calculated on the basis of one full day or, preferably, two half days in the week. It is possible that the Fisher Act put the figure too high for general consumption at 8 hours a week and it is provisionally suggested that the basis should be 2 half days of $3\frac{1}{2}$ hours per week, or 280 hours in the year. This would facilitate the staffing arrangements.

(d) In order to guard against the difficulty experienced under the Fisher Act, the Appointed Day for the operation of the Act should be the same for all areas constituting single industrial and commercial regions; e.g., London and the Home Counties, the West Midlands, Merseyside, South Lancashire, the West Riding, Tyneside and South Wales. Great progress has been made in the formation of Regional Councils and other methods of co-operation between Authorities in the sphere of technical education, and it is reasonable to expect that the machinery so created will make collaboration for this purpose much easier and more effective than it was in 1920.

Buildings

18. A serious handicap to the earlier Day Continuation Schools was the frequent use of shoddy and inconvenient buildings. Suitable housing and amenities, including proper provision for physical training and games, are essential to the internal efficiency of the schools and their public repute. Further, they must be so equipped as to afford all the necessary facilities for technical and commercial work. While new buildings will in some cases be unnecessary, a heavy building programme is inevitable.

The Work of the Schools

19. The details of the curriculum will need careful working out, but one or two fundamental considerations may be mentioned. It will have to be remembered that the pupils have gone out into the world of employment and are rapidly widening their practical knowledge and experience, with a corresponding development of

their points of view, their interests and their pursuits. These facts will have to be reflected not merely in the subjects of instruction, but, even more, in their treatment, and the wider the experience and the less academic the outlook of the teacher the better. Continuation Schools will not be vocational schools in any narrow sense, but to many of the pupils who are in employment instruction bearing on their work will make a direct appeal. Again, special arrangements will have to be made for advanced technical and commercial students, and for those who before the arrival of Continuation Schools would have been released by their employers for day-time attendance.

20. The Day Continuation School should be something more than an institution that simply provides one day's education a week : it must be a real entity with its own corporate life, recognised as in some sense a Community Centre for Youth or a Young People's College. It should have all the facilities necessary to enable all kinds of activities, recreative and cultural, including school societies and clubs, to be developed in and around it outside the actual hours of instruction. Workshops and other rooms should be kept open in the evenings for the benefit of pupils following technical or commercial courses and also for the prosecution of hobby activities in the form of various handicrafts. All this will mean that the school buildings will be fully occupied throughout the week, both in the daytime and in the evenings.

CHAPTER 3.—THE SERVICE OF YOUTH

21. The development within the sphere of the public system of education of facilities to meet the social and recreative needs of young persons, now commonly referred to as the "Service of Youth," has its origin in Section 17 of the Fisher Act of 1918 (Section 86 of the Education Act, 1921), which gave Local Education Authorities powers to supply or maintain, or aid the supply or maintenance of, facilities for social and physical training whether in the day or evening. This gave recognition to the need for reinforcing the work of the schools and for preventing waste of educational effort by providing ample opportunities for the happy and healthy use of leisure.

22. At the time this was a new departure extending the influence of the Education Authorities beyond the walls of the schools and outside school hours into the leisure hours of their pupils and young persons. While restricted originally to children and persons attending schools or educational institutions, the power was extended by

Section 6 of the Physical Training and Recreation Act, 1937, to cover persons irrespective of age and irrespective of attendance at any educational institution.

23. A wide field of social welfare, within which Education Authorities can operate, has thus been opened up. As so often in this country, voluntary effort had for many years already pointed the way, and the value of the work among both adolescents and adults carried on by the great national organisations—such as the Boys' and Girls' Clubs, the Scouts and Guides, the Y.M.C.A. and other bodies and, not least, by the Churches—cannot be over-rated.

24. But voluntary effort alone could not provide—and cannot be expected to provide—a national service : on the other hand, the powers to make such provision given to Local Education Authorities have hitherto been exercised somewhat sporadically, and facilities of the kind contemplated have tended, perhaps, to be regarded rather as an "extra" than as an essential element in an ordered system of educational provision for the adolescent.

25. A new stage was marked by the announcement in November, 1939 of the policy for a "Service of Youth," accompanied by the setting-up within the Board of a special branch to foster and develop it. In this way recognition was given to the training and welfare, outside their working hours, of young people who have ceased full-time education, as an integral part of the national system of education. Clearly in this field, as elsewhere in education, what is essential is co-operation between voluntary effort on the one side and the statutory authorities on the other, and steps have been taken to secure this by the setting up of Local Youth Committees which are Committees of the Local Authorities for higher education including representatives of the local voluntary organisations and the other interests concerned. At the centre, similar contact is established between the Board and the voluntary organisations through the National Youth Committee.

26. The services for leisure hours which it is thus hoped to promote will not, however, stand by themselves. They will be supplementary, or rather complementary, to the Day Continuation Schools in which young workers will continue to receive a measure of education, including physical training, within their normal working hours. For the first time, a complete system covering the educational and physical and social welfare of adolescents can be brought into operation. Properly organised and directed, the Day Continuation School will develop a social life of its own and become a Youth Centre, which should be closely linked up with all the units—whether statutory or voluntary—of the Youth Service in the area which it serves.

Its establishment will carry with it the extension of medical super-vision for all young people up to the age of 18, with proper facilities for physical recreation under competent supervision, and will thus obviate once and for all the deterioration experienced in the past of the habits of healthy living formed in the schools.

27. The period up to 18 years of age will be regarded as still essentially an educational period. The young "earner" will still be the young "learner". If this principle is accepted, it may well be that other services should be more closely co-ordinated with the education of the adolescent. Thus, education is in part preparation for employment and should carry some responsibility for placing in employment. At present the responsibility for Choice of Employment work is undertaken by only about half of the Local Education Authorities, and it may well be that a coherent system of adolescent training requires that Choice of Employment should be administered locally by those responsible for the administration of education. It may further be a matter for consideration whether other aspects of juvenile welfare should not be more closely associated with the general provision for adolescent education : for example, the Approved Schools and the Probation Service—the latter in particular —should clearly be closely linked with the Service of Youth.

28. The central problem in the development of education for the adolescent, whether in the Day Continuation School or in the volun-tary work outside school hours, will be the provision of the best kind of teacher or leader. Both the compulsory and the voluntary sides should work as complementary parts of one whole, and should share common ideals and purposes. In some degree the men and women concerned to carry on this work will have to share much in their training. They should feel themselves to be part of a single whole, however diverse the parts may be. As the schools serve as practising grounds for the Training Departments and Training Colleges, the clubs and other youth organisations will no doubt serve as training grounds for those who require the newer training for adolescent education, and it will be essential to secure that the voluntary organisations continue to be assisted to maintain their activities as part of the national system.

29. A planned system of education on these lines, providing for education in the strict sense of the term, for the maintenance of physical fitness and the meeting of recreational interests, founded upon the work of the full-time schools and based both on the resources of the Local Authorities and on the nation's rich variety of voluntary effort, should go far to eliminate the waste of adolescent life that has unfortunately too often prevailed in the past. It should

produce a generation of future citizens well equipped to undertake
the tasks before them.

CHAPTER 4.—THE FURTHER EDUCATION OF THE ADOLESCENT AND THE ADULT

30. The present Chapter is concerned with education after full-
time schooling is finished. The field covered is wide and hetero-
geneous, including all ages from the school leaving-age upwards
and every variety of subject. The instruction is largely vocational,
but there is also a substantial body of continued liberal education
for both young people and adults. The common features are that
nowhere is the student under compulsion to attend and that, apart
from a limited amount of full-time work, the instruction is part-
time, usually given in the evening after the day's work is done.

It is not proposed to review this wide field in detail, but only to
draw attention to certain features which will demand consideration
in any scheme of educational reconstruction or development.

(i) Evening Institutes

31. Evening Classes or Evening Institutes had their origin in an
appreciation of the necessity to provide some means of continuing
general education for young people—little more than children—
who had finished their schooling at an early age, or for older persons
who desired to make good the deficiencies of a limited elementary
education and to learn something bearing on their occupation.
So far as younger students are concerned, the evening class was
definitely a continuation class, to continue an education still
"elementary" and far from sufficient.

32. With a minimum leaving age of 14 and the growing effective-
ness of instruction in the Elementary Schools the continuation of
"elementary" education has become less important. There has been
a further development of courses designed to prepare students to
enter on more advanced part-time vocational study at about 16
years of age in the Technical and Commercial Colleges and Schools
of Local Education Authorities, but the gap created by the decreasing need for the teaching of the rudiments of knowledge has not, in
general, been satisfactorily filled. Tradition dies hard and the objectives of Evening Institutes have often become confused, with the
result that the system has failed in two directions. There is a heavy
wastage and it is clear that a satisfactory bridge to the Technical
and Commercial Colleges has not been provided, while many

students who enter looking for something other than purely vocational study drift away bored and unsatisfied.

33. With a minimum leaving-age of 15 and statutory Continuation Schools the whole problem takes on a new aspect. It might be suggested that for a large majority of young people there will no longer be either need or incentive to attend Evening Classes—there will in effect be a transfer of education from evening to daytime hours. This, however, in itself at once creates a new problem—that of increased leisure. Ineffective as much of the work of the Evening Institutes may be, they have at least provided some occupation in the evenings for numbers of young persons who would otherwise be at a loose end. Something will still be required to meet this problem of the "unoccupied hours".

34. At the same time, there will be a number of young persons anxious to proceed to more advanced studies as a means of improving their qualifications for employment, and they will want evening instruction for a year or so in preparation for the senior courses in the Technical and Commercial Colleges. The genuine and ambitious student offers no difficulty. The problem arises over the great majority who have neither desire nor occasion to pursue courses leading to advanced study.

But here again the situation will be radically affected by the establishment of Continuation Schools which, as described in Chapter 2, will have a dual part to play in the evenings. On the one hand they will be the centre of "out of school" activities of all kinds in the shape of their pupils' clubs and societies; on the other they will make provision for those of their pupils who want industrial or commercial courses and who are not attending a college.

35. Clearly the demand may easily exceed the accommodation of the individual Continuation School, whose clientele will be five times its capacity. The Evening Institutes will still be needed for adolescents as well as for older persons; but the Continuation School, for the area it serves, might well form the central point from which, in co-operation with the Institutes and the neighbouring voluntary organisations, a complete network of provision for young people might be developed. The Local Youth Committees already in existence, which represent Local Education Authorities and voluntary organisations, provide the machinery through which co-operation can be secured.

(ii) Technical and Commercial Education

36. There is urgent need, in the interests of the industrial and commercial prosperity of the country, to secure an improved system

of technical and commercial training. Four questions are of out-standing importance—the training of apprentices and other young workers; relations with industry and commerce; the provision of build-ings and equipment; and the development of regional organisation.

(a) *The training of young workers*

37. Apart from the pre-entry training now provided in Junior Technical and Commercial Schools and such training as is given in the course of employment, the technical and commercial training of young workers has hitherto depended in the main on the system of Evening Classes, and therefore on the enterprise and tenacity of the individual student. This has produced many young men and women of high intelligence and sturdy character, but the system—if it can be called a system—is haphazard and ill-adapted to the requirements of today.

38. The advent of Continuation Schools will of course go a con-siderable way to better the position. They will provide a measure of vocational training related to their employment or occupation for all young persons, and this may suffice for a large majority. In the case of those who should be encouraged to go further and proceed to more advanced forms of training, some relief will be given from the burden of study after the day's work, although some evening work will still be required.

39. The senior and advanced courses, designed to equip those who should fill responsible posts in industry and commerce, extend from 16 to 19 or 21 years of age. After the age of 18, therefore, when the student would finish with the Continuation School, there would be no statutory provision for daytime study, and he would be thrown back entirely on evening attendance, with a necessarily smaller allowance of time just when he has reached the most advanced stages of his studies.

40. It is true that a number of progressive firms release their apprentices and learners during working hours for attendance at Technical Schools, the number so released in 1938 being 41,000, of whom 13,000 came from the engineering industry. This, however, only touches the fringe of the problem of an ordered system of industrial and commercial training. It is a question whether a training policy, at any rate for selected industries, can be worked out in consultation with those industries and whether such a policy would be voluntarily adopted, or would have to be imposed as part of a national industrial policy.

(b) *Relations with Industry and Commerce*

41. In any case, much closer relations should be established

between educational and industrial and commercial interests. In many areas there is a measure of local co-operation, *e.g.*, local employers and representatives of Trade Unions serve on advisory committees associated with local Technical institutions. But, in general, the Technical Schools have not been integrated as they should be with our industrial and commercial life. Again, at the centre, while the Board are in close contact with the professional institutions, such as the Civil and Mechanical Engineers, they have not established any such close association with industry or commerce in their productive and trading capacities. Something in the way of a national advisory council—or possibly separate councils for industry and commerce—seems to be required. Fully representative bodies would be quite unwieldy and it might be best to appoint special advisory committees for each of the most important industries and branches of commerce and a small council of persons of acknowledged standing in industry and commerce, representing both employers and employed, who would collaborate with the Board in discussing broad issues of policy.

(c) *Buildings and Equipment*

42. The standard of Technical College buildings in this country is, in far too many instances, deplorably low, and only a few compare with the institutions found in Germany and elsewhere abroad. Moreover, equipment must be brought and kept up to date. In the absence of any statutory obligation on Local Education Authorities to make such provision, progress is distressingly slow. Before the war a survey was made and a programme of new building was being planned, to complete which, at pre-war prices, would involve a capital outlay of not less than £12 to £15 million.

The extension and improvement of buildings for technical and commercial education will be an essential feature not only of educational but indeed of economic reconstruction. How far the provision of technical education, particularly in its higher ranges, can properly continue to be left to depend on local initiative, and what should be the arrangements for its organisation and administration, are matters which will need careful consideration in the light of industrial conditions and requirements after the war.

(d) *Regional Organisation*

43. Industrial organisation takes no cognisance of the organisation of local government, and, with Technical Schools provided by Local Education Authorities, it is not easy to adjust provision to the real needs of a wider industrial region. There is always a danger of overlap or mal-distribution. The need for co-operation and associa-

tion has for some time been recognised by Local Education Authorities and a number of co-ordinating or advisory councils are already in being, e.g., the Yorkshire Council for Further Education, the South Wales Advisory Council and the West Midland Regional Advisory Council.

44. It is possible that changes in the layout of local government may affect this problem; otherwise, it will be essential to develop regional association between Authorities on the lines indicated in order to secure that technical education is properly related to the needs of industry.

(iii) Art Education

45. It is unnecessary to deal separately with provision for art education. *Mutatis mutandis* the considerations indicated above apply to the provision for art education. The two mean points which require to be pursued are the provision of better accommodation and the development of art instruction for industrial purposes in closer association both with industry and technical education. The brevity of this reference to art education must not be taken as representing the weight that should be attached to the importance of its further development. Quite apart from any questions of cultural values, there is no doubt that much remains to be done to secure that the Art Schools shall make their due contribution to production in the sphere of design.

(iv) Adult Education

46. The following paragraphs deal with the service recognised under the Board's Adult Education Regulations, namely, courses "designed for the liberal education of adults," that is, persons of at least 18 years of age. These courses are of several types, including University Tutorial Classes, University Extension Courses and Lectures, and other courses organised under the aegis of voluntary bodies such as the Workers' Educational Association. It must, however, be remembered that this does not represent the whole range of educational facilities for adults. In addition, provision is made by Local Education Authorities largely, of course, in the form of vocational education, but also, in some areas, of a kind comparable in character and content to that conducted under the Adult Education Regulations. Considerable provision is also made of classes in practical subjects, including handicrafts and the practice of music and art.

47. The Adult Education movement has a long history. It has steadily developed and in the ten years 1928–38 the number of classes and students recognised under the Adult Educational Regu-

lations approximately doubled. There is, however, no cause for complacency, as the universities and voluntary bodies would be the first to agree. Provision is too much a matter of bits and pieces. In many areas it is insufficient to meet the potential demand, while even where a number of classes are in existence their range is often restricted, with the result that the freedom of choice of the students is also restricted. What is needed is the development of the service on systematic lines throughout the country, not merely to fill the obvious gaps, but also to secure that classes may be differentiated properly, both in grade and in subject.

48. There are two main factors in the problem. In the first place, correlation of the activities of universities and voluntary bodies and Local Education Authorities is often imperfect; so much so that in the greater part of the country adult education could hardly be called an organised service at all. Where a measure of co-ordination of effort has been secured by one means or another its results are clearly apparent in the larger volume and greater variety of the work. In the second place, while there are some notable exceptions of Local Education Authorities who have been active in establishing adult education classes comparable with those provided by the universities and the voluntary bodies, the large majority, while giving some assistance to the voluntary organisations, have done little or nothing in the way of direct provision themselves.

49. The only satisfactory solution will, it is suggested, be found in the mapping of England and Wales into regions, for each of which a Regional Council would be responsible. These Councils should be composed of representatives of all the bodies who are, or should be, effectively concerned with the provision of adult education in the region, i.e., the Universities, University Colleges, the Workers' Educational Association and other voluntary bodies, and the Local Education Authorities for higher education. These Councils would be responsible for ascertaining and stimulating local demand and for drawing up and carrying out programmes for courses and classes to meet it; and the Board's grant would be paid to them.

50. Reconstruction of the service along these lines would call for a very real measure of readjustment and some limitation of the independence now enjoyed by the universities and the several voluntary organisations. If, however, the patchwork character of the present arrangements is admitted, and if account is taken of the promising student-material which is at present not reached at all, the case for such readjustment is a very strong one. When the Militia Act was passed and consideration was given to means

of providing a measure of education for young men during their period of militia training, and later when war broke out and provision was required for education for men in the Armed Forces, it was found both necessary and possible to form regional committees for education in the Forces much on the lines above indicated, which offer a precedent for closer co-operation in the field of civilian education also. It is not suggested that the regional scheme now associated with education for the Army should necessarily be followed in detail when applied to civilian conditions. The regional layout might be different, and in any case would have to be the subject of full consultation with all the interests concerned.

51. One further point should be added. The closer association of Local Education Authorities with the universities and voluntary bodies in this field may assist to promote the development of adult education along institutional lines. In many quarters there is a feeling that there is room for the development in the larger centres of population of institutions provided as such for the liberal education of adults; an example may be found in the City Literary Institute in London. While there is no doubt whatever of the value of the personal contacts and social interest which centre on the existing individual classes, there are also values in a corporate institution which brings together people of rather diverse interests, and these values might be secured by the development of institutions of the type in question.

CHAPTER 5.—THE AVENUE TO THE UNIVERSITIES AND SIMILAR TYPES OF INSTITUTION

52. The path of the poor scholar to the university has been made broader and less difficult during the past twenty years. The State, Local Education Authorities, Universities and Colleges, City Companies, many charities and trusts and a large number of schools contribute towards a bewildering multiplicity of scholarships and maintenance allowances which enable young people to obtain a university education.

A.—Present Position

53. Pupils from Secondary Schools who have the necessary academic qualifications and who are willing to commit themselves, at about 17 or 18 years of age, to the teaching profession are assisted by grants made under the Board's Regulations for the

Training of Teachers to take a four year course at the university. The first three years consist of a course for a degree, usually in arts or pure science, and the fourth is a course of professional training. (*See* Chapter 7.)

54. The award of other university scholarships by the State, that is "State Scholarships", dates from 1920. Their object is to strengthen the connection between Secondary Schools and the universities and to diffuse more widely the benefits of university education. In the first instance provision was made for the award of 200 scholarships annually to pupils from grant-earning Secondary Schools. The number now offered annually for award is 360 and they are open to pupils in all Secondary Schools, grant-aided or otherwise. They are tenable for three or four years; and there are, therefore, in normal times, about 1,100 State Scholars in the universities. State Scholarships are not tenable at universities abroad.

55. State Scholarships are awarded on the recommendation of the several Examining Boards which conduct the Higher School Certificate Examination, and the allocation as between boys and girls is related to the number of pupils of each sex entering for that examination. The maximum value of a State Scholarship is £100 per annum in respect of maintenance plus the payment of approved fees. The actual award in each case, however, is determined, subject to the maximum, in relation to the financial circumstances of the scholar and his parents. At each university a "standard local maximum" is fixed for grants for maintenance: that is to say a sum is agreed upon by the Board and the university authorities which represents what a State Scholar should receive from all sources to meet the ordinary expenses of university life.

56. The "standard local maximum" at Oxford and Cambridge is £175 per anuum. At other universities it is lower, but in every case, save one, it is higher than the maximum of £100 payable as a State Scholarship. In practice, however, many State Scholars hold other awards, and the parents of many are also able to make a contribution. The awards are reviewed annually, and if necessary reassessed, in the light of any change in the scholar's financial position. Small additions to the "standard local maximum" are allowed in special cases.

57. The number and value of Senior or Major Scholarships awarded by Local Education Authorities to enable local pupils to proceed to a university, and the basis upon which they are assessed, vary considerably in different areas. The maximum

value of these awards may exceptionally reach £250 per annum; an average figure would be about £80 or £100. There are probably 5,000 students at the universities holding senior awards made by Local Education Authorities, but many of the students concerned hold State and other scholarships as well; it is thus not possible to say how many beneficiaries are solely dependent upon their Local Education Authorities. The expenditure of Local Education Authorities on senior awards in 1936–39 was some £300,000 compared with the expenditure of the Board on State Scholarships of about £130,000. A pupil's chances of securing the aid necessary to take him through a university course vary very widely according to the area in which he happens to reside, and this in spite of the general effect of State and other scholarships in levelling local inequalities.

58. Still more haphazard in their incidence are the scholarships and exhibitions given by universities, colleges, schools and outside bodies. No information is readily available as to the number or total value of these awards, but the proportion of students receiving some form or other of financial assistance is known. Out of 10,778 students in residence in Oxford and Cambridge in 1937–38, 4,819, or 44.7 per cent were receiving financial assistance. The proportion of assisted students in London was 26.4 per cent; in the English universities as a whole 38.5 per cent and in Wales 58.8 per cent. Out of a total student population in England and Wales of 39,000, nearly 16,000 students were in receipt of financial aid.

59. Local Education Authorities also make awards to enable students to attend Technical Colleges. The only Scholarships other than State Scholarships awarded by the Board consist of a small number of Royal Scholarships in Science tenable at the Imperial College of Science and Technology (University of London), scholarships in Art tenable at the Royal College of Art and a limited number of studentships for teachers.

B. Objections to the Present System

60. It is clear that a considerable measure of public and private assistance is extended to young people who wish to attend a university and who are able, in competition with other pupils, to win a scholarship or exhibition. But there are objections to the present system.

(a) Even though it may not be desirable that every pupil who desires to pursue a university course should be encouraged to do so, it is nevertheless probable that the amount of public aid available for the purpose throughout the country as a whole is not adequate to meet legitimate demands.

(b) It is not right from the point of view of public policy that a promising pupil living in one area should have less chance of securing the benefits of a university education than a pupil of no great promise living in another area.

(c) It is illogical to have as a maximum State Scholarship maintenance figure a sum less than the cost of living at a university. It should not be assumed that every candidate worthy of a State Scholarship will necessarily obtain an additional scholarship, or that the parent of every scholar is able to make some contribution to university expenses.

(d) The fact that as many as three bodies, the Board, a Local Education Authority and a college, may each make an award to the same scholar, results in excessive administrative work when making original assessments and when adjusting the awards, if necessary, year by year. Naturally, neither Local Education Authorities nor colleges are willing that the whole of the saving should accrue to the Board. The Board have adopted a system of co-ordinating awards, but the work involved is disproportionate to the purpose it achieves.

(e) It is educationally disastrous that boys and girls should have to go scholarship hunting; first the Higher School Certificate Examination in July for a local award, a State Scholarship or both, then an Open Scholarship examination in December and perhaps again in March, to say nothing of other competitive examinations.

(f) The intensely competitive nature of the majority of examinations upon which scholarships to the university are awarded encourages an excessive devotion to academic study, particularly on the part of candidates with meagre financial resources, just at a time when boys and girls should be encouraged to maintain any interest they may have in those occupations and activities which are, fortunately, not susceptible of examination. The result is that after a year or two at the university there may be a reaction; and scholarship holders not infrequently find themselves played out for lack of any real foundation to their academic and social life.

(g) The system of earmarking grants at the undergraduate stage for intending teachers is extremely undesirable. No one has a good word to say for it, though the modern universities are keenly aware that, broadly speaking, it keeps their faculties of arts and science alive. It requires students to commit them-

selves to the teaching profession at much too early an age, and
some students so commit themselves because it is the only way
in which they can hope to secure a university degree. (*See*
Chapter 7.)

(*h*) There is no provision, as there ought to be, for assisting
a specially selected and limited number of boys and girls to
attend universities in the Dominions and the United States of
America.

C—Proposals for Reform

61. It would be impossible to make detailed proposals for reform
without consulting all the bodies concerned, and particularly the
universities whose work does not come within the province of the
Board's administration. But a reasonable case can be made for
the view that universities are national rather than local institutions,
and that in a democratic system of education the State should make
itself wholly responsible for seeing that promising Secondary School
boys and girls, regardless of the area in which they live and of the
financial position of their parents, are enabled to pursue university
studies up to the stage of their obtaining a first degree. If responsibility for ensuring this measure of higher education were
undertaken by the State, it would perhaps be reasonable for
university and college scholarships to be devoted to post-graduate
work and research. It is probable that, in so far as the universities
are failing to make their full potential contribution to the advancement of science and learning, the reason is partly because the
emoluments which they are able to offer to tempt brilliant students
to devote their time for a period after graduation to advanced
work or research are inadequate.

62. Whether or not it is practicable to aim at such a diversion
of university scholarships, it is both desirable and practicable that
the existing local and state scholarships should be merged and be
administered centrally by the Board of Education. That is to say
that steps should be taken to establish some uniform system
throughout the country for selecting promising pupils in Secondary
Schools; and these should receive State awards rather than local
awards. The whole cost need not fall on the Exchequer. An appropriate charge could be levied on all Local Education Authorities
which provide Secondary Schools by means of a deduction from the
exchequer grant otherwise payable to them. Under such an arrangement the maximum award payable to a State Scholar would of
course be the maximum required for the university he was to attend.
His actual award would depend upon his parents' financial resources
and his other scholarships, if any.

63. The question of the examination or other test on which State awards should be made is a matter for further consideration; as is also the question of a centralized system of awards for Technical Colleges. Further, steps would have to be taken to prevent an undue proportion of scholars seeking admission to Oxford and Cambridge. These and many other problems could only be decided in consultation with the schools, Local Education Authorities and particularly the universities.

64. In simple terms, the prime reform proposed is an extension of the present State Scholarship system, so as, among other things, to absorb (a) the awards now made by Local Education Authorities and (b) the grants now made by the Board to undergraduates under the Regulations for the Training of Teachers. Such an extended scheme should be on a scale sufficient to ensure an intake to the universities adequate to provide, amongst other things, the graduate teachers required for the public system of education; and should include provision whereby specially selected students were able to proceed to universities in the Dominions and the United States.

65. It is a pre-requisite of any national scheme of awards to universities and similar types of institution that the fiinancial assistance made available to the scholar should not be the bare minimum necessary for him to maintain himself and pursue his studies, but should be fixed at a figure which has regard to the expenses which a full participation in the corporate life of the university inevitably involves. The present arrangements are not such as to secure this.

CHAPTER 6.—THE HEALTH AND PHYSICAL WELL-BEING OF THE CHILD

The School Medical Service

66. Under Section 80 of the Education Act, 1921, it is the duty of Local Education Authorities to provide for the medical inspection of all children in Public Elementary Schools, Secondary Schools and certain other schools and to make arrangements for the medical treatment of children in Public Elementary Schools. In the case of schools other than Public Elementary Schools Authorities have the power but not the duty to provide for medical treatment of the children.

67. So far as medical inspection is concerned, the ground is more or less adequately covered (apart from inadequacy of staff in certain areas) and the only matter for consideration is whether more of the

routine supervision of children might not be left to school nurses, the medical staff being used among other things for more detailed forms of inspection than can be practised under existing arrangements. Whatever system may be adopted, it is of importance to secure that children are medically inspected on first admission to school, before or at the time of their transfer from the sphere of primary to secondary education, and again about a year before they finally leave school. If the proposal made in paragraph 69 below is adopted, it would, of course, be essential to ensure that children are kept under medical and nursing supervision before the age of 5.

68. Provision for medical treatment is made by all Local Education Authorities, though in some areas facilities are far more complete than in others. In some few areas it includes only treatment for defects of teeth, eyes, ears, nose and throat, and for minor ailments, while in others it extends to orthopædic treatment, certain forms of chronic as distinct from acute illness, the supervision and convalescent treatment of rheumatism and its effects, and the treatment of maladjusted children through child guidance clinics or otherwise. These inequalities are in part inevitable in any system of local government, but are in large measure due to the absence of a sufficiently specific definition of the duty of providing for medical treatment. Persuasion is and will always be insufficient, and equally of opportunity so far as the health services of education are concerned can only be secured by requiring Local Education Authorities by statute to provide or secure adequate arrangements for the treatment of certain specific defects and illnesses. These would include all those mentioned above, for which provision is already made in some areas, and also such other forms of treatment as the Central Authority might from time to time direct. If such provision were made a statutory duty on Local Education Authorities the main task of the Board would then be to ensure that the provision made in each area was adequate to its needs.

Legislation on these lines should apply in the sphere of elementary and higher education alike and would make the provision of facilities for these forms of treatment obligatory in respect of children and young persons up to the age of 18 receiving full-time education in any form of grant-aided school.

69. Provision for medical inspection and treatment is at present restricted to children actually attending schools provided, maintained or aided by Local Education Authorities, and certain other schools, the Governors of which may ask for such provision to be made. Experience has shown that large numbers of children acquire in the pre-school years the defects which are only discovered when

they reach the age of 5 and become liable to school medical inspection. The responsibility for attending to the health of children in the first few years of their life rests with the Minister of Health, and the Maternity and Child Welfare Authorities, and these Authorities have provided throughout the country Maternity and Child Welfare Centres (often associated with school clinics) to which mothers may bring their children for medical advice and attention. They have also appointed Health Visitors whose duty it is to visit the homes and assist the parents with advice in the care of young children. Effort has, however, been as a rule concentrated on the first year of life, with the intention, and happily also with the result, of greatly reducing the infant mortality rate. A further result, however, has been that less effort has been applied to the later years, and that the School Medical Service is confronted year by year with the problem of dealing with large numbers of children entering school already suffering from malnutrition, deformities, skin diseases, pediculosis, and other defects which have arisen between the age of one and the date of first admission to school. In many cases these defects are remediable, though early neglect prolongs the time required for cure. In some cases irreparable damage has been done.

It is of vital importance that the gap should be bridged between the upper limit of effective provision by Maternity and Child Welfare Authorities, that is to say, at about the end of the first year of the child's life and the lower limit of provision by Local Education Authorities, i.e., at the age of 5 or at whatever earlier age a child first attends school. It is suggested that this can best be done by extending the responsibility of Local Education Authorities, which has hitherto been confined to children attending school, downwards so as to include all children above a certain age.

The precise age at which the transfer of responsibility should be made is a matter for discussion, but it is thought that the sphere of Local Education Authorities might appropriately begin at the age of 2. Transition from one Authority to another would be facilitated by requiring the medical records of the youngest children to be handed on by the Welfare Authority to the Education Authority and by extending the practice already adopted in many areas whereby the school nurse also acts as health visitor.

Social Training and Education of Children under 5 in Schools, Classes or Nurseries

70. Responsibility for the social care and training of children below the age of compulsory school attendance is at present shared

between different Authorities and (omitting special types of provision designed to meet war needs) provision made for them may take any of the following forms :—

(i) Day Nurseries provided by Local Authorities under the Maternity and Child Welfare Acts or by voluntary bodies and recognised by the Ministry of Health. These may admit children of any age before 5 but most of the children are under 2. They are staffed by nurses and, except in some instances where children between 2 and 5 attend, no teachers are employed and there are usually no educational arrangements. The number of Day Nurseries is understood to be decreasing.

(ii) Nursery Schools provided by Local Education Authorities or voluntary bodies and recognised by the Board under Section 21 of the Education Act, 1921. There are about 120 of these Schools with nearly 10,000 children between the ages of 2 and 5 in attendance. The aim of the Nursery Schools is to secure the healthy physical and mental development of the children coming in the main from homes where housing conditions are bad or where many mothers go out to work. These schools are generally open from about 8.30 a.m. to 5 p.m., the children remaining in them throughout the day in the care of trained teachers, nurses and others, and being provided with a mid-day meal and given plenty of rest in addition to carefully planned activities and training.

(iii) Nursery Classes in Public Elementary Schools which provide for children from 3 to 5. Before the war some 170,000 children attended Nursery Classes, of whom less than one quarter were between 3 and 4 years old and over three-quarters between 4 and 5. These classes form part of the Infants' Departments of Public Elementary Schools and have the normal hours of opening of such schools, that is to say roughly from 9 to 4 with an interval at mid-day. They are staffed by qualified teachers and enjoy a curriculum suited to the ages of the children, with opportunity for play and rest. They receive frequent visits from school and other nurses and are under general medical supervision.

71. There is frequently much overlapping between these various types of provision, though the objects of all of them are similar. There is room for a wide expansion in this provision. For a variety of reasons this expansion could not be met merely by an increase in the number of Nursery Schools. If provision for more than a

small fraction of the children who would benefit from it is to be made in any reasonable period of time, it must be by some other means. Much could be done by an extension of Nursery Classes and in many areas provision of this sort may meet the needs. In other areas, these could best be met by the continuance in peace time, under the auspices of Local Education Authorities, of simple types of Nursery conducted on the lines of Nursery Centres for evacuated children and War Nurseries for children of mothers in employment. These types of Nursery which, as a war measure, are being administered by Maternity and Child Welfare Authorities, are, so far as children from 2 to 5 are concerned, more in the province of the Education Authorities.

It is accordingly suggested that Local Education Authorities should be charged with the duty of making such additional provision as may be necessary for attending to the physical and mental development of children over 2 and under 5 years of age in Nursery Schools or classes or such other forms of Nursery as may be approved by the Board of Education. Such provision would carry with it the corollary that, as suggested in paragraph 69, the functions of Maternity and Child Welfare Authorities should not extend beyond the age of about 2 years.

Care and Education of Handicapped Children

72. The statutory provision for the elementary education of blind, deaf, physically and mentally defective and epileptic children is contained in Part V of the Education Act, 1921, and further provision may be made for their continued education beyond the age of compulsion under Sections 70 and 71 of that Act. Broadly, the position is that the parents of such children are required to keep them at Special Schools until the end of the term in which they attain the age of 16, and that Local Education Authorities for elementary education are under a similar obligation to provide or secure suitable education for them up to that age. Beyond the age of 16 there is no obligation on Authorities or parents, though in point of fact the large majority of the blind continue to receive training and further education for anything up to four or five years, while a few proceed to a Secondary School course. A certain proportion of deaf, cripples and those suffering from severe epilepsy also receive training and further education after they reach the age of 16.

73. So far as Special Schools for children up to the age of 16 are concerned, provision has hitherto been somewhat haphazard. The number of handicapped children of any one type (excluding delicate

children) within the area of all but the largest Local Education Authorities is far too small to justify the establishment of a Special School for children from that area only. The small day school is in any case ineffective, and for satisfactory education a unit of not less than four, or preferably five or six, classes should be regarded as the minimum. Having regard to the proportion of handicapped children in the child population, it is found in practice that the smallest area which could justify the establishment of a Special School to meet its own need is one containing a population of from one to several millions according to the category of defect. This being the case it has not been practicable for the Board to enforce the law upon individual Local Education Authorities, and though co-operation between Authorities has occasionally been effective, the Board have had to rely on the initiative of the more enterprising Authorities and on voluntary effort. Numbers of residential schools for all types of defective children have been established under voluntary management.

74. Each of the several categories of handicapped children presents its own problems which it would be beyond the scope of this Memorandum to discuss in detail. Broadly, the position is that though accommodation for the blind and deaf, including the partially sighted and partially deaf, is more or less adequate, it is ill-distributed and much of it is old and inconvenient. War-time conditions have led to the evacuation of a number of these schools, generally to their great advantage. In any scheme of reconstruction the opportunity should be taken of reorganising these schools on a regional basis and removing them from the towns to the country, and at the same time of implementing the recommendations of the special committees which have recently examined the problems presented by these children.

Additional Residential Special School accommodation for children suffering from rheumatism and its effects and for delicate and debilitated children is also required and the residential provision for mentally defective children is gravely inadequate. So far as the care of the mentally defective is concerned, little has so far been done to carry out the recommendations of the joint committee of the Board of Education and Board of Control, which reported in 1929. For the large majority of these children and also of the delicate children now certifiable as physically defective, provision will have to be, and should properly be, made within the Public Elementary School system and separate Special Schools are unnecessary.

Some additional accommodation in residential hospital schools is also required for children suffering from crippling defects. Casualties due to enemy action may well increase the number of cripples requiring orthopædic treatment. Some of the additional hospital accommodation which has been provided to meet war conditions may become available after the war and could be used for these children and for other categories of handicapped children for whom residential provision will be required.

75. There are also certain types of handicapped children who are not covered by Part V of the Act for whom special provision is needed—the maladjusted or problem child and the convalescent. For the former, as mentioned in paragraph 68 above, provision may be made by Local Education Authorities under Section 80 of the Act for treatment in child guidance clinics or by sending the child to one or other of the few private residential homes designed to deal with these cases. It is desirable that the scope of Part V should be enlarged so as to include maladjusted children and that a small number of residential Special Schools should be provided for them on a regional basis. It is also desirable that Authorities should be allowed under Section 80 of the Act to send children convalescing after illness to residential homes where they would receive the rest and treatment they require before returning to the ordinary schools, but it is not suggested that such institutions should be provided by Authorities or certified as Special Schools.

76. It has long been felt that the differentiation between the upper age limit for compulsory education in Special Schools and Public Elementary Schools respectively is unnecessary and undesirable, except in the case of the blind and deaf, whose educational handicap is so much greater than that of normal children. The raising of the age of compulsory education for normal children to 15 should, it is suggested, be accompanied by lowering that for physically and mentally defective children to the same age. On the other hand, the upper age for blind and deaf children should remain at 16, and the limitation which now exists on retention after the statutory age in all types of Special School should be withdrawn. By this means continuity of education after 15 or 16 will be secured and development of the curricula towards the needs of a vocation will be facilitated.

At the same time the whole of Part V of the Act, which is based on a series of earlier enactments dating back to 1893 should be revised and brought up to date. Among other things, the provisions of this part of the Act and those of the Mental Deficiency Acts should be brought into line, and a fresh delimitation made of the respective functions of Local Education Authorities and Local Mental Deficiency Authorities. It is also desirable that the present requirement should be reconsidered under which all types of defective children must be formally certified as defective before proper arrangements can be made for their educational care.

The recommendations contained in the preceding paragraphs will fail of their purpose unless the education and care of these handicapped children are organised on a wide geographical basis. Given the necessary co-operation between Authorities there is no reason why adequate provision for all the various types of afflicted children should not be forthcoming within a relatively short time.

Provision of meals

77. Broadly speaking, Local Education Authorities have power under various sections of the Education Act, 1921, to provide meals for children attending any grant-aided school.

In the case of Public Elementary Schools these powers derive from Sections 82 to 84 of the Act, the general effect of which is (a) that if there are undernourished children in the schools the Authority may provide them with free meals in case of need, and (b) that they may also provide meals on payment by the parents. Where payment is demanded, it is usually limited to the cost of the food only, the overhead expenditure falling on the Authority.

Free meals for necessitous children attending Secondary and Technical Schools may be provided by the Local Education Authorities for higher education, whether under Section 71 (c) as a form of maintenance allowance, or under the general power given by Section 70 (1) to supply or aid the supply of higher education. In many of these schools meals are also provided on payment by the parents of a sum which represents something more than the bare cost of the food.

In Nursery Schools, under Section 21, meals are provided as part of the normal routine of the school, the parents paying what they can afford.

In the case of Special Schools certified under Part V of the Act, meals are usually provided and parents are expected to pay for them if they are in a position to do so.

78. It will be seen that there is a distinction between Public Elementary Schools on the one hand and all other types of school on the other, so far as provision of free meals is concerned. In the former, the view has been taken that meals may be provided free only if (a) the children are undernourished and (b) the parents are necessitous; while in the latter, the only criterion is the means of the parents. The necessity of satisfying both criteria in the case of Public Elementary Schools has been a fruitful cause of difficulty

in administration and delay in actual provision. There can be no justification for a procedure which allows a well nourished child attending a Secondary or Special School to have meals free if its parents are poor, while withholding this provision from a similar child of equally poor parents if he happens to be at a Public Elementary School. Apart from this anomaly, recent investigations have made it clear that medical opinion on what constitutes under-nourishment is not well defined, and that no hard and fast line can be drawn between the varying degrees of malnutrition on which a decision can be properly based whether free meals should be given.

79. The rapid development of provision of meals for school children that has taken place during the war and the expected wide-spread institution of communal feeding for the general public may produce a marked change in the social habits of the people. It may well be that the provision of a midday meal will become and will remain a normal element in public education.

There is much to be said for the view that midday dinners should be regarded as an integral part of full-time education and, as such, provided free. If this view is not accepted, there remains the question on what basis to determine whether parents are to be required to pay for the meals. At present the income scales on which the decision is reached vary widely from area to area, and it is suggested that if the charge for meals is in future to be based upon the parents' income, the anomalies which exist at present would be reduced by the institution of a national income scale such as is in operation in the case of the National Milk Scheme. The whole question is, however, one that requires much consideration and it is possible that the solution lies rather in the introduction of some system of family allowances than in remission of the cost of meals on the basis of parental income.

80. There still remains the question whether provision of meals should be a power or a duty of Local Education Authorities. So long as it remains a power the exercise of which lies in the discretion of the Authority, it seems probable that there will always be some areas in which no meals are provided, even for the children most clearly in need of supplementary nourishment. In these cases the Board will have no remedy. The provisions of Sections 82–84 of the Education Act, 1921, which are open to more than one interpreta-tion, should in any case be amended and clarified. It may well be felt that this opportunity should be taken of making it obligatory for Local Education Authorities to make or otherwise secure the provision of meals for all children for whom such provision is neces-sary in order that they may derive full benefit from their education.

CHAPTER 7.—THE RECRUITMENT AND TRAINING OF TEACHERS

A.—Present Position

(Temporary adjustments due to the War have been disregarded.)

(a) *Training*

81. There are two main types of institution engaged in the training of teachers, namely :—(a) Training Colleges, referred to as T.C.s. and (b) Training Departments of Universities and University Colleges, referred to as U.T.Ds. There are some 80 Training Colleges, 50 of them provided by voluntary bodies (mainly the churches) and the remainder by Local Education Authorities. There are about 20 Training Departments of Universities and University Colleges.

82. The T.Cs. provide a two-year course of combined academic and professional study (at the Domestic Science T.Cs. the course is three years), the minimum age of admission to which is 18. The U.T.Ds. provide a four-year course, the first three being a course for a university degree, and the fourth year being devoted to professional training. The minimum age of admission to this four-year course is 17.

83. There are certain divergences from this pattern. The Froebel Colleges provide a three-year course, only the last two of which are recognised by the Board. Some T.Cs. provide third-year courses in special subjects, which a few students take, either immediately following the completion of their two-year course or after they have had some years of practical experience as teachers. There are also one or two specialist colleges for the training of teachers of physical training and teachers of handwork. There is also a system of training, very little used, known as school-centred training, in which graduates are attached to specially selected Secondary Schools and secure their training at those schools. But these special types of training, though important, do not materially affect the main picture.

84. The annual output of trained teachers from the T.Cs. is about 5,000, and from the U.T.Ds. about 1,600. The T.C. course does not, save in a few exceptional cases, lead to a university degree and the students from these Colleges teach almost exclusively in Public Elementary Schools. The U.T.D. course involves graduation, and some 40 per cent. of the output obtain posts in Secondary Schools. The remainder teach in Public Elementary Schools, mainly in the Senior Schools.

85. Both types of training are subsidised by grants. The Board pay 50 per cent. of the net expenditure which Local Education

Authorities incur in providing and maintaining T.Cs.; they pay capitation grants in the form of tuition and maintenance grants to or on behalf of students in voluntary T.Cs.; and, subject to need, they pay tuition fees and maintenance grants in respect of students taking the four-year course at the U.T.Ds. The annual expenditure by the Board on capitation grants to voluntary T.Cs. and U.T.Ds. is roughly £700,000 a year. If the 50 per cent. grant to Local Education Authorities were isolated and added to the above figure it would probably show that the total annual expenditure by the Board on the training of teachers was about £900,000. The Local Education Authorities which provide T.Cs. (other than Domestic Science T.Cs.) receive a subsidy raised from those which do not.

86. Students admitted either to T.Cs. or U.T.Ds. normally have had a full secondary education, and if they seek grant aid (that is are not admitted as private students training at their own expense) they sign a declaration acknowledging that they are taking advantage of public money in order to be trained as teachers and asserting their intention to complete the course and thereafter follow the profession of teacher.

87. In the main there are separate T.Cs. for men and women, though there are some "mixed" colleges. The U.T.Ds. with the exception of Cambridge, like the universities themselves, admit both men and women. The T.Cs. are, in the main, residential institutions where the students are segregated by profession, and, as indicated above, generally by sex. There are a few day students living at home at some colleges. The U.T.Ds. are residential in the sense that there are hostels attached to the universities, but a number of students live at home or in lodgings.

88. The scales of salary of the staffs of the T.Cs. are approximately the same as the scales of Secondary School teachers. The scales in U.T.Ds. conform to university standards. In the T.Cs. not only are the students resident, but in general the staff also. No doubt in the men's T.Cs. married men teachers live outside the college, but in the women's T.Cs. the staff with few exceptions are unmarried and in general reside in college.

89. The preceding paragraphs deal with what may be called pre-employment training. There is a system, very spasmodic and fluctuating, of post-employment training which takes the form of short courses sometimes extending over three months and sometimes over only a fortnight or even a weekend, designed to serve as refresher courses for serving teachers. These courses are conducted by T.Cs. and U.T.Ds., by Local Education Authorities and by independent organisations; and for many years the Board have themselves

organised courses of about a fortnight's duration conducted by their Inspectors. There is, however, no requirement that a teacher, trained or untrained, shall attend a refresher course; on the other hand, the number of courses provided is by no means equal to the demand for them.

90. There is very limited provision whereby serving teachers who wish to devote any period up to a year away from their schools, in order to undertake a special study or investigation, may receive a sum, based on need, not exceeding £200. The money available for promoting this form of "Sabbatical Year" has never exceeded £1,500 a year. There are occasional "interchanges" between T.C. lecturers in this country and in the Dominions.

(b) *Recognition*

91. The regulations governing Public Elementary Schools require that teachers shall be recognised in some specific category namely as Certificated Teachers, Uncertificated Teachers or Teachers of Special Subjects. (In rural schools Supplementary teachers may in certain circumstances be employed.) A Certificated Teacher now means a trained teacher, that is a teacher who has satisfactorily completed a course of training of the kind already described. There is a class of Certificated Teachers diminishing in number year by year, who are not trained. These are a relic of the days when the Certificate could be obtained by examination only.

92. The regulations governing Secondary Schools do not require the recognition of teachers by category and do not prescribe any precise academic or professional qualifications. They provide that the teaching staff of a school must be "suitable and sufficient in number and qualifications for providing adequate instruction in each subject of the curriculum." In practice, teachers in Secondary schools are normally graduates and many of them are trained. The regulations governing Technical Schools are similar in character, but except in the case of Art teachers the teachers in Technical Schools are seldom "trained teachers." The Board make provision for a course of training for teachers of art, but there is no obligation on teachers in Art Schools to have taken such training.

93. For historical reasons and because of the Regulation requirements governing the recognition of teachers in Public Elementary Schools, the only recognition granted by the Board to teachers who have been trained, even though they may have been trained specifically for work in Secondary Schools, is "recognition as a Certificated Teacher for the purposes of the Code," that is for the purpose of teaching in a Public Elementary School.

94. The courses which a student has to take and the examinations

which he has to pass in order to be recognized as a Certificated Teacher are as follows :—

(a) At T.Cs. The T.Cs. are arranged in groups round the various universities; and Joint Boards, representative of the T.Cs. and the particular university concerned, conduct examinations on courses and under a system which the Board approve. The Board accept the recommendations of the Joint Boards about the certification of individual students. There is a Central Advisory Committee, representative of all the interests concerned, which advises the Board about minimum requirements in the way of subjects; and thus a rough parity, though not necessarily identity, of qualification is required throughout the country for certification.

(b) At U.T.Ds. The Board accept a university degree as adequate evidence of academic attainment and they accept success in the examination for the university Diploma in Education (or Teaching Diploma) as sufficient for professional purposes. If specially recommended by the university, a student who fails in his final degree examination may nevertheless take the fourth professional year with a view to certification; and a graduate who fails to obtain the university Diploma in Education may in certain circumstances, nevertheless, be recognized as a Certificated Teacher.

In both the T.Cs. and the U.T.Ds. the Board reserve the right to be the final assessor whether a student has acquitted himself well enough in practical teaching to justify recognition as a Certificated Teacher. The Board inspect the T.Cs., but to a lesser extent and, in effect, only on request, the U.T.Ds.

95. Every Certificated Teacher has to serve one probationary year before his recognition as a Certificated Teacher can be confirmed. In cases of incompetence recognition is withdrawn. The system of probation does not, of course, apply to trained teachers who take posts in Secondary Schools, since "certification" has no meaning for those schools.

(c) *Supply*

96. The Board control the supply of Certificated Teachers by fixing annually the quota of students at T.Cs. and U.T.D.s. whom they are prepared to recognize as Certificated Teachers on the conclusion of the course.

97. But both T.Cs. and U.T.Ds. admit students outside this quota. The T.Cs. sometimes admit students from the Colonies, who intend to return to their own country, and the U.T.Ds. admit students whose sole object is to be trained for teaching in Secondary Schools,

and to whom therefore recognition as a Certificated Teacher is irrelevant.

B.—Objections to the Present System

98. The weaknesses of the present system are briefly as follows :—

(*a*) Young people are committed to the teaching profession at too early an age; and—a specialised aspect of this—enter the profession before they have had any experience of life other than that of a pupil at school or a student at college.

(*b*) The two-year course at T.Cs. is inadequate. The amount of academic and professional work required is such that students have insufficient opportunity to mature as individuals.

(*c*) Students at the T.Cs. are all preparing for the same profession and, in general, are segregated by sex. This tends to a narrowness of outlook. Further, some of the colleges have a tradition of supervision and discipline not appropriate to young people, especially young people who, on leaving college, will at once enter upon an independent life as teachers.

(*d*) Training is too uniform in character. For instance, no extensive use has been made of school-centred training, which in its present form is inadequately financed.

(*e*) Recruitment of the staffs of T.Cs. is not on a satisfactory basis. Some of the lecturers have little or no experience of work in Public Elementary Schools, and the present salary arrangements are not such as to attract the well-established teacher with considerable school experience. There is too much "immobility." Teachers should not only come into T.C. work from the schools, but should also go out from T.Cs. to specially responsible work in the schools. In short, appointment to the staff of a T.C. should not generally be regarded as a permanency.

(f) Training, though it may be for Secondary Schools, issues in a "recognition" which is relevant only to Public Elementary Schools. This is troublesome now and will be quite impossible to justify or administer when schools are organized as primary up to eleven years of age and secondary thereafter.

(*g*) There is no adequate system of short post-employment refresher courses of training to enable serving teachers to review and improve their professional practice or to acquire the knowledge and technique necessary for developments which are new to them.

(*h*) There is no regularized or extensive system of "Sabbatical Years"; that is, arrangements whereby teachers can get away from their own schools or colleges for a year in order to teach or study elsewhere. This kind of "refreshment" is very necessary, and particularly for teachers on the staffs of T.Cs.

(*i*) The Local Education Authorities, except the few which provide T.Cs., and the schools generally, except those in the neighbourhood of T.Cs. which are used as practising schools, have no educational responsibility for, and take no part in, the training of the teachers who will ultimately serve them.

(*j*) There is no provision for the training of teachers of technical subjects who serve in the Technical Schools and Colleges.

C.—Proposals for Reform

99. It will always be desirable, apart from the needs of Technical Schools, to have teachers of two broad classes : graduates and non-graduates. To require every teacher to take a university degree course would be to deprive the schools, and particularly the Infant and Junior Schools, of some of the persons best qualified by character and natural endowment to be teachers. It follows that the broad division into T.Cs. providing non-graduate courses, and U.T.Ds. providing courses after graduation, should not be disturbed. But there must be added a new category of training institution, namely training departments of Technical Colleges.

100. The following are the main proposals for reform as regards T.Cs. and U.T.Ds. :—

(*a*) The course at T.Cs. should be a three-year course, and on the satisfactory completion of his training a student should be recognized as a "trained teacher" without the necessity of serving a year on probation. No teacher should be recognized as a trained teacher before his 21st birthday. This provision would make unnecessary any precise minimum age for admission to a T.C., which always involves hardship on those a few days or weeks under the age.

(*b*) The second or middle year of the course, except possibly in the case of students at the Domestic Science Training Colleges, should be spent away from college, at least six months of the year being spent in teaching in a school under supervision as a paid "untrained teacher in training". The remaining part of the year should be spent either in teaching or in some other work of approved character.

(*c*) No student should be called upon finally to commit himself to teaching or to sign any declaration until the beginning of his third year. He should be free to give up training for the profession, and the Board or the college should be free to require him to give up such training, at any time up to the end of his second year.

(d) The four-year course, as such, at the U.T.Ds. should be abolished, no grants being earmarked for intending teachers at the undergraduate stage. The money now spent on earmarked grants to undergraduates, with further sums if necessary, should be allocated to the universities or some other appropriate body to be used for the purpose of enabling qualified but needy students to pursue a university degree course (see Chapter 5). No university student should be required to decide whether he intends to be a teacher or to sign a declaration on the matter until he has graduated.

(e) There should be a reasonable capitation grant in respect of graduates who sign a declaration of their intention to be teachers and who take a year's professional course in a U.T.D. (that is the equivalent of the existing fourth year of the four-year course).

(f) The system of school-centred training for graduates as an alternative to training at U.T.Ds. should be encouraged.

(g) The ideal is "every teacher a trained teacher or a teacher under training." But until this ideal can be reached teachers should be regarded as classified under two broad heads: "trained teachers" and "untrained teachers". Each of these two classes is naturally divided into two sub-clauses, thus :—

Trained Teachers :—
    (a) Graduates—from U.T.Ds. or school-centred training.
    (b) Non-graduates—from T.Cs.
Untrained Teachers :—
    (a) Graduates—from the Universities.
    (b) Non-graduates—from the Secondary Schools and elsewhere.

(h) The term Certificated Teacher, as implying a trained teacher, should disappear. But some of the existing Uncertificated Teachers in the Public Elementary Schools might, in virtue of long and meritorious service, be raised to a grade called Certificated Teachers.

(i) The training of specialist teachers of practical subjects such as domestic science and handicraft needs separate consideration. The position of the Froebel Colleges, which at present have a three-year course, only the last two of which are recognized by the Board, would also require special consideration.

(*j*) The salary arrangements for the staffs of T.Cs. should be revised so as to encourage the recruitment of a more appropriate and distinguished staff, and thus give the T.Cs. a more significant place in the hierarchy of educational institutions.

(*k*) Thehe should be members of the staff in every T.C. who are not appointed to permanent posts but are serving the T.Cs. in virtue of their special qualifications, for a limited period of years on their way to headmasterships or other responsible and well-paid posts in schools. Further, part-time appointments should be encouraged whereby (i) specially experienced teachers in schools could, while still continuing their school teaching, make some contribution to the work of the T.Cs.; and (ii) married women could play a part in the training of women teachers.

(*l*) The Board should ensure (i) adequate provision of refresher courses for teachers and (ii) a system of Teacher Studentships which allow annually a substantial number of teachers, particularly teachers on the staffs of Training Colleges, to enjoy a "Sabbatical Year." Interchange arrangements between the T.Cs. themselves and with the Dominions and U.S.A. should be encouraged.

101. Provision must be made for the training of Teachers in Technical Colleges and Schools and Day Continuation Schools. In such institutions teachers, both full-time and part-time, are broadly of two types, namely : teachers of technical and ancillary subjects and teachers of general subjects. The training of teachers of general subjects presents no special difficulties and requires no special provision outside the provision which is already made or could be made by U.T.Ds. and T.Cs.

102. But the training of teachers of technical subjects involves new provision. These teachers, if part-time, are employed in, and if full-time have been employed in, industry or commerce. Such industrial or commercial experience is an essential part of their professional equipment, and is, indeed, an integral part of their training as teachers of technical subjects. But they seldom have been trained in teaching methods. Moreover, the full-time teachers may need not only courses of training in method but also courses designed to bring their knowledge of industrial and commercial conditions and practice up to date. Further, part-time teachers of ancillary subjects, e.g., science, who are often teachers in Elementary or Secondary Schools, need a knowledge of the technique required for dealing with technical students, the majority of whom are in employment.

103. None of the forms of training mentioned in paragraph 102

can be provided either by the U.T.Ds. or the T.Cs., whose knowledge of or contact with industry or commerce is as a rule negligible. It is necessary therefore that Training Departments should be established at selected Technical Colleges and should provide full-time and part-time courses of training to meet the varied needs of teachers of technical and ancillary subjects. Experiment should also be made with school-centred training, whereby a teacher with adequate academic qualifications and with industrial or commercial experience would be attached for training to a Technical College or School.

104. The classification of teachers, mentioned in paragraph 100 (g), into "trained teachers" and "untrained teachers" would apply equally to teachers of technical subjects. But teachers of technical subjects with certain academic qualifications, e.g. a National Certificate or Diploma, plus adequate industrial or commercial experience, should rank in the hierarchy of teachers as equivalent to the graduate rather than to non-graduate.

105. The intensive refresher and other courses which it will be necessary to establish on a considerable scale immediately after the war in order to provide the initial staff of teachers and "leaders" for the two new and inter-related services, namely : (a) Day Continuation Schools, and (b) Youth Centres, are not here described in detail. Rapid improvisation will be called for, and the resources of the U.T.Ds., T.Cs. and Technical Colleges will be taxed to the full. But, in course of time, the training of teachers and "leaders" for these new services will form an integral part of the normal work of the universities (including the Social Science Departments and the U.T.Ds.), the T.Cs. and the Technical Colleges.

Conclusion

106. The objections which could be raised against, and the difficulties which would have to be faced in giving effect to, these reforms, particularly as regards the T.Cs. and U.T.Ds. are chiefly as follows :—

(a) The T.Cs. might complain that if the second year of a three-year course were spent in school, resulting in no two consecutive years being spent at college, there would be a loss of continuity in the study of students and a weakening of the corporate spirit of the college. In a sense, however, this loss and this weakening are desirable. The students suffer from continuity of study and the Colleges lack the breath of fresh air which would be provided if each year there returned to the college young men and young women of at least 20 years of age who had spent a year of independence in being tested as potential teachers in the schools. It is not corporate spirit but maturity, experience of life and a considered choice of the profession that young teachers lack when they begin their careers as trained teachers.

(b) The Local Education Authorities might complain at being compelled to employ for six months or a year half-baked teachers in training. But training will never be what it ought to be until the schools themselves play a significant part in the training. The Local Education Authorities, and it may be added H.M. Inspectors, would have to shoulder a responsibility never placed upon them hitherto.

(c) The universities would complain unless the national scholarship provision, enabling qualified but needy students to pursue a degree course without committing themselves to any particular profession, were really adequate. At present the Faculty of Arts, and to some extent the Faculty of Pure Science, in practically all the modern universities, is kept alive by the earmarked grants for students who pledge themselves to be teachers at 17 or 18 years of age.

107. It is essential, if what is called "Youth Work" becomes an integral part of the national educational system, that the training of Youth "leaders" should not be divorced from the training of teachers, and that there should be interchangeability, for suitable posts, between trained teachers and trained leaders; and this involves something in the nature of equivalence of salary and superannuation arrangements.

CHAPTER 8.—THE UNITS OF LOCAL EDUCATIONAL ADMINISTRATION

108. The present units of local educational administration were laid down in the Education Act, 1902, but to understand them it is necessary to go back to 1896. In that year Sir John Gorst's abortive Education Bill entrusted the administration of all types of education to the Councils of Counties and County Boroughs. This proposal was vehemently opposed by the non-County Boroughs and Urban Districts, and the 1902 Act accordingly provided for two types of Local Education Authority—one for elementary education and another for higher education. They are—

Authorities for Elementary Education (Part III Authorities):
(315 in number) :—

> (i) Non-County Boroughs with a population of over 10,000, according to the 1901 Census;
> (ii) Urban Districts with a population of over 20,000 according to that Census;
> (iii) County Boroughs;
> (iv) Counties in respect of the County areas, exclusive of the areas mentioned in (i), (ii) and (iii).

Authorities for Higher Education (Part II Authorities):
(146 in number) :—

> (i) County Boroughs;
> (ii) Counties in respect of the County areas, exclusive of County Boroughs.

109. Past history makes it clear, therefore, that the institution of two types of Local Education Authorities was determined by considerations of political expediency rather than of its suitability to the educational system, and the development of the educational system during the years that have elapsed since 1902 has demonstrated in ever-increasing measure that this artificial dichotomy is a serious bar to educational progress.

110. The inconveniences arising from this dual system of local educational administration were described in a memorandum submitted in 1927 by the Board to the Royal Commission on Local Government in the following paragraph :—

> "The immediate practical difficulty which arises out of the position stated above related to the type of school known as a central school. The recent Report of the Board's Consultative Committee on 'The Education of the Adolescent' clearly contemplates the development of the provision of such schools, under the name of 'modern' schools, as a separate and distinct form of full-time post-primary education alternative and supplementary to the existing secondary schools and junior technical schools. The question therefore immediately arises whether this particular type of post-primary education should be provided under powers relating to higher or to elementary education. Central schools at present fall within the sphere of elementary education and can be provided and administered only by the Authority for elementary education, and under the regulations for the time being applying to public elementary schools. This distinction in the position of central (or 'modern')

schools as compared with that of other types of institution providing post-primary education may be unfavourable to their development as a separate and individual contribution to the supply of education of post-primary character. Moreover, in those areas which, so far as elementary education is concerned, are administered as autonomous areas, there is the possibility of unprofitable competition or overlapping between the Part II and Part III Authorities in the supply of post-primary education, unless the Authority concerned take steps to co-operate closely in providing the education facilities necessary and suitable to the needs of the particular geographical area. Such co-operation is, of course, possible under section 6 of the Education Act, 1921."

111. But it is easier to diagnose a malady than to prescribe its cure. As has been well said by a Permanent Secretary of the Board* :—

"In view of the past history of this matter it would be hazardous to prophesy how or how soon the obstacle to educational organisation presented by the incoherence of administrative areas will be overcome. It is to be hoped that realisation of the great and increasing inconveniences of the present arrangements will lead, whether by way of central or local action, to a real effort to overcome them."

112. To look for reform by way of local action is idle. Civic pride will rarely allow a Borough or an Urban District to admit that its functions could be better discharged by another Authority, and the full force of vested interests will be marshalled in support of the maintenance of the *status quo*.

113. That nothing has been done by way of central action is certainly not the fault of the Board's Consultative Committee. Both the Hadow Report, "The Education of the Adolescent" and the Spens Report, "Secondary Education" dealt with the matter at some length.

114. The Hadow Report recommended advance by two, or possibly three, stages, viz. :—

(i) co-operation between Part III and Part II Authorities, with the object of securing by mutual agreement that, just as representatives of a Part III Authority already take part in the initiation and administration of Secondary Schools maintained in its area by the Part II Authority, so the Part II Authority

*Sir Amherst Selby-Bigge's "The Board of Education," 1927, p.54.

should be fully consulted before Senior Schools are developed by a Part III Authority;

(ii) legislation transferring to Part II Authorities powers and duties of those Part III Authorities whose areas do not reach a certain minimum standard of population, and vesting with full Part II powers those Part III Authorities whose areas attain that standard;

and possibly later on—

(iii) legislation creating new provincial Authorities in which Part III and Part II Authorities will both be merged.

115. The Spens Report went into less detail. It gave general support to the Hadow mode of progress, except that it expressed the view that the third step would not command any measure of support and recommended that the problem should be remitted to a Departmental or Inter-departmental Committee.

116. The May Committee on National Expenditure, reporting in 1931, came out with the following categorical recommendation :—

"First among the changes which we consider necessary in the interests of efficient administration we would place the reduction in the number of Authorities by the concentration of all educational functions, as far as Local Authorities are concerned, in the hands of the County and County Borough Councils."

117. As recently as 1939 the Select Committee on Estimates recommended in the interests of economy and efficiency what is in effect the Hadow second step, with the modification that, in addition to the factor of population, financial capacity to discharge all the powers and duties should be a factor in determining whether an existing Part III Authority should be vested with full Part II powers.

118. The general arguments in favour of a single type of Local Education Authority are strongly reinforced by the proposals in regard to the lay-out of the educational system, so far as the full-time education of the child is concerned, contained in Chapter 1 of this Memorandum. If all Schools for children over 11 are to be regarded as secondary and dealt with under a single code of regulations, then the field of elementary education will be limited to education for children up to the age of 11 and, for the time being, such children over that age as of necessity have to remain in all-age Elementary Schools. In the words of the Select Committee on Estimates, the suggestion that the functions of Authorities for elementary education should be limited to the education of children up to 11 "is only to be made to be rejected."

119. The precise method of constituting Local Education Authorities, assuming that the principle of a single type of Authority is accepted, is outside the scope of this Memorandum. It may be that the solution lies in the direction suggested by the Board's Consultative Committee, the May Committee, and the Select Committee on Estimates. On the other hand account will need to be taken of the growing volume of opinion in favour of larger units of administration, constituted on a regional basis. This solution, however, raises wide general questions of local government which cannot profitably be pursued here.

CHAPTER 9.—THE DUAL SYSTEM AND ALLIED PROBLEMS

120. Since the Education Act, 1902, Public Elementary Schools have been divided into provided (or council) and non-provided (or voluntary) schools. The maintenance of schools of both types is a statutory duty of the Local Education Authority, but in the case of non-provided schools the necessary repairs, alterations and improvements are the responsibility of the Managers, the Local Education Authority having no power to spend money for these purposes, except in respect of fair wear and tear. The power given temporarily to Local Education Authorities under the Education Act, 1936, to make grants for voluntary school building for senior children is referred to in paragraph 126 below.

121. The powers of control of Local Education Authorities over non-provided schools are limited. In particular (a) the Managers appoint the teachers, subject to the Authority's consent, which, however, must not be withheld except on educational grounds, and (b) while the Local Education Authority have the control of secular instruction, they have no general power to alter the organisation of a non-provided school in such a way, for instance, as to convert a school for children of all ages into a school for juniors only or for seniors only; (the power given by Section 34 of the 1921 Act to redistribute children among two or more schools of the same denomination in the same locality is of very limited application).

122. The legal safeguards and the divided responsibilities of the dual system have given rise to endless complications in administration, which retard educational progress, engender friction and consume time and energies which could be spent to much better purpose. The system is inconsistent with proper economy and efficiency since, for example—

(i) a non-provided school with 30 or more pupils cannot be closed, however much spare accommodation there may be in neighbouring Council schools, unless there is another school of the same denomination to which its pupils can go;

(ii) a new non-provided school may be set up although the children who will attend it are adequately accommodated already in Council schools;

(iii) the Authority cannot ensure that a vacancy in the staff of a non-provided school is filled not by a new appointment but by the transfer to it of a redundant teacher from another school in the area, so that without dismissals of teachers, which are contrary to the practice of Authorities, reasonable and economical adjustments of staffing cannot be ensured.

123. Most non-provided schools are in old buildings and very few have any financial resources, such sums as can be raised by church collections and the like barely sufficing in many cases to keep the existing premises in reasonably good repair. It is quite impossible, therefore, for most Managers to find the money for enlargements or improvements, and still less for the rebuilding or replacement which are essential if the schools are to be kept abreast, not only of present-day educational requirements, but also of modern standards of hygiene, ventilation and the like.

124. The following figures illustrate the results of Managers' lack of funds and of Local Education Authorities' lack of control over the organisation of voluntary schools :—

(a) of the 753 schools still remaining on the Board's Black List of schools with defective premises (issued in 1925 and now very much out-of-date) 541 are non-provided schools;

(b) on the 31st March, 1939, 62 per cent. of the children of 11 years of age and over in Council schools were in Senior Schools or departments specially organised for children of that age, while the corresponding figure for non-provided schools was 16 per cent.

125. The scope of the problem is shown by the following figures. On the 31st March, 1938, the latest date for which reliable statistics are available, there were 10,533 non-provided schools with an average attendance of 1,374,000 pupils; on the same date there were 10,363 Council schools with an average attendance of 3,151,000. Thus only 30 per cent. of Public Elementary School children are in non-provided schools, although these schools are more numerous than Council schools. They are, therefore, in general very much smaller than Council schools, tending to less economy and efficiency

in organisation and administration, though due allowance must be made for the fact that a considerable proportion of non-provided Elementary Schools are rural schools. It is interesting to note that in 1902 the children attending non-provided schools were in a majority, there being 3,074,000 in 14,275 schools against 2,344,000 in 5,875 Council schools or 56 per cent. in non-provided schools.

126. With the development from about 1926 of Hadow reorganisation, which involves separate Senior Schools or departments for children of 11 and over with proper facilities for handicraft and domestic subjects, for science, physical training and games, and with the prospect of the raising of the school leaving age to 15, the position of the non-provided schools became acute. Managers could not afford to make suitable provision for their older children and many would not consent to the decapitation of their school so that the seniors might attend a Senior School provided by the Council. To meet this situation the Education Act, 1936, enabled, but did not compel, Local Education Authorities for a limited period to pay not less than 50 per cent. and not more than 75 per cent. of the cost of new non-provided school building for senior children. The building proposals and organisation had to be of a standard approved by the Authority and the Board and the teachers in the school aided under the Act had to be appointed and dismissed by the Authority, subject to the right of the Managers to be satisfied as to the fitness and competence of certain of the teachers (called "reserved" teachers) to give denominational religious instruction. Owing to the inability of many Managers to raise their share of the cost, to the dislike by some of the increased control given to Local Education Authorities and to the unwillingness of a few Local Education Authorities to subsidise denominational schools, only 519 proposals were put forward under the 1936 Act (289 of these were in respect of Roman Catholic Schools), providing for some 136,000 of the 400,000 or more senior children now in non-provided schools. Of these proposals only 37 have materialised and the remainder cannot now be proceeded with without further legislation.

127. It will be evident from what has been said that, under the existing law, non-provided schools will be required, if they are to continue, to shoulder a financial burden far in excess of their capacity. In the first place, Senior Schools will be unable to conform to the suggested policy of equal standards in all forms of secondary education. Secondly, the need for modernisation or replacement of much of the non-provided school accommodation for junior and infant children, a larger number of whom are housed in conditions little short of scandalous, faces the Churches with a

financial problem greater in extent and no less urgent than that in respect of senior children, a problem which they have shown themselves quite unable to meet in recent years and which they are less than ever likely to be able to meet after the war.

128. If large numbers of children are not to be deprived of healthy and decent school conditions—to say nothing of equal educational opportunities—there is no disguising the fact that, unless a considerable number of voluntary schools are to be brought to an end and replaced by new provided schools, some further assistance from public funds must be found towards the maintenance and improvement of the premises, where such improvement is possible. It is believed that, generally, public opinion would not tolerate what might mean the large-scale abolition of non-provided schools, but would look rather for some measure of extended financial assistance, accompanied, as it must be, by such extended public control as is necessary, not simply to secure a *quid pro quo*, but to ensure the effective and economical organisation and development of both primary and secondary education. Further, it is believed that public opinion will take the view that in framing proposals for such control the services of the churches to the community as pioneers in public education, as the protagonists of Christian teaching in schools and as having for many generations voluntarily spent large sums on the provision and upkeep of premises for this purpose, cannot justly be disregarded.

129. There are, too, indications that the sectarian and political interests which have obstructed the many attempts which have been made for more than 30 years to solve the problem are now less intransigent, and with the passage of time there is a wider recognition of the educational and social importance of changing the present system. Proposals for a solution may now, therefore, be advanced with more hope of success. A basic element in all proposals for extended financial assistance and extended public control for non-provided schools has been, and must continue to be, the transfer of the power to appoint and dismiss teachers from the Managers to the Local Education Authority, combined with measures for continuing denominational religious instruction. If denominational religious instruction is to continue to be given by teachers, the important issue is raised that in the new circumstances this would involve "religious tests" for teachers appointed by Local Education Authorities to schools wholly maintained from public funds. If, however, denominational instruction is to be given adequately, or even at all, in many schools, it is inevitable

that it should be given by teachers, among whom are to be found many men and women keenly interested in the work whose debarring from it would be felt as a real loss by themselves and to the schools.

130. A method of meeting this difficulty may be found in the provisions of the Education Act, 1936, for the reservation of teachers. Under Section 9 and 10 or the Act the appointment of all teachers in non-provided senior schools to which the Local Education Authority made a building grant was placed in the hands of the Authority, who, however, had to consult the Managers before appointing certain of the teachers (named "reserved" teachers) the number of whom was specified in the building grant agreement and of whose fitness and competence to give the appropriate denominational religious instruction the Managers had the right to be satisfied. The application of these principles to existing non-provided schools would call for some procedure, in substitution for the procedure through the negotiation of a building grant agreement, for determining the number of teachers to be reserved. It is to be hoped that this question would generally be settled by agreement, but in the event of dispute ascertainment of the wishes of parents as to the religious education of their children would appear to be necessary and could be carried out by means of an approved form of inquiry circulated by the Authority to all parents concerned.

131. A new factor to which reference has been made and which is of great importance in considering possible solutions of the denominational problem, is the policy of equality of status for all education of children over 11 years of age. It follows from the principles laid down in Chapter 1 that all schools for pupils over 11 should be equally classed as secondary, and in consequence that Modern Schools hitherto administered as Senior Elementary Schools under Part III of the Education Act, 1921, should in future fall within the scope of higher education. Generally speaking, there need be no great difficulty in bringing them within the framework of the law applicable to higher education. The Local Education Authority which, under the proposal contained in Chapter 8, will be the Authority for all types of education, will, as indicated in paragraph 6, have a general duty to provide for the secondary education of children for whom sufficient and suitable provision is not otherwise made. Provided Modern Schools will take their place in this system of secondary education side by side with Grammar and Technical Schools, and will be subject to similar

conditions with them as regards provision, control and maintenance.

132. But certain problems do arise from the transfer of non-provided Modern Schools into the field of higher education. Higher education is mercifully free from the problems and embarrassments of dual control. In non-provided schools of higher education, management and control are vested in the Governing Body, on which the Local Education Authority are represented but without a majority. The Local Education Authority have the power, but are under no duty, to aid the schools in respect of repair, enlargements, etc., of their premises and their maintenance costs, without any corresponding restriction on the Governors in respect of the appointment of teachers and control of education. It would clearly be most undesirable to import into the field of higher education any of the restrictions and limitations which are so fruitful a source of trouble and difficulty in the elementary sphere. The question is whether non-provided Modern Schools can be left to the operation of the law relating to higher education or whether special provisions applicable to them will be required.

133. The width of the gulf which would need bridging if precise equality of treatment were to be enjoyed by non-provided Modern Schools on the one hand and non-provided Grammar Schools on the other is shown in the following comparisons :—

Non-provided Modern Schools	*Non-provided Grammar Schools receiving their grant from the Local Education Authority.*
1. The Local Education Authority is under a statutory obligation to maintain the school and keep it efficient.	1. The Local Education Authority's aid, usually given on a deficiency basis, is discretionary and can be withdrawn if the Local Education Authority so desire.
2. The Managers are required to carry out the directions of the Local Education Authority as to the secular instruction.	2. The secular instruction is in the hands of the Governors.
3. The power vested in the Managers to appoint and dismiss teachers is limited by the requirement that the consent of the Local Education Authority to their appointment and dismissal must be obtained.	3. The appointment and dismissal of teachers rests with the Governors.

4. The Local Education Authority are precluded by statute from paying for or contributing to the cost of repairs (other than fair wear and tear), alterations, and improvements of the buildings. (The Act of 1936 furnishes an exception to this general rule.)

4. The Local Education Authority have a free hand to meet the whole or part of the cost, if they so desire.

134. The new obligation on Local Education Authorities in regard to the provision of secondary education referred to in paragraph 131 will clearly have to include an obligation to maintain existing non-provided Modern Schools. But this obligation would need to be accompanied by a power vested in the Local Education Authority to cease to maintain unnecessary schools, subject to the consent of the Board in case of dispute. As regards new schools, promoters will in general find it difficult to raise the money needed to build a new Modern School, the provision of which, in accordance with the principles of equality of standards for all Secondary Schools, will be no less costly than a Grammar School of the same size. None the less, it would be a manifest injustice if the fact that Senior Schools are to be renamed Modern Schools and lifted from the field of elementary to that of higher education, and that the standard of accommodation and amenities for such schools is to be materially improved, were to deprive denominations of their existing right, subject to certain safeguards, to provide denominational schools for children between 11 and the statutory leaving age and to look to the Local Education Authority for their maintenance. For these reasons, it is essential that Local Education Authorities should be under an obligation to maintain not only existing but such new non-provided Modern Schools as may be determined by the Board to be necessary.

It is not necessary to place on Local Education Authorities an obligation to maintain existing aided Grammar Schools since part of the cost of the maintenance of such schools is found by the Governors. It is true that this part will be substantially reduced by the abolition of fees in aided Grammar schools, proposed in paragraph 6, but it can be left to Authorities to decide whether in these altered circumstances they will continue to aid the school on the present basis or will demand, as a condition of continued aid, a greater measure of control in the governance of the school.

135. It is unlikely that public opinion would tolerate, and

educational considerations would not support, the suggestion that, on the transfer of non-provided Modern Schools to the field of secondary education, the Managers should enjoy unrestricted powers in respect of the appointment of teachers and the control of secular instruction, while the Local Education Authority are called upon to bear the whole cost of maintenance. At the same time it would be inappropriate that the powers and responsibilities of the Managers should be in any way diminished when the status of their schools is changed.

136. It is a natural corollary of the assimilation of Modern Schools with Grammar and other schools of higher education that the provisions in regard to religious instruction should not differ in the different types of secondary education. At preset, denominational religious instruction is prohibited in provided Elementary Schools by the Cowper-Temple Clause (Section 28 of the Education Act, 1921), but is allowed in all schools of higher education (Section 72). Uniform conditions for all Secondary Schools will demand not that the restriction now in force in Modern Schools should be imposed on Grammar and Technical Schools but that the arrangement whereby denominational teaching may be provided in schools of the latter type should be extended to Modern Schools.

137. Abrogation of the Cowper-Temple clause in provided Modern Schools and the continued power of the Governors of non-provided Modern Schools to appoint their own teachers should go a long way to compensate the Churches for the increased measure of public control over non-provided Primary Schools, the necessity of which has been indicated. With these provisions the Churches would have fuller opportunities than they have now of presenting their distinctive doctrines to children at an age when they are most likely to be able to apprehend them. The reasons for assimilating the conditions of religious instruction in Modern Schools to those now obtaining in Grammar Schools do not apply to Primary Schools. In this connection, it has to be remembered that there are many—and among them staunch Churchmen—who hold that children of Primary School age are not ready to receive denominational formularies. Their case can best be met by the teaching of the Bible story and of the common principles of the Christian faith which the agreed syllabuses aim at providing. Such teaching will serve as a foundation for instruction at a later age in the tenets of particular denominations.

138. At the present time in provided schools, while it is the almost universal practice to have undenominational religious

observance and instruction, such instruction is required neither by statute nor by regulation. There is a growing volume of opinion that the time has come when the place of religion as an essential element in education should be specifically recognised. It is accordingly suggested that there should be religious observance and instruction enjoined by statute in all provided Primary and Secondary Schools.

139. To give effect to the suggestions outlined in the preceding paragraphs, legislation might be shaped on the following lines :—

(i) General Provisions applicable to Primary and Secondary
Schools

(a) Religious observance and instruction in accordance with an agreed syllabus to be given in provided schools in school hours by teachers suitable and willing to give it, subject to a conscience clause and provision for the withdrawal of pupils for religious observance or instruction elsewhere.

(b) Agreed syllabus instruction to be given in non-provided schools on the school premises and during school hours to children whose parents desire them to receive it.

(c) No teacher, other than a reserved teacher, to be required to give religious instruction or to be in a better or worse position by reason of giving or not giving it.

(ii) Special Provisions applicable to Non-Provided Primary
Schools

(a) The Local Education Authority to have power to appoint and dismiss all teachers, subject to (d) below.

(b) The Local Education Authority to have the duty to keep the premises (existing and future) in repair and the duty to make necessary alterations and improvements.

(c) The Local Education Authority to have the power, with the consent of the Board of Education—

(i) to cease to maintain an unnecessary school;
(ii) to alter the organisation or age range.

(d) Denominational religious observance and instruction to be under the control of the Managers and, in so far as it is given by teachers, to be given only by teachers fit and competent to give it and appointed after consultation with the Managers. The procedure for the appointment of such teachers and for determining disputes with respect to their appointment or dismissal to be on the lines of the provisions of the Education Act, 1936, relating to reserved teachers.

(iii) Special Provisions applicable to Non-Provided Modern Schools

(a) The management of the school to be in the hands of a Governing Body constituted in accordance with the Regulations applicable to Secondary Schools generally.

(b) The appointment and dismissal of teachers to rest with the Governors, subject to the consent of the Local Education Authority, which consent shall not be withheld except on educational grounds.

(c) The Local Education Authority to be responsible for and have the control of secular instruction.

(d) The Local Education Authority to have the duty to maintain and keep the school efficient.

(e) The Governors to be under an obligation to provide the school house, keep it in good repair, and make necessary alterations and improvements. Should the Governors, however, at any time be unable or unwilling to fulfil their obligations in regard to repairs, alterations or improvements, the Local Education Authority to be under a duty to fulfil those obligations, and the power of appointing and dismissing teachers to pass from the Governors to the Local Education Authority, with provision for the appointment of reserved teachers.

(f) The Local Education Authority to have the power, with the consent of the Board of Education, to cease to maintain an unnecessary school.

140. The provisions suggested above for religious observance and instruction largely meet the views announced on February 12th, 1941, by the Archbishops of Canterbury, York and Wales in consultation with Free Church leaders; their two minor recommendations—i.e., the abrogation (a) of the provisions of Section 27 (1) (b) of the Education Act, 1921, that religious observance and instruction should be confined to the beginning or end or to the beginning and end of the school meeting (a provision designed to facilitate the withdrawal of children) and (b) of the provision of Section 27(1)(c), that it shall be no part of the duties of His Majesty's Inspector to inspect religious instruction, would be met so far as Modern Schools are concerned by the assimilation suggested above of the conditions for religious instruction in Modern Schools to those now obtaining in schools of higher education, where these restrictions do not apply. If this were acceptable, the abolition of the restrictions in the Primary Schools also would naturally fall for consideration.

141. It would be idle to expect that these, or indeed any other suggestions for the reform of the Dual System, will escape criticism. But that reform there must be, if the policy of equality of educa-

tional opportunity for all is not to be an empty slogan, cannot be questioned. It is in the belief that all interests will be ready to make sacrifices to secure the fulfilment of this policy, and that there is a unity of the Christian faith which transcends denominational divisions, that these suggestions are put forward.

CHAPTER 10.—SALARIES OF TEACHERS

142. Under Section 148(1) of the Education Act, 1921, "a local education authority may appoint necessary officers, including teachers, to hold office during the pleasure of the authority, and may assign to them such salaries or remuneration (if any) as they think fit."

143. While, under this Section, the salaries of teachers may be determined by each Authority at will, in practice the salaries of teachers in schools provided or maintained by Local Education Authorities have for over twenty years been governed by agreements reached between representatives of teachers and of Local Education Authorities sitting together on the Burnham Committees, which were set up in 1919 to bring some national order out of a variety of conflicting and competing scales of pay.

144. The salary scales so agreed (and approved by the Board for grant purposes) cannot be enforced by the Board in terms and directly, but they are supported by the Board's Grant Regulations, which provide that, if the scales of pay are less than the recognised scales, and if in the Board's opinion educational efficiency in the area is thereby endangered, the Board may make such deductions from the grant as will, in their opinion, secure that the expenditure by the Authority falling to be met from the rates shall not be less than such expenditure would have been if the scales of salary in question had been in accordance with the recognised scales.

145. The scales now in force are based on three separate Reports, for teachers in Public Elementary Schools, teachers in Secondary Schools and teachers in Technical and Art Schools respectively, though the basic scales for Secondary and Technical Schools are the same. The scales are thus related to the type of school in which a teacher is serving and tend to emphasise the division between different types of school, or at least the division between Elementary and Secondary or other schools in the sphere of higher education. It is clear that, if a policy is to be adopted to secure a greater unification of the educational system and to break down the old distinctions too often redolent of social prejudice, it will be desirable to unify, so far as may be, the teaching profession and to find some

alternative to a series of differentiated scales which are based on distinctions which it is desired to remove.

146. It is, of course, true that, in so far as the spheres of primary and post-primary education may be re-defined, and Elementary Senior Schools transferred to the province of higher education, teachers in Senior Schools would find their position automatically assimilated under the present system to that of Secondary School teachers. There would, however, still be anomalies which call for consideration.

147. In the case of elementary teachers, the existing scales are three in number :—II, III and IV. (Scale I (the lowest), which at one time existed, was abandoned in 1936.) Scale IV is the scale in force in the London area which, in addition to the London County Council area, includes the whole of the County of Middlesex and with one exception the boroughs and urban districts of the metropolitan parts of Essex, Kent and Surrey. Scale III is the predominant scale covering the county boroughs and boroughs, Scale II operating mainly in rural areas. The differentiation was due to the fact that the scales, when framed, were in some measure related to the differing rates of pay current at the time in different types of area, which no doubt reflected a presumed difference in local costs of living. On the other hand, the scales for teachers in Secondary and Technical Schools provide only two scales—a London scale for the London County Council, Middlesex, East and West Ham and Croydon, and a provincial scale for the rest of the country. The questions how far there are good grounds for greater refinement in the case of elementary teachers may call for examination.

148. Some of what may be termed the "personal" anomalies to which the present scales give rise can best be illustrated by two or three sample cases showing the application of the scales to teachers possessing the same paper qualifications but serving in different types of school under the same Authority. In the examples which follow the salary figure selected for illustration is the minimum of the scale in the London area.

149. A trained graduate man teacher who has completed a four-year course—three years for his degree and one year professional training—on entering an Elementary School receives a starting pay of £216. A teacher with the same qualifications entering a Secondary School would receive £291. In practice the teacher in the Elementary School, if in a Senior School, might be teaching boys who were older than those in the junior form being taught by his colleagues in the Secondary School.

150. The ordinary two-year trained certificated man teacher in the elementary School starts at £192 per annum. In a Secondary or Junior Technical School he would rank as a non-graduate assistant and would receive £204. On the other hand, a non-trained graduate who would start in a Secondary School with £276 per annum would, in an Elementary School, rank only as an uncertificated teacher with a starting pay of £117.

There is something artificial in the differentiations thus made which reflect something artificial in the gradings of our educational system.

151. The remuneration of teachers is not simply a matter of clear-cut scales. Round the scales has grown up a large accretion of "case law" : there are special arrangements for the payment of head teachers, allowances for posts of special responsibility, etc. It would be impossible, therefore, in this note to review the working of the scales in detail, nor, indeed would such a review serve any immediate purpose. The recasting of teachers' salaries to fit any new educational layout is not a matter primarily for the Board of Education. It is a matter which, in the first instance, must be dealt with through the machinery of the Burnham Committees.

152. There are, however, one or two principles which, while not necessarily the only ones the application of which might rationalise the remuneration of teachers, may nevertheless at least point the way towards the greater unification of the teaching profession that appears desirable. In the first place, it is suggested that one general principle to be adopted should be to relate basic salary to qualifications, irrespective of the type of school in which a teacher may be serving—thus a graduate teacher would be paid graduate scale, whether serving in a primary or in a post-primary school. In the second place, there must be some recognition of posts (specialists, heads of departments, and headships) carrying special responsibility or normally filled by teachers with special qualifications. In some measure, therefore, pay must be related to the job and not solely to qualifications. This principle is already recognised in the case of both Elementary Schools and institutions for higher education in the special scales payable to principals, heads of departments and head teachers and in the allowances over and above scale salaries for teachers whose service is of exceptional value or who are discharging special responsibility or possess special academic attainments.

153. How these two principles can best be developed and adjusted is not a matter to pursue here. It is, however, believed that along

some such lines as those indicated a way may be found to create a greater professional unity and with it, a greater unity in the educational system.

CHAPTER II—THE FINANCE OF EDUCATION

Part I—Grants to Local Education Authorities

154. The present grant system provides for payment of grants to Local Education Authorities under the following heads :—

(a) Elementary Education

The grant formula for elementary education up to the outbreak of the present war was derived from that recommended by the Kempe Committee before the last war, as modified by Mr. Fisher after the passing of his Education Act. It was extremely elaborate, containing a number of different percentages of grant in respect of different types of expenditure and two other factors not related to expenditure. The first of these latter factors was a capitation grant of 36s. per child in average attendance, which was added to the amounts of grant determined as percentages of expenditure. From the total grant thus ascertained was deducted the second factor, which was the product of a 7d. rate in the area.

In September, 1938, however, at the time of the Munich crisis, provisional agreement was reached between the Board and the Treasury on a simpler formula to be applied in the event of war. The simplification took the form of assessing the grant for elementary education to Local Education Authorities at the same proportion in each case of the net recognisable expenditure as the grant for the year 1937–38 bore to the net recognisable expenditure of that year. This revised formula was put into operation, after the outbreak of war, for the year beginning April 1st, 1939, with the result that Local Education Authorities now receive a grant from the Board varying from 6 to 72 per cent. of the net recognised expenditure. The advantage of this simpler formula was that it greatly reduced the amount of clerical and administrative work, both locally and centrally, and that Authorities knew where they were financially. It resulted in a substantial addition, considerably over £500,000, to the total Exchequer Grant to Local Education Authorities. It may be taken for granted that the experience of this simpler formula has rendered a return to the original complicated formula at once undesirable and impracticable.

Unfortunately, from the point of view of simplicity, the desire of the Government that Local Education Authorities should carry out urgently certain special types of work has resulted in the modification and complication of the new formula in the following respects :—

(i) As from April 1st, 1939, any expenditure upon air-raid precautions attracted a grant of 50 per cent. if the standard rate was less than that figure.

(ii) As from October 19, 1940, any expenditure for this purpose attracted grant at the rate of 100 per cent. where the Board were satisfied that the shelter provided would be available to the public at all times when it would not be required for school purposes.

(iii) As from July 1st, 1940, in respect of expenditure on the provisions of meals under Sections 82 to 84 of the Education Act, 1921, a minimum grant of 50 per cent was substituted for the standard percentage and in cases where the standard percentage was not less than 30 per cent., 20 per cent. was added to it.

It should be noted that the all-over result of this simpler formula (without taking account of the modifictions mentioned above) has been to meet by grant 50 per cent. of the total net recognised expenditure of Local Education Authorities, although, as indicated above, the actual percentage in the case of any given Authority may and does vary from this mean.

(b) Higher Education

Grant in respect of higher education is based upon the net recognised expenditure of Local Education Authorities and is assessed at 50 per cent. The only exception to this general rule is that as from October 19th, 1940, expenditure upon air-raid shelters attracted grant at the rate of 100 per cent. under the same conditions as those applicable to elementary education (see (a) (ii) above). There is a trifling additional grant of £70,000 payable to certain Authorities who maintain Training Colleges. As, however, deductions of the same total amount are made from the grants to those other Authorities who do not maintain Training Colleges, other than those for Domestic Science, this element may be ignored.

A Revised Grant System

155. Any revision of the grant system must be largely conditioned by the nature and number of the Authorities who administer the public system of education and receive grants, a subject which is more fully dealt with in Chapter 8. It is there suggested that a

reduction in the number of Local Education Authorities is inevitable and that the reduced number must be Authorities for all types of education—Part II Authorities. There are at present 146 such Authorities, composed of the administrative County Councils and the County Borough Councils. On financial grounds alone it may be doubted whether some of the smaller Counties and County Boroughs are well suited to discharge even the present functions of Local Education Authorities for higher as well as elementary education and their fusion in some larger area would undoubtedly be beneficial, but in practice the retention of the existing Part II Authorities must probably be accepted. It has, however, been agreed by the Committees which have considered this problem, that it would be advisable to add to their number a few of the larger existing Authorities for elementary education only (Part III Authorities), whose promotion would on all grounds be highly desirable. It would be necessary to scrutinise closely all proposals for such promotion from the financial as well as the administrative point of view. Any new Part II Authority would have to be of sufficient financial capacity and stability to undertake the provision and supervision of higher education, and at the same time its area would need to be very carefully defined in order not to cripple the County in which it is situated by the withdrawal from the latter of too large a part of its present rateable value.

Assuming that the total number of Part II Authorities were thus to reach some such figure as 180, the administrative task of providing for the various types of education would be greatly simplified and it should be possible at the same time to secure a corresponding simplification in the finance of education. If each of the new Local Education Authorities is to be charged with the provision and supervision of all types of education and if elementary education is to be confined to the education of children up to the age of 11 instead of, as at present, to the statutory leaving age, the need for two separate education accounts and two separate grant formulae seems also to disappear. A single unified grant system would mark a financial advance equivalent to and consequent upon the administrative advance marked by the institution of single Authorities for all types of education. Such a system would need to take account of and provide for all branches of the Authority's educational work and should therefore, it is submitted, properly take the form of a block grant.

156. The proposal that the present grant system should be superseded by a block grant needs some definition. It is suggested that a proper system of Exchequer grants should

(a) recognise that a fair contribution should be made from the Exchequer to the cost of local services :

(b) ensure that Local Authorities have complete financial interest in their administration :

(c) be adapted in its working to the needs of the areas :

(d) permit the greatest freedom of local administration and initiative : and

(e) provide for sufficient general control and advice from the Central Department to ensure a reasonable standard of performance.

The experience of the general block grant for local government services administered by the Ministry of Health shows that such a system has, on the whole, met the five cardinal requirements in a satisfactory way. The introduction of this block grant was held to be justified by the effect of derating on the financial position of Local Authorities generally. The suggested reduction in the number of Local Education Authorities and the extension to each of them of the supervision of all types of State-aided education within its area offers the opportunity for a similar financial reform.

For this purpose a block grant may be taken to be a grant of which the total amount is determinable by the Government for a period of years, there being a statutory regulation of the amount of the grant. This total amount is then distributed among Authorities upon a basis designed to take account both of the amount of the work to be done in each area and of the capacity of each area to pay for it. The basis of the distribution would aim at securing *ultimate* distribution solely by reference to the relative needs of the various areas and their ability to meet those needs out of the rates. In order to avoid violent fluctuations of rates at the inception of the scheme, provision would need to be made for the new basis of distribution to be brought gradually into effect over a substantial period of years and some new Exchequer money would be necessary to facilitate the process of transition from the old system to the new.

As regards the basis of distribution, there is no reason to suppose that the fundamental factors used in the computation of the Ministry of Health block grant would be unsuitable to a block grant for education, although it would probably be necessary to adapt the weighting additions to meet the special needs of that service. It will probably be conceded that unemployment, sparsity and the rateable value per head of population are all elements which will be properly taken into account in fixing an education grant. When it comes, however, to the weighting to be derived from the proportion of children in the population of the area, it will probably be necessary to adopt as the weighting factor the proportion to the total population of children under the new minimum school leaving age of 15; it might even be desirable to extend this to the age of 18, so as to take into account the full range of the new Authorities' responsibilities.

It will be borne in mind that the suggested scheme would be brought in at a period of expansion. Account will have to be taken of this in considering the amount of any new Exchequer money brought in in order to launch the scheme. It is understood, however, that there has been no suggestion that the periodical revision of the Ministry of Health block grant brings the grant too slowly to the aid of developing services. Indeed, the problem of providing for periods of subsequent expansion seems to be satisfactorily met by the provision in the Local Government Act, 1929, that the *minimum* amount of the general Exchequer contribution for each period shall be determined by reference to a prescribed percentage of the rate- and grant-borne expenditure in the penultimate year of the preceding fixed-grant period. It must also be borne in mind that *new* services put into operation during a fixed-grant period would be directly grant-aided at their inception, the grant being absorbed in the revision for the next fixed-grant period.

Part II—Grants to Bodies other than Local Education Authorities

(a) *Technical Education*

157. Seventeen Technical Colleges and five Art Schools are recognised for direct grant under the Board's Regulations for Further Education. The grant in each case is determined by the Board after consideration of the character, efficiency, volume and cost of the work of the school; in other words, it is assessed *ad hoc*. These grants, however, are only of the order of £40,000 a year, and the institutions in question are likely, with the passage of time, to become absorbed into the public system of education as aided by Local Education Authorities. It is therefore suggested that no change need be made in the present system so far as they are concerned.

(b) *Schools of Nautical Training*

There are seven Schools of Nautical Training which receive grants under the Board's Regulations for Further Education. This grant is assessed in the same way as for the institutions mentioned in (a) above. The annual grant to these institutions amounts to some £13,000 a year. As their name indicates, they are non-local in character and it would be unreasonable to expect any Local Education Authority to adopt them as part of its general system owing to the accident of locality. It is therefore suggested that here again no change need be made in the present system.

(c) Special Schools and Schools for Blind and otherwise defective children

Grant is paid upon a capitation basis to Special Schools for defective children and also in respect of the higher education of such children. The total sum involved is of the order of £30,000 a year, and these schools are, generally speaking, non-local in character. It may be that with the extension of the provision for these defective children they will gradually become absorbed by Local Education Authorities, but it is not considered desirable to hasten this process by any change in the present grant system.

(d) Adult Education Classes

University Tutorial Classes and other forms of adult education such as are currently associated with the Workers' Educational Association receive grant at the rate of approximately £100,000 a year. The grant is assessed on a basis related to the fee paid to the tutor of the class subject to certain requirements as regards the regular attendance of the students. The grant system will require adjustment to the changes in local organisation suggested in Chapter 4.

(e) Training of Teachers

There are 73 voluntary Training Institutions, including the University Training Departments, which receive grant, broadly speaking, on a capitation basis for the students in training. The grants to these Institutions are of the order of £700,000 a year. The voluntary Training Colleges are one of the earliest integral parts of the system of public education. They are for the most part denominational in character, and therefore unsuitable for incorporation in the system of the Local Education Authorities, and they may be regarded as fulfilling an essential function. They are also definitely non-local in character and there seems to be no justification for their correlation with any block grant system.

(f) Play Centres and Nursery Schools

Grant is paid to these institutions, which are under the charge of bodies of voluntary Managers, on the basis of 50 per cent. of the recognised net expenditure, amounting in all, at present, to £18,000 odd a year. These institutions are the latest product of the voluntary movement in English education. No change in the arrangements for financial assistance is called for.

(g) Direct Grant Secondary Schools

There are 235 of these schools which receive grant direct from the board of a capitation basis. The grant involved is of the order of £700,000 a year.

These schools may be said to form a more or less irreducible "hard core" of voluntary effort within the Grammar School system, as is shown by the fact that their numbers have for many years remained constant. It is unlikely that they would be willing to accept deficiency aid from local funds, with the local control which such a step would involve, and indeed the variety of tradition which this relative financial autonomy has enabled them to preserve is an element of great and characteristic value in English education.

Assuming, therefore, that their financial status remains unaltered, it remains to consider what allowance, if any, should be made for the provision which they supply in their various areas, when assessing any form of block grant to the respective Local Education Authorities. At first sight it might be urged that the fact that 18 per cent. of the total number of pupils in Grant-aided Secondary Schools are in Direct Grant Schools implies a relief to Local Education Authority expenditure of which account should be taken. It must, however, be borne in mind that over 10 per cent. of those pupils are boarders and do not, therefore, diminish local expenditure, while in urban areas the proportion of extra-district day pupils in such cases as that of Manchester Grammar School is substantial, and any reduction of the block grant to Manchester in such a case would hardly be equitable.

On the whole, therefore, it is suggested that in dealing with these schools their financial autonomy should be respected and that the amount of Exchequer grant thus disbursed would in the case of any one Authority be relatively so small as to be negligible when the block grant for the area is being fixed.

SUMMARY OF MAIN SUGGESTIONS

Foreword

1. Educational machinery must be adjusted to serve educational needs and not vice versa.

Full-time Schooling

2. The school leaving age to be raised to 15 without exemptions (para. 5).

3. The area of elementary education to be redefined. Education will then fall into three stages :—

Primary : covering Nursery Schools and Classes, Infant Schools and Junior Schools ending at the age of 11+.

Secondary : covering Secondary Schools of all types—the Modern School, the Grammar School and the Technical School with leaving ages ranging from 15+ to 18.

Further Education : covering Day Continuation Schools, full-time education in Senior, Technical and Commercial Colleges, part-time technical and commercial education in the day or evening and Adult Education (para. 5).

4. A single type of Local Education Authority to be established for both elementary and higher education (paras. 6 (*b*) and 118).

5. Provision of secondary education to be a duty and not simply a power of Local Education Authorities (para. 6 (*c*)).

6. All schools at the secondary stage to be on an equality and under one Code of Regulations (para. 6 (*d*)).

7. All Secondary Schools, provided, maintained or aided by Local Education Authorities to be free (para. 6 (*e*)).

8. The Special Place Examination at 11 to be abolished. Children to proceed to Secondary Schools of different types on the basis of their record in the Primary School, supplemented by suitable intelligence tests (para. 6 (*f*)).

9. A genuine review, with a re-sorting as may be necessary, to take place at the age of 13. To facilitate this interchange the content of the education for the age group 11–13 to be generally the same in all types of Secondary School (para. 6 (*f*)).

Day Continuation Schools

10. Day Continuation Schools to be established for young persons up to the age of 18 (paras. 13–20).

11. The hours of attendance at Day Continuation Schools to be 280 per year, preferably on two half days of 3½ hours each per week (para. 17 (*c*)).

12. The Appointed Day for the operation of the Act setting up Day Continuation Schools to be the same for all areas constituting single industrial and commercial regions (para. 17 (*d*)).

13. Day Continuation Schools should develop a corporate life related to the social and recreational activities of young persons and to their further leisure-hour educational interests (para. 20).

The Service of Youth

14. The Service of Youth, utilising to the full the assistance of the voluntary organisations, to be developed as supplementary or complementary to the work of the Day Continuation Schools. In

this way a complete system may be built up covering the social, physical and educational welfare of adolescents (paras. 26–29).

The Further Education of the Adolescent and the Adult

15. With the introduction of Day Continuation Schools the character and scope of the work of Evening Classes and Evening Institutes for younger students will require reconsideration (paras. 33–35).

16. There is an urgent need in the interests of industry and commerce to secure an improved system of technical and commercial training; in particular, the training of young workers calls for attention and an ordered scheme (para. 36).

17. Closer relations need to be established between education and industry and commerce. Advisory committees representing industry and commerce should be set up to collaborate with the Board in framing policy (para. 41).

18. No development can be secured without extended and improved accommodation. The building programme planned before the war should be completed (para. 42).

19. Association on a regional basis between Local Education Authorities will be essential to secure that technical education is properly related to industrial needs (paras. 43, 44).

20. Art education to be developed, in particular to assist production on the side of design (para. 45).

21. The provision of adult education needs overhaul; further development should be secured by regional organisation on the lines now in operation for meeting the needs of the Armed Forces (paras. 49, 50).

22. The development of adult education on institutional lines should also be considered (para. 51).

The Avenue to the Universities

23. The system of ear marking grants at the undergraduate stage for intending teachers is extremely undesirable (para. 60 (g)).

24. Existing Local Authority awards and State Scholarships should be merged and administered by the Board, an appropriate charge being levied on all Authorities. This would give some uniformity throughout the country and even up opportunity (para. 62).

25. The scheme of awards should be on a scale sufficient to ensure an intake to the universities adequate to provide, amongst other things, the graduate teachers required for the public system of education; it should include provision whereby specially selected students may proceed to universities in the Dominions and the United States (para. 64).

26. The financial assistance made available to the scholar should be fixed at a figure which has regard to the expenses which a full participation in the corporate life of the university inevitably involves (para. 65).

The Health and Physical Well-being of the Child

27. Local Education Authorities to be required by statute to provide or secure adequate arrangements for the treatment of certain specific defects and illnesses of children in the spheres of elementary and higher education alike (para. 68).

28. The gap between the upper limit of the effective provision by Maternity and Child Welfare Authorities (about one year of age) and the lower limit of provision by Local Education Authorities (five years of age) must be bridged. To secure this the responsibility of Local Education Authorities hitherto confined to children attending school should be extended downwards to include all children, say from the age of two (para. 69).

29. Local Education Authorities to be charged with the duty of making such provision as may be necessary for attending to the physical and mental development of children over two and under five years of age in Nursery Schools or Classes or such other forms of Nursery as may be approved by the Board of Education (para. 71).

30. The provision of schools for handicapped children should be reorganised on a regional basis and the schools transferred from town to country (para. 74).

31. Part V of the Education Act, 1921, should be extended to include maladjusted children. This part of the Act should be revised and brought up to date (para. 76).

32. When the age of compulsory education for normal children is raised to 15 the age of compulsory education for physically and mentally defective children should be lowered from 16 to 15. The upper age for blind and deaf children should remain at 16 (para. 76).

33. It should be made obligatory on Local Education Authorities to make or otherwise secure the provision of meals for all children for whom such provision is necessary in order that they may derive full benefit from their education (para. 80).

Recruitment and Training of Teachers

34. The Two-Year Training College Course to be extended to three years, the second year of which would, at any rate in part, be spent in teaching (para. 100 (*a*), (*b*)).

35. The Four-Year Course as such at University Training Departments to be abolished, no grants being earmarked for intending teachers at the undergraduate stage. A year's professional training course to be made available for graduates with appropriate grants (para. 100 (*d*), (*e*)).

Units of Local Educational Administration
36. A single type of Local Education Authority covering all types of education to be established. The precise method of constituting such Authorities will need to be determined in the light of any general decision that may be taken affecting the reorganisation of local government (paras. 118, 119).

The Dual System
37. The reform of the Dual System is essential if real equality of educational opportunity and sound and economical organisation are to be secured (paras. 121–128). Detailed suggestions for the reform of the system are contained in para. 139.

Salaries of Teachers
38. The remuneration of teachers should be reviewed in order to replace the present differential scales by a more uniform system of pay appropriate to a united profession and a more unified system of education (paras. 152, 153).

The Finance of Education
39. The present elementary grant formula and the percentage grant for higher education to be replaced by a single block grant to be determined for a period of years. The direct grants payable to various bodies other than Local Education Authorities to be continued (paras. 155–157).

REFERENCES

Chapter 1   The Start Of It All

1 Peter Laslett, "New Light on the History of the English Family", *The Listener*, 17 February 1966, p. 223.
2 P. W. Musgrave, "The Relationship Between The Family and Education", *British Journal of Educational Studies,* vol. XIX, 1, February 1971, pp. 17–31.
3 W. Shakespeare, *The Taming of the Shrew*, 1596, Act V scene I.
4 G. Clark, *The Wealth of England*, 1946, p. 192.
5 Fox Bourne, *Life of John Locke*, vol. 11, pp. 383–5, from C. Birchenough, *History of Elementary Education*, 1927, p. 73.
6 B. Mandeville, *The Fable of the Bees*, 1772, vol. I, pp. 214–7.
7 Mrs Trimmer, *Reflections upon the education of children in charity schools*, 1792, pp. 4–31.
8 J. Henry Harris (Ed.), *Robert Raikes: A Man and His Works*, 1899, pp. 40–3 and pp. 303–5.
9 J. J. Finlay, *Arnold of Rugby*, 1898, p. 39.
10 E. J. R. Eaglesham, *The Foundations of 20th-Century Education in England*, 1967, ch. 9.
11 R. V. Jones, "The Advancement of Science" (lecture to the RSA), 1964, p. 4. Lytton Strachey, *Eminent Victorians* (Essay on Dr Arnold), 1918.
12 *The Teaching of English in England*, HMSO, 1921, pp. 13–15.

Chapter II   The Nineteenth Century to 1870

1 Newcastle Commission, 1859, Evidence of Mr Lingen.
2 Report of the Select Committee on Education, 1865.
3 Hansard-Com. Vol. 188/10 July 1867/Cols. 1317, 1346 and 1348.
4 Hansard-Com. Vol. 188/19 July 1867/Cols. 1317–42.
5 Report of the Children's Employment Commission, 1863, para. 338.
6 J. A. Banks, *Prosperity and Parenthood*, 1954, ch. X and p. 374. W. L. Guttsman (Ed.), *The English Ruling Class*, 1969, Section 5—Education.
7 J. S. Mill, *On Liberty*, 1859.
8 Hansard-Com. Vol. 190/2 December 1867/Cols. 478–506.

9 Percy Wilson, *Views and Prospects from Curzon Street*, Blackwell, 1961, p. 7.
10 Schools Inquiry Commission (Taunton Commission), 1868, Vol. 1, pp. 637–42.
11 Hansard-Com. Vol. 190/14 February 1868/Cols. 742–52 and 770–4.
12 Hansard-Com. Vol. 190/17 March 1868/Cols. 1816–26.
13 Hansard-Com. Vol. 190/14 February 1868/Cols. 734–75.
14 Hansard-Com. Vol. 192/24 June 1868/Col. 2006.
15 Hansard-Com. Vol. 188/10 July 1867/Cols. 1317–66 and Vol. 203/4 August 1870/Cols. 1558–60.
16 Hansard-Com. Vol. 202/24 June 1870/Cols. 895–904.
17 Mr W. E. Forster, Vice-President of the Committee for Education introduced the Elementary Education Bill to Parliament on 17 February 1870; it received the Royal Assent on 9 August 1870. See Hansard-Com. Vol. 199/17 February 1870/Col. 438 and Vol. 203/9 August 1870/Col. 1729.
18 John Morley, *The Struggle for National Education*, 1873, p. 103.
19 Hansard-Com. Vol. 199/17 February 1870/Cols. 438–466.
20 Hansard-Com. Vol. 203/19 July 1870/Col. 492.
21 Hansard-Com. Vol. 199/20 June 1870/Cols. 476, 478 and 483–4 and Vol. 202/26 February 1870/Cols. 560–6, 862 and 1156–60.

Chapter III   1870–1902

1 Cecil Woodham-Smith, *The Great Hunger*, 1962.
2 John Prebble, *The Highland Clearances*, 1963.
3 Terry Coleman, *The Railway Navvies*, 1965. Harold Perkin, "The Age of the Railway", 1970.
4 L. Paul, "The Deployment and Payment of the Clergy", Church Information Office, 1964; A. P. M. Coxon, "Patterns of Occupational Recruitment : The Anglican Ministry", *Sociology*, vol. 1/1 January 1967, pp. 73–9.
5 Hansard-Com. Vol. 229/18 May 1876/Cols. 929–65.
6 Hansard-Com. Vol. 229/18 May 1876/Col. 929.
7 Hansard-Com. Vol. 233/5 July 1880/Cols. 1615–21.
8 London School Board v Duggan 1884. A leading case summarized in *B. J. of Edn'l Studies*, vol. 18/No. 2/June 1970/p.175. "The Education Act of 1870 as the start of the modern concept of the child" by Nigel Middleton.
9 Board of Education Report 1900–1. Vol. II. BPP 1901 XIX II p. 359.
10 Stanley Baldwin, "The authentic note of democracy". Speech

delivered 14 July 1930. See collection *This Torch of Freedom*, 1935, p. 47.

11 Adam Smith, *Wealth of Nations*, 1767.

12 R. V. Jones, *The Advancement of Learning*, 1964, p. 4.

13 T. H. Huxley, "A Liberal Education and Where to Find It", in *Science and Education*, 1895, p. 97.

14 Reports of the Education Department, 1878–81.

15 B. Keith-Lucas, *Local English Government Franchise*, ch. IV.

16 Beatrice Webb, *Our Partnership*, Longmans, 1948, p. 77.

17 R. V. Jones, *op. cit.*, p. 16. Bryce Commission Vol. III Q. 2736 (Evidence of Sidney Webb and Dr Garnett); Vol. II, p. 256–7, 29 May 1894 and pp. 276–7, Q. 2737, 29 May 1894.

18 Science and Department Report 1895–6; Board of Education Report 1901–2.

19 Special Report of the Education Department, 1898, vol. II; Board of Education Report 1899–1900, vol. III, p. 173–4.

20 Board of Education Reports 1909–10.

21 Education Department Report 1897–98, p. xvi.

22 Bill 269, 8 April 1892, Part 1 Section 3(e).

23 Report of a Conference on Secondary Education in England, 10 and 11 October 1894, Clarendon Press, 1894.

24 G. A. N. Lowndes, *The Silent Social Revolution*, OUP, 1937, pp. 65–70.

25 Parliamentary Paper, No. 381 of 1898.

26 B. M. Allen—*Sir Robert Morant—A Great Public Servant*, 1934, pp. 123–51.

27 Ministry of Education file, "Advanced Elementary Education", Secretary's Clerks Papers, Minute dated 6 April 1900.

28 G. A. N. Lowndes, *The Silent Social Revolution, op. cit.*, pp. 88–9; "The Education of the Adolescent", Hadow Report, 1926, p. 10; D. Lockwood, *The Blackcoated Worker*, 1958, p. 26.

29 High Court before Mr Justice Wills and Kennedy, 20 December 1900, and Appeal Court, April 1901.

30 Cabinet Memorandum from Lord President of the Council (Duke of Devonshire); Secretary's Clerks' file on Board of Education Act, 1899, Memo dated 26 January 1898.

31 First draft of the Education Bill dated February 1898, with legal opinion given by Sir Courtney Ibbert, the Solicitor General. (Ministry of Education file on 1899 Bill—Secretary's Clerks' papers.)

32 Letter from "Unionist" to *The Times*, February 1898. Reproduced in a précis of opinions on the Board of Education Bill by Morant, Ministry of Education file—Secretary's Clerks' papers.

33 Hansard-Com. Vol. 84/26 June 1900/Col. 1031–44.
34 Fabian Society, *Essays In Socialism*, 1889; S. Webb, "Historic Perspective", p. 55.
35 Fabian Tract No. 106 of January 1901; S. Webb, *The Educational Muddle and the Way Out.*
36 C. Silvester Horne, "A Popular History of the Free Churches", 1903, pp. 393–410.
37 *Ibid*, p. 412.
38 Brian Gardiner, *Mafeking—A Victorian Legend*, Cassell, 1966.
39 Beatrice Webb, *op. cit.*, p. 240.
40 Ministry of Education notes dated 17 December 1900 and 21 March 1902.
41 Letter Bishop of Rochester to Lord Salisbury dated 4 December 1901 (Ministry of Education file).
42 Rev. E. C. S. Gibson, Vicar of Leeds, to R. Morant in letter dated 4 November 1901 (Ministry of Education file).
43 The Percentage of people living in poverty :
    C. Booth, *Life and Labour of the People in London,* 1889–1902;
    B. S. Rowntree, *Poverty—A study of life in York,* 1901;
    D. H. Macgregor, "Poverty Figures", *Economic Journal,* 20 December 1910, pp. 569–72;
    W. H. Beveridge, *Full Employment in a free society,* 1944, pp. 40–6.

Chapter IV 1902–1918

1 Minutes of the Anson Bye-Law dated April 1903 in Education Bill 1913, file Memo. No. 12;
  Board of Education Circular No. 512 of 1904;
  A 1908 Court decision, Blencome *v* Northants CC, 1907 (1 Chancery, 504);
  Anson Bye Law adopted in 38 out of 63 counties, 11 out of 75 county boroughs, 39 out of 134 boroughs and 14 out of 50 urban districts.
  Evidence in 1913 suggested very few withdrawals, mostly RCs in non-Catholic schools. (Education Bill 1913 Memo. No. 12 dated March 1931.)
2 Augustine Birrell speech of 13 November 1906 (Published as a Liberal Party Publication).
3 George Dangerfield, *The Strange Death of Liberal England,* 1935, paperback, p. 27; J. A. Spender, *Life of Campbell Bannerman,* 1926, pp. 302–4; G. K. A. Bell, *Randall of Durhams,* 1938, pp. 526–7.

4 Education Bill of 9 April 1906;
The McKenna Bill of February 1908 and Runciman's Bill November 1908;
Education (Local Authorities) Bill of 3 February 1908.

5 Bentley B. Gilbert, *Evolution of National Insurance in Great Britain*, 1966, pp. 102–17;
F. Le Gros Clark, *The Social History of the School Meals Service*, 1948, p. 4;
M. E. Bulkley, *The Feeding of School Children*, 1914, pp. 15–20;
Nigel Middleton, *When Family Failed*, 1971, pp. 43–74.

6 Royal Commission on the Poor Laws (BPP 1909/39/Q.246–54).
Mr Adrian QC, Legal Adviser to the Local Government Board.

7 Bentley B. Gilbert, *op. cit.*, pp. 131–58.

8 Royal Commission on the Poor Laws, 1909;
Consultative Committee on Attendance, 1907–9;
Interdepartmental Committee on Partial Exemption from School Attendance, 1909.

9 E. J. R. Eaglesham, *The Foundations of 20th-Century Education in England*, Routledge, 1967, p. 91.

10 Beatrice Webb, *op. cit.*
This is a recurrent theme; see pages 157–9, 160–2, 167 and 337.

11 Special Reports on Educational Subjects, vol. III, 1898, p. 47.

12 Secondary Education, Spens Report, 1938, pp. 70–71.

13 *Ibid.* p. 67.

14 Code for Elementary Schools for 1904 and 1905;
A. M. Kazamias, *Politics, society and secondary education in England*, 1966. Statistics p. 152 compiled from annual reports.

15 Conversation with Mr T. O. Wilson CBE, formerly Director of Education for Oxfordshire, 1920–45, who was an education officer in Berkshire, 1904–20.

16 G. A. N. Lowndes, *op. cit.*, p. 100.

17 E. J. R. Eaglesham, *op. cit.*, p. 59.

18 Conversation with Mr T. O. Wilson, CBE.

19 Report of the Ministry of Education, "Education 1900–1950", 1951, p. 250.

20 Secondary School Regulations for 1904 (Preparatory Memo. p. 8 para. V c).

21 Olive Banks, *Parity and Prestige in English Secondary Education*, 1955.

22 Education (England and Wales) Bill 1911.

23 R. B. Haldane addressing : The Manchester Reform Club, 10 January 1913; *Manchester Guardian*, 11 January 1931; The

National Union of Teachers March 1913; Education Estimates Debates, Hansard-Com. Vol. 51/10 April 1913/Cols. 1458–1508.

24 Rt Hon. J. A. Pease, President of the Board of Education, Commons speech of 22 July 1913 published as a Liberal Party Pamphlet, 1913.

25 Elementary Code 1904, Ch. 1, para. 3.

26 Draft of a Bill to make further provision with respect to Education in England and Wales, XX(7), dated 2 May 1914. Discussions started in Cabinet Committee 1 December 1912 among members Lord Crewe, Lloyd George, Runciman and Acland.

27 Education Draft Bill 1914 (Sections 18, 19 and 20).

28 A. M. Kazamias, *op. cit.*, p. 210 date from Board's statistics.

29 The Consultative Committee on Scholarships for Higher Education, Chairman, Mr Dyke Acland; Set up in March 1913, Interim Report June 1916.

30 Report of Departmental Committee on Juvenile Education in Relation to Employment after the War, Lewis Committee, 1917, pp. 3 and 9. BPP 1917–18/XI.

31 Lewis Committee, *op cit.*, p. 13 (Para. 22).

32 Opposition was mainly from the cotton and wool areas of the north, *Yorkshire Post*, 9 and 10 October 1917. (Based on memo. by Spurley Hey for Manchester Education Com.); *Manchester Guardian*, 19 September 1917 (Dr M. E. Sadler on Provincial Associations).

33 *The Tablet*, August 1917.

34 Address by Archbishop Whiteside to the Catholic Young Men's Society at Liverpool on 30 September and 29 October 1917.

35 Results communicated to the President of Board at a conference of textile employers and workers, with Lancashire MPs present. (Ministry of Education file, 2F–16.)

36 Memorandum by the Education Committee of the Federation of Industries based on a questionnaire circulated to members on their views of the proposed education reforms. A copy was sent to Fisher on 30 August 1917 (Ministry of Education file, 9c(1)–(10).);
Address given by Sir Henry Hibbert on 10 November 1917. There was support for a local option to adopt the alternative scheme in *The Times Educational Supplement*, 17 May 1918 (Ministry of Education file 28 (1)–120); Tootal Broadhurst, Lee and Co. in March 1918 (Ministry of Education file 30 (iii) b).

37 H. A. L. Fisher in a letter to *The Times*, 17 December 1917, explained the Bill was not dead but had been withdrawn to save Parliamentary time while certain amendments were made;

Evidence of protest in Ministry of Education files, 2F(10) A, E. H, B. 2F(8) and 2F(5).

38 The debate on the Second Reading of the Bill deals with these issues. See Hansard-Com Vols 104–108/May–July 1918. NB Vol 104/13 & 18 March 1918/335–447 & 674–779. Vol 105/ 7 May 1918/1989–2120.

39 House of Lords Debates, 23 July 1918/Cols. 1007–14.

40 Hansard-Com. Vol. 120/5 June 1918/Cols. 1105–11.

41 Catholic opposition Ministry of Education files 2e (ii) 17; Hansard-Com. Vol. 121/2 July 1918/Cols. 1567–8 (HAL Fisher); *The Tablet*, 27 July 1918.

42 The Education Act 1918 (Section 4 (4)).

43 The National Society commentary on "The Education Act", 1918, p. 17, by Sir Montague Barlow and Richard Holland.

44 Richard Burdon Haldane, *An Autobiography*, 1929, pp. 218–9. Lord Crewe mentioned was another Liberal leader.

Chapter V *1918–1936*

1 Electoral facts from D. Butler and J. Freeman, *British Political Facts* 1900–67, 1968; 1910 electorate 7.7 million. 1918 electorate 21.4 million.

2 Report of Departmental Committee "The teaching of English in England", 1921, p. 17.

3 A. Piepe *et al.*—"The Location of the Proletarian and Deferential Worker", *Sociology*, vol. 3/2 May 1969, pp. 239–44.

4 W. H. Beveridge, *Full Employment in a Free Society*, 1944, p. 47.

5 M. Branson and M. Heinemann, *Britain in the Nineteenth Thirties*, 1971, p. 148.

6 T. Wilson, "The British Election of 1918", *J. of Modern History*, vol. 36/i/March 64, pp. 28–42.

7 H. A. L. Fisher, Diary Entry for 3 December 1918; C. Petrie, *The Chamberlain Tradition*, 1938, p. 227 (Ll. George/Austen Chamberlain conversation).

8 *The Times* dated 18 November 1965. Letter from Prof. J. Dover Wilson.

9 R. H. Tawney, *Secondary Education for All*, Allen and Unwin, 1924.

10 The Committee on National Expenditure, BPP 1921/Cd. 1190, The Geddes Report.

11 The Departmental Committee on the Free Place and Scholarship System, 1920, 11,000 excluded because they failed to win a free place; many who did win places forced by family circum-

stances to leave before the end of the course because parental circumstances could not afford to let them stay on; a further 10,000 excluded because there was no room for them.

12 Secretary's clerks' papers. File, Reconstruction 197(13c), "Memorandum on Facilities to Scholars in Public Elementary Schools for a Continuance of their Full-Time Education beyond the age of 14", dated 29 November 1918. Selby-Bigge argued that a secondary system was "essential to a sound system of national education".

13 Consultative Committee Reports.
"Differentiation of the Curriculum for Boys and Girls respectively in Secondary Schools", 1923;
"Psychological Tests of Educable Capacity and their possible use in the public system of education", 1924.

14 Discussion between delegation from the Consultative Committee and the Secretary on 22 November 1923 to discuss the terms, Min. of Education file 4(4) (ix)(9) papers dated 23 November 1923.

15 Different departments of the board suggested for investigation by the Consultative Committee the following topics: the place of central schools in the education system; should elementary education cease at 14; was there a place for intermediate schools between the elementary and the secondary; the meaning and scope of commercial education; the problem of rural areas on advanced instruction for elementary schools, Min. of Education file, 4(4) (ix)(9) for 1923.

16 Hadow reference signed 19 December 1923 (File as above).

17 *The Times Educational Supplement*, 11 March 1966, "Still Small Voice at the Hustings".

18 Min. of Education files 4(4) (ix)(9), Papers dated January–May 1924.

19 Correspondence between the President and Sir Henry Hadow, 16–23 December 1926, Min. of Education file 4(4) (ix)(9).

20 Board of Education Circular No. 1397 dated 18 May 1928; "The New Prospect in Education", Board of Education Pamphlet No. 60—1928.

21 Board of Education File Secretary's clerks' papers, No. 36, "Bills, General". See papers leading to Education (School Attendance) Bill 1929.

22 Board of Education File Secretary's clerks' papers No. 10 C. dated October 1928 *et seq.*

23 Based on Ministry of Labour Memorandum Secretary's clerks' Papers, File No. 36/1929. In the Midlands and London little

juvenile unemployment, but much in the areas of heavy industry (mining and cotton textiles). After 1934 if the school leaving age was raised there would be nearly a million less juveniles available for industry; this would have different effects in different areas.

24 Min. of Education file, Secretary's clerks' papers No. 36, Education (School Attendance Bill 1929); Government Actuary information in Board of Education Circular No. 1395.

25 Labour Party Manifesto for the General Election of 1929, Subtitled "Labour's Appeal to the Nation".

26 Trevelyan sent the chief H.M. inspectors to explore the issue with Directors of Education. (Memorandum by President dated 24 June 1929 in file 36.)

27 Trevelyan argued that raising the school-leaving age would keep 450,000 children at school in 1931. About 250,000 would have found employment; it was estimated 2½ children equalled one adult at work, thus it was expected to take 100,000 out of the unemployed. This would relieve the expenditure on relief and "dole" by about £4.5 million a year. (File 36—Memorandum by President dated 24 June 1929.)

28 Charity Commissioners Report, 1883.

29 Public Records Office Papers. Educational file No. 12/262. Extracted from a manuscript attached to a minute dated 26 August 1920.

30 Hansard-Com. Vol. 223/4 December 1928/Cols. 1029–32; 11 December 1928/Cols. 1902–5 and 2081–seq.; 18 December 1928/Cols. 2306, 2607 and 2817; 20 December 1928/Cols. 3307–8.

31 Hansard-Com. Vol. 229/13 November 1929/Col. 2076 (Miss Eleanor Rathbone).

32 Min. of Education file Secretary's clerks' papers File No. 36, 1929. The President had tried to obtain a 75 per cent contribution towards the local authority costs, to be counted as a government contribution towards the relief of the unemployed.

33 Min. of Education Secretary's Clerks' File No. 2015 (Papers leading to the Education Act of 1936). Preliminary discussions on raising the school-leaving age and assistance to voluntary schools. (Secretary's Review, 2 August 32.) Bill introduced by Mr Thomas Davies and Mr Holland of the National Society privately assisted in the drafting.

34 Board of Education Files, No. 2015; Education Bills—1929–31; Pelham Review February–August 1932 in preparation for the Education Act of 1936.

35 White Paper, "Terms of Agreement", BPP 1930/Cmd. 3551.

36 Board of Education File No. 2015, Flat rate of 5/- per week from fourteen to fifteen. An income of under £3 a week with two children would qualify for grant. Ceiling being £3/5/- for three children, £3/15/- for four, £4/5/- for five etc.

37 "Proposals for Aid to Non-Provided Schools", Conference 13 and 14 January 1931 (Cmd. 3786).

38 Report of Committee on National Expenditure (Cmd. 3920) (May Report published 11 September 1931); Below quoted—paras. 501 and 502.

39 Board of Education, Economy Committee, 1931, File "Y".

40 Board of Education files, Consultative Committee 4(4) (xii), Period 8 February–October 1933. There was a consensus of opinion within the board for an investigation into secondary and technical schools, the area specifically excluded from the Hadow inquiry.

41 Board of Education file, Secretary's Clerks' Papers, No. 2015. Educational issues for the next election were discussed in December 1933 and Cabinet memoranda were circulating early in 1934.

42 Board of Education file, Secretary's Clerks' Papers No. 2011 and 2013. Draft memo on raising the school-leaving age—January 34. Revised policy notes Minutes of Cabinet—Educational Policy Meetings of 14 February and 1 March 1934.

43 Board of Education File, Secretary's Clerks' Papers No. 2011. The estimate of £1 million (£0.7 from the Treasury and £0.3 from the rates) was arrived at by excluding maintenance grants from the Trevelyan figures; an allowance was made for the exemptions through beneficial employment. It was thought the numbers concerned in school would be few. (Draft of 5 January 1934) Reference back to cabinet—(see minutes of Cabinet Education Policy Meeting dated 6 November 1934 (Ref : E(34) 3rd Meeting).

44 Board of Education file, Secretary's Clerks' Papers, No. 2011. "Cabinet Education Policy Committee" (E (34) 3rd Meeting dated 6 November 34).

45 Board of Education, File No. 2014, "Report on Raising the School-leaving age",
　　(a) Committee chaired by the Permanent Secretary (Sir H. Pelham). Terms of reference Papers dated 13 November 1934;
　　(b) Minute dated 20 November 1934 by H. Ramsbotham to the President and the Permanent Secretary. NB Ramsbotham later President, and was in effect President, because Irwin (Halifax) was employed elsewhere;

(c) Agreed findings in papers dated 20 February 1935. (See A. Campbell-Johnson, *Viscount Halifax,* 1941, pp. 343–4 and 373).

46 Board of Education, Files No. 2012 and 2015. Preliminary discussions on raising the school leaving-age and assistance to voluntary schools : "Education Act 1936".

47 Board of Education File, Secretary's Clerks' Papers, No. 2011, (E(34) (6); Cabinet Memorandum by Oliver Stanley dated 27 June 1935; "Compulsory Education beyond 14".

48. *Ibid.*

49 Board of Education File No. 1070 ("1936 Education Bill"). Collection of cuttings and letters reacting to the measure. A varied bag, from some saying the Act "went too far" while others thought it "niggardly and unsatisfactory".

50 Education Act 1936 (Clauses 12 and 13).

51 Hansard-Com. Vol. 308/13 February 1936/Col. 1236 (Mr. Somerville).

52 Hansard-Com. Vol. 312/26 May 1936/Cols. 1883–87, 1926–7 and Vol. 312/27 May 1936/Cols. 2050, 2055 and 2058–62. (Duchess of Atholl.)

Chapter VI 1936–1939

1 Board of Education file, No. F 645/37 (Papers dated 27 April 1937). Interim Report of the Committee on the Building Programme of Government Departments, March 1937. Suggestions communicated to authorities in C.1456 of June 1937.

2 37th Annual Conference of Labour party at Bournemouth 4–8 October 1937.

3 Hansard-Com. Vol. 336/7 May 1938/Col. 1221.

4 *Education,* 3 June 1938, article "Week by week".

5 *The Schoolmaster and Woman Teachers' Chronicle,* 9 June 1938; *The Teachers World,* 15 June 1938.

6 With the NUT were the WEA, the New Educational Fellowship, and the Ten Year Plan. Details of deputation discussion of 13 June 1938 from Board of Education Files No. E 599 and P/S 25B (1) Part 6 (London Staffing File).

7 *Daily Herald* of 14 June 1938. Details of local authorities completed. Hansard-Com. Vol. 336/16 June 1938/Cols. 2217–18.

8 *Education,* 10 June 1938; *The Tablet,* 11 June 1938; *Universe* 17 June 1938.

9 *Daily Herald,* 20 June 1938.

10 Hansard-Com. Vol. 337/20 June 1938/Col. 778 on.

11 Discussions between the Treasury and the Board of Education on the possibility of extension beyond 1940. (File No. s.38505). Board of Education Minute to the Treasury Minute on file No. 2078. Treasury to Secretary, Reply on 16 June 1938.

12 Response to Ministry of Health letter C.1687 of 6 May 1938, which asked authorities to survey the field of their capital expenditure and submit a complete programme for five years 1938–42, in order of priority, showed the authorities were placing all capital expenditure on elementary education in the years 1938 and 1939, postponing the bulk of other capital expenditure to last three years of the period. This was obviously because of the conditions on which the educational grants had been made. (Board of Education draft letter to Treasury dated 30 June 1938 on file F.1180/38.)

13 References of letter series : Board of Education to Treasury of 27 July 1938 on File E.1180/38; Treasury to Board of 28 July 1938 on File s.40282; Board to Treasury of 29 July 1938 on file 38/2880Y. Percentage of expenditure on new schools was : 1935–6 = 28.3, 1936–7 = 19.0 and 1937–8 = 10.8 (Average for 1935–38 = 19.3 per cent).This was £0.99 million on new schools for the three years, as against £2.7 millions on new premises and £2.66 millions on extensions and improvements.

14 Board of Education file No. F.1180/38. The Treasury agreed to the extension on 2 August but it was to "be administered with discretion and would not be applied in any automatic and universal way". Interested departments were informed in confidence and welcomed the extension as easing the difficulties in local arrangements. Circular 1464 which promulgated this policy was issued on 14 October. On 12 October instructions had been sent to staff and His Majesty's Inspectors to refrain from pressing local officials to execute projects for which there was not "a genuine and urgent educational need".

15 The Times, 28 October 1938, reported the speech.

16 Daily Herald of 5 November 1938—LCC stoppages on secondary schools linked with the issue of C.1464, a fortnight after Munich and about ten days after the Minister of Health's speech.

17 Board of Education file, Secretary's Clerks' Papers, No. 2110.

18 Hansard-Com. Vol. 341/8 November 1938/Cols. 19–21 and subsequent debate. Col. 30 Chamberlain's speech.

19 Hansard-Com. Vol. 341/14 November 1938/Cols. 465 on (Debate on the Address from the throne); Motion by Mr Pethwick Lawrence on the condition of the people; WEA Annual Conference at Blackpool on 12 November 1938.

20 Secondary Education : Spens Report, 1938, Introduction XIX-XXII and Ch. XX, 345, also p. 291 and Ch. IX generally.
21 *Ibid*, Ch. VII.
22 *Ibid.,* Ch. IX (Equality of Status), Introduction Sections III, IV and Ch. VIII (Vocational schools).
23 *Ibid.,* Ch. IX, Part VII.
24 Circular 1463 of 18 July 1938, Approved certain modification of the School Certificate Examination; Circular 1473 of 2 August 1938, Organization of secondary schools with promise of detailed pamphlet on curriculum reorganization.
25 Board of Education Report for 1939 (Unpublished) provides details of development of technical education while other educational building curtailed. Also Board of Education file 2110, Papers dated 31 July 1938.
26 Board of Education file No. 2132, Papers dated 31 March 1939.
27 Board of Education file E–484/21, Papers dated 31 December 1938.
28 Board of Education file No. C.1468, Papers dated 9 May 1939. Criticism of too solidly built schools. This applied to work before the first world war, but not afterwards. LEA's encouraged to try for lighter structures. Longer loan facilities given in Circular C.1468 of 9 May 1939. Circular 1471 of 21 July 1939, Encouragement to use new standards. Circular 1475 of 31 August 1939. Problems to be faced on outbreak of war.
29 Board of Education, Circular C. 1477 dated 26 September 1939.
30 Hansard-Com. Vol. 352/10 October 1939/Cols. 255–60.
31 John Vaizey, *The Cost of Education,* 1958, p. 90.
32 Return of Accommodation in Elementary Schools at 19 December 1924. BPP 1924–5/XXI dated 10 February 1925.
33 M. Morris, *The People's Schools,* 1939, p. 56.
34 L. G. E. Jones, *The Training of Teachers in England and Wales,* 1924, p. 446.
35 Accounts of supplementary teachers and monitresses. Marjorie Wise, *English Village Schools,* 1931, pp. 31–5; Miss Read, *Country School,* 1955; A. W. Ashby and P. G. Byles, *Rural Education,* 1923, pp. 62–5; M. K. Ashby, *The Country School,* 1929, pp. 228–36.
36 Board of Education Annual Report for 1958.
37 G. C. Leybourne and K. White, *Education and the Birth Rate,* 1940, pp. 144–6.
38 John Vaizey, *The Costs of Education,* 1958, p. 74.
39 G. A. N. Lowndes, *The British Educational System,* 1955, p. 65.
40 Board of Education Pamphlet No. 110, 1937, pp. 8–16.

41 *The Education of the Adolescent*, 1926, p. 135. Hansard-Com. Vol. 174/15 May 1907/Col. 1054 (Stephen MacKenna).

42 R. J. Montgomery, *Examinations*, 1965, pp. 109–13.

43 London Statistics, Vol. 41, 1938, p. 57 and p. 75; Charity Organisation Handbook for 1938.

44 G. G. Leybourne and K. White, *op cit*. pp. 127–9.

45 John Vaizey, *op. cit.*, p. 74.

46 Annual Report of the Board of Education, 1938, pp. 13 and 206; G. G. Leybourne and K. White, *op. cit.*, Appendix "E".

47 Public Record Office file, Edn. 11/251 E 432/10. "1937—General information on pupils in public elementary schools staying beyond the usual age limit." See papers supporting the Minute dated 7 January 1938.

48 Secondary Education (Spens Report—1938), p. 102.

49 G. G. Leybourne and K. White, *op. cit.*, p. 111.

50 Annual Report of the Board of Education, 1938, p. 17.

51 G. G. Leybourne and K. White, *op. cit.*, p. 259; LCC set the limit at £800 p.a.

52 More detail can be found in : J. Burnett, *Plenty and Want*, 1966; Noreen Branson and Margot Heinemann, *Britain in the Ninteeen Thirties*, 1971, Ch. VII. Nigel Middleton, *When Family Failed*, 1971, Ch. VII.

53 Brinley Thomas articles in *Economics* : "The Movement of Labour into South-East England—1920–32", Vol. 1/2/May 1934, pp. 220–41; "The Influx of Labour into London and the South East—1920–36, Vol. 4, 15 August 1937, pp. 336–72; "The Influx of Labour into the Midlands 1920–37", Vol. 5, 2 November 1938, pp. 410–34.

54 "Health of the School Child", 1925, p. 116, Report of the School Medical Service, Medical Research Council No. 106, 1926.

55 "Health of the School Child", 1926, p. 97.

56 *Medical Officer*, 6 May 1933.

57 "Health of the School Child", 1927, p. 110.

58 Public Record Office File—M. of H. 57/3/130282/3/30. See papers dated 14 November 1930 to 16 January 1931.

59 The most widely used minimum diet was the one published by the British Medical Association in November 1933. Surveys : John Boyd Orr, "Food Health and Income", 1936; Seebohm Rowntree, "Poverty and Progress", 1941, Survey of York; P. Sargant Florence, "Nutrition and size of family", 1939, Birmingham area. For the account of attempts to muzzle Orr see his autobiography *As I recall*, 1942.

60 Recent work on children affected by starvation in Biafra has

shown the difficulty of measuring the adverse effects is still shown that the difficulty of measuring the adverse effects is still severe at certain vital periods of physical development which affected the growth of the brain.

Chapter VII   January 1940–July 1941

1 Examples of articles advocating far reaching social changes : *Christian Newsletter*, 31 January 1940; *The Times Educational Supplement*, 10 February 1940, p. 53, leader on restoration of compulsory attendance. National Executive of the Labour party issued a statement of peace aims on 10 February 1940. Published as pamphlet : "Labour's Home Policy—The War and After", May 1940; Hansard-Com. Vol. 358/5 March 1940/Cols. 242–351 (Education debate); *The Times*, "Looking Forward", leading article of 6 March 1940; *The New Era*, June 1940; *Teachers World*, July 1940; *The New Statesman*, 24 August 1940; also series of articles in *The Times Educational Supplement*, March–November 1940.

2 Lords—Vol. 115/7 February 1940/Cols. 467–511 (Archbishop of Canterbury Cosmo Lang) also reported with comment *The Times Educational Supplement*, 10 February 1940, p. 50.

3 Marjorie Reeves, "Education after the War", *The New Era*, June 1940; *The Times*, 2 November 1940.

4 Lords—Vol. 115/7 February 1940/Cols. 467–511 (Lord Addison).

5 Hansard-Com. Vol. 353/16 November 1939/969–71 (John Morgan).

6 Hansard-Com. Vol. 358/5 March 1940/Col. 310 (Mr Cove) and Col. 306 (Mr Creech Jones).

7 L. Thompson, *1940—Year of Legend*, 1966, p. 65—Gallup poll details.

8 *Ibid.*, pp. 139–40—Summary of Gallup poll results.

9 Michael Hughes, *Cartoons from the General Strike*, 1968; Julian Symons, *The General Strike*, 1957.

10 Report of Trade Union Congress Meeting of 9 October 1940.

11 Resolution of the Executive Committee of the Workers Education Association dated 30 November 1940.

12 Ministry of Education file, Secretary's Clerks' Papers (No. 2152 (A)I documents dated November 1940).

13 Meeting of the Executive Committee of the Workers Education Association, 30 November 1940.

14 R. J. Minney, *The Private Papers of Hore-Belisha*, 1960.

15 Ministry of Education file (No. 2152 (A) (1), Principal Assistant Secretaries. Committee. Papers dated 25 November 1940.

16 Report of speech in *The Times Educational Supplement*, 1 March 1941.

17 Ministry of Education file—No. 2152(A) (I). Papers dated 17 March 1941.

18 S. J. Curtis, *History of Education in Great Britain*, University Tutorial Press, 1953, p. 374.

19 W. Kenneth Richmond, *Education in England*, Pelican, 1945, p. 145.

20 Green Book—Ch. II (Section 155 and 156).

21 The Memorandum submitted by the Board was published as a White Paper "Memorandum with regard to the existing Grant System". (BPP 1926/xxii/Cmd. 2571.)

22 Green Book—Ch. II Part II (Sec. 157 (a) to (g).

23 *Ibid.*, Ch. 9 (Sec. 125).

24 *Ibid.*, Ch. 9 (Sec. 124). Of the 519 proposals, 289 were from Roman Catholic Schools. The 519 schemes provided for 136,000 of the 400,000 senior children in non-provided schools.

25 *Ibid.*—Ch. 9 (Sec. 124(a)). The Black List was drawn up in 1925 with 2,800 condemned schools. In 1928 it had been reduced to 1,800 and it was forecast another seven years would clear these, but there were still 753 in use in 1939.

26 *Ibid.*—Ch. 9, "The Dual System and Allied Problems".

27 *Ibid.*—Ch. 9, Sec. 130 and Education Act 1936 (Sec. 9 and 10).

28 B. Gardner, *Churchill in his time: A study in a reputation 1939–45*, 1968; R. R. James, *Churchill: A study in failure 1900–1939*, 1970; G. M. Thomson, *Vote of Censure*, 1968.

29 *The Lancaster Observer and Morecambe Chronicle* of 5 September 1941.

Chapter VIII   July 1941–June 1943

1 For biographical details : Francis Boyd, *Richard Austen Butler*, 1965; Ralph Harris, *Politics Without Prejudices*, 1956; Gerald Sparrow, *R.A.B. Study of a Statesman*, 1965; R. A. Butler, *The Art of the Possible*, Hamish Hamilton, London, 1971; Viscount Templewood (Samuel Hoare), *Nine Troubled Years*, 1954, pp. 71–2, refers to Butler's qualities and his uncle's last words to Templewood when he visited him on his death bed were : "Look after my nephew, Rab, and help him in his newly-started political career".

2 Robert Skidelsky, *Gold Standard and Churchill: The Truth*, *The Times*, 17 March 1969.

3 M. Keynes, *The Economic Consequences of Mr Churchill*, 1930.

4 Ministry of Education (2152 (1) (i)) President's Papers. Letter from Butler at the Foreign Office to Ramsbotham thanking him for the Green Book dated 12 July 1941.

5 R. A. Butler—"Lord Butler Looks Back", television interview in *The Listener* (Vol. 76/No. 1948/28 July 66/p. 112); R. A. Butler, *The Art of the Possible*, p. 90; R. R. James (ed.), *Chips: The Diaries of Sir Henry Channon*, 1967, Penguin, p. 377.

6 Brian Jackson, "Short of Change", *New Statesman*, 12 November 1971, p. 643.

7 Janet Beveridge, *Beveridge and his Plan*, 1954, p. 114.

8 Personal papers of Geoffrey Faber, letter dated 26 June 1941.

9 Memorandum H. Brooke to G. Faber dated 25 October 1944 (Faber Personal Papers).

10 Francis Boyd, *op cit.*, p. 75; Ministry of Education file (No. 2152 (1) (i)) President's Papers dated 15 August 1941.

11 Ministry of Education file (No. 2152 (1) (i)) President's Papers dated 12 September 1971.

12 R. A. Butler, *The Art of the Possible*, Hamish Hamilton, London, p. 71.

13 Lord Butler on Cabinet Government (Conversation with Norman Hunt), *The Listener*, 12 November 1965, pp. 407–11.

14 Terry Coleman, *The Railway Navvies*, 1965.

15 Marjorie Cruickshank, *Dual System Reform 1941–44*, University of London MA 1950, pp. 55–8.

16 Letter from Dr Scott Lidgett to Sir Maurice Holmes dated 30 January 1942; Ministry of Education file, No. 2152.

17 Ministry of Education file, No. 2152 (1) (i), The President's Papers dated 5 September 1941.

18 Ministry of Education file, No. 2152: Minutes of meeting 2 January 1942 Workers' Educational Association; Green Book Discussions, Minutes No. 20 dated 21 October 1942.

19 Sir Frederick Mander, President of the National Union of Teachers. "The Religious Instruction Controversy", *The Schoolmaster*, January 1942.

20 Interview Butler and Mander on 30 January 1942 (Butler's papers). Series of articles by F. Mander in *The Schoolmaster*, January–February 1942. Published by the NUT as "The Religious Instruction Controversy"; Ministry of Education file "Green Book Discussions" Minutes No. 22 dated 2 April 1943.

21 "Educational Reconstruction"—NUT Pamphlet (1942); R. A.

Butler, *The Art of the Possible*, Hamish Hamilton, London, 1971, p. 99; Report of the proposals of the executive of the NUT sent to the Board on 3 February 1942 with draft of pamphlet "Educational Reconstruction".

22 Meeting of Sir Maurice Holmes and representatives of the Association of Directors and Secretaries of Education; Green Book Discussions, Minutes dated 5 February 1942.

23 The County Councils Association Green Book Report dated April 1942; The Education Committee of the Association of Municipal Corporations sent in Green Book comments dated 1 April 1942; Roman Catholic support for their proposals—See *The Universe* of 2 October 1942.

24 Meeting of the deputation of Association of Education Committees on 19 March 1942. See Ministry of Education file Green Book Discussions (Minutes No. 11), note especially para. 7.

25 Association of Education Committee Minutes of meeting dated 19 March 1942; Report of Executive dated April 1942. Free Church views : Dr Scott Lidgett interview at Board 14 April 1942; Chuter Ede comments on Ministry of Education file, "The Religious Question" dated 27 April 1942.

26 Butler's notes on interview with Lord Selborne, prominent in the National Society, dated April 1942.

27 Ministry of Education file; Bishop of Derby—"Note on Education" dated 24 April 1942; Bishop of London's letter to Archbishop of Canterbury dated 11 April 1942, passed to Board of Education; Bishop of Woolwich Record of interview with Chuter Ede dated 20 May 1942.

28 F. A. Iremonger, *William Temple—His life and letters*, 1948; See reports on the Conferences on Christian Politics, Economics and Citizenship held in Birmingham in 1924, usually called the COPEC Conferences.

29 William Temple, "Our Trust and Our Task", Presidential address at the annual meeting of the National Society on 3 June 1942.

30 Marjorie Cruickhsank, *Church and State in English Education*, 1963, pp. 151–3; F. A. Iremonger, *op cit.*, p. 572, letter to Canon Tatlow.

31 Bishop of Hexham and Newcastle in his Advent Pastoral letter in 1942.

32 Cardinal Hinsley in *The Times*, letter dated 2 November, 1942.

33 R. A. Butler, *The Art of the Possible*, Hamish Hamilton, London, 1971, p. 107.

Chapter IX   July 1943–August 1944

1 A. F. S. Ross, *Parliamentary Representation*, 1943, pp. 81–3; D. Butler and J. Freeman, *British Political Facts 1900–1967*, 1968, pp. 142 and 159.

2 Sir Henry Morris-Jones, *Doctor in the Whips' Room*, 1955, p. 110. Labour M.P.'s fainting from underfeeding.

3 A. F. S. Ross, *Parliamentary Representation*, 1943, p. 236—Cost of being an MP. Memoirs of the period bristle with examples of the case of adoption of the candidate with money; Harold Nicolson, *Diaries and Letters 1930–39*, 1966, pp. 215–20; R. R. James (ed.), *Chips: The Diary of Sir Henry Channon*, 1967.

4 Alan Bullock, *Ernest Bevin and his times*, 1967, Vol. II, p. 224 –5; Janet Beveridge, *Beveridge and his plan*, 1954, p. 114.

5 Hansard-Com. Vol. 380/9 February 1943/Cols. 1201–2 (Ernest Bevin).

6 R. A. Butler, *The Art of the Possible*, 1971, pp. 109–16 (Gathering the material); Elizabeth Nel, *Mr Churchill's Secretary*, 1958, p. 96—(Dictation in the car.)

7 R. A. Butler, *The Art of the Possible*, 1971, p. 117; Lord Boyle, "Lord Butler's vivid work of art"—Review of the above in *The Times* of 12 July 1971.

8 Harold Laski, *Faith, Reason and Civilization*, Gollancz, London, 1943, pp. 162–3.

9 *The New Statesman and Nation* of 24 July 1943, p. 51.

10 Hansard-Com. Vol. 391/29 July 1943/Col. 1863 (Mr Sexton of Barnard Castle).

11 *Ibid.*, Vol. 391/29 July 1943/Cols. 1984–5 (Mr Guy of Poplar).

12 *Ibid.*, Vol. 391/29 July 1943/Col. 1859 (Sir Harold Webbe of Westminster Abbey); 30 July 1943/Col. 2044 (Mr Chuter Ede—Parly. Sec. Bd. of Education).

13 *Ibid.*, Vol. 391/29 July 1943/Cols 1835–7 (Mr Butler).

14 *Catholic Herald* of 6 August 1943.

15 Lords—Vol. 128/4 August 1943/Col. 1006 (Archbishop of Canterbury).

16 Hansard-Com. Vol. 391/29 July 1943/Col. 1870 (Mr Lakin of Llandaff and Barry).

17 *Ibid.*, Vol. 29 July 1943/Col. 1845 (Mr Creech Jones of Shipley); 30 July 1943/Col. 1937 (Mr Arthur Greenwood of Wakefield).

18 The religious antagonisms are well sketched out in Margaret

Cruickshank, *Church and State in English Education,* MA London University (1950), pp. 170–89).

19 The *Manchester Guardian.* Articles by "Artifex", October 1943; Bishop of Chelmsford article in *Education* (17 October 1943).

20 *The Tablet,* 24 July 1943 and 4 September 1943 (Cardinal Hinsley); *The Church Times,* 30 July 1943; *The Times,* 2 November 1943 (Bishop of Gloucester).

21 *The Times Educational Supplement* of 31 July 1943 (NUT attitude to Para. 39).

22 D. W. Dean—"Problems of the Conservative Sub-Committee on Education 1941–45", *Journal of Educational Administration and History,* Vol. III/I/December 1970, pp.26–37.

23 *The Catholic Herald,* 6 August 1943, Archbishop Amigo.

24 *The Tablet* of 28 August 1943.

25 Lord Butler's personal notes on the meeting dated 30 August 1943.

26 Press accounts of the campaign against the White Paper : Large public meetings *The Times* of 18 October 1943 (Liverpool); *The Catholic Times* of 1 October 1943 (Newcastle). *The Universe* of 27 August 1943 (London). Campaign at other meetings *The Catholic Times* of 1 October 1943; Catholic Parents' Association—*The Universe* of 13 August 1943 and *The Catholic Times* of 1 October 1943.

27 Hansard-Com. Vol. 397/25 February 1944/Col. 1166 (Mr Walkden of Bristol South).

28 *The Catholic Herald* of 17 September 1943. Report of NUT meeting.

29 Lord Butler's Personal Papers. Memorandum dated 9 September 1943.

30 R. A. Butler *The Art of the Possible,* 1971, pp. 106–7; Draft letter Butler to Sir John Anderson, Chancellor of the Exchequer, dated 28 September 1943; Ministry of Education file (President's papers).

31 Lord Butler's personal papers. Memorandum dated 19 October 1943.

32 Herbert Morrison, *An Autobiography,* Odhams, London, 1960, p. 230.

33 Major Pethwick at a regional Conservative Conference as reported in the *Sheffield Telegraph* of 2 October 1942.

34 D. W. Dean—"Problems of the Conservative Sub-Committee on Education", 1941–5, *Journal of Educational Administration and History,* Vol. III, December 1970, pp. 266–7.

35 Hansard-Com. Vol. 391/15 February 1944/Col. 46 (Sir Geoffrey Shakespeare of Norwich).

36 Hansard-Com. Vol. 397/15 February 1944/Col. 47 (Mr Loftus of Lowestoft). See other speakers—Cols. 51–74.

37 Hansard-Com. Vol. 397/15 February 1944/Col. 65 (Prof. Gruffydd, University of Wales).

38 Hartmut Kopsch, *The approach of the Conservative Party to social Policy,* London University Ph.D., 1970, pp. 260–3; Hansard-Lords Vol. 132/18 July 1944/Col. 960 (Lord Rankeillout); Hansard-Com. Vol. 396/8 February 1944/Cols. 1647–65 (Debate on title of Minister) and Vol. 397/9 March 1944/Cols. 2447–8 and 1654–5; Education Act 1944 (Sec. 1(1) and Sec. 68; Geof. Faber letter to W. Byng Kenrick of 7 January 1944 (Faber Papers Box 1) Resistance to upgrading the department to ministerial rank).

39 Hansard-Com. Vol 397/9 March 1944/Cols. 2258–9 (Kenneth Lindsay, MP for Kilmarnock).

40 *Ibid.*

41 Hansard-Com. Vol. 397/9 March 1944/Cols. 2267–9 (Prof. Gruffydd).

42 *Ibid.,* March 1944/Cols. 2270–79 (Mr R. A. Butler).

43 *Ibid.,* 15 February 1944/Col. 127 (Mr Chuter Ede).

44 *Ibid.,* 16 February 1944/Cols. 206–9 (Mr R. A. Butler).

45 Debate on school equipment : Hansard-Com. Vol. 397/15 February/Cols. 100–20; Playing field notion—Admiral Sir William James (Portsmouth North); Audio visual equipment and radios —Mr Kenneth Lindsey (Kilmarnock).

46 Hansard-Com. Vol. 396/19 January 1944/Cols. 235–7 (J. Parker —MP Romford); Cols. 268–9 (John Wilmot—MP Kennington); Cols. 454–5 (Mollwyn Hughes—MP Carmarthen) and Col. 471 (Lewis Silkin—MP Peckham).

47 Committee—Abolition of fee paying; Hansard-Com. Vol. 398/28 March 1944/Cols. 1264–1312 (Capt. Cobb); Cols. 1284–89 (W. G. Cove-Aberavon); Cols. 1300–7 (R. A. Butler).

48 Hansard-Com. Vol. 398/4 April 1944/Col. 1922 (W. G. Cove).

49 Hansard-Com. Vol. 397/16 February 1944/Col. 226 (Dr Haden Guest) and Col. 227 (Mr Cove).

50 *Ibid.,* 24 February 1944/Col. 1072 (Mr Gallacher) and Col. 1074 (Prof. Gruffydd).

51 *Ibid.,* 25 February 1944/Col. 1137 (Mr R. A. Butler).

52 *Ibid.,* 25 February 1944/Col. 1142–6)Mr Tinker of Leigh).

53 Hansard-Com. Vol. 398/4 April 1944/Col. 1919 (Mr Stokes).

54 Hansard-Com. Vol. 397/10 March 1944/Col. 2442 (Mr Chuter Ede).

55 *Ibid.,* 17 February 1944/Col. 324 (Parliamentary Question Mr Mander to Mr Butler).

56 Harold Nicolson, *Diaries and Letters,* 1939–45, Collins, London, 1967, p. 360; Lord Butler, *The Art of the Possible,* 1971 pp. 120–3; Michael Foot, *Aneurin Bevan Vol. I,* 1962, pp. 470–1; Hansard-Com. Vol. 398/30 March 1944/Cols. 1578–1656, 29 March 1944/Cols. 1452–57, 28 March 1944/Cols. 1355–96.

57 *Ibid.,* 30 March 1944/Col. 1616 (Earl Winterton), 1620 (Mr Maxton, 1630 (Aneurin Bevan).

58 W. S. Churchill, *My Early Life,* 1930; R. A. Butler, *The Art of the Possible,* London, 1971, pp. 108 and 115; *The Listener,* of 28 July 1966, p. 112.

59 Thelma Gazalet Keir, *From the Wings,* 1967, pp. 112–3.

Chapter X 1945–1972

1 *The Times,* 28 March 1945 (letter).

2 Minutes to the Cabinet, Memorandum on Raising the School-leaving Age dated 16 August 1945 on File No. 2223/4; Memorandum by the Minister of Education and the Secretary of State for Scotland to the Cabinet on Raising the School-leaving Age dated 28 August 1945; Cabinet Paper No. 45/117 dated 30 August 1945.

3 Ministry of Education Memorandum to the Cabinet dated 18 December 1946; The Scottish Office concern became apparent in a draft memo dated 5 December 1946 which was addressed to the Cabinet. A copy was sent to education and after discussion it was revised and submitted to the Lord President's Committee on 10 December 1946 (Ministry of Education File No. 2223/5).

4 Francis Williams, *The Triple Challenge,* 1948, pp. 128–132; *The Times Educational Supplement,* Vol. 37, 6 July 1946. (Parliamentary Debate on Educational Vote 2 July 1946); Vol. 38, 6 February 1947, p. 78 (Miss Wilkinson—Obituary).

5 F. Blackburn, *George Tomlinson,* Heinemann, London, 1954; An anecdotal biography which shows both the subject's limitations and his special ability to achieve good public relations.

6 Rodney Barker, *Education and Politics* 1900-1951, OUP, London, 1972, ch. V, pp. 81–97.

7 Oliver Marriott, *The Property Boom,* Hamish Hamilton, London, 1967; Hunter-Davis, *The Rise and Fall of Jake Sullivan,* 1968, a fictional account of the scramble for the exploitation of urban sites.

8 Lord Eccles, *Life and Politics—A Moral Diagnosis,* Longmans, 1967, pp. 114–16.

9 The Crowther Report, "15 to 18", Vol. I and II, HMSO, 1959. Appointed March 1956. Reported July 1959. Published December 1959.

10 The Carr Report, "Recruitment and Training of Young Workers in Industry", HMSO, 1958; Andrew Shonfield, "Apprenticeship and Training Conditions", *The Observer* of 4 June 1961; The Coldstream Report, "National Advisory Council on Art and Education", 1960; The McMeeking Report, "Report by the Advisory Committee on Further Education and Commerce", HMSO, 1959; The Jackson Report, "The Supply and Training of Teachers for Technical Colleges", HMSO, 1957.

11 The Beloe Report, The Secondary Schools Examination Council of the Ministry of Education, "Secondary School Examinations other than G.C.E.", HMSO, 1960.

12 The Albermarle Report, "The Youth Service in England and Wales", HMSO, 1960.

13 The Wolfenden Report, Committee appointed by the Central Council of Physical Education who also published the report, "Sport and the Community", 1960.

14 Women's Group on Public Welfare, *Our Towns—A Close-up,* OUP, 1943; The Curtis Report, "The Care of Children", HMSO, 1946.

15 The Younghusband Report, "Social Workers in the Local Authority Health and Welfare Services", HMSO, 1959.

16 Ingleby Report, "Report on Children and Young Persons", HMSO, 1960.

17 M. Kogan, *The Politics of Education,* 1971, pp. 90, 162.

18 Newsom Report, "Half Our Future", HMSO, 1963.

19 David Coates, "The Teachers' Association and the Restructuring of Burnham", *British Journal of Educational Studies,* Vol. XX, 2 June 1972, pp. 192–204.

20 Conservative Party Campaign Guide, 1970, p. 385.

21 Richard Spielelberg, "Parliamentary Business", *The Times,* 3 July 1970; Barry Turner, "Margaret Thatcher Wins Her Colours", *The Observer,* 7 February 1971; Margaret Thatcher

interviews, *The Spectator,* 8 and 15 July 1972; Stephen Jessel "Review of the Year", *The Times,* 31 December 1971.

22 *Daily Mirror* leader, Saturday, 16 June 1971.

23 Hansard-Com. Vol. 809/21 January 1971/Cols. 1236–44 (Schoolchildren—sandwich meals); Brian Jackson, "Where Labour Went Wrong", *New Statesman,* 4 June 1971, p. 760.

SELECT BIBLIOGRAPHY

History of Education

W. H. G. Armytage, *Four Hundred Years of English Education* (1964).

Olive Banks, *Parity and Prestige in English Secondary Education* (1955).

Rodney Barker, *Education and Politics 1900–1951* (1972).

H. C. Barnard, *A Short History of English Education* (1947).

Charles Birchenough, *History of Elementary Education* (1927).

Margorie Cruickshank, *Church and State in English Education* (1963).

S. J. Curtis, *Education in Britain since 1900* (1952).

——, *History of Education in Great Britain* (1953).

H. C. Dent, *1870–1900—Century of Growth in English Education* (1970).

E. J. R. Eaglesham, *The Foundation of 20th-Century Education in England* (1967).

T. L. Jarman, *Landmarks in the History of Education* (1951).

L. G. E. Jones, *The Training of Teachers in England and Wales* (1924).

R. V. Jones, *The Advancement of Learning* (1964).

A. M. Kazamias, *Politics, Society and Secondary Education in England* (1966).

G. C. Leybourne ad K. White, *Education and the Birth Rate* (1940).

G. A. N. Lowndes, *The British Social Revolution* (1937).

——, *The Silent Social Revolution* (1937).

M. Mathieson and M. T. Whiteside, "The Secondary Modern School in Fiction", *BJES*, Vol. XIX, October 1971, p. 283–93.

Nigel Middleton, "The Education Act of 1870 as the start of the modern concept of the child", *BJES*, Vol. XVIII, June 1970, pp. 175–85.

M. Morris, *The People's Schools* (1939).

Michael Parkinson, *The Labour Party and the Organisation of Secondary Education 1918–65* (1970).

Ivor Morrish, *Education since 1800* (1970).

F. H. Pedley, *The Educational System in England and Wales* (1964).

W. Kenneth Richmond, *Education in England* (1945).

R. J. W. Selleck, *English Primary Education and the Progressives 1914–39* (1972).

Brian Simon, *The Politics of Educational Reform 1920–1940* (1974).

W. A. S. Stewart, *Progressives and Radicals in English Education 1750–1970* (1972).

Background Material

B. M. Allen, *Sir Robert Morant—A great public servant* (1934).

Stanley Baldwin, *This Torch of Freedom—Speeches* (1935).

J. A. Banks, *Prosperity and Parenthood* (1954).

Janet Beveridge, *Beveridge and his Plan* (1954).

W. H. Beveridge, *Full Employment in a Free Society* (1944).

Lord Birkenhead, *Halifax—The Life of Lord Halifax* (1965).

Charles Booth, *Life and Labour of the People of London* (1889–1902).

F. Blackburn, *George Tomlinson* (1954).

Francis Boyd, *Richard Austen Butler* (1965).

N. Branson *et al., Britain in the Nineteen Thirties* (1971).

M. E. Bulkley, *The Feeding of School Children* (1914).

Alan Bullock, *Ernest Bevin and His Times* (Vol. II) (1967).

J. Burnett, *Plenty and Want* (1966).

John Burrows, *Darwin and the Origin of the Species* (1972).

D. Butler *et al., British Political Facts* (1968).

R. A. Butler, *The Art of the Possible* (1971).

F. Le Gros Clark, *The Social History of the School Meals Service* (1948).

G. Clark, *The Wealth of England* (1946).

Terry Coleman, *The Railway Navvies* (1965)

George Dangerfield, *The Strange Death of Liberal England* (1935).

D. W. Dean, "Problems of the Conservative Sub-Committee on Education", *Journal of Educational Admin. and History,* vol. III, December 1970, pp. 226–37.

Lord Eccles, *Life and Politics—A Moral Diagnosis* (1967).

S. M. Ferguson *et al., Studies in the Social Services* (1954).

J. J. Finlay, *Arnold of Rugby* (1898).

P. Sargant Florence, *Nutrition and Size of Family* (1939).

Michael Foot, *Aneurin Bevan, Vol. II* (1962).

Brian Gardiner, *Mafeking—A Victorian Legend* (1966).

Bentley B. Gilbert, *Evolution of National Insurance* (1966).

——, *British Social Policy 1914–39* (1970).

Richard Haldane, *An Autobiography* (1929).

Ralph Harris, *Politics Without Prejudice* (1956).

C. Silvester Horne, *A Popular History of the Free Churches* (1903).
Michael Hughes, *Cartoons from the General Strike* (1968).
F. A. Iremonger, *William Temple—His Life and Letters* (1948).
R. R. Jones (ed), *Chips—The Diary of Sir Henry Channon* (1967).
Thelma Cazalet Keir, *From The Wings* (1967).
Harold Laski, *Faith, Reason and Civilization* (1943)
Peter Laslett, *The World We have Lost* (1965).
D. Lockwood, *The Blackcoated Worker* (1958).
Oliver Marriott, *The Property Boom* (1967).
Nigel Middleton, *When Family Failed* (1971).
John Morley, *The Struggle for National Education* (1873).
Henry Morris-Jones, *Doctor in the Whips' Room* (1955).
Herbert Morrison, *An Autobiography* (1960).
Harold Nicholson, *Diaries and Letters 1930–39* (1966).
John Boyd Orr, *Food, Health and Income* (1936).
——, *As I Recall* (1950).
L. Paul, *The Deployment and Payment of the Clergy* (1964).
Harold Perkin, *The Age of the Railway* (1970).
John Prebble, *The Highland Clearances* (1963).
A. F. S. Rose, *Parliamentary Representation* (1943).
B. S. Rowntree, *Poverty* (1901).
Seebohm Rowntree, *Poverty and Progress* (1941).
Adam Smith, *Wealth of Nations* (1767).
Julian Symons, *The General Strike* (1957).
Gerald Sparrow, *RAB—Study of a Statesman* (1965).
Lytton Strachey, *Eminent Victorians* (1960).
R. H. Tawney, *Secondary Education for All* (1924).
L. Thompson, *1940—Year of Legend* (1966).
Richard M. Titmuss, *Poverty and Population* (1938).
——, *Problems of Social Policy* (1950).
John Vaizey, *The Cost of Education* (1958).
Beatrice Webb, *Our partnership* (1948).
Sidney Webb, *The Educational Muddle and the Way Out* (1901).
M. M. Wells *et el.*, *The New Law of Education* (1944).
Francis Williams, *A Prime Minister Remembers* (1961).
——, *The Triple Challenge* (1952).
Women's Group on Public Welfare, *Our Towns—A Close Up* (1943).
Cecil Woodham-Smith, *The Great Hunger* (1962).

General Sources

The Times

The *Times Educational Supplement*
The *Sunday Times*
The *Daily Herald*
The *Observer*
The *Guardian*
The Listener
The Tablet
The Universe
The *New Statesman*
Education
The Teachers World
The School Master
The Charity Organisation Handbook
The Family Welfare Organisation Handbook
Annual Reports of the Trades Union Congress
Annual Reports of the National Union of Teachers
Annual Reports of the main political parties
Party Manifestos issued at elections

Official Periodic Sources

Annual Reports of the Education Department
The Health of the School Child
Periodic circulars issued as instruction to local authorities

Special Official Reports

These are numerous and well known, so only a few of the lesser known are listed :

Report of the Children's Employment Commission (1863).
Children under Five Years of Age in Public Elementary Schools (1906).
School Attendance of Children below the Age of Five (1908).
Royal Commission on the Poor Laws (1909).
Playgrounds of Public Elementary Schools (1912).
Partial Exemption from School Attendance (1909).
Medical Inspection and Feeding of Children attending Public Elementary Schools (1906).
Education (Provision of Meals) Bill 1906 (1906).
Reports on working the Education (Provision of Meals) Act (1910, 1911, 1914).
Employment of School Children (1902).

Juvenile Education in Relation to Employment (The Lewis Report) (1918).
The Teaching of English in England (1921).
National Expenditure (The Geddes Report) (1922).
Accommodation in Elementary Schools (1924).
Psychological Tests of Educable Capacity (1924).
The New Prospect in Education (1928).
National Expenditure (May Report) (1931).
Local Expenditure (Ray Report) (1932).
Proposals for Aid to Non-Provided Schools (1931).

INDEX

by
PETER FORD